"For the first time, this important work by prominent German liturgists Albert Gerhards and Benedikt Kranemann has been made readily available to English-speaking readers. True to the tradition of Liturgical Press, which has brought significant liturgical works from European scholars to wider audiences since its founding, Linda M. Maloney offers her translation of an informative and comprehensive volume attending to the history, theology, and pastoral practice of the liturgy. Gerhards and Kranemann's *Introduction to the Study of Liturgy* provides an excellent foundational resource for those interested in liturgical studies while exposing readers to the best in contemporary German scholarship."

— Katharine E. Harmon
Assistant Professor of Theology
Marian University

"Here two renowned scholars, Albert Gerhards and Benedikt Kranemann, attempt to bring together the essential elements for an introduction to liturgical studies. They do so with brilliance. This book should now be considered a work of reference. It is sensitive to contexts and history, written in an interdisciplinary way—in short, essential to its field."

— Gilles Routhier
Professor and Dean of Theology and Religious Sciences
Université Laval
Québec, Canada

"A crucially important introduction to liturgical studies from two experts in the field. Their collaborative effort succeeds at being both vastly informative and surprisingly succinct; it is rooted in a deep knowledge of historical developments but also in an attentiveness to new ways of inquiring into liturgy. The book is bound to become a foundational text."

— Teresa Berger
Professor of Liturgical Studies and Thomas E. Golden Jr.
Professor of Catholic Theology
Yale Divinity School

Introduction
to the Study of Liturgy

Albert Gerhards

Benedikt Kranemann

Translated by

Linda M. Maloney

A PUEBLO BOOK

Liturgical Press   Collegeville, Minnesota

www.litpress.org

A Pueblo Book published by Liturgical Press

Publication of this work was made possible in part by a gift in memory of Kathleen M. O'Brien, a dedicated student of liturgy and an accomplished liturgical musician who practiced her ministry in Washington, DC, and at US Air Force bases throughout the world in partnership with her husband John L. O'Brien.

1	2	3	4	5	6	7	8	9

Library of Congress Cataloging-in-Publication Data

Names: Gerhards, Albert, author. | Kranemann, Benedikt, author. | Maloney, Linda M., translator.
Title: Introduction to the study of liturgy / Albert Gerhards, Benedikt Kranemann ; translated by Linda M. Maloney.
Other titles: Einführung in die Liturgiewissenschaft. English
Description: Collegeville, Minnesota : LITURGICAL PRESS, 2017. | Series: A pueblo book | "Original edition "Einführung in die Liturgiewissenschaft", 3rd edition 2013 by WBG (Wissenschaftliche Buchgesellschaft), Darmstadt, Germany." | Includes bibliographical references and index.
Identifiers: LCCN 2017006245 (print) | LCCN 2017029828 (ebook) | ISBN 9780814663370 (ebook) | ISBN 9780814663127
Subjects: LCSH: Liturgics. | Catholic Church—Liturgy. | Catholic Church—Doctrines.
Classification: LCC BV176.3 (ebook) | LCC BV176.3 .G4813 2017 (print) | DDC 264/.02—dc23
LC record available at https://lccn.loc.gov/2017006245

Contents

Appendixes

Introduction

Liturgical studies (liturgics), as a theological discipline, concerns itself with the history, theology, and pastoral practice of liturgy. It investigates the multifaceted celebrations of different Christian liturgies. The forms of faith expression that are the object of scholarly interest include the whole spectrum of linguistic and nonlinguistic liturgical sign-actions throughout history and in the present, in various confessions and cultures. In this introductory work, that breadth of content is confronted with the requirement of brevity. Therefore we can address only certain basic themes, placing accents here and there, and giving pointers and encouragement for the reader's own further reading. Though this book can treat many subjects in only fragmentary fashion, it still intends to offer a critical picture of Christian worship and to awaken interest in liturgics.

The book begins with a sketch of the function and interpretation of liturgy within its social context. A second chapter introduces liturgics as a discipline and is followed by a longer chapter (still merely a survey) on the history of the Roman liturgy. Here again, the brevity of the presentation requires us to concentrate on basic information. The history of liturgy is a field that is as central to liturgics as the theology of liturgy, some basic themes of which will be developed. On the basis of history and theology, then, elements and expressions of worship can be described: Sacred Scripture in liturgy, prayer as the central liturgical language-act, the language of worship, hymnody and music, as well as the signs and symbolic character of the liturgy. We will deal with fundamentals, because it is against that background that an active event like liturgy must be understood.

An appendix with a few textual examples and schemata, as well as an extensive bibliography, will be an aid to the use of this book as a textbook.

This introductory work is addressed to readers interested in theology and cultural studies; therefore less attention is paid to pastoral liturgy than to theological and historical questions. Besides, those who are familiar with the history and theology of the liturgy will be able to develop their own criteria for pastoral use.

Finally, we should point to the confessional limitations of the book. This introduction is written from the perspective of Roman Catholic theology in Germany. Liturgics has been ecumenical for many decades; consequently, voices from the scholarly tradition in other confessions must be heard as a matter of course. The authors are aware of their obligation to an ecumenical liturgics, but for this brief publication they have been forced to restrict themselves to a presentation of their own tradition.

We are indebted to our colleagues in the chairs of liturgics at the Catholic theological faculties of Bonn and Erfurt, especially Dipl. theol. Birgit Hosselmann, Annika Bender, Christopher Tschorn, and Dr. Stephan Wahle, for ideas and redactional assistance.

Albert Gerhards
Benedikt Kranemann

CHAPTER 1

Liturgy in Its Social Context

1.1 Christian Liturgy and the Multiplicity of Liturgical Celebrations

The simple word "liturgy" covers a multitude of forms of celebration that are associated in a broad variety of ways with the life of the church, society, and individuals, and are given a great many different interpretations. "Liturgy" is a concept that in the abstract and at a distance is illuminating to analysis and knowledge, but at the same time always demands to be enriched with the specifics and differences of concrete liturgical celebrations. Our introduction to liturgics proceeds accordingly: it collects the statements and insights about the phenomenon of "liturgy" that can be formulated in general terms and applies them to concrete liturgical actions.

Here we offer a quick summary of examples of the multiform liturgical life of the church.

First example: Liturgy responsible to the church

Central to a Catholic congregation is the Sunday Eucharist, the celebration of Christ's resurrection: a liturgy with a clear reason and purpose (the weekly celebration of the Easter mystery as the center of Christian existence) on a fixed day (Sunday) and usually in a particular place (parish church), with, as far as the participants are concerned, a relatively clearly constituted and confessionally limited group of attendees and a division of offices and roles determined by church rules. This liturgy must follow the guidelines and texts (readings, orations, canon, etc.) of liturgical books—lectionaries, gospel books, missals. It is thus a church-determined liturgy, even though there is broad latitude in its presentation. The reasons for the church's prescribed order are related to the necessary structuring of a human gathering, to the effort to preserve orthodoxy in the liturgy, which is the expression of the church's faith, and to the incorporation of the liturgy within the church and the securing of its theological and cultural level.[1] Additional variations among the liturgies of various local churches derive either from inculturation (the interaction of different cultures) or self-chosen freedom in presentation. Liturgy is subject to the duty to constitute the church, which ought to be constantly renewed by the Eucharist. Thus the liturgy has a powerful significance within the church but is also accepted and tolerated within society as the action of a social group.

If we look solely at the multitude of expressions of such a church-regulated liturgy we will encounter a great many "liturgies." These include such different celebrations as the Mass, with Liturgy of the Word and Eucharist; the Liturgy of the Hours (Lauds, Vespers, Compline, Matins, and the lesser hours), with songs and readings drawn from the Old and New Testaments as well as prayers; the Easter liturgy with its complex structure (a vigil with celebration of light, Liturgy of the Word, baptism, and Eucharist); a simple Benediction (blessing) with Scripture reading, prayer of blessing, petitions, and closing prayer; or a burial liturgy in which through readings, prayer, and symbolic actions we take leave of and express hope for the dead. This catalogue could be expanded to include many other forms of celebration, traditional and contemporary, most certainly if we expand our view to include the ecumenical world and the numerous ways in which we can celebrate ecumenical worship. Thus today "liturgy" is not limited to the Mass but includes all forms of church-sanctioned worship services, with their differing theological significance and varied ritual *habitus*.

---

[1] Martin Klöckener, "Freiheit und Ordnung im Gottesdienst: ein altes Problem mit neuer Brisanz," *Freiburger Zeitschrift für Philosophie und Theologie* 43 (1996): 368–419.

Second example: Worship services occasioned by community events

A very different type of liturgy is constituted by worship services occasioned by events within the community: for example, those connected with catastrophes.[2] They are celebrated because of certain events and are usually organized jointly by church and state institutions and based on certain ritual repertoires. Such celebrations are not "church" events but have an explicitly public character. Ultimately there are no clear guidelines for who may participate, even though, for example, mourning over the victims of the catastrophe unites the participants. The celebration functions as an aid to articulation of and dealing with sorrow and to holding the community together. Some groups will interpret the event as confessionally religious, others more as an act of civil religion. The role-players vary and in German-speaking regions are not determined altogether by ecclesial-theological specifications. As a rule such celebrations are interconfessional, more and more often interreligious. The shape of the celebration also varies, although certain elements (biblical texts, instrumental music, blessings, etc.) commonly appear. The place for such worship services depends on the circumstances: churches, public plazas, even sports stadiums. These celebrations attract a large media presence; as a result, various forms of participation are possible, either through personal presence or via the media. Depending on whether a confession of God is uttered in such a service, and whether there is explicit recognition of God as a partner in contact with humans, one may speak of liturgy or more generally of a religious service. This brings to light a differentiation within the Christian culture of celebrations, something that grows whenever the church acts beyond its own circle of members through new rituals performed in society. The expanding number and variety of forms of celebration, and ultimately of liturgy as well, constitutes an especially urgent demand on a church that understands itself as part of a pluralistic society.

---

[2] *Disaster Ritual: Explorations of an Emerging Ritual Repertoire*, ed. Paul Post, Liturgia condenda 15 (Leuven: Peeters, 2003).

Third example: Church liturgies with plural meanings

Infant baptism remains the most frequent form of initiation for Roman Catholics in Western societies. Baptism (in combination with confirmation and Eucharist) means that the baptized are made participants in the death and resurrection of Christ and members of the church. The liturgy of baptism is given a clear interpretation in ecclesiology and sacramental theology. As a liturgy of initiation, that is, as a rite of passage in the religious sense[3] or a rite of transition from the status of unbaptized to that of baptized, it acquires a different significance within the church than that of Eucharist, for example, which presupposes that status. But at present these liturgies are assigned other meanings by their participants, meanings that apparently are considered essential, and this is important for our understanding of the many perceptions of liturgy. Infant baptism, in particular, is widely interpreted as a ritual that affirms and sacralizes the religious identity of the family. Baptism is understood as a private matter and the connection to church and congregation is minimized. In the foreground[4] stands the affirmation, interpretation, and exaltation of an everyday reality. But at the same time baptism is conducted according to a church-sanctioned liturgical book and involves an assignment of roles. The parents make a deliberate decision to accept this church liturgy but interpret it in the context of family. The maintenance of tradition in the ritual goes hand in hand with the break with tradition in its interpretation.

It is evident from this example—something similar could be said for marriage and burial—that a number of very different pointers for interpretation may be concealed within the liturgy, and it is important to reflect theologically on the legitimacy and relationship of those signals. Thus the concept of "liturgy" is associated with a great variety not only of forms but also of interpretations, so that one and

---

[3] Arnold Van Gennep, *The Rites of Passage*, trans. Monika B. Vizedom and Gabrielle L. Caffee (Chicago: University of Chicago Press, 1960 [first pub. 1909]); Victor W. Turner, *The Ritual: Structure and Anti-Structure* (Chicago: Aldine, 1969).

[4] According to Michael N. Ebertz, "Einseitige und zweiseitige liturgische Handlungen. Gottes-Dienst in der entfalteten Moderne," in *Heute Gott feiern. Liturgiefähigkeit des Menschen und Menschenfähigkeit der Liturgie*, ed. Benedikt Kranemann, Eduard Nagel, and Elmar Nübold, et al., Pastoralliturgische Reihe in Verbindung mit der Zeitschrift "Gottesdienst" (Freiburg: Herder, 1999), 89.

the same celebration is interpreted very differently.[5] The history of liturgy is filled with such pointers to interpretation of theological meaning, but in the modern situation of religious pluralism they acquire greater relevance and plausibility.

Secularization

The variety of worship experiences today[6] must be seen in the context of the development of religion, and thus of Christianity, in western Europe. What follows refers primarily to western Europe, and Germany in particular. Religions are taking a different course of development in other parts of the world. The current paradigm is "secularization." The role of religion in the secularization of western European societies is characterized, with reference to the work of the American sociologist José Casanova,[7] by three factors that may be regarded "in matters of religious development as the great exception in need of explanation."[8]

1. The secularization that characterizes the development of modern society is marked by a separation between the secular and religious spheres. Politics, economics, science, and religion have become autonomous; society has distinguished them. Religion has not lost its function thereby, but that function has changed.

2. In addition, in western Europe secularization means that the traditions and practices of religion have been eroded. This is evident in

---

[5] Lawrence A. Hoffman, "How Ritual Means: Ritual Circumcision in Rabbinic Culture and Today," *Studia Liturgica* 23 (1993): 78–97; Stephan Winter, "'Wir übergeben den Leib der Erde . . .' Überlegungen zu mystagogischer Bestattungsliturgie," *Arbeitsstelle Gottesdienst* 16 (2002): 12–25.

[6] On this see also Winfried Haunerland, "Authentische Liturgie. Der Gottesdienst der Kirche zwischen Universalität und Individualität," *Liturgisches Jahrbuch* 52 (2002): 135–57, at 141–50.

[7] José Casanova, "Religion und Öffentlichkeit. Ein Ost-/Westvergleich," in *Religion und Gesellschaft. Texte zur Religionssoziologie*, ed. Karl Gabriel and Hans-Richard Reuter, UTB 2510 (Paderborn: Schöningh, 2004), 271–93; see his *Public Religions in the Modern World* (Chicago: University of Chicago Press, 1994).

[8] Karl Gabriel, "Säkularisierung und öffentliche Religion. Religionssoziologische Anmerkungen mit Blick auf den europäischen Kontext," *Jahrbuch für christliche Sozialwissenschaften* 44 (2003): 13–36, at 16.

regard to liturgy: in recent decades the worship practices of German Catholics have changed markedly. According to statistics provided by the Conference of German Bishops, the percentage of attendees at Roman Catholic Sunday services fell from 44.7% (in West Germany) in 1962 to 10.4% in 2015. There are declining numbers especially of baptisms and marriages. The number of burials, on the other hand, has remained constant over the decades. In contrast, the number of baptisms of school-age children and of adults has risen. Erosion can be observed also in regard to familiarity with different liturgical rites and pious practices.[9]

3. Finally, a third aspect of secularization is the privatization of religion. This tendency is constant in Europe, as can be empirically proven, even though the shift of religion from the public to the private sphere is not a necessary consequence of modern social development.

These data on the relationship between religion and the public sphere also affect the celebration of liturgy. The differentiation of forms and interpretations of liturgy is connected with the radically changed role of religion; that change also influences what liturgy means in detail and how it is perceived.

1.2 "Liturgy"—History of an Idea

Ultimately, the diversifications we have noted are reflected in history and reveal the plurality of liturgical traditions even within the Catholic Church. The names for the many kinds of worship celebrations have a very complex conceptual history, within which the concept of "liturgy" came into use quite late.

Terms for the "katabatic" and "anabatic" dimensions

Thus we encounter terms referring to functions within the service, such as *ministerium, munus, officium, opus*—from the Latin *opus Dei*, hence the English term "service"—although it remains an open question whether this refers to God's service to humankind or human service for God or both. The case is clearer with equally common

---

[9] See "Zahlen und Fakten" on the home page of the Conference of German Bishops, www.dbk.de.

terms such as *mysterium* or *sacramentum*, which echo God's offer of salvation (the soteriological dimension or *katabasis*, from Greek καταβαίνειν, descend), emphasizing God's action toward humankind, or concepts such as *cultus*, *devotio*, or *religio*, which foreground reverence toward God or the worship humans owe to God (*latreia* dimension or *anabasis*, from Greek ἀναβαίνειν, ascend). Besides these there are terms that point more directly to the external forms of worship, such as *ceremoniae* and *ritus*.

The term "liturgy"

"Liturgy" is derived from Greek λειτουργία, a composite of ἔργον (work) and λαός (people). In its original meaning it described services performed by citizens for public and social purposes, that is, service for the common good and so for the people as a whole (donations for feeding the poor, financing of cultural and athletic events). The word first appears in a cultic context in the second century BCE. In the Septuagint, the Greek translation of the Old Testament, λειτουργία described service in the Jerusalem temple (representing עֲבֹדָה). In the New Testament the word group has a variety of meanings, sometimes referring to the Old Testament priesthood (Luke 1:23; Heb 9:21; 10:11), but it also has the old meaning of taxes (Rom 13:6) and caritative service (Rom 15:27; 2 Cor 9:12; Phil 2:30) and is used in reference to sacrificial service for the apostles (Rom 15:16; Phil 2:17). Only Acts 13:2 uses it to refer to a Christian worship assembly ("while they were worshiping the Lord [λειτουργούντων] and fasting"). This last meaning, with reference to worship and liturgical offices, became dominant in the post-apostolic period (*1 Clem.* 41.1; *Did.* 15.1; Eusebius, *Hist. Eccl.* 3.13.4; *Apost. Const.* II, 25.5, 7; VIII, 4.5; 18.3; 47.15, 28, 36). As early as the *Euchologion* (11.3), a collection of prayers handed down under the name of Serapion of Thmuis (d. after 362), the term is used only for the Eucharist. This constriction prevailed in both East and West. It is only since the age of Humanism that the word "liturgy" has been used in the West; in 1540 the Humanist Beatus Rhenanus wrote "liturgia" in an edition of the Liturgy of St. John Chrysostom. A year later Georg Witzel used the Greek term in German, speaking of "liturgy." At first it was applied only in the narrower sense, to the Mass, but since the eighteenth century it has been more broadly used for all worship services. Today the concept is current in a variety of Christian churches.[10]

Preconciliar ideas of liturgy

We have already named the two essential aspects of the act-event of liturgy: "katabasis" and "anabasis." There were phases in the history of liturgy in which anabasis, and thus the cultic dimension of worship, was placed very prominently in the foreground. Two older definitions of liturgy that are very important for Vatican II's understanding make this clear. The Codex Iuris Canonici (CIC) of 1917 defines (in canons 1256–57) that the worship is called "public" that is "carried on in the name of the Church by persons legitimately deputed for this and through acts instituted by the church." Otherwise it is "private." It is said to be solely a matter for the Apostolic See both to order the sacred liturgy and to approve liturgical books. The concept of *cultus* (from Latin *colere*, "cultivate," "venerate"), here used in place of the word "liturgy," emphasizes only the worship of God. Cult is part of the *habitus* of religion. The actualization of salvation history in worship, the action of God on human beings, and thus above all their sanctification (cp. chap. 4), as an event believed to be present in divine worship, remain unspoken or recede into the background. In addition, public cult is only what church authority has instituted with regard to the acting persons and the actions to be performed. Ludwig Eisenhofer, in his important *Handbuch der katholischen Liturgik*, wrote: "Catholic liturgy is the external, public cult whose basis was given by Christ and the details of whose performance are regulated by the church."[11] Here we can observe a further refinement: the prescribed course of the liturgy is regulated in detail. Only a liturgy performed in this way is regarded as valid and as a cult appropriate to God. One consequence of such a clear definition

---

[10] Emil Joseph Lengeling, "Liturgie," *Handbuch Theologischer Grundbegriffe* 3 (1970): 77–100 (first pub. 1962); idem, "Liturgie/Liturgiewissenschaft," *Neues Handbuch Theologischer Grundbegriffe* 3 (1991): 279–305; Albert Gerhards, "Liturgie," *Neues Handbuch Theologischer Grundbegriffe* 3 (2005): 7–22.

[11] Ludwig Eisenhofer, *Handbuch der katholischen Liturgik*, 2 vols., 2nd ed. (Freiburg: Herder, 1941), 1:6.

was the attempt to set public and private cult, liturgy, para-liturgy, and "pious exercises" (*pia exercitia*) apart from one another. The idea of a cult owed to God also demanded the presumption that the sacrifice of the Mass in particular was to be offered by the priest alone, and while it made sense to have participation by the community, that was not absolutely necessary. "The priest alone suffices for a valid celebration without any requirement that the community of the faithful be present." All that was needful was "that the one who performs the worship service must be truly regarded as a legitimate representative of a body, here the church."[12]

The concept of liturgy in the conciliar tradition

Current liturgical theology begins from a different angle. It has developed out of the Liturgical Movement and is expressed primarily in the Constitution on the Sacred Liturgy of Vatican II, *Sacrosanctum Concilium (SC)*, the definitive document for Roman Catholic liturgy in the present time (see appendix 4). The concept of "liturgy," which combines katabasis and anabasis, is therefore programmatic. The third paragraph of *SC* 7 describes the event of liturgy as follows:

> It involves the presentation of [human] sanctification [*sanctificatio hominis*] under the guise of signs perceptible by the senses and its accomplishment in ways appropriate to each of these signs. In it full public worship is performed by the Mystical Body of Jesus Christ, that is, by the Head and his members.

Primarily, the liturgy—as interpreted by the Liturgy Constitution—is God's action toward human beings, the immediate consequence of which is worship of God, the cultic dimension of liturgy. Glorification of God is the response to the new reality opened to human beings by God. In *SC* 7 the Constitution links this to the presence of Christ in the worship service. It makes it clear how both katabasis and anabasis in worship form an event that happens through and with Christ. Liturgy is thus in a special way a place of the presence of Christ. The council names the paschal mystery, and in particular the passion,

---

[12] Ibid., 1:18.

death, resurrection, and exaltation of Christ, as the center of the liturgy that gives it its meaning.

Liturgy as communication event between God and humans

To come closer to language that describes what is celebrated, one might characterize the basic event of liturgy as a "dialogue between God and the human,"[13] a communication event or encounter. It is important that this is about an event that takes place between God and the human whose fundamental ritual features are listening to God's word and responding to it. Hence the basic structures of the liturgy are said to be the reading, as a sign of the presence of Christ, and the prayer, as a sign of the listening and responding community.[14] As complex as liturgy seems, at its heart some very fundamental and simple actions can be seen as "elementary."

Agents of the liturgy

The Liturgy Constitution emphasizes that liturgy is an event affecting the whole church and enacted by it. Thus in the fourth paragraph of *SC* 7 it says:

> From this it follows that every liturgical celebration, because it is an action of Christ the Priest and of his Body, which is the Church, is a sacred action surpassing all others. No other action of the Church can equal its efficacy by the same title and to the same degree.

It is no longer only the priests, but all the baptized who cooperate in producing the liturgy. This corresponds to the axiom of "active participation," which today is essential for the liturgy and appears repeatedly in the Liturgy Constitution as a sustained theme: the baptized are to cooperate in celebrating the liturgy and so experience their dignity as such.

---

[13] See Emil Joseph Lengeling, *Liturgie: Dialog zwischen Gott und Mensch*, ed. Klemens Richter (Altenberge: Telos, 1988).

[14] Angelus A. Häussling, "Gottesdienst III. Liturgiegeschichtlich IV. Liturgisch-theologisch," in *Lexikon für Theologie und Kirche* 4 (1995): 891–903, at 902.

Sensible signs

The Constitution also emphasizes that the liturgy is essentially an event by means of signs that not only serve as pointers but also, and primarily, have an effective, actualizing character. *SC* 7 speaks of sensible signs. These correspond to the sense-nature of human perception. The postconciliar liturgical reform focused especially on the renewal of the sign-dimension of liturgy and gave a new weight to the nonverbal aspects alongside the verbal.

1.3 The Rediscovery of the Ritual Dimension of Liturgy

Especially in German-language discussions over recent decades there has been little attention paid to an aspect that emerges in descriptions of the phenomenon of liturgy: that liturgy is ritual.[15] For liturgics, whether applied to theology, history, or pastoral questions, attention to the ritual nature of worship services is indispensable if an essential dimension of these celebrations is not to be ignored.[16] At the same time, rituals within society are attracting new interest, and that also should be a subject of reflection for liturgists.

What is a ritual?

The concept of "ritual" is used in such an inflated manner today that some aspects must be emphasized: in liturgics, "ritual" means a structured, usually repeatable and stylized action sanctioned by a group. Rituals are actions authorized by a community for use in key life situations, especially at transition points (transition rituals), in crises (crisis rituals), and at fixed points in the calendar (calendared rituals). Individually, they enable individuals and groups to carry out a life transition, to deal with a crisis, and to ground and renew

---

[15] Nathan Mitchell, *Liturgy and the Social Sciences*, American Essays in Liturgy (Collegeville, MN: Liturgical Press, 1999); Paul Post, "Ritual Studies: Einführung und Ortsbestimmung im Hinblick auf die Liturgiewissenschaft," *Archiv für Liturgiewissenschaft* 45 (2003): 21–45.

[16] Andreas Odenthal, *Liturgie als Ritual. Theologische und psychoanalytische Überlegungen zu einer praktisch-theologischen Theorie des Gottesdienstes als Symbolgeschehen*, Praktische Theologie heute 60 (Stuttgart: Kohlhammer, 2002).

collective identity. In addition, rituals give symbolic expression to experiences that cannot otherwise be adequately articulated; still more, "rituals are . . . the active mode of symbols."[17] In particular they are a primary medium of religious expression. What is crucial from the point of the reception of liturgy is that they place a special accent on the nonverbal dimension of action and thus on sensibility and physicality. Without wanting to diminish the significance of verbal elements in rituals, we should say that here the essential element is the expressive act-event. In baptism, such crucial rites are the pouring of water or immersion, anointing with chrism, clothing with the baptismal garment, and presentation of the baptismal candle. While the transition to the new status of Christian is stated in the texts, it is received by the senses in the baptismal actions. In the burial liturgy we find impressive biblical texts and prayers, but the farewell to the dead and hope for her or him is expressed emotionally in thick action: the lowering of the coffin into the grave, sprinkling with water (aspersion) or censing, casting earth on the coffin, and the sign of the cross over the grave. Language contributes primarily by interpreting the ritual for the congregation's understanding. Thus the pouring of baptismal water is not primarily an act of cleansing or refreshment; rather, it is an event within the framework of salvation history as interpreted by Christians, as the blessing of the water and the baptismal formula articulate. The burial of a dead person is not only interment and farewell but the expression of a faithful hope for resurrection, something that can be identified in the accompanying texts. Consequently, rituals such as we find in the liturgy are about complex actions with very different internal structures and meanings.

Significance of tradition and formalization

A number of different characteristics of religious ritual contribute to this complexity.[18] As a rule such rituals are designed as group ac-

---

[17] Thomas Luckmann, *Die unsichtbare Religion*, 3rd ed. (Frankfurt: Suhrkamp, 1996), 177; a version of this book is available in English as *The Invisible Religion: The Problem of Religion in Modern Society* (New York: Macmillan, 1974).

[18] Bernhard Lang, "Ritual/Ritus," *Handbuch religionswissenschaftlicher Grundbegriffe* 4 (1998): 442–58.

tions and thus have a collective character. They are strongly influenced by tradition and regulations. The link to tradition guarantees that the rituals are tied to the central traditions of the religious group in question. Catholic theology today gives the paschal mystery of Jesus Christ as the center of all liturgy, thus making it clear that all liturgical celebrations are linked to the passion, death, resurrection, and exaltation of Jesus Christ; that is, in the broad sense they are bound up in salvation history from creation to consummation of which the Old and New Testaments speak. These rituals are thus about symbolic action that cannot be described solely in functional terms but contains a "more," a "surplus," and participates in another reality. The church regulates the form and content of these celebrations by means of a set of rules, some broad and some more strictly defined. The liturgical rituals are formalized: thus, for example, certain models of action and speech occur frequently while roles and the sequence of actions are fixed. This makes the rituals repeatable—an essential feature of liturgy as such, though it does not exclude variations and different types of presentation.

Association, emotion, and intuition, among other things, play a major role in rituals. They thus possess qualities not necessarily found in other expressions of religion. Hence rituals always remain polysemous and ultimately inaccessible to a fully fixed order and interpretation. Their surplus of signs opens them to associations and connotations that make these rituals dynamic and accessible to ever-new perceptions.

Functions of rituals

The liturgy also participates in a series of different functions of such rituals, though some liturgies must be distinguished from others. We may mention coping with life transitions through the rites of passage, with their three aspects of separation, transition, and incorporation.[19] One of those life transitions is inclusion in the church and the Christ-event, carried out in baptism; other such transitions are marriage, celebrated in the wedding, or dying and death, for which prayers for the dying, viaticum, and burial offer help, fulfilling a function of release. Rituals can distill complex realities, as in the case

[19] Van Gennep, *Rites of Passage* (see n. 3 above), 11.

of the Eucharist or in the Easter celebration of the Christ-event. At the same time, they enact beliefs, for example, in processions whereby a faith conviction of the church community is given public expression. This presentation of beliefs can at the same time have a reverse effect on human actions and so influence behavior, so that one can attribute an ethical function to rituals.

Tendency to immutability

The consistently shaped action supports the development of these functions, and thus the effectiveness of rituals. It enables people to surrender themselves to the ritual and trust it, for ritual is not newly created every time but appears as traditional and unchangeable; the extent to which that is really the case for individual rituals must be judged in each instance. In general, rituals have a tendency to present themselves as inalterable. But a glance at the changes and upheavals that have taken place in the course of the history of liturgy and at "invented," that is, new rituals in the present time should warn us to be cautious here.

Multiplicity

On the whole, one may speak of rituals as symbolic actions with their own rationale, functioning according to their own grammar and, as complex processes, in need of both critical scientific-theological reflection and pastoral prudence. There are different rituals corresponding to the multiple situations and needs in the lives of groups and communities, as in those of individuals. This multiplicity of rituals corresponds to the manifold liturgical celebrations.

Introduction of new rituals

At the same time, increasing interest in liturgical rituals corresponds to the rediscovery of rituals in the larger society. It seems that rituals are coming to play a new role in the public realm and also in individual lives. Instability in relationships, feelings of emptiness, lack of order within one's life—such things as these have led to a rebirth of traditional rituals (sometimes in new contexts and with altered content and form) but also call for the creation of entirely new ones.

These are characterized especially by individuality and creativity—individuals create rituals for themselves—and independence of institutions. Describing such rituals already shows how clearly they are different from "traditional" ones in their form. They are different in their functions as well, which include not only spiritual growth but the ordering of life and its environment, as well as overcoming crises and gaining self-knowledge.[20] Such rituals can be flexibly shaped and may be combined with a variety of religious ideas.

Such phenomena are of interest to liturgists for two reasons: first, they document an increased interest in symbolic actions, something that for a long time was satisfied by liturgy in all its variety. Devotions, blessings, processions, and pilgrimages were essential expressions of Catholic faith. The loss of such a variety of forms is problematic, all the more so when nowadays people seek something in new rituals that was originally provided by the rituals of the church.

Christian questions to secular rites

A second point of interest is the way in which ritual phenomena have mutual effects. What is sought in the new rituals at the same time poses a challenge to traditional liturgy and influences both its form and its interpretation. It is all the more necessary, then, for students of liturgy to analyze the revived rituals and the different perceptions of them. This demands a critical view of rituals, no matter their provenance. It would constitute a misunderstanding to view them primarily under aspects such as therapy, healing, or aids to living. Likewise, the suggestive and manipulative power of rituals in the service of all kinds of ideologies must not be overlooked. The image of the human in different rituals must be examined. In the social context, the *proprium* of Christian rituals must be acknowledged: Christian ritual makes present the truth that human beings are involved with God in a history of salvation and are called to the freedom to share in that history. That God-given freedom is proclaimed to humanity in solemn forms; they are encouraged to accept their freedom and make it the basis for their

---

[20] Dorothea Lüddeckens, "Neue Rituale für alle Lebenslagen. Beobachtungen zur Popularisierung des Ritualdiskurses," *Zeitschrift für Religions- und Geistesgeschichte* 56 (2004): 37–53.

own existence. Christian ritual cannot exist without this reference to salvation history; it would lose its very center.[21] This is an essential difference from secular rituals in pluralist society that must be kept in mind when discussing rituals. Theology makes a contribution to pluralism by making the *proprium* of its own liturgy a challenge to ritual forms and content that contradict Christian convictions and the idea of an enlightenment rooted in what is Christian.[22]

Reverse effects of secular and church rituals

At the same time, the new rituals lead to a refinement of the church's culture of celebration and an expansion of its repertoire. These new forms of ecclesial celebration attempt to respond to changes in society and altered ideas about faith, value systems, and ways of life. We encounter rites of blessing for infants, blessings for the children of unbaptized parents, rituals for life's turning points instead of the dedication of youth,[23] different rites for mourning and remembering the dead, new forms of the Liturgy of the Word as well as Christian festivals that have to be re-created or adapted for celebration in cities or a secular milieu, and many other such things.[24] These are attempts to perceive religious pluralism as a possible mode of authentic faith, even in the church's forms of celebration. Ties to the community of faith are altogether voluntary. "Pluralism does not weaken faith . . . but can even strengthen it under certain conditions."[25] It must be accepted as a challenge for liturgy as well.

[21] Karl-Heinrich Bieritz, "Einladung zum Mitspielen? Riten-Diakonie und Ritualtheorie: Anregungen und Einwürfe," in *Die diakonale Dimension der Liturgie,* ed. Benedikt Kranemann, Thomas Sternberg, and Walter Zahner, Quaestiones disputatae 218 (Freiburg: Herder, 2006), 284–304.

[22] Benedikt Kranemann, "Die Wiederentdeckung des Rituals. Ein kulturelles Phänomen in liturgiewissenschaftlicher Perspektive," *Religionsunterricht an höheren Schulen* 48 (2005): 24–35.

[23] Reinhard Hauke, "Die Feier der Lebenswende. Eine christliche Hilfe zur Sinnfindung für Ungetaufte," in *Gott feiern in nachchristlicher Gesellschaft. Die missionarische Dimension der Liturgie,* ed. Benedikt Kranemann, Klemens Richter, and Franz-Peter Tebartz-van Elst (Stuttgart: Katholisches Bibelwerk, 2000), 2:32–48.

[24] See ibid.

[25] Hans Joas, "Glaube und Moral im Zeitalter der Kontingenz," in idem, *Braucht der Mensch Religion? Über Erfahrungen der Selbsttranszendenz* (Freiburg: Herder, 2004), 32–49, at 45.

1.4 The Complex Field of Liturgy as the Subject of Liturgics

At the present time also, the concept of "liturgy" designates a highly complex field. A simple glance at the characteristics of rituals helps us to see the specifics of different liturgical celebrations whose investigation in light of the religious sociological conditions of the present is indispensable for liturgical analysis. Thus there are various liturgical celebrations that differ not only in their individual rites but also in their significance and their importance for the life of the church and for individuals. Liturgy is not a uniform fabric but is itself pluriform. Correspondingly, quite different interpretations are given to particular liturgical celebrations, and their number and variety is increasing in a plural and religiously open society and a church with plural forms for living the Christian life. These interpretations correspond to different possibilities for participation—from active involvement through common prayer and song in worship services, but also by the assumption of roles (altar servers, lectors, ministers of communion, cantors), and by simple forms of presence characterized by a fundamental openness to worship but not expressed in any visible form of participation. At the same time, very different expectations are attached to liturgy, from one extreme that demands creativity and a centering on groups and themes to the other that insists on traditionalism and preservation of the cultural treasure of the liturgy.

Liturgics must acknowledge, reflect on, and give theological evaluation to both the different interpretations and possibilities for participation and the expectations placed on liturgy. In addition, a partly different understanding of religion,[26] in this case of Christianity and its lived expressions, leaves its mark on the perception of liturgy. Those who are more strongly influenced by a functional idea of religion will also judge Christian liturgy according to its functions for the individual, church, or society. Others, who see religion more in substantive terms, that is, who look to God or the Holy as the fundamentals of religion[27] and thus its essential content, will expect above all that the central statements of faith will be articulated in the

---

[26] Klaus Hock, *Einführung in die Religionswissenschaft*, 4th ed. (Darmstadt: Wissenschaftliche Buchgesellschaft, 2011), 10–21.

[27] Fritz Stolz, *Grundzüge der Religionswissenschaft*, 3rd ed., UTB 1980 (Göttingen: Vandenhoeck & Ruprecht, 2001), 13–22.

liturgy. In a society that displays a great variety of attitudes toward religion, liturgics encounters a no less varied field of worship celebrations and rites.

Hence the determination of the nature of liturgy is altogether more complex as soon as one leaves the internal sphere of theology or church and seeks that determination in society and culture. But since liturgy itself is also shaped by society and culture both past and future, liturgics cannot be blind to that context when reflecting on the liturgy (see chap. 2). This is true in particular of worship in the Roman Catholic Church, which—for example, in the Pastoral Constitution *Gaudium et Spes* of the Second Vatican Council—has opened itself to the world and emphasized the necessity of dialogue between the church and the world: "Thus the Church, at once 'a visible association and a spiritual community,' goes forward together with humanity and experiences the same earthly lot which the world does. She serves as a leaven and as a kind of soul for human society as it is to be renewed in Christ and transformed into God's family" (*GS* 40).

Accordingly, dialogue and openness require knowledge of one's own center as well as a readiness to question one's own worship practice within the social environment. Corresponding to this, liturgics must develop standards to be applied in judging the legitimacy of the different forms of worship life and their place in church and society. It formulates these criteria primarily with reference to the history and theology of the liturgy.

CHAPTER 2

History, Outline, and Methods of Liturgics

2.1 Liturgics from Within

In Catholic, Protestant, and Orthodox theology

Liturgics is the discipline within the field of theology that concerns itself with the expression of Christian faith in the various forms and traditions of public worship. It is an independent discipline within Catholic theology, with its own research methods and corresponding responsibilities for teaching. In Protestant theology, liturgical theology is the province of the department of practical theology. Orthodox theology also has a liturgics, but it regards liturgical experience as much more important than is the case in Western theology; for the Orthodox, liturgy is the norm and source of all theology.[1] These different scholarly cultures express the traditions and characteristics of the various Christian traditions.

Methodology

Liturgics is characterized by an engagement with Christian worship as an action-event. Its interest is thus not solely in speech-acts but equally in symbols and symbolic actions; at the same time it encompasses such aspects as space, vestments, sounds, colors, etc.

---

[1] For Catholic and Protestant theology see *Liturgie lernen und lehren. Aufsätze zur Liturgiedidaktik*, ed. Jörg Neijenhuis, Beiträge zu Liturgie und Spiritualität 6 (Leipzig: Evangelische Verlags-Anstalt, 2001); for Orthodoxy see Karl Christian Felmy, *Einführung in die orthodoxe Theologie der Gegenwart*, Lehr- und Studienbücher zur Theologie 5 (Münster: LIT, 2011).

It investigates a complex ritual in which Christians exercise their faith in expressive fashion. The methodological approach of liturgics is very strikingly distinguished from those of other theological disciplines by the fact that it investigates Christian faith in terms of its ritual, thereby incorporating the sense-aspect of the faith. This is clear when we examine, for example, the center of the eucharistic celebration, the Eucharistic Prayer (see appendix 2.2). In order to rightly interpret such a prayer and its basic structure, grounded in liturgical theology, one must inquire about its genesis, its present function in connection with the eucharistic celebration and the Mass as a whole, the accompanying symbolic actions, and the pragmatics of the prayer text. We may list the relevant questions and the methods that address them: How did the text originate? (history of liturgy); What theological statements do we find there? (liturgical theology); What criteria should be applied in shaping and celebrating the liturgy today? (pastoral liturgy).

German-speaking liturgiologists formulated their own scholarly profile in a position paper prepared in 1991. According to this, liturgics is a discipline reflecting the anthropology and theology of divine worship; its essential aspects are tradition, ecumenism, and inculturation. Alongside the traditional historical, systematic theological, and pastoral methodologies, the paper mentions those of the humanities that deal with human beings and their forms of expression.[2] These must be expanded today to include the cultural sciences as well.

2.2 Historical Development of the Study of Liturgics

Interpretations of Christian worship and critical reflection on its history are not a modern invention; even in Christian antiquity there were theological discussions of individual aspects of worship and interpretations of whole services. Scholars of the Middle Ages devoted themselves intensively to a spiritual analysis of the liturgy. In the modern period, since 1800, we find a number of very different approaches to the pastoral aspect of liturgy. The establishment of professorships devoted partly or exclusively to liturgics did not originate in the twentieth century,

---

[2] Albert Gerhards and Birgit Osterholt-Kootz, "Kommentar zur 'Standort-bestimmung der Liturgiewissenschaft,'" *Liturgisches Jahrbuch* 42 (1992): 122–38.

certainly not since Vatican Council II, but is attested here and there as early as the eighteenth century. Even the distinction of fields of study that is common today—theology, history, pastoral liturgy—was shaped by a centuries-long history, even though the decisive implementation took place only in the early twentieth century.

Overlap with other disciplines

The following brief introduction to the history of the subject and its predecessors points to the multitude of approaches by means of which divine worship can be observed according to its forms and expressions. There are a number of reasons for this multiplicity: hermeneutical and methodological renewals in theology also influence reflection on liturgy and its instruments. Thus, for example, the medieval allegorical explanation of liturgy cannot be understood apart from Neoplatonism; the development of scholarship interested in practical questions of worship around 1800 was influenced by the late phase of the Enlightenment; the approaches to liturgy influenced by the human sciences in the twentieth century would have been unthinkable apart from the "anthropological turn" in theology. Changes in associated disciplines, especially psychological and cultural studies, also affect liturgics. This involves such subjects as music, theater, art, and also religious studies, disciplines whose fields of study overlap with that of liturgics. In recent years liturgics has developed paradigms of investigation, in discussion with "ritual studies," that lead to a different and sharper perception of liturgy itself in its ritual nature.[3]

Ritual dynamics

Liturgy, as a celebratory event, is a cultural artifact shaped by anthropology, theology, art, music, etc., that, despite its ties to tradition, changes constantly. We speak of ritual dynamics. The changing liturgy

---

[3] Paul Post, "Liturgical Movements and Feast Culture: A Dutch Research Program," in *Christian Feast and Festival: The Dynamics of Western Liturgy and Culture*, ed. idem, Gerard Rouwhorst, Louis van Tongeren, and Anton Scheer, *Liturgia condenda* 12 (Leuven: Peeters, 2001), 3–43; *Modern Ritual Studies as a Challenge for Liturgical Studies*, ed. Benedikt Kranemann and Paul Post, *Liturgia condenda* 20 (Leuven: Peeters, 2009); see also chap. 1.2 above.

poses ever-new tasks to liturgics. The spectrum of tasks for liturgics shifts according to whether the liturgy is regulated, as something formalized and rubricized, or is seen as something to be shaped according to certain conditions; the same is true for innovations and radical changes in liturgical theology, attitudes, and piety, the division of roles between laity and clerics, changes in individual elements, etc. Knowledge of different interpretive models for liturgy contributes to a better understanding of the stages in the history of liturgy and of individual phenomena.

Cult and liturgy in the Bible

In terms of its past, liturgics looks back over a long prehistory. Hints of an engagement with cult and liturgy can be found even in the Bible. According to the Old and New Testaments, prayer, cult, and worship were not only carried out and celebrated but also subjected to theological reflection and critique. The Old Testament formulates a long series of cultic regulations, especially in Leviticus, Numbers, and Deuteronomy. The prophetic critique of the cult in Amos 5:21-24; Isaiah 1:10-17; Jeremiah 6:20, and elsewhere names the presuppositions and consequences of a cult that could exist and endure before God. The New Testament critique of cult takes as one of its starting points the double commandment of love of God and neighbor. John 4:20-24 speaks of prayer in spirit and truth as the goal of true prayer. In 1 Corinthians 11, Paul criticizes the practice of the Lord's Supper in the Corinthian congregation and describes an order for the Supper that corresponds to Christ's command. The letter to the Hebrews interprets divine worship as "service of the word" in the sense of an event of address and answer.[4]

Survey: History of liturgics

Thus divine worship has been the subject of thorough reflection, but—at least in the early Christian communities—it did not need to be

[4] Claus-Peter März, "Das 'Wort vom Kult' und der 'Kult des Wortes.' Der Hebräerbrief und die rechte Feier des Gottesdienstes," in *Wie das Wort Gottes feiern? Der Wortgottesdienst als theologische Herausforderung*, ed. Benedikt Kranemann and Thomas Sternberg, Quaestiones disputatae 194 (Freiburg: Herder, 2002), 82–98, at 98.

legitimated because its social milieu did not question it. Moreover, the relationships between contemporary culture of celebration and daily life and that of worship were so close that individual worship events spoke for themselves. There had not yet been any far-reaching revolution in cultural interpretation to make liturgy opaque and in need of explanation. That happened only when Christian liturgy, shaped primarily in the Mediterranean region, took root in other cultural spaces. While at first mystagogy, as the interpretation of liturgy as celebrated, was in the foreground (see 2.2.1.1), since the Middle Ages it has been allegoresis, a hermeneutics interested primarily in spiritual interpretation (chap. 2.2.1.2). Only with the advent of Humanism was a basis developed for sustaining a broad interest in the historical sources of worship (chap. 2.2.2). The rubricism of the late Middle Ages and early modern era described the legal regulation of liturgical rites that, if followed, promised a safe ritual certitude (chap. 2.2.3). With the eighteenth century and the Catholic Enlightenment there was a stronger engagement with pastoral liturgy; the critically reflective potential of "liturgics" was growing (chap. 2.2.4.1). The late nineteenth and early twentieth centuries produced a series of instructional handbooks (chap. 2.2.4.2). The division of labor into history, theology, and practice/reflection, whose fundamentals are still accepted today, was formulated in the early twentieth century (chap. 2.2.5). Catholic liturgics, now elevated to a major theological subject, also received a special shape from the Second Vatican Council (chap. 2.2.6). In the second half of the twentieth century the subject continued to develop its methodology and the objects of its study (chap. 2.2.7).

2.2.1 Explanations of Liturgy in the Ancient Church and in the Middle Ages

2.2.1.1 Early Christian Examples of Reflection on Christian Worship

Postbaptismal catechesis

One medium of early Christian explanation of liturgy was the catecheses. Mystagogical catecheses given after the celebration of initiation with baptism in water, anointing by the bishop, and first Eucharist were intended to disclose the content of the mysteries at the heart of the liturgical celebrations and lead believers to a deeper exploration of the meaning of the sacraments. Symbolic interpretation and metaphorical disclosure served this purpose. There were close connections between catechesis and liturgical celebration, between theological interpretation and liturgical doxology. That is why Cyril of Jerusalem attributed a greater power of persuasion to seeing over hearing. Only after the newly baptized had celebrated and experienced baptism, the preacher as mystagoge led them into the meaning of what had happened to them.[5] According to Ambrose of Milan the light of the mysteries poured more freely into the unknowing neophytes than it would if they were instructed prior to baptism.[6] The pilgrim Egeria, who visited Jerusalem and Palestine, among other places, in the fourth century, reports that no unbaptized person in Jerusalem was allowed to listen to the post-Easter catechesis on the baptismal liturgy; access to the *anastasis* (Basilica of the Holy Sepulchre) was forbidden them.[7]

Function of mystagogical preaching

Post-baptismal catecheses were held not on catechetical but on theological motifs. Ambrose regarded baptism as the completion of faith: it was only the grace of baptism that made possible an understanding of the mysteries.[8] Mystagogical preaching explained the spiritual content of a liturgy; it also had a worship character. It was not a matter of reflecting on liturgy on a meta-level.

Thus in *De sacramentis* Ambrose explained the core event of the Eucharist, participation in the Blood and Body of Christ, with textual citations from the Old and New Testaments intended to show

---

[5] St. Cyril of Jerusalem, *Catecheses* 1.1, in *Select Library of Nicene and Post-Nicene Fathers of the Church* 2, vol. 7: *Cyril of Jerusalem, S. Gregory Nazianzen*, ed. Philip Schaff (Grand Rapids: Eerdmans, 1989).

[6] Ambrose of Milan, "The Mysteries," 1.2, in *Ambrose: Theological and Dogmatic Works*, trans. Roy J. Deferrari, Fathers of the Church 44 (Washington, DC: Catholic University of America Press, 1963).

[7] See *Egeria: Diary of a Pilgrim*, trans. George E. Gingras, Ancient Christian Writers 38 (New York: Newman Press, 1970), 47.2.

[8] Ambrose of Milan, "The Sacraments," 1.1; 3.15, in *Ambrose: Theological and Dogmatic Works*.

the believers how much the heavenly word—here the consecratory prayer—effected. While later centuries inquired about the genesis of the Eucharistic Prayer or argued in terms of systematic theology, Ambrose was concerned with spiritual exploration of the consecration. For its interpretation he pointed to the word of God through which creation came to be,[9] to the new creation in Christ,[10] to the word of Christ that transformed all creatures,[11] to the miracle of the exodus that Moses brought about at God's command,[12] etc. This hermeneutic was sustained by analogies. What happens in the sacrament of the Eucharist can be understood in the light of salvation history, which continues it in the present and is staged ever anew in the liturgical celebration. Cyril of Jerusalem interprets similarly, showing with reference to Old and New Testaments that the eucharistic bread is the Body of Christ.[13]

Prebaptismal catechesis

Certainly there were also pre-baptismal catecheses in the early church that were aimed more at initiation in the practice of the Christian life. With the crisis of the catechumenate, the time of preparation for baptism, because of an excessive number of candidates for baptism and the frequent practice of delaying baptism—people registered as baptismal candidates but waited until much later to be baptized—pre-baptismal catecheses became increasingly common; examples are the baptismal catecheses of John Chrysostom[14] and Theodore of Mopsuestia.[15] Theodore explains the importance of pre-baptismal catechesis by saying that those who know the basis for

[9] Ibid., 4.15.
[10] Ibid., 4.16.
[11] Ibid., 4.17.
[12] Ibid., 4.18.
[13] St. Cyril of Jerusalem, *Catecheses* 4 (see n. 5 above).
[14] *St. John Chrysostom: Baptismal Instructions*, trans. Paul W. Harkins, Ancient Christian Writers 31 (New York: Paulist Press, 1963).
[15] Theodore of Mopsuestia, *Katechetische Homilien*, trans. Peter Bruns, *Fontes christiani* 17 (Freiburg and New York: Herder, 1994–1995). For selections in English see Frederick G. McLeod, *Theodore of Mopsuestia*, Early Church Fathers (London and New York: Routledge, 2009), 158–70.

the liturgy can participate all the more devoutly in the liturgical act. The meaning of the sacraments must be clarified in order that what happens in them can be received.[16]

Homilies

Besides the catecheses that played a role in the context of initiation we should mention the very many homilies that interpreted the sacraments and feasts. Theologians like Melito of Sardis, Peter Chrysologus, Caesarius of Arles, and others sought to open to the faithful a more profound spiritual access to the liturgy. But we can also observe an effort to explain the origins of rites. Thus Origen writes concerning kneeling at prayer and facing the East that, while everyone does these things, the reason for them is not known to everyone.[17]

Early forms of liturgics

But on a meta-level as well, we find reflections on liturgy even in the ancient church. Thus there are discussions, explanations, comparisons, and contrasts of the different usages in various local churches regarding fasting, communion, baptism, the catechumenate, etc. We find such early forms of liturgics in Augustine's letters to Januarius, in which he touches on precisely these questions and considers norms for the liturgical life of different churches,[18] and in discussions on the date of Christmas in a Christmas sermon by John Chrysostom,[19] in a letter from Pope Innocent I to Bishop Decentius of Gubbio[20] about, among other things, the action of consecration (confirmation) and the anointing of the sick, etc. The different forms of reflection bequeathed a variety of results. At present they primarily give impetus to spiritual interpretation and presentation of the liturgy. They shed light

---

[16] Theodore of Mopsuestia, *Ketechetische Homilien* 12.1.

[17] Origen, *Homilies on Numbers*, trans. Thomas P. Scheck, ed. Christopher A. Hall, Ancient Christian Texts (Downers Grove, IL: IVP Academic, 2009), 5.1.4.

[18] Augustine, *Letters, Vol. 1 (1–82)*, trans. Sr. Wilfrid Parsons, Fathers of the Church 12 (Washington, DC: Catholic University of America Press, 2008 [1951]), Letters 54, 55.

[19] John Chrysostom, "Homily on the Birth of Christ," PG 49:351–62.

[20] Innocent I, *Epistle* 25, PL 20:554B–55A; 559B–61A.

on the existential significance of liturgy for the faithful, something that must in turn be explored. In addition, they are an impetus to theology as mystagogy.

2.2.1.2 Medieval Explanations of Liturgy

The usual method of interpreting liturgy in the Middle Ages was allegorical. It is closely associated with the name of Amalar of Metz (775–ca. 850),[21] though in the West it preceded him. Other important witnesses for this procedure in explaining the liturgy are Rupert of Deutz (1075/76–1129),[22] Sicard of Cremona (1150/55–1215),[23] and William Durandus of Mende (ca. 1230–1296).[24]

Changes in the liturgy

The spread of this method was preceded by profound changes in the liturgy in contrast to the practice of the ancient church. Historically, the community liturgy gave way to the clerical liturgy, and at the same time the emphasis on doxological moments retreated behind a view of liturgy that looked primarily to the graced effects of liturgy and was more interested in individual formulae and rites than in the ritual as a whole. Nevertheless, the complex ritual of, for example, a Mass had to be interpreted for believers. This was accomplished through allegorical explanation, which interpreted the liturgy against the background of Christ's passion.

Examples of allegory

Allegory is applied to Christ in various ways, as some examples from Rupert of Deutz's *Liber de divinis officiis* clearly show. The

---

[21] *Liber officialis*, StT 138–40.

[22] *Ruperti Tuitiensis Liber de divinis officiis*, ed. Rhabanus Maurus Haacke, Corpus Christianorum, Continuatio Mediaevalis 7 (Turnhout: Brepols, 1967).

[23] *Sicardi cremonensis episcopi Mitrale, sive De officiis ecclesiasticis summa*, PL 213:9–436.

[24] Gulielmus Durandus, *Rationale divinorum officiorum*, ed. Anselme Davril and Timothy M. Thibodeau, Corpus Christianorum, Continuatio Mediaevalis 140, 140A, 140B (Turnhout: Brepols, 1995–2000).

Eucharist is interpreted in terms of selected passages. Thus the Canon of the Mass (which Rupert calls the *secreta* and is known today as the Eucharistic Prayer) is a remembrance of Christ's passion (*memoria dominicae passionis*).[25] Individual parts of the canon are related to events of the passion: from *Te igitur* to *Qui pridie* is said to reflect the time from Jesus' entry into Jerusalem to his betrayal by Judas. The priest's fivefold sign of the cross over the bread and wine is said to indicate the five wounds of the Crucified.[26] Rupert interprets the fact that the priest speaks the words *nobis quoque peccatoribus* softly as a recollection of the confession of guilt by the thief crucified with Christ and his response.[27] Three additional signs of the cross commemorate the completion of the passion. The corporal, which covers the chalice, is elevated because the curtain of the temple was torn.[28] Comparable interpretations are applied to the whole liturgy. We can systematically distinguish four different types of interpretation that may be combined in a variety of ways:

Interpretation	Definition	Example
Re-memorative interpretation	Explanation of the liturgy as a memorial of the life of Jesus	The altar signifies the cross, the chalice the tomb, the paten the stone before the tomb, the corporal the shroud that covered Jesus, etc.[29]
Typological interpretation	Fulfillment of the Old Covenant in the liturgy of the New Covenant	Gestures of blessing over bread and wine: Melchizedek's blessing of the sacrificial gifts of bread and wine.[30]

[25] *Ruperti Tuitiensis Liber de divinis officiis* 2.5.

[26] Ibid., 2.12.

[27] Ibid., 2.14.

[28] Ibid., 2.15.

[29] Franz Rudolf Reichert, *Die älteste deutsche Gesamtauslegung der Messe. Erstausgabe ca. 1480*, Corpus catholicorum 29 (Münster: Aschendorff, 1967), 103.

[30] Ibid., 106.

Anagogical interpretation	Eschatological explanation of the liturgy	The mixing of wine and water in the preparation of the gifts: the union of the people with Christ in the sacrament.[31]
Tropological interpretation	Moral explanation of the liturgy	The whiteness of the host: the purity and integrity of the one who desires to receive the sacrament.[32]

These interpretations (the examples are taken from the earliest German overall explanation of the Mass, from about 1480)[33] were used to a different extent by different authors and in different regions (East and West).

Purpose of allegory

Allegorical explanations of liturgy do not focus on the salvation-bringing anamnetic quality of liturgy but on awakening remembrance of the life of Jesus, more specifically his passion, and drawing consequences for one's own life. The achievement of such allegorical explanation is its clarification of the hidden meaning of the rites, which are bearers of meaning. From today's point of view, however, one may ask whether it was really about *explaining the liturgy* or instead an *explanation of statements of faith* that are brought to mind by the ritual. Recent studies emphasize that such explanations strengthen the essential anamnetic character of the liturgy by linking biblical and liturgical actions. The explanation is interpreted as a mnemotic technique; the commentary keeps the rite alive in the tradition.[34]

[31] Ibid., 101.

[32] Ibid., 99.

[33] See n. 29; see also Gary Macy, "Commentaries on the Mass during the Early Scholastic Period," in *Medieval Liturgy: A Book of Essays*, ed. Lizette Larson-Miller, Garland Reference Library of the Humanities 1884, Garland Medieval Casebooks 18 (New York: Garland Publications, 1997), 25–59.

[34] Thomas Lentes, "*A maioribus tradita*. Zur Kommunikation von Mythos und Ritus im mittelalterlichen Messkommentar," in *Literarische und religiöse Kommunikation in Mittelalter und Früher Neuzeit*, ed. Peter Strohschneider, DFG-Symposion 2006 (Berlin and New York: de Gruyter, 2009), 324–70.

This way of explaining liturgy did not remain unchallenged in the Middle Ages. Florus of Lyons (d. 860), who saw not only *knowledge* of salvation but its *reality* mediated by the liturgy, achieved the condemnation of Amalar at the regional council of Quierzy in 838.

Here and there we find other forms of explanation of liturgy. Thus we encounter the first efforts to understand liturgy in terms of its historical origins; this approach is represented by Walafrid Strabo (807–848) with his *Libellus de exordiis et incrementis quarundum in observationibus ecclesiasticis rerum*, also described as the first history of liturgy, and Radulf of Rivo (1340–1403), whose work *De officiis ecclesiasticis*, among others, was devoted to the ancient Roman liturgy.

2.2.2 Humanist Collections of Liturgical Resources and Commentaries

New interest in history

Humanism and the Counter-Reformation (Catholic Reformation) led the Roman Catholic Church to publish a large number of source editions and commentaries on the liturgy, for a variety of reasons. A new interest in history, especially ancient history, is evident. There was also an effort to obtain a more effective tool for persuasion in the context of theological controversies through a better explanation of the liturgy, and this also played a role. In addition, it was desirable to emphasize the authority of one's own liturgy by reference to historical witnesses. The possibilities offered by the printing press also benefited scholarly engagement with the history of liturgy.

Examples

In the following years the Humanists developed a tradition of philological work that contributed to the increase of liturgical scholarship; that tradition continues to the present day and is an indispensable basis for research. Great editions were produced, represented by names such as those of Melchior Hittorp (1525–1584), Jakob Pamelius (1536–1587), or Antonio Ludovico Muratori (1672–1750). Individual theological writings and commentaries, such as those of Georg Cassander (1513/1516–1566), sought to mediate among the emerging confessions. A number of liturgies were annotated, as in Giovanni

Bona's (1609–1674) work on the Mass liturgy. Survey works were published, such as the one by Jean-Étienne Durant (1534–1589) on church building, sacred vessels, the Mass, and the Liturgy of the Hours. There were outstanding achievements especially by members of the French Benedictine congregation of St. Maur, which devoted itself particularly to scholarly work; these included Nicolas-Hugues Ménard (1585–1644), Jean Mabillon (1632–1707), and Edmond Martène (1654–1739). Their editions, for example, of sacramentaries, Roman *ordines*, and sources for the Old Gallican liturgy, remained for many years the standard source works. An extensive *oeuvre* on liturgy containing editions, tractates, and programmatic writings was the work of Martin Gerbert (1720–1793), who after 1764 was the prince-abbot of St. Blase. Liturgies of other churches were also treated. Research on liturgies of the Eastern churches was the achievement especially of Jakob Goar (1601–1653), Eusèbe Renaudot (1648–1720), and Joseph Aloysius Assemani (1710–1782). Cornelius Schulting (1540–1604) collected Lutheran and Calvinist liturgies for purposes of theological argument.

Special mention should go to Pope Benedict XIV (1675–1758), who produced a series of important works that touched on liturgy in the broad sense; his works were based on his interest in source studies and liturgical history. Benedict XIV promoted liturgics institutionally as well by founding *Scholae Sacrorum Rituum*. He also commissioned, among other works, a handbook for the study of liturgy.

2.2.3 Rubricism in the Early Modern Era

What is "rubricism"?

As the understanding of liturgy changed, so that it was now seen primarily as an action of the church that was legally regulated by the appropriate authority, the rubricism that had arisen as early as the fourteenth and fifteenth centuries gained in importance. The term "rubricism" itself points to the approach employed by this way of comprehending liturgy. Rubrics are instructions, written in red ink (Latin *ruber*) for conducting liturgical celebrations. Rubricism explains liturgy according to its legal form. Liturgical books, decrees, and instructions from Roman and other ecclesiastical authorities, among others, were consulted. From the sixteenth century onward, rubricism achieved real importance and maintained it until well into the twentieth century. Explaining liturgy on the basis of liturgical law is still a task of liturgics today but, differently from classical rubricism, it is now conducted for theological and pastoral reasons.[35] Authors of important works who should be mentioned are Bartolomeo Gavanti (1569–1638), Giuseppe Catalani (1698–1764), Giovanni Michele Cavalieri (end of the seventeenth century to 1757), and more recently Philipp Hartmann and Georg Kieffer.

Twentieth-century examples

One example of Kieffer's rubricism from the twentieth century shows how this approach to liturgy functioned but also reveals the focus that could be associated with it. The mixing of wine and water during the preparation of the gifts is described in minute detail: the priest takes

> the wine cruet presented by the altar server and, on the side of the purificator, pours as much wine into the chalice as he is inclined to do for this purpose, as much as one can drink in one or at most three swallows at communion. After returning the cruet to the altar server he makes a sign of the cross with his right hand over the water cruet while saying: *Deus, qui humanae substantiae,* etc. Then he takes the small spoon, extracts a few drops from the cruet, and lets them fall into the chalice with the words: *da nobis per huius aquae et vini mysterium;* he replaces any residual drops in the cruet, dries the spoon on the purificator with his left hand, and places it alongside the corporal or chalice veil.[36]

For rubricism the theology and history of this ritual are of no interest. Its aim is to secure the "correct" liturgy through a precise application of the instructions. Its real goal is the uplifting celebration of the

---

[35] Stefan Rau, *Die Feiern der Gemeinden und das Recht der Kirche. Zu Aufgabe, Form und Ebenen liturgischer Gesetzgebung in der katholischen Kirche,* Münsteraner theologische Abhandlungen 12 (Altenberge: Oros, 1990).

[36] Georg Kieffer, *Rubrizistik oder Ritus des katholischen Gottesdienstes nach den Regeln der heiligen römischen Kirche,* 9th ed., Wissenschaftliche Handbibliothek (Paderborn: Schöningh, 1947), 161.

worship service for the glory of God and edification of the faithful.[37] However, such rule books encourage a legalization of the liturgy as well as scrupulosity.

2.2.4 Shift to an Independent Discipline of "Liturgics"

In the late eighteenth and in the nineteenth century, scholarly preoccupation with liturgy set some decisive new courses. Various trends and developments in church, society, and scholarship participated in this shift. The Catholic Enlightenment should be mentioned, as well as Restoration and Ultramontanist trends. In the wake of a strict differentiation of theological disciplines, especially the beginnings of pastoral theology, liturgy was seen in a new light as a subject of study. At the same time church historians developed new programs of research into questions of divine worship. When, in the course of the nineteenth century, separate handbooks of "liturgics" were published, the path to an independent discipline of "liturgical studies" was prepared.

2.2.4.1 Liturgics since the Eighteenth Century

Interest in an anthropology of liturgy

The Catholic Enlightenment of the late eighteenth and early nineteenth centuries helped to shape the later subject of "liturgics." At least for those who regarded themselves as enlightened, the liturgy was no longer an undisputed matter. It was scrutinized, if not altogether called into question. That was reason enough to engage in a study of the content and form of traditional liturgy. Critical examination of liturgy, and consequently of the tradition, was characteristic of liturgics during the Catholic Enlightenment. The liturgy was supposed to contribute to the happiness of humankind and a virtuous life before God. The engagement with the theology and history of worship was accompanied by an interest in the anthropology of liturgy. Suggestions for the reform of worship were developed whereby

---

[37] Ibid., 11.

the engagement with liturgy acquired a very practical and pastoral character.[38]

The Theresian and Josephite reform of studies

No small factor behind this development was, among other things, the reform of studies initiated under Empress Theresa and Emperor Joseph. The fundamental programmatic work of Franz Stephan Rautenstrauch (1734–1785), *Entwurf zur Einrichtung der theologischen Schulen*, which appeared first in 1774 and thereafter in numerous edited versions, saw liturgics as well as catechetics as tasks of pastoral theology. The theological course of study was reformed, and the practical education of those studying for the priesthood was promoted. Emphasis was placed on the relevance of theology for action; the theologian Franz Giftschütz (1748–1788) defined pastoral theology as "pastoral instruction" and thus as an applied science.

The Catholic Enlightenment's concept of liturgy was shaped by theologians such as Beda Pracher (1750–1819), Benedict Maria Werkmeister (1745–1823), and Vitus Anton Winter (1750–1814). An influential figure was the General Vicar of Constance, Ignaz Heinrich Freiherr von Wessenberg (1774–1869), who set in motion an extensive work of reform with a view not only to the replacement of individual liturgical books but also to education for the priesthood and continuing education for priests.

Practical consequences

It is typical of the liturgy of this period that people did not limit themselves to theoretical discussions but also undertook changes in practice. Hymnals and prayer books as well as ritual books in great numbers were revised or newly conceived and introduced into the

---

[38] Franz Kohlschein, "Liturgiereform und deutscher Aufklärungskatholizismus," in *Liturgiereformen. Historische Studien zu einem bleibenden Grundzug des christlichen Gottesdienstes*, vol. 1: *Biblische Modelle und Liturgiereformen von der Frühzeit bis zur Aufklärung*, ed. Martin Klöckener and Benedikt Kranemann, Liturgiewissenschaftliche Quellen und Forschungen 88 (Münster: Aschendorff, 2002), 511–33.

congregations, especially in southwestern Germany. Reform there took its place alongside the explanation and presentation of liturgy. The goal was a worship service that could both instruct and edify the congregation and was structured for that purpose. The faithful should be able to participate in the liturgy. Basic standards, such as compatibility with reason, were derived, *inter alia*, from Sacred Scripture and from early Christian liturgy (which was seen in a very idealistic perspective). It was hoped that recourse to the latter would yield clear liturgical structures, but above all an unadulterated liturgy.

Education was to prepare for a corresponding practice in worship. A number of periodicals were available, containing articles and reviews, to serve the purpose of continuing education; some of these were published by individual dioceses. Pastoral conferences also took place, some of them with thematic intent; apparently these were organized in very authoritarian fashion but also quite efficiently.[39]

The Catholic Enlightenment collapsed with the advent of Romanticism; it was destroyed by social upheavals and resistance within the church, not the least of which came from Rome.

Dom Prosper Guéranger

Without explicitly favoring liturgics, Dom Prosper Guéranger (1805–1875), the re-founder of the Abbey of Solesmes, helped to shape the engagement with liturgy. As an Ultramontanist, the Benedictine abbot was dedicated to the Roman liturgy, which for him was an expression of the apostolic beginning:

> Be wise, then, ye children of the Catholic Church, and obtain that largeness of heart which will make you pray the prayer of your mother. Come, and by your share in it fill up that harmony which is so sweet to the ear of God. Where would you obtain the spirit of prayer if not at its natural source?[40]

---

[39] *Liturgiewissenschaft. Studien zur Wissenschaftsgeschichte*, ed. Franz Kohlschein and Peter Wünsche, Liturgiewissenschaftliche Quellen und Forschungen 78 (Münster: Aschendorff, 1996).

[40] Prosper Guéranger, *The Liturgical Year*, 15 vols. (Westminster, MD: Newman Press, 1951–1955). General Preface, available at www.liturgialatina.org/lityear.

Starting at Solesmes, Guéranger began a reform of worship in France that led, by 1875, to the demise of all the local diocesan liturgies in favor of the Roman. It should be possible to experience the church in the liturgy, according to Guéranger, and therefore he greatly valued the originality, universality, authority, etc., of the liturgy. The program at Solesmes included engagement with the history of liturgy and especially the renewal of Gregorian chant. Among Guéranger's influential works were *Institutions liturgiques* (1840, 1841, 1851) and *L'année liturgique* (1841–1861), both of which were shaped by his recourse to tradition. Guéranger demanded a liturgy in which the congregation participated because only in that way could believers live from celebrating the mysteries of the faith.[41]

Oxford Movement

In the same period the Oxford Movement in the Church of England (after 1833) sought to renew the church by referring back to the apostolic tradition. A great many theological studies, including the so-called "Tracts," strove for a reform of liturgical life. Theology, ecclesiology, and liturgy were again brought into close relationship.[42]

Other theologians in that period also looked back to the Middle Ages and their liturgies: for example, the British Catholic theologian and historian Daniel Rock (1799–1871). "Rock can be seen to be in the mainstream of Romanticism which looked with nostalgia on the medieval past which many Christians, both Catholics and Anglicans, wished to transform into a restoration of medieval liturgical and devotional practices."[43]

---

[41] Arno Schilson, "Erneuerung aus dem Geist der Restauration. Ein Blick auf den Ursprung der Liturgischen Bewegung bei Prosper Guéranger," *Rottenburger Jahrbuch für Kirchengeschichte* 12 (1993): 213–34.

[42] Teresa Berger, *Liturgie. Spiegel der Kirche. Eine systematisch-theologische Analyse des liturgischen Gedankenguts im Traktarianismus*, Forschungen zur systematischen und ökumenischen Theologie 52 (Göttingen: Vandenhoeck & Ruprecht, 1986).

[43] See John D. Crichton, *Lights in Darkness: Forerunners of the Liturgical Movement* (Collegeville, MN: Liturgical Press, 1996), 85.

2.2.4.2 The Beginning of Handbooks in the Nineteenth and Twentieth Centuries

In the nineteenth century, in German-speaking lands, there appeared handbooks on liturgy, some of them quite extensive; these attracted interest far beyond the time of their publication. They were written in a variety of spiritual and church-historical contexts, and they unmistakably represent different directions in theology. These books were an expression of efforts toward a theory of liturgical scholarship and the sign that study of liturgy was becoming an academic subject. Among the most influential of these handbooks were the following:

Handbooks by Schmid and Hnogek

The handbooks by Franz Xaver Schmid (1800–1871) and Anton Adalbert Hnogek (1799–1866) were still influenced by the Catholic Enlightenment but set themselves clearly apart from it. They treat the anthropology of services of worship, the expression and arousal of religious feelings, the aesthetics of ceremony; purposefulness and clarity are regarded as values. But there is also a clear interest in the objective, salvation-historical purpose of the liturgy; it reveals inner religion and mirrors a religious truth.[44] Schmid already refers to the "science of liturgy"[45] and distinguishes it from a pure "practical science."

Handbooks of the Tübingen School

A second group of handbooks was created around the Tübingen School. Here the liturgy was interpreted in terms of salvation history and explained through revelation theology. The standard work was a liturgics by Johann Baptist Lüft (1801–1870). Lüft endeavored to derive general principles from liturgical institutions going back to Christ and the apostles but also resting on human nature itself. He was not primarily concerned with pastoral instruction. Jakob Fluck (1810–1864) tried to describe the divine wisdom reflected in the liturgy. His interest lay in a systematic treatment of the divine truth present in the liturgy. He began by describing the sacramental cult

---

[44] Franz Xaver Schmid, *Grundriss der Liturgik der christkatholischen Religion* (Passau: Friedrich Winkler, 1836), 13–24.
[45] Ibid., 30.

that mediates salvation, seeing as its direct consequence the cultic *latreia* that glorifies God.

Handbooks by Thalhofer and Eisenhofer

The handbooks of Valentin Thalhofer (1825–1891) and Ludwig Eisenhofer (1871–1941) also represent their individual approaches to content. Thalhofer describes not only historical and theological but also anthropological and psychological elements of worship. Eisenhofer, who revised Thalhofer's handbook, concentrated almost exclusively on history and rubricism. He gave less attention to the theology of the liturgy. The differing evaluations of the relationship between liturgics and pastoral theology by the two authors are worth noting. Thalhofer classified liturgics as pastoral theology and did not regard it as an independent branch of theology. Eisenhofer categorically rejected such an ordering and defined liturgics as "the science of the *Ecclesia orans et sanctificans*.[46] Eisenhofer's Handbook was re-edited by Joseph Lechner, and that edition was also translated into English.[47]

The handbooks are still especially useful today as historical sources. They are helpful, among other reasons, because of the many details of liturgical history they describe. In particular, Eisenhofer's handbook therefore remains an important compendium.

2.2.5 Objectives of the Study of Liturgics in the Early Twentieth Century

Fields of study

Three fields of work within the study of liturgy crystallized in the early twentieth century. Their concrete relationship and content are frequently discussed, but their combined effect is part of the indispensable specific of the subject of liturgics.[48] The study of the history of liturgy, theology of liturgy (also called "systematic liturgics"), and

---

[46] Ludwig Eisenhofer, *Handbuch der katholischen Liturgik*, 2 vols., 2nd ed. (Freiburg: Herder, 1941), 55.

[47] See Joseph Lechner, *Liturgy of the Roman Rite*, trans. Edward Francis Peeler and Harold Edgar Winstone (Freiburg: Nelson, 1961).

[48] *Gottesdienst als Feld theologischer Wissenschaft im 20. Jahrhundert. Deutschsprachige Liturgiewissenschaft in Einzelporträts*, ed. Benedikt Kranemann and Klaus

pastoral liturgy are at the same time different approaches to divine worship and fields of study within liturgics. There are complementarities among them. The methods and goals of research within the individual fields of study vary, sometimes greatly. Only a correspondingly nuanced instrument for investigation can do justice to the multiple aspects of such a complex action-event as the liturgy.

2.2.5.1 Multiple Methods in Liturgical Study

Extensive research programs for the study of liturgy were developed around the turn of the twentieth century; these anticipated a systematic investigation of the historical sources.[49] Here liturgics presented itself as a discipline operating with a critical philological method. Three different methodological approaches attempted to satisfy this concept of a scholarly discipline. The historical-genetic method, that of comparative study of liturgical history, and an inquiry more strongly directed to intellectual history—these three are still regarded today as formative, but they must be pursued critically and augmented by new sources and methods.

The historical-genetic method

The historical-genetic method is associated with the name of Josef Andreas Jungmann (1889–1975); his work on the history of the eucharistic celebration (*The Mass of the Roman Rite* [*Missarum Sollemnia*]), still the standard today, with its subtitle *A Genetic Explanation of the Roman Mass*, was shaped by that approach.[50] It addresses the question: How did the original liturgical forms develop into more and more complex elaborations? In the foreword to the first edition of his

---

Raschzok, Liturgiewissenschaftliche Quellen und Forschungen 98 (Münster: Aschendorff, 2011).

[49] Benedikt Kranemann, "Liturgiewissenschaft angesichts der 'Zeitenwende.' Die Entwicklung der theologischen Disziplin zwischen den beiden Vatikanischen Konzilien," in *Die katholisch-theologischen Disziplinen in Deutschland 1870–1962. Ihre Geschichte, ihr Zeitbezug*, ed. Hubert Wolf, Programm und Wirkungsgeschichte des II. Vatikanums 3 (Paderborn: Schöningh, 1999), 351–75, at 356–72.

[50] The English translation bears the less specific subtitle "Its Origins and Development."—Trans.

book Jungmann describes his working method, an overview of the sources in historical sequence, which made it possible to trace the development of the Mass and ultimately yielded an overall picture:

> The medieval development, I found, would have to be worked out anew from the sources. For, although by and large the phenomena were all connected by a common tie, still a more precise insight into origins and motive forces could be gained only by carefully determining the place of provenance and the stage of development of the texts that have come down to us, texts which in some particulars were still further disparate and divided. From what the sources had to offer . . . excerpts had to be made systematically. The rows of paragraphs and chapters began to grow, in parallel columns that stretched out yard after yard, and with dozens and even hundreds of smaller strips; and, to make it easier to establish relationships and basic forms, all shimmering in every color of the rainbow! By thus collating the texts I could at last arrive at a thorough understanding of the evolution of a given piece.[51]

The analysis of the structures of liturgical formularies in light of their development was Jungmann's real interest. This is clear from the set of questions he developed for the history of the *Kyrie eleison*. "Why this repeated cry, and why precisely a ninefold repetition? What is the derivation of this simple cry, so indeterminate in contents? Why in Greek? And who was originally the petitioner?"[52] Jungmann shows from the sources how this cry of worship and petition maintained its present form and significance from early times. He incorporates various liturgical families, points to the crucial upheavals in the time of Gregory the Great, explains the process of musical development of the *Kyrie*, etc. A chapter on the *Agnus Dei* begins with observations on contradictions in current practice, ending with the question: "What is really the original meaning of the *Agnus Dei*?"[53]

Jungmann's real interest was not the reconstruction of history but the exposition of the structures and internal plan of the liturgy:

---

[51] Josef A. Jungmann, *The Mass of the Roman Rite: Its Origins and Development (Missarum Sollemnia)*, 2 vols., trans. Francis A. Brunner (New York: Benziger, 1951–1955), 1:vi.

[52] Ibid., 1:333.

[53] Ibid., 2:333.

"We will proceed in a more historical-genetic manner, observing how liturgical forms have grown and continue to grow, from simple beginnings to ever-richer unfolding."[54] Ultimately, Jungmann was pursuing what in the broadest sense would be called a pastoral interest. His intent was to renew the practice of the faith, something for which knowledge of the history and thus of the foundations of the liturgy was indispensable. We might call this a historical approach with practical consequences for the liturgy.[55]

Other authors (including Alois Stenzel and Bruno Kleinheyer) adopted Jungmann's genetic-liturgical approach; it shapes study of the history of the liturgy to this day. Although some details and individual conclusions of his studies on liturgical history have had to be revised in the meantime, Jungmann's outstanding contribution to the twentieth-century reform of the liturgy is unmistakable. The historical-genetic method represented a revolution in study of the history of liturgy to the extent that it emphatically illustrated the variants and varieties within the Roman liturgical tradition. In doing so it went beyond a pure historical positivism and rendered the history of liturgy a subject for discussion—at first within liturgics, then in theology, and finally in all the humanities. Jungmann described the history of liturgy as an event in process in which continuity and change interacted. This opened new possibilities for action in theology and in the church because it became clear that the current form of the liturgy was the outcome of a long history, and thus subject to change.

Certainly, over the course of time the limitations of this method have also become clear. It concentrates too much on the history of text and event. Changes in written liturgical sources are taken into account, but the underlying mentalities, social and ecclesial preconditions,

---

[54] Jungmann, *Liturgische Feier. Grundsätzliches und Geschichtliches über Formgesetze der Liturgie* (Regensburg: Pustet, 1961), 54. English: *Liturgical Worship*, trans. by a monk of Saint John's Abbey (New York: Pustet, 1941).

[55] Jungmann, "Vordringliche Aufgaben liturgiewissenschaftlicher Forschung. Referat auf der Studientagung der Liturgikdozenten des deutschen Sprachgebietes in München (28 März 1967) [Urgent Tasks for Research in Liturgics. Lecture at the Conference of Teachers of Liturgy in the German-Speaking Regions at Munich]," introduced, transcribed, and explained by Rudolf Pacik, *Archiv für Liturgiewissenschaft* 42 (2000): 3–28.

reception of the worship event, its performance, and so on are scarcely or not at all the subject of inquiry by this method.

Comparative study of liturgy

Anton Baumstark (1872–1948) was even more emphatic than Josef Andreas Jungmann in formulating his scholarly approach as method: in this case it was comparative study of liturgical history. While Jungmann, as a rule, concentrated on a single family of rituals and thus—as one of his titles illustrates—tried to explain "how liturgy came to be," Baumstark devoted himself to the process of the evolution of liturgy in different liturgical families. Structural analyses, philological investigations, and comparison of different ritual families were to be used to expose the strands of development of divine worship. Comparative studies and synopsis, the inclusion of pagan cults and Jewish liturgy, consideration of ethnic-cultural contexts all shaped this approach. Baumstark and his students even attempted to formulate laws that applied to the evolutionary process of the liturgy.

> The earth itself furnishes the primary source material for the science of geology, material that functions in that science as archives do in the [historical study of diplomacy]. The earth's present-day crust provides evidence in its own stratification for the violent upheavals that produced it. In the same way, the liturgy also displays—both in its present form and in those forms evident in this or that older liturgical document—traces of the very process that brought it into being. To meticulously pursue these traces and to compare them with evidence from external sources in order to discern links is also of importance. Above all in this regard, it is crucial to test for an intrinsic conformity to patterns governed by laws: whether or not, and to what extent, from the treasure trove of material available for examination, that conformity can be discerned also in liturgical development. On the strength of such regularity, liturgical development would more or less fall in line with linguistic and biological development.[56]

Baumstark's works are important for both historiography and philology. Mention should be made especially of, besides *Liturgie*

---

[56] Anton Baumstark, *On the Historical Development of the Liturgy* (Collegeville, MN: Liturgical Press, 2011), 45–46; altered translation LMM.

comparée,[57] his brief work *On the Historical Development of the Liturgy*, quoted above, a monograph on the Roman Missal,[58] and *Nocturna laus*,[59] a study of Christian vigils. These works were important for the historical study of liturgy also because they intensively researched the liturgical life of the Eastern churches. And by no means least, they strongly influenced the philological *instrumentarium* of the field.

Authors writing in English also sought rules according to which liturgy had developed. Adrian Fortescue (1874–1923), who studied the Eastern churches as well,[60] wrote in his book *The Mass* of "the constant tendency of the greatest days to keep older arrangements."[61]

Baumstark's method led to the development of a genuine school, as witnessed, for example, by studies on the eucharistic prayers by Hieronymus Engberding and Fritz Hamm.

Certainly Baumstark's approach also encountered criticism that pointed, for example, to the danger that a historical approach that equated the development of liturgy, as an evolutionary process, too simply with natural history would overlook the particular determinants of the development of liturgy as a cultural system.[62] Historical reality and intellectual construction must not be confused, especially in historical writing. This was also true of the application of the text-critical method to genres of texts that were obedient to the laws

[57] Anton Baumstark, *Liturgie comparée. Principes et méthodes pour l'étude historique des liturgies chrétiennes* (Chevetogne: Éditions de Chevetogne, 1939; 3rd ed., 1953). English: *Comparative Liturgy*, rev. Bernard Botte, ed. F. L. Cross (London: Mowbray, 1958).

[58] Anton Baumstark, *Missale Romanum. Seine Entwicklung, ihre wichtigsten Urkunden und Probleme* (Eindhoven-Nijmegen: Wilhelm van Eupen, 1929).

[59] Anton Baumstark, *Nocturna laus: Typen frühchristlicher Vigilienfeier und ihr Fortleben vor allem im römischen und monastischen Ritus* (Münster: Aschendorff, 1957).

[60] See Adrian Fortescue, *The Orthodox Eastern Church* (New York: B. Franklin, 1969); idem, *The Lesser Eastern Churches* (Piscataway, NJ: Gorgias Press, 2001).

[61] Adrian Fortescue, *The Mass: A Study of the Roman Liturgy* (London and New York: Longmans, Green, 1912), 270.

[62] Fritz West, *The Comparative Liturgy of Anton Baumstark*, Alcuin/Grove Joint Liturgical Studies 31 (Nottingham: Grove, 1995).

of liturgical transmission.[63] From today's point of view no scholarly approach is any longer acceptable that leaves out of account the liturgical history of the churches of the Reformation, as Baumstark did. He could not have included them because there was no place for them within his model of a continually growing liturgy; rather, they represented an upheaval.[64] The philosophical premises of the approach advocated by Baumstark must therefore be subjected to critical reflection, but that in no way represents a fundamental challenge to his comparative approach. In light of the necessarily ecumenical foundation of liturgical study, comparative liturgy is indispensable, both methodologically and hermeneutically.

Considerations presented by Robert Taft on the methodology of liturgical studies and comparative liturgics lead us further. He sees the latter's task as primarily uncovering all the possible developments in the history of liturgy, and in doing so he strongly emphasizes the ecumenical significance of such an approach, by means of which we may, among other things, overcome the controversial theology of the past.[65]

Study of the intellectual context

Anton Ludwig Mayer's works proceed from the thesis that every change and development in the liturgy took place under the influence of intellectual forces. Consequently, he investigates liturgy in the context of its intellectual milieu. Unlike the comparative historians or the method oriented to the genesis of liturgy, Mayer inquires about the formation and deformation of the liturgy in its cultural context. In his essay, "Die geistesgeschichtliche Situation der Liturgischen Erneuerung in der Gegenwart [The Present Intellectual Situation of Liturgical Renewal]," first published in 1955,[66] his approach is evident:

---

[63] Achim Budde, *Die ägyptische Basilios-Anaphora. Text, Kommentar, Geschichte,* Jerusalemer Theologisches Forum 7 (Münster: Aschendorff, 2004), 50–51.

[64] Friedrich Lurz, *Die Feier des Abendmahls nach der Kurpfälzischen Kirchenordnung von 1563. Ein Beitrag zu einer ökumenischen Liturgiewissenschaft,* Praktische Theologie heute 38 (Stuttgart: Kohlhammer, 1998).

[65] Robert Taft, "Über die Liturgiewissenschaft heute," *Theologische Quartalschrift* 177 (1997): 243–55, at 248.

[66] In *Archiv für Liturgiewissenschaft* 4 (1955): 1–51. Reprinted in Anton L. Mayer, *Die Liturgie in der europäischen Geistesgeschichte. Gesammelte Aufsätze,* ed. Emmanuel von Severus (Darmstadt: Wissenschaftliche Buchgesellschaft, 1971), 388–438.

Can the liturgical renewal, like pious attitudes and cultic ideas of the past, be integrated into a broad intellectual context—as symptom and partial phenomenon of that context—and thus show itself to be a supra-individual, driving, or compensatory cultural factor? In other words: are there phenomena, correspondences, and parallels within intellectual culture that show us and may convince us that the liturgical renewal, precisely in these times and in this cultural milieu, emerging from its long prehistory of development, its esoteric, monastic, and scholarly stages, is able to become part of the public world, to enter into the life of the church and individuals and help to structure and fulfill that life? What, after all, has happened in the spheres that, for us, are determinative of an intellectual culture, in the arts, in literature, in scientific and ideological thought?[67]

The themes with which Mayer engaged in his publications evidence his scholarly program: "Renaissance, Humanismus und Liturgie [Renaissance, Humanism, and Liturgy]," the essay just quoted, and "Der Wandel des Kirchenbildes in der abendländischen Kulturgeschichte [The Changing Image of the Church in the History of Western Culture]."[68] Art and literature, for example, became sources for understanding and interpreting the changes in the liturgy within the framework of Western cultural history. This approach to liturgical history networks liturgics with other fields in the humanities. Regrettably, it was not pursued. Even though many of Mayer's conclusions and positions must be regarded as passé in light of subsequent research,[69] the demand for an intellectual and cultural profile of liturgical study remains unfulfilled.

Important liturgical-historical works in English included those of Edmund Bishop (1846–1917). A convert from Anglicanism to Catholicism in 1867, he worked closely with the Benedictines of Downside Abbey in southern England. His studies of medieval liturgical history appeared posthumously under the title *Liturgica historica*.[70] The

---

[67] Ibid., 389.

[68] All in Mayer, *Die Liturgie in der europäischen Geistesgeschichte* (n. 66 above).

[69] See Arnold Angenendt, *Liturgik und Historik. Gab es eine organische Liturgie-Entwicklung?*, 2nd ed., Quaestiones disputatae 189 (Freiburg: Herder, 2001), 64–75; 171.

[70] Edmund Bishop, *Liturgica Historica: Papers on the Liturgy and Religious Life of the Western Church* (Oxford: Clarendon Press, 1918).

most important essay was "The Genius of the Roman Rite."[71] Other important liturgical historians of a later generation include Edward Yarnold, SJ (1926–2002), and Godfrey Diekmann, OSB (1908–2002), both of whom focused primarily on the liturgies of the ancient church.

2.2.5.2 Liturgics as a Theological Discipline

Important initiatives for both liturgical theology and a theology of liturgy came from English-speaking liturgical scholars. Theological proposals from various confessions were received with ecumenical interest. They described the relationship between *lex orandi* and *lex credendi* in a variety of ways (see below). While the theology of liturgy is often shaped by principles of systematic theology, the theology of liturgy takes a different tack. Dorothea Haspelmath-Finatti, a German Lutheran theologian, has written that "American liturgical theology illuminates the foundational meaning of worship for the God-human relationship and for academic theology from a variety of perspectives, kaleidoscopic and often couched in easily understood, poetic language."[72] The crucial theological projects were those, among others, of Alexander Schmemann (1921–1983), Aidan Kavanagh, OSB (1929–2006), Gordon Lathrop, Geoffrey Wainwright, and Edward J. Kilmartin, SJ (1923–1994).

Romano Guardini

With his 1921 essay, "Über die systematische Methode in der Liturgiewissenschaft [On Systematic Method in Liturgical Studies],"[73] Romano Guardini exercised a decisive influence on the further development of the field, and of *liturgical theology* in particular. He claimed that

---

[71] In ibid., 1–19. This essay was the inspiration for Keith F. Pecklers, *The Genius of the Roman Rite: On the Reception and Implementation of the New Missal* (Collegeville, MN: Liturgical Press, 2009).

[72] Dorothea Haspelmath-Finatti, *Theologia Prima. Liturgische Theologie für den evangelischen Gottesdienst*, Arbeiten zur Pastoraltheologie, Liturgik und Hymnologie 80 (Göttingen: Vandenhoeck & Ruprecht, 2014), 84.

[73] Romano Guardini, "Über die systematische Methode in der Liturgiewissenschaft [On Systematic Methods in Liturgics]," *Jahrbuch für Liturgiewissenschaft* 1 (1921): 97–108.

liturgics is theology, thus expanding its spectrum, since heretofore historical research had been central. In addition, Guardini described the object of this theology in a way that was unusual within the overall field of theology: liturgics should concern itself with the church that carries out the sacred mysteries in the liturgy: "The object of systematic study of liturgy is thus the church that is living, sacrificing, praying, and carrying out the sacred mysteries, in its actual practice of worship and its binding statements about these expressions."[74]

Guardini's concern is with the living, sacrificing, praying church. The object of investigation should be actual worship practices, that is, the liturgy itself, and what the church says about those practices. But, according to him, interest should ultimately focus on the supernatural reality that is expressed in them and be applied to a way of life that the church proclaims.

> It is about theology, that is, teaching about supernatural revelation and transmission of life. Its content is established, both theoretically and practically, by the church's binding teachings, essential regulations, and concrete actions. Thus the work of liturgical theology focuses first on the governing supernatural truth and order of life conveyed by the church. But while the church's laws focus on the active life of the church, liturgics is directed to its contemplative or cultic life, as well as to the supernatural truth and reality of grace thus expressed.[75]

Systematic liturgics

Guardini saw systematic liturgics as clearly contrasted to exegesis and dogmatic theology, for its task is to formulate not systematic doctrine but the teaching content of worship. "It well may be that it also extracts the teaching content of cultic life, but not in order to present a system or teaching on faith or morals; rather, it seeks to understand the living reality of the church's worship from various sides. It is methodical investigation of the real church in its life of prayer."[76] He distinguished a special study of liturgics designed to investigate

[74] Ibid., 104.
[75] Ibid.
[76] Ibid., 108.

both the individual parts and the whole of the liturgy from a general study that would concentrate on "the fact of liturgy as such,"[77] thus the concept of the liturgical, the relationship of liturgy to individual and communal devotion, to the religious life of the spirit, and so on.

Here *lex orandi* and *lex credendi*, the church's liturgy and its faith, were again brought into relationship. The newly strengthened sense of the liturgy as the locus of faith in the contemporary liturgical movement was now affecting theology. However, for a long time, and especially in German-speaking countries, the systematic study of liturgy was not pursued in the way its scholarly scope deserved.

Theology of the mysteries

The most important liturgical-theological initiative of the twentieth century, adopted in many works by other theologians, came from Odo Casel (1886–1948).[78] Casel introduced the theology of mystery into the liturgical and sacramental theological discussion. He interpreted the celebration of the liturgy, especially against the background of patristic studies, as a panegyric recollection and making-present of the paschal mystery.[79] Casel developed an idea of liturgy according to which believers at worship share in the unique yet currently present saving deed of Christ. In the celebration of the liturgy those taking part become, in sacramental fashion, contemporaries of the mysteries (cf. 4.3.3 below); they dwell in God's saving work in Christ. In addition, the liturgy is again becoming the center of Christian existence. The core of Christian identity is God's saving action celebrated in the liturgy. Casel's theology strongly influenced the Constitution on the Sacred Liturgy, *Sacrosanctum Concilium*, and the work of liturgical studies as a whole.

---

[77] Ibid., 107.

[78] See Arno Schilson, *Theologie als Sakramententheologie. Die Mysterientheologie Odo Casels*, Tübinger theologische Studien 18 (Mainz: Matthias Grünewald, 1982); Angelus A. Häussling, "Odo Casel—noch von Aktualität? Eine Rückschau in eigener Sache aus Anlass des hundertsten Geburtstages des ersten Herausgebers," *Archiv für Liturgiewissenschaft* 28 (1986): 357–87.

[79] Odo Casel, *Die Liturgie als Mysterienfeier*, Ecclesia Orans 9 (Freiburg: Herder, 1922), 130–31.

2.2.5.3 Pastoral Liturgy's Promotion of Liturgical Life

Pastoral care as object of liturgics

The concept of "pastoral liturgy" was shaped in the 1920s. Athanasius Wintersig (1900–1942) used the term to describe a branch of liturgics that would concern itself with the significance of the liturgy for pastoral care. "Besides the questions 'what was it like?' and 'what does it mean today?' the comprehensive treatment of liturgy raises the questions: 'does it have practical significance for pastoral care, and if so, what?' and 'how can I fulfill, through pastoral care, the obligation that underlies the cultic validity of the liturgy?'"[80] He regarded historical study and theology of liturgy as preconditions for pastoral liturgics, but he thought that all three fields within liturgics should exist as equals alongside one another. According to Wintersig the task of pastoral liturgics is the teaching, exercise, and promotion of the liturgical life of the congregation in its ideal form.[81] Certainly the theological meaning should always be in the foreground because, according to Wintersig, the subject is ultimately the church celebrating the liturgy for the salvation of humans. The questions to be addressed concern the liturgy and its relationships to congregational life (general pastoral liturgy) and its individual forms and methods of performance (special pastoral liturgy). "The goal of the journey is a systematic presentation of the situation and of the challenges for a religious congregational life that really corresponds to the liturgy as valid form of worship, and a fundamental instruction on how to respond to those challenges in a variety of circumstances, in accordance with the essence of liturgy and pastoral care."[82]

Wintersig's very proposal for this dimension of the subject reveals the claim to interdisciplinarity: philosophy, psychology, and the social sciences are to be incorporated. It is also worth noting that, in addition

---

[80] Athanasius Wintersig, "Pastoralliturgik. Ein Versuch über Wesen, Weg, Einteilung und Abgrenzung einer seelsorgswissenschaftlichen Behandlung der Liturgie," *Jahrbuch für Liturgiewissenschaft* 4 (1924): 153–67, at 157.

[81] Ibid.; see also Birgit Jeggle-Merz, *Erneuerung der Kirche aus dem Geist der Liturgie. Der Pastoralliturgiker Athanasius Wintersig/Ludwig A. Winterswyl*, Liturgiewissenschaftliche Quellen und Forschungen 84 (Münster: Aschendorff, 1998).

[82] Wintersig, "Pastoralliturgik," 166.

to precise scientific reflection, Wintersig also mentions community life and practice of worship as methods of pastoral liturgical work: "The value of pastoral liturgy emerges from the value of the liturgy itself. Christ's mission is that of a priest-king who as such is also prophet and teacher. His offices and dignities are incorporated in his character as priest-king. The liturgy, as Christ's continued high-priestly life in the church, the sacred mystery, is therefore the true center of the religious life of the believing community."[83] Pastoral liturgy has shown itself to be a highly productive field. The new demands on liturgics imposed after the Second Vatican Council have allowed it to develop further and in new directions.

In English as well, many people engaged, for pastoral reasons, in the promotion of liturgical life. One important figure was Virgil Michel, OSB (1888–1938), of Saint John's Abbey, a center of liturgical renewal in the United States. His liturgical ambitions were encouraged by Abbot Alcuin Deutsch, OSB (1877–1951), who in turn had contact with, among others, the German Benedictine abbeys of Maria Laach and Beuron, and so to the German liturgical movement. In 1926, Virgil Michel, together with well-known theologians of the liturgical renewal such as William Busch (1882–1971) and Gerald Ellard, SJ (1894–1963), founded the journal *Orate Fratres*, now called *Worship*. This became the vehicle for publications of such authors as Hans Anscar Reinhold (1897–1968), a priest from Germany and a committed combatant on behalf of reforms in the liturgy. Reynold Hillenbrand (1904–1979), who was very active on behalf of liturgical education, was also in contact with Michel. He and Reinhold repeatedly pointed to the connection between liturgy and social justice.[84]

Another representative of pastoral liturgy was Martin Hellriegel (1891–1981), who was, with others, a founder of the national Liturgical Conference in the United States. There were also women who engaged in very different ways on behalf of a new liturgical celebration.[85] These included Dorothy Day (1897–1980), Estelle

[83] Ibid.

[84] See Keith F. Pecklers, *The Unread Vision: The Liturgical Movement in the United States of America; 1926–1955* (Collegeville, MN: Liturgical Press, 1998).

[85] For a work calling for attention to women's role in liturgical history see Teresa Berger, *Gender Differences and the Making of Liturgical History: Lifting a Veil on Liturgy's Past* (Farnham, England, and Burlington, VT: Ashgate, 2011).

Hackett, OP (1888–1948), Justine Ward (1879–1975), and Louise Walz, OSB (1864–1944).[86]

Immigrants from Europe (Germany, Ireland, and Poland) produced important initiatives for the Liturgical Movement and the development of liturgics in the United States. "German immigrants, whose liturgical traditions were not as impoverished as those of the Irish, found themselves better prepared for the liturgical revival in the United States. They had brought with them from Germany a strong tradition of congregational participation, particularly in terms of liturgical music. Likewise, they had a strong sense of community, and with that, an active social consciousness."[87]

2.2.6 Evaluation of the Discipline of Liturgics by the Second Vatican Council and in the Postconciliar Period

Revaluation of the field

The Second Vatican Council (1962–1965), in the Constitution on the Liturgy, issued on 4 December 1963, elevated liturgics to a major subject within the theological curriculum (*SC* 16) and described a broad field for its endeavors, corresponding to the multiple dimensions of the liturgy itself. Thus not only theology and history but also the spiritual, pastoral, and juridical aspects of liturgy are to be taught. This corresponds to the council's revaluation of the liturgy as a source of faith: liturgy is the "summit toward which the activity of the church is directed; it is also the source from which all its power flows" (*SC* 10). Therefore the liturgy is the subject not only of liturgics; rather, all theological subjects—dogmatics, exegesis, spirituality, and pastoral theology are explicitly named—should "expound the mystery of Christ and the history of salvation in a manner that will make clear the connection between their subjects and the liturgy" (*SC* 16).

Other conciliar and postconciliar documents accordingly emphasized the significance of the liturgy for the whole of theology, as well as the value of the study of liturgics; these included the conciliar decree on the education of priests, *Optatam Totius* (*OT* 4, 16), the fundamental curriculum for priestly education, *Ratio fundamentalis* (1970),

---

[86] Pecklers, *The Unread Vision*, discusses these.
[87] Ibid., 37.

51

the apostolic constitution *Sapientia christiana* on studies at Catholic universities and in theological faculties and how these should be carried out, and an instruction on the liturgical education of candidates for the priesthood (1979). Overall, these ecclesial documents underscore the significance for Christian existence of doxology, the praise and glorification of God in the celebration of faith. In doxology the faith of the church and of individuals is articulated. It is the task of theology ("the science of faith") to reflect on it; the duty of liturgics is to consider it in the historical and present forms of worship life. Thus at the same time these documents make it clear that liturgics is before all else a theological discipline. Its subject is the church at prayer (Romano Guardini). While this for a long time seemed indisputable, it has been called into question especially by the crisis of faith and of belief in God in the twentieth century. Liturgics is therefore challenged to reflect on Christian belief and the life of faith in this context. It takes up the questions posed to liturgy by contemporary culture and, against the background of what the liturgy celebrates, it offers critical counter-questions to that culture.

2.2.7 Liturgics Today

2.2.7.1 Liturgy in a Changed Ecclesial and Social Context

The second half of the twentieth century saw fundamental changes both in the church's worship life, as regards its theology and celebratory practice, and also in the social and ecclesial context of the liturgy. This affects liturgics, which is now faced with different questions from those present even in the first half of the twentieth century and at the time of the council. The basic features of these changes are, among others, as follows.

Liturgy as dialogue and rationale
- The understanding of what it means to celebrate liturgy was changed by Vatican II; a notion of worship oriented primarily to cult was replaced by a theological model that interprets liturgy as an event of dialogue and encounter. Central to liturgical theology is now the interplay of *katabasis* and *anabasis*, the sanctification of the human and the glorification of God,

with emphasis on the primacy of God's action through Christ in the Holy Spirit. The actions of worship in which this event is performatively accomplished are the proclamation of the word, song, and prayer, as well as symbolic action. In the liturgy, the human being before God comes into the picture in an entirely new way. Correspondingly, emphasis is now placed on the participation of the initiates in the liturgy, and the distribution of liturgical roles has been newly defined: the guiding paradigm is the renewal of the congregational liturgy. This has consequences for the form of the assembly and the distribution of roles, for liturgical language, for the configuration of actions, etc. Liturgics is now tasked with the study of the anthropology of liturgy, because the multifaceted cooperation of human beings in the worship of God is now to be considered in light of theology and the configuration of the liturgy itself.

Liturgical reforms

- Emphasis on participation of the faithful in the liturgy changes perception of worship in still other ways. The illusion of a static and unchanging liturgy (which is a fiction even historically) is shattered. The council implicitly affirms a liturgical celebration that changes as believers change. Since the human ability for prayer and liturgical celebration changes, as well as faith and the capacity for devotion, we must reckon with consequences for the form of the liturgical celebration. Alongside the unchangeable aspects of liturgy, SC 21 names the "elements subject to change." Liturgical reform thus became a topic for liturgics.[88] It is to reflect historically on the corresponding processes and accompany them in theological-critical fashion into the future. It must concern itself with the crisis of prayer and be open to the people of its time. With regard to the liturgy it must address the question of contemporary experiences of God and so protect the church from a solely system-immanent way of thinking.[89]

[88] *Liturgiereformen* (see n. 38 above).
[89] For liturgics as a critically reflective theological discipline see Angelus A. Häussling, "Liturgiewissenschaftliche Aufgabenfelder vor uns" [1970], in idem,

- The initiation of inter-Christian ecumenism also influenced the development of liturgics, as Vatican II—especially in *Unitatis Redintegratio*, the Decree on Ecumenism—made efforts toward Christian unity a central concern. The Liturgy Constitution also contained stimuli for ecumenism (beginning with *SC* 1) by opening the liturgy to reforms, locating it within salvation history, and emphasizing God's saving action through its dialogical concept of liturgy. At the same time the Constitution recognized influences stemming from the churches of the Reformation, such as emphasis on the proclamation of the word, as well as influences from Orthodoxy; in this case, for example, the stronger emphasis on pneumatology.[90] Documents developed after the council by the Christian churches together, such as the Lutheran/Roman Catholic Joint Commission's *The Eucharist* (1978), or *Baptism, Eucharist, and Ministry*, the "Lima Declaration" (WCC Faith and Order Paper 111, 1982), were able to work out many credal convergences, and these also influenced liturgy. Knowledge of what we have in common and interest in what is distinctive in the other churches grew. For liturgics, which could already look back at a long history of study especially of the Orthodox and

---

Christliche Identität aus der Liturgie. Theologische und historische Studien zum Gottesdienst der Kirche, ed. Martin Klöckener, Benedikt Kranemann, and Michael B. Merz, Liturgiewissenschaftliche Quellen und Forschungen 79 (Münster: Aschendorff, 1997), 321–33; in the same volume see also idem, "Die kritische Funktion der Liturgiewissenschaft" [1970], 284–301; "Liturgiewissenschaft zwei Jahrzehnte nach Konzilsbeginn. Eine Umschau im deutschen Sprachgebiet" [1982], 302–20.

[90] Teresa Berger, "'Erneuerung und Pflege der Liturgie'—'Einheit aller, die an Christus glauben.' Ökumenische Aspekte der Liturgiekonstitution," in *Gottesdienst—Kirche—Gesellschaft. Interdisziplinäre und ökumenische Standortbestimmungen nach 25 Jahren Liturgiereform*, ed. Hansjakob Becker, Bernd Jochen Hilberath, and Ulrich Willers, Pietas liturgica 5 (St. Ottilien: EOS, 1991), 339–56. See also Balthasar Fischer, "Östliches Erbe in der jüngsten Liturgiereform des Westens," *Liturgisches Jahrbuch* 27 (1977): 92–106; Frieder Schulz, "Gottesdienstreform im ökumenischen Kontext. Katholische Einflüsse auf den evangelischen Gottesdienst," *Liturgisches Jahrbuch* 47 (1997): 202–20.

Eastern churches, there now began a development in the direction of an ecumenical liturgics that continues to be pursued.[91]

Liturgy and Judaism

- In addition to its appreciation of inter-Christian ecumenism, the council revised the Catholic Church's attitude toward Judaism and developed a new theology of Israel,[92] expressed in the conciliar declaration *Nostra Aetate*, which dealt with the relationship to non-Christian religions, in many succeeding documents, and in changes in the liturgy, especially the Good Friday litany. Emphasis was placed on God's enduring covenant with Israel; commonalities in theology and spirituality were sought, and knowledge and respect for Judaism were called for. This revision of the relationship to Judaism, whose importance is obvious against the background of a centuries-long history of persecution and the Shoah, touches the new image of Israel in liturgical theology and the treatment of biblical texts that are also read in the synagogue, and demands, among other things, an absolute clarity about the confession of one God in trinitarian prayers. The revision also casts new light on the history of liturgy, especially the Jewish origins of Christian liturgy and the relationships and distinctions between Jewish and Christian worship services.[93] A broad sphere of inquiry with manifold questions was opened,

[91] Friedrich Lurz, "Für eine ökumenische Liturgiewissenschaft," *Trierer Theologische Zeitschrift* 108 (1999): 273–90; Benedikt Kranemann, "Gottesdienst als ökumenisches Projekt," in *Liturgisches Kompendium*, ed. Christian Grethlein and Günter Ruddat (Göttingen: Vandenhoeck & Ruprecht, 2003), 77–100.

[92] Daniela Kranemann, *Israelitica dignitas? Studien zur Israeltheologie Eucharistischer Hochgebete*, Münsteraner theologische Abhandlungen 66 (Altenberge: Oros, 2001).

[93] Gerhard Rouwhorst, "Christlicher Gottesdienst und der Gottesdienst Israels. Forschungsgeschichte, historische Interaktionen, Theologie," in Karl-Heinrich Bieritz, et al., *Theologie des Gottesdienstes: Gottesdienst im Leben der Christen. Christliche und jüdische Liturgie*, Gottesdienst der Kirche 2.2 (Regensburg: Pustet, 2008), 491–572.

and it influenced the hermeneutics of liturgical study.[94] The marginalization of Jewish liturgy by the liturgics of the first half of the twentieth century is increasingly being overcome; still, too little attention is being paid to the liturgies of contemporary Judaism.

Crisis of faith

• The ecclesial and social context in which celebration takes place today in broad stretches of Western Europe has altered profoundly in the decades since the council. In general we must note, in the German-speaking countries, first the broadly based dissolution of what was formerly a very homogeneous Catholic milieu, with close ties to liturgy and a very lively practice of devotion. The associated handing on of faith and liturgy, considered a matter of course at least over several generations, had already been in crisis since the 1950s. The absence of a thoroughgoing organization of religious life[95] touched liturgy as well; the gradual result was a drastic decline in frequency of participation in Sunday Mass and—to varying degrees—in the other sacraments as well. Over the long term the alienation of many members of the congregation from the church's liturgy has posed a problem; the preconditions for "active participation" are often no longer present. Thus secularization has its effects not only in the social milieu but also in the churches. In point of fact, we must speak of a crisis of God and faith that does not spare the liturgy.

---

[94] Albert Gerhards, "Impulse des christlich-jüdischen Dialogs für die Liturgiewissenschaft," in *Methodische Erneuerung der Theologie. Konsequenzen der wiederentdeckten jüdisch-christlichen Gemeinsamkeiten*, ed. Peter Hünermann and Thomas Söding, Quaestiones disputatae 200 (Freiburg: Herder, 2003), 183–211.

[95] Urs Altermatt, "Von der Volksreligion zur Massenreligiosität," in *Liturgie in Bewegung/Liturgie en mouvement. Beiträge zum Kolloquium Gottesdienstliche Erneuerung in den Schweizer Kirchen im 20. Jahrhundert 1.–3. März 1999 an der Universität Freiburg/Schweiz//Actes du Colloque Renouveau liturgique des Églises en Suisse au XXᵉ siècle. 1–3 mars 1999, Université de Fribourg/Suisse*, ed. Bruno Bürki and Martin Klöckener, with Arnaud Join-Lambert (Fribourg: Universitätsverlag; Geneva: Labor et Fides, 2000) 33–51, at 43.

The situation is decidedly more difficult to describe in the English-speaking world. Whereas, for example, in Canada we can observe a society in which attachment to church and religious practice are clearly growing weaker, in broad regions of the United States church and liturgy continue to play a powerful role. Still, in those places also the liturgy bears—as Charles Taylor says—the marks of a secular age.[96] By this he means a society in which, even for religious people, faith is one among many options. That is a challenge for liturgy as well, and one that liturgics must address.

Uncodified rituals

- At the same time we may observe a new religious productivity outside the churches, expressed, among other things, in a rediscovery of rituals, not only in occult or esoteric circles but in altogether different spheres of society. The church's liturgy is affected to the extent that increasingly—especially at weddings and funerals, but also in the giving of names—non-Christian liturgies for key points in people's lives are establishing themselves. They are becoming a challenge to the church's liturgy. One consequence, already observable today, is a pluralizing of the church's liturgy, which increasingly is no longer limited to the principal forms, the sacraments. New forms of divine worship are developing, applicable to life situations and participant groups and often comparable to the sacramentals.[97]

Individualization

- In addition, people's expectations of ritual are changing; these are no longer accepted as given but are understood, in the context

[96] See Charles Taylor, *A Secular Age* (Cambridge, MA: Harvard University Press, 2007).
[97] German examples of various services of blessing and Christian celebrations with the unbaptized can be found in *Gott feiern in nachchristlicher Gesellschaft. Die missionarische Dimension der Liturgie*, ed. Benedikt Kranemann, Klemens Richter, and Franz-Peter Tebartz-van Elst (Stuttgart: Katholisches Bibelwerk, 2000; first published 1998–99).

of individualism, as personal expressions by those participating in the ritual (biographical effect). This notion of ritual differs from the church's liturgy because the community of faith is obligated to transmit the faith, and liturgy is regarded in a theological sense as the action of God; thus what is celebrated in the liturgy is seen as a gift to human beings.

These tensions, thus briefly sketched, extending as they do far into the church's internal "space," raise questions of objectivity and subjectivity for liturgics, of the personal dimension in worship, of predetermined shaping of liturgy versus a free hand, etc.[98] More and more frequently the forms of liturgy established by the church are encountering new—ecclesial or nonecclesial, religious or secular—rituals.[99]

2.2.7.2 Consequences for Method

Recent discussions of method in research and teaching do not question the fields of work for liturgics described above. The primary discussion is about priorities and the relationship of historical research and liturgical theology on the one hand to pastoral liturgy on the other. There is critique of the fact that, in the wake of the twentieth-century liturgical reforms, liturgics in many ways sacrificed liturgical theology and a methodologically refined study of the history of liturgy and instead assumed the mantle of an applied study. The concept of new models of worship or the transmission of competency in liturgical actions thus became the primary tasks of liturgics. But the subject matter of liturgics is, it is said, a theologically responsible

---

[98] Albert Gerhards, "Gottesdienst und Menschwerdung. Vom Subjekt liturgischer Feier," in *Markierungen. Theologie in den Zeichen der Zeit*, ed. Mariano Delgado and Andreas Lob-Hüdepohl, Schriften der Diözesanakademie Berlin 11 (Berlin: Morus, 1995), 275–92.
[99] Paul Post, "Überfluss und Unvermögen. Ritualkompetenz oder Kompetenzverlust: rituell-liturgische Erkundungen im Lichte der Ritual Studies," in *Wiederkehr der Rituale. Zum Beispiel die Taufe*, ed. Benedikt Kranemann, Gotthard Fuchs, and Joachim Hake (Stuttgart: Kohlhammer, 2004), 47–71.

scholarly reflection on faith.[100] Therefore alongside the historical and systematic-theological study of liturgy, instead of a pastoral liturgy supposedly directed to practical constructions, these scholars posit a "critical science of liturgy" that would measure the actual performance of worship against the *lex orandi* and propose criteria for the carrying out of worship.[101]

Fundamentally it must be maintained that the multifaceted nature of the liturgical event and the different liturgical celebrations in past history and today, in East and West, are not adapted to a single investigatory perspective. Liturgics therefore always includes multidisciplinary research perspectives and inter- and intra-disciplinarity.[102]

Study of Liturgical History

New approaches

The history of liturgy is no longer studied in liturgics solely from written liturgies (manuscripts or printed books), although the liturgical manuscripts and books retain essential aspects of Christian liturgy. More multifaceted approaches to liturgical history are being sought. The different social and ecclesial factors in the origins (production) of these sources must be taken into account, and their differing receptions, according to region, time, and participating group, must be attended to. The awareness that image, song, space, vestments, liturgical vessels, etc., are at least as crucial to the liturgical act-event as are texts is also fundamental for liturgical history. The liturgy consists of complex rituals that must be investigated by means of a correspondingly refined set of scholarly instruments.

Liturgy does not consist solely of the Roman type, nor can it be described only on the level of various liturgical families (on this, see chap. 3). The focus can be equally on the worship situation in an individual diocese, city, or church. An ideal liturgy can be described,

---

[100] Gabriele Winkler and Reinhard Messner, "Überlegungen zu den methodischen und wissenschaftstheoretischen Grundlagen der Liturgiewissenschaft," *Theologische Quartalschrift* 178 (1998): 229–43.

[101] Reinhard Messner, *Einführung in die Liturgiewissenschaft*, 2nd ed., UTB 2173 (Paderborn: Schöningh, 2009), 26.

[102] Paul Post, "Liturgical movements and feast culture" (see n. 3 above).

that is, what a particular church formulates in its liturgical books and instructions as the norm for liturgy. But the object of investigation is equally the actual practice of liturgy. Then the question is how concrete worship practice has been shaped. The history of liturgy, in addition, is concerned not only with the actions of the clergy but also with monastic communities and laity who have participated in the liturgy in various ways throughout the centuries. Every participant in worship and her or his particular form of participation can be brought into the picture. At the same time, the object of study is not limited to high liturgical forms such as those of the sacraments or the breviary or Liturgy of the Hours; it may also encompass public devotions, veneration of the saints, and processions, which were the really significant acts of divine worship for the faith of the people in many epochs of liturgical history.

Expanding the horizon of the question: Contextual studies

Consequently, liturgics cannot be conducted exclusively in terms of philology. Approaches through psychological and sociological studies must be included alongside ecclesial and religious studies if we are to do justice to the various dimensions of worship. For a liturgical examination of the Mass it is not solely a matter of interest in which texts from a missal were prayed by a church or its clergy. The life-circumstances of the people in an agrarian, urban, or industrial culture, their worldview or perspective on the world, the church's teaching about liturgy at that time, the value of religious and secular rituals, etc., all help to shape the worship event. A contextual study of liturgy will do justice to this multidimensionality.

From among the approaches to the study of liturgical history already mentioned, comparative liturgics and the historical-genetic method continue in use today, but the content of these methods varies in relation to the history of research and is still developing today.

Philology, ritual criticism, and the history of conflict

A number of very different concepts of *comparative liturgics* have presented themselves in recent times. Gabriele Winkler describes a philological research program that inquires into the structures, texts, and historical developments of Eastern and Western liturgy.[103] The respective rites are to be explained in terms of their own conceptuality. The comparison of the liturgies should not only describe the strands of development in their history but also yield a critique of the rites. Robert Taft advocates a broadening of the investigative field when he urges that, besides the study of church-approved texts and rites, research should be done on actual celebrations of liturgy with consideration of the socio-cultural environment, thus going far beyond a purely philological perspective.[104] Karl-Heinrich Bieritz sketches the model of a comparative liturgics that is to be pursued as a history of conflict and, by including theological and social motifs, seeks the radical changes, abandonments, and innovations in the various liturgical traditions throughout history.[105]

For the Eucharist, Winkler compares texts and ritual structures of, for example, the Eucharistic Prayer in order to make theological statements about shapings, dependencies, and developments. With Taft the researcher asks how Eucharist was actually celebrated in the different liturgical families and what were the motives for doing so. With Bieritz one compares the changes in individual churches' liturgical celebrations in order to arrive, by means of understanding the liturgical-theological ruptures, at a mutual understanding of the different liturgies.

Text, reception, performance

The question of the development of a rite, that is, *historical-genetic research*, also retains its significance as it seeks to sketch the development of the elements of the worship service. This method applies itself closely to the liturgical formularies and inquires about the basic lines of structure and content. However, it does not do justice to its object when it concentrates exclusively on philological questions and texts while neglecting the reception and performance of the liturgy. In this way, for example, it is impossible to grasp that a

---

[103] Winkler and Messner, "Überlegungen" (see n. 100 above).
[104] Robert Taft, "Über die Liturgiewissenschaft heute" (see n. 65 above), 254.
[105] Karl-Heinrich Bieritz, "Liturgik II. Forschungsstand," *Religion in Geschichte und Gegenwart* 5 (2001): 452–57, at 454.

liturgical rite may not have changed its fixed written form over centuries although, on the basis of altered presuppositions in the church, theology, and society, new meanings have long since been assigned to it. Historical-genetic research therefore needs to be methodologically broadened if it is to describe the actual performance of the liturgy.[106]

In addition, we should mention *ecclesial-historical approaches*; these interpret the different liturgical celebrations within the framework of the church's life. The meaning of the liturgy for various scenarios in church life, changes in the liturgy resulting from instructions of councils and synods, interpretations of liturgy in theology and devotional practice, the function of the liturgy for the church's faith, etc., are all objects of investigation.

Pluralism in method

In addition, research in the field of liturgics applies a multitude of methods that belong more broadly to the fields of cultural and social studies. Because there is no corresponding dialogue, but also because of the special demands of the object of investigation, we frequently encounter a methodological pluralism in liturgical studies. Seldom does one find a clear methodological system. In particular, questions of *religious history* or *religious studies* are pursued, examining the liturgy in the context of concrete religiosity—that is, allowing the religious expressions of a particular era to speak for themselves and interpreting liturgical phenomena against this background. Arnold Angenendt has repeatedly been able to show how the archaic religious idea of giving and receiving (*do ut des*; the human being gives God something and receives a gracious gift from God in return) worked itself out, for example, in the "penances" given in medieval Christian penitential practice or in the sacrificial character of the Mass; how the medieval juridicizing of rituals drove a concomitant juridification of the liturgy; how the idea of the inevitable and predetermined character of law promoted the idea of an automatic ritual effect; and possibly also the increasing codification of an originally freer liturgy. A conversation with theology regarding

[106] Friedrich Lurz, *Erlebte Liturgie. Autobiografische Schriften als liturgiewissenschaftliche Quellen*, Ästhetik, Theologie, Liturgik 28 (Münster: LIT, 2003).

the results of religious-historical research is desirable; such a dialogue would emphasize the nature of Christianity and its liturgy as a gift, an endowment, and inquire about the nature of enduring Christian identity.[107] A study of liturgics interested in *intellectual history* or the *history of worldviews*[108] seeks ideas typical of a particular time, hidden prejudices and attitudes toward action, consciousness-determining factors—in other words, the mentality of an era as distinct from major events and their influence on liturgy. The history of everyday life and that of popular culture are of particular interest; they in turn open up other themes and sources. Alongside the *festa chori*, exclusively liturgical, *festa fori*, public festivals, are now of special interest. In contrast to the history of events, long-lasting convictions and influences (*longue durée*) are being examined—factors that must be reckoned with especially for liturgy and liturgical reform.[109]

"Ritual Studies"

Cultural-anthropological approaches to liturgics have a different focus. Here, inspired by the very multifaceted "Ritual Studies" movement,[110] the investigation of ritual and symbol is in the foreground. Under the umbrella of "Ritual Studies" fall research projects with a variety of origins and a number of different methods; what they have in common is their engagement with the phenomenon of "ritual." Opinions are correspondingly varied about which qualities of rituals

---

[107] Arnold Angenendt, *Geschichte der Religiosität im Mittelalter*, 3rd ed. (Darmstadt: Wissenschaftliche Buchgesellschaft, 2005); idem, *Liturgik und Historik* (n. 69 above); idem, *Liturgie im Mittelalter. Ausgewählte Aufsätze zum 70. Geburtstag*, ed. Thomas Flammer and Daniel Meyer, Ästhetik, Theologie, Liturgik 35 (Münster: LIT, 2004).

[108] French "histoire des mentalités."

[109] Pierre-Marie Gy, "Les réformes liturgiques et la sociologie historique de la liturgie," in *Liturgiereformen* 1 (see n. 38 above), 262–72.

[110] See Benedikt Kranemann and Paul Post, eds., *Modern Ritual Studies* (n. 3 above); Andréa Belliger and David J. Krieger, eds., *Ritualtheorien. Ein einführendes Handbuch*, 5th ed. (Wiesbaden: Verlag für Sozialwissenschaften, 2013); Paul Post, "Ritual Studies. Einführung und Ortsbestimmung im Hinblick auf die Liturgiewissenschaft," *Archiv für Liturgiewissenchaft* 45 (2003): 21–45.

merit study ("high rituals" or those of everyday life); whether or not rituals are unchangeable; how ritual and myth, ritual and sacrality, ritual and power are related; and many other such questions. Among the themes of such an approach are the relationship between the carrying out of the rite and the social structure of the community that performs it, the assorted meanings accorded to a rite, and the relationship between performance and text.[111] Likewise, liturgical rituals, as cultural phenomena, are investigated with respect to the way they function and what they mean within the construction of reality. Ritual Studies opens a new approach for liturgics and new insights into liturgy as ritual; in particular, this discipline expands its methodology.

An *intellectual-historical* study of the history of liturgy, which inquires into the crucial and principal spiritual and intellectual ideas of an epoch and their effects on liturgy, has not been pursued since the work of Anton Ludwig Mayer. Many factors in the intellectual-historical context of liturgy have been scarcely studied, or not at all, which has proved to be a handicap for the study of the history of liturgy.

Liturgical Theology

Liturgy as an event effected by the Spirit

Catholic liturgics today understands liturgy, notwithstanding all the different models of interpretation, as an event between God and humanity that is to be understood as enabled by God, as pneumatic—that is, of the Spirit. Liturgy is the celebration of the paschal mystery of Jesus Christ. It is the place where the church is repeatedly constituted anew, and this can be experienced symbolically in worship celebrations (forms of congregational participation; ministerial office in service to the gathered community; inclusion of congregations in the *ecclesia catholica* through petitions, intercessions, a common order of prayer). Liturgy is tightly interwoven with witness, the handing on of the faith (*martyria*) and faith lived on behalf of others (*diakonia*). Together, these three fundamental acts shape the identity of the community. Liturgy is therefore important for the existence and life

---

[111] Martin D. Stringer, "Liturgy and Anthropology: The History of a Relationship," *Worship* 63 (1989): 503–21.

of the Christian, who is strengthened by it and constantly brings something new into it. The theology of the liturgy therefore concerns itself not only with the theology of the celebration of sacramental liturgies and thus the internal constitution of the liturgy. Because relationship with God, being church, and the Christian's identity are all made real in the liturgy, liturgical theology formulates its own independent contributions, for example, to anthropology, Christology, and ecclesiology.[112] That the liturgy is the celebration of faith and thus the ritual realization of the relationship between God and humanity makes it mandatory for liturgics to reflect on liturgy in an explicitly theological perspective. Still more: the liturgy itself must again become a source for theology.[113] The ancient church was aware of that; Orthodoxy still today employs a substantially stronger recourse of theology to liturgy as a *locus theologicus* than is the case in the West.[114] Vatican II pointed the way to a new qualification of worship by calling it the source and summit of the church's action (*SC* 10; *LG* 11). A distinction is drawn between a liturgical theology and a theology of the liturgy; each has its own separate spectrum of questions to address.

Liturgical theology

As proposed by the Orthodox theologian Alexander Schmemann[115] and represented by, *inter alia*, Aidan Kavanagh,[116] the Lutheran theologian Gordon Lathrop,[117] and Reinhard Messner,[118] *liturgical theology*

---

[112] Helmut Hoping and Birgit Jeggle-Merz, eds., *Liturgische Theologie. Aufgaben systematischer Liturgiewissenschaft* (Paderborn: Schöningh, 2004).

[113] Klemens Richter, et al., eds., *Liturgie: ein vergessenes Thema der Theologie?*, 2nd ed., Quaestiones disputatae 107 (Freiburg: Herder, 1987).

[114] Karl Christian Felmy, *Einführung in die orthodoxe Theologie der Gegenwart*, Lehr- und Studienbücher zur Theologie 5 (Münster: LIT, 2011).

[115] Alexander Schmemann, *Introduction to Liturgical Theology* (Crestwood, NY: St. Vladimir's Seminary Press, 1986).

[116] Aidan Kavanagh, *On Liturgical Theology*, The Hale Memorial Lectures of Seabury-Western Theological Seminary 1981 (New York: Pueblo, 1984).

[117] Gordon Lathrop, *Holy Things: A Liturgical Theology* (Minneapolis: Fortress Press, 1993).

[118] Reinhard Messner, "Was ist systematische Liturgiewissenschaft? Ein Entwurf in sieben Thesen," *Archiv für Liturgiewissenschaft* 40 (1998): 257–74.

starts from the event and experience of faith that happens in the liturgy and from which Christian faith lives.[119] It is theology's task to reflect on this pneumatic event. According to an axiom of Prosper of Aquitaine (d. ca. 455), whereby the rule of prayer shapes the rule of life (*legem credendi lex statuat supplicandi* [*DH* 246]), the question is that of the relationship between *lex orandi* and *lex credendi*: the liturgical rite is the foundation of a norm of faith.[120] Kavanagh calls the liturgy "primary theology" (*theologia prima*). In the liturgical celebration God acts in the Holy Spirit. According to Kavanagh the liturgy comes from God just as does Sacred Scripture. It is the foundation for all reflection, for "secondary theology" (*theologia secunda*), and is constitutive for a theology that inquires particularly about the actions of liturgy, about word and symbol. A theology is to be developed out of the central act of faith, that is, the Doxology: a theology that is not filtered or alienated by means of a hermeneutics that is foreign to liturgy. Liturgical theology is assigned a paradigmatic significance for all of theology.

Theology of liturgy

To be distinguished from the above is a *theology of liturgy*, which is clearly distinct from the other approach. On the basis of material from systematic theology it develops a theology characterized by its reference to liturgy as the fundamental way of living out Christianity. This is a theology *of* liturgy, not a theology *from* liturgy. The Methodist Geoffrey Wainwright, for example, in the first part of his *Doxology*, follows dogmatic tractates in treating sequentially the image of God, Christ, the Holy Spirit, and the church.[121] Edward J. Kilmartin presents a trinitarian theology of Christian liturgy, thus orienting his work

---

[119] Julia Knop, *Ecclesia orans. Liturgie als Herausforderung für die Dogmatik* (Freiburg: Herder, 2012).

[120] Martin Stuflesser, *Memoria Passionis. Das Verhältnis von lex orandi und lex credendi am Beispiel des Opferbegriffs in den Eucharistischen Hochgebeten nach dem II. Vatikanischen Konzil*, Münsteraner theologische Abhandlungen 51 (Altenberge: Oros, 1998), 23–26.

[121] Geoffrey Wainwright, *Doxology: The Praise of God in Worship, Doctrine and Life; A Systematic Theology* (New York: Oxford University Press, 1980).

to systematic theology. But what is critical for him is also that it is especially in worship that the redeeming event in Christ is communicated and shared.[122] Josef Wohlmuth has developed a mystagogical Christology based on texts and actions of the liturgical celebration, but he chooses as his hermeneutical approach an aesthetics drawn from contemporary philosophy.[123] His work presents a conversation between systematics and liturgy that takes the liturgy, and thus the aesthetic form of faith, as its starting point. Emil Joseph Lengeling has presented some noteworthy works on liturgical theology.[124] His aim was a theological reflection on the post–Vatican II work of reform, especially the theological saturation of the congregational liturgical celebration. Studies like Lengeling's were particularly influential in the development of the Constitution on the Liturgy.

A liturgical theology reflects and argues entirely from the liturgy, while the theology of liturgy pursues materials not derived from liturgy. Both approaches have their strengths. Thus in particular liturgical theology offers an original contribution within theology and radicalizes the idea that liturgy is the source of faith. Given the importance of liturgy for the church, this strand of theology must be accorded a prominent place. At the same time it must be taken more seriously in other theological disciplines in order that long-buried dimensions of the theological traditions be given new validity. Finally, liturgics, if it takes its theological task seriously, can ensure an enduring awareness of the doxological character of theology.

Still, the limitations of both approaches should not be overlooked. Thus we should consider the question whether, and if so to what extent, the *theologia prima* construct is also a *theologia secunda*, implying that liturgical theology is also subject to unreflected presuppositions. The disadvantage of a theology of liturgy is that its criteria are not drawn directly from the liturgy, but at the same time it offers more space for a critical distancing from the liturgy.

---

[122] Edward J. Kilmartin, *Christian Liturgy: Theology and Practice*, vol. 1: *Systematic Theology of Liturgy* (Kansas City, MO: Sheed & Ward, 1988).

[123] Josef Wohlmuth, *Jesu Weg, unser Weg. Kleine mystagogische Christologie* (Würzburg: Echter, 1992).

[124] Emil Joseph Lengeling, *Liturgie: Dialog zwischen Gott und Mensch*, ed. Klemens Richter (Altenberge: Telos, 1988).

However, both forms of theology attend to the special character and density of event in liturgy. The foci between which they move are on the one hand the praxis of liturgy, toward which they assume a reflective attitude, and on the other hand the theological theory whose limitations they keep in mind, measuring them against doxology. The reflective exposure of the celebration and the reference to the still greater mystery beyond all reflection characterizes such a theology as mystagogical.[125]

Ecumenical liturgics

The task of any liturgical theology, and ultimately of liturgics as a whole, is also to orient itself to the ecumenical context.[126] It is theologically grounded, which implies not only an interdisciplinarity between the theologies of varied confessional origins. The center of every Christian liturgy is the celebration of the Christ-mystery. That celebration unfolds in the differently developed historical forms of expression of the different Christian churches. According to Friedrich Lurz, ecumenical liturgics takes the perspective of understanding, shaped by the "hermeneutics of another liturgy."[127] The foundation of faith common to all Christians allows us to reflect on and try to understand the liturgies of other churches. At the same time it offers the criterion by which the theological legitimacy and quality of the various liturgies can be measured and by which deficiencies can be made clear, but multiplicity can also be valued. Perception and understanding of other liturgies, investigations of their genesis, structure, and theology, as well as critical comparison and dialogue that at the same time implies self-critique in an ecumenical context: these are the tasks of such an ecumenical liturgics that knows itself obligated to the tension between multiplicity and unity.

[125] Arno Schilson, "'Gedachte Liturgie' als Mystagogie. Überlegungen zum Verhältnis von Dogmatik und Liturgie," in *Dogma und Glaube. Bausteine für eine theologische Erkenntnislehre. Festschrift für Bischof Walter Kasper*, ed. Eberhard Schockenhoff and Peter Walter (Mainz: Matthias Grünewald, 1993), 213–34, at 234.
[126] Michael Meyer-Blanck, ed., *Liturgiewissenschaft und Kirche. Ökumenische Perspektiven* (Rheinbach: CMZ, 2003).
[127] Lurz, "Für eine ökumenische Liturgiewissenschaft" (see n. 91 above), 208.

Practical-Theological Liturgics

A set of criteria accompanying praxis

The subject of liturgics is nowadays located primarily within the field of practical theology. This gives it a special assignment: liturgics reflects the Christian faith in light of the church's fundamental action, liturgy.[128] As in the case of pastoral liturgics, this is therefore not about shaping praxis but about developing a set of criteria that can serve to accompany praxis. The anthropologically oriented theology that developed, with Vatican II, into an influential theological paradigm seeks to understand God's revelation in and through the human. Along with anthropology, attention to the human sciences has increased within theology. Liturgics also looks more acutely than before at the human who appears before God in the liturgy. Liturgy is understood as a communication between God and the individual, and between God and the assembly, although for theological reasons the communicative models of the human sciences are informative only in an analogous sense. The human being and her or his participation in the liturgy are even called the paradigm of liturgy.[129] At the same time an intensive dialogue with the various cultural and human sciences has begun, as in the past with sociology, linguistics, and psychology: human experience is being discovered as a dimension of worship and reflected on with the aid of a variety of scientific discoveries. There is study of the conditions of human celebration, religious speech, human assembly, the theory of signs, etc.

---

[128] Andreas Odenthal, "'. . . et communicatio sancti spiritus sit cum omnibus vobis.' Thesen zu einer praktisch-theologischen Liturgiewissenschaft im Kontext der 'Kommunikativen Theologie,'" in *Communicative Theology: Approaches, Discussions, Differentiation*, ed. Matthias Scharer, Bradford E. Hinze, and Bernd Jochen Hilberath, Communicative Theology: Interdisciplinary Studies 14 (Vienna: LIT, 2010), 108–29.

[129] Angelus A. Häussling, "Liturgiereform. Materialien zu einem neuen Thema der Liturgiewissenschaft" [1989], in idem, *Christliche Identität aus der Liturgie* (see n. 89 above), 41–43.

Inclusion of the cultural and human sciences

More generally, one may say that criteria for investigation of the human capacity for liturgy, and the possibilities and preconditions for a liturgy suitable to be the order of prayer for the present time, are being formulated in dialogue with other sciences relating to humanity. Insights into worship that could not be achieved with reference only to historical or theological approaches can now be gained. But this heuristic can also be described as pertaining to liturgics in the narrower sense when it pays attention to the fundamental liturgical-theological event, because only in this way can there be a valid assertion of what is specific to the liturgy: its being primarily an event that comes from God.

Practical-theological liturgics has in the recent past been able to show the relevance of the symbolism and sign-character of the liturgy anew, develop criteria for the shaping of liturgical spaces, and present models for the inculturation of liturgy. In the process, discoveries in the human sciences have come into conversation with liturgical theology.

The current task of practical-theological liturgics is to analyze the ongoing process of inculturation of liturgy, reflect on it against the background of liturgical history and theology, and provide a scholarly basis for its current application. Accordingly, the task is one of reflection on contemporary worship acts and development of systems of criteria for the shaping and revision of the liturgy. Levels of communication, competencies for action, the aesthetics of the liturgy, the relationship between culture and liturgy, and the role of the liturgy in the church's life are all subjects of investigation. In the second half of the twentieth century there was increased application of social-science and human-science approaches and instruments for the purpose of giving an adequate assessment of the theological and anthropological dimensions of the action-field that is worship. More recently, empirical means have been employed to arrive at statements about the celebrating community, its attitudes, and its expectations.[130] There is recourse to the methods of linguistics for

[130] Bernhard Meffert, *Liturgie teilen. Akzeptanz und Partizipation in der erneuerten Messliturgie*, with an introduction by Albert Gerhards, Praktische Theologie heute 52 (Stuttgart: Kohlhammer, 2000).

analyzing the language forms and speech processes in liturgy,[131] and semiotic methods are broadening our perceptions of nonverbal communication.[132] Psychoanalytic considerations reveal the symbolic event of worship and inquire about convergences between and within worship and the lived human reality.[133] This pluralism of method corresponds to that of practical theology and is associated with the claim to investigate human experiences as an essential dimension of worship celebrations. The goal is reflection on transmitted experiences (tradition) and empirically perceivable and describable present experiences (situation) in order to move toward innovative shaping in light of new experiences.[134]

Interdisciplinarity and what is proper to theology

The problem facing practical-theological liturgics when it has recourse to nontheological methods and approaches is that of their relationship to theology. A number of possibilities exist: the non-theological sciences can be subordinated to theology (*ancilla* paradigm) or adopted by theology as a complete theoretical structure (foreign prophecy paradigm). Alternatively, it is possible to employ the paradigm of "converging options," which aims at an equality, ability to dialogue, and convergence between theology and the human sciences in order to facilitate interdisciplinarity through the integration of different fields of scholarship. Thus liturgics can take its proper place in scholarship as part of the practical theology of liturgy as a symbolic mediation of the revelation of God and human

---

[131] Michael B. Merz, *Liturgisches Gebet als Geschehen. Liturgiewissenschaftlich-linguistische Studie anhand der Gebetsgattung Eucharistisches Hochgebet*, Liturgie-wissenschaftliche Quellen und Forschungen 70 (Münster: Aschendorff, 1988).

[132] Karl-Heinrich Bieritz, *Liturgik* (Berlin and New York: de Gruyter, 2004).

[133] Andreas Odenthal, *Liturgie als Ritual. Theologische und psychoanalytische Überlegungen zu einer praktisch-theologischen Theorie des Gottesdienstes als Symbolgeschehen*, Praktische Theologie heute 60 (Stuttgart: Kohlhammer, 2002).

[134] Heribert W. Gärtner and Michael B. Merz, "Prolegomena für eine integrative Methode in der Liturgiewissenschaft. Zugleich ein Versuch zur Gewinnung der empirischen Dimension," *Archiv für Liturgiewissenschaft* 24 (1982): 165–89.

experience.[135] In contrast, a preliminary clarification of the theological *proprium* of liturgics is called for from the other side, one that can, as such, be constitutive for interdisciplinarity with the human sciences. As a science of faith, the field reflects liturgy as a work of faith relying on God's self-revelation in Christ. The associated claim to truth must also have its rightful place within interdisciplinarity.[136] However, this does not contradict the principle of converging options, since these depend on the perception and description of symbolic agency.[137]

2.3 How Should We Interpret Liturgy?

The hermeneutic of liturgics

Liturgics operates hermeneutically, that is, it intends to interpret liturgy and contribute to its understanding. It concerns itself with speech-acts composed of verbal and nonverbal elements of varied origins and historical-cultural provenience that mutually interpenetrate one another. With liturgical celebrations such as baptism, confirmation, Eucharist, Liturgy of the Hours, and feasts such as Christmas or Easter, or with such devotions as Benediction, it investigates complex situations of communication: the participants are a community, sorted by sophisticated means according to anthropological and theological criteria; the feasts and ceremonies are celebrated as events between the assembly of the faithful (the community, the church) on the one hand and God on the other, and they are structured within themselves according to units of meaning and function; beyond the particular celebration, they are incorporated within the whole of the church's liturgy.

[135] Albert Gerhards and Andreas Odenthal, "Auf dem Weg zu einer Liturgiewissenschaft im Dialog. Thesen zur wissenschaftstheoretischen Standortbestimmung," *Liturgisches Jahrbuch* 50 (2000): 41–53.

[136] Martin Stuflesser and Stefan Winter, "Liturgiewissenschaft—Liturgie und Wissenschaft? Versuch einer Standortbestimmung im Kontext des Gesprächs zwischen Liturgiewissenschaft und Systematischer Theologie," *Liturgisches Jahrbuch* 51 (2001): 90–118.

[137] Andreas Odenthal, *Liturgie als Ritual* (see n. 133 above).

Semantics, syntactics, pragmatics

Liturgy makes use of very different means of communication: verbal text, song, and music; gestures, mimicry, and movement; space; color; vessels; etc. To put it another way: it has recourse to verbality, imagery, sound, and embodiedness.[138] None of these means of communication exists in and for itself; each is incorporated within a larger liturgical structure of meaning. Liturgy is never accomplished solely in the text. It makes use of the multiple means of communication just listed and at the same time unites human beings in the event through every available communicative and sensual means. Even the written forms of liturgy—for example, those contained in liturgical books, which of course attend to and describe these means of expression—contain only certain aspects of liturgy. Ultimately, the proper object of investigation is the performance of the worship-event. It is about the carrying out of the worship service and the experiences associated with it. In order to be able to understand the liturgy in this perspective we must consider not only theology but such things as piety, spirituality, and mind-set, social and cultural context, etc.

The concepts of "performance" and "performative" are used today in cultural studies in a number of ways.[139] They are of elementary significance for liturgics because they concern fundamental actions of liturgy. In the first place, they describe *a speech-act that is effective in and of itself*. But the same concept also designates a *dramatic* performance.[140] The participants in a ritual use very different media for dramatization and presentation; at the same time, for those participating, such a kind of performance involves intensive experience. It is a matter of representative or illustrative action. This aspect of performance is also noteworthy for a liturgy such as that of the Easter Vigil, with its multiple verbal and nonverbal dramatic elements. Such rituals are events that, among other things, alter human perception, that as "frames" enable meta-communication within which

[138] Rainer Volp, *Liturgik. Die Kunst, Gott zu feiern*, vol. 1: *Einführung und Geschichte* (Gütersloh: Gerd Mohn, 1992), 154–55.

[139] Uwe Wirth, ed., *Performanz. Zwischen Sprachphilosophie und Kulturwissenschaft* (Frankfurt: Suhrkamp, 2002).

[140] See Stanley J. Tambiah, "A Performative Approach to Ritual," *Proceedings of the British Academy* 65 (1979): 113–69, at 119.

other actions and messages can be understood; these activities effect change.[141]

Thus liturgics inquires about the semantics, syntax, and pragmatics of the different elements in the speech-act "liturgy." It investigates the meaning of the liturgical elements, their internal structure, and their integration in parts or the whole of a liturgical celebration, as well as their effects and their usage in and through the liturgy. A meaningful liturgics approach to sources of worship can pursue very different questions; these determine the particular methodology and concrete procedure. But some steps are indispensable if we occupy ourselves with liturgies in the present and in history. In what follows we will illustrate this in terms of certain elements from the baptismal liturgy.

First approach to the source

An interpretation of the elements adduced must deal with a variety of questions. In any case, with any text, no matter what kind, the first concern is with an adequate study of the source as such, following philological standards. In the case of a liturgical text, no matter whether historical or contemporary, one begins with a translation or an analysis of the original form of the text and a determination of the literary genus. In liturgy, language is not something external but is one of the essential means of communication. The linguistic form is always also to be examined in terms of the text's meaning. The translation or careful study of the form of the language calls attention to these linguistic features (cf. 5.3). In the case of a sign-action one will correspondingly take care to obtain an exact description in order to be able really to understand it. Additionally, the meaning of the source must be critically assessed: who is behind this source? Who, insofar as this can be determined in the case of liturgical texts, is its author? What is its function? To whom is it addressed and who would use it? Source criticism is necessary especially in dealing with *liturgica*. Thus the type of source must be clarified: is this a liturgical book in the sense of a collection of liturgical texts and necessary sequences of

---

[141] Catherine Bell, *Ritual: Perspectives and Dimensions* (New York and Oxford: Oxford University Press, 1997), 72–76.

actions, as for example in a baptismal ritual? Does the book, such as a *Liber ordinarius*, serve to describe sequences of liturgical actions? Is this writing, as the name "church order" already indicates, intended to order ecclesial life and describe an ideal liturgy? The question of reception is in order not only for historical sources. *Liturgica* in particular (also) transmit bodies of tradition that may possibly be (or have been) unimportant for liturgical practice. Hence a critical dealing with the source may protect us against wrong assessments of actual liturgical practice.

History of liturgical speech-acts

Historical studies of texts and sign-actions have different foci, depending on the question. Liturgical texts in particular, because they are embedded in an ongoing process of tradition, can be called "living literature." Historical study, especially of the genesis of text and action, inquires about the place and time of origin and the original situation in which these were used. Current Catholic liturgy for the baptism of children uses texts and ritual actions for the signing of the infant on the forehead, litany and petitions, prayer for liberation (exorcism), and anointing with the oil of catechumens, all elements whose genesis, function, and present interpretation can only be given a correct scholarly analysis if we know their history. Their original locus was the catechumenate for the initiation of adults. When the baptism of infants developed out of that rite, the named elements were retained. If we know that background we can interpret these speech-acts today as catechumenal, and with that an indispensable dimension of Christian initiation comes into view.

Thus we must ask about possible developments and functional alterations in texts and actions because they can explain why a text or sign is used in this or that place and because such a diachronic approach facilitates understanding. However, the cultural and theological history behind the texts and actions must also be investigated. Thus knowledge of the history of theological discussions contributes to our understanding of christological or pneumatological statements in liturgical texts. In the baptismal ritual, knowledge of the religious-historical and theological significance of exorcisms is helpful for understanding their function, development, and alteration in modern times. Basically, we should expect that, in liturgy, elements from the faith tradition will be practiced at a later time under different social, cultural, and spiritual presuppositions, that is, they will be received within a different faith situation.

Individual speech-acts as parts of the whole ritual

The embedding of a text in a broader ritual unit or the ritual as a whole needs to be investigated. Thus we should inquire about factors that shape the performance of liturgy beyond verbal expression. Who speaks the text, and who hears? What gestures accompany it? What physical attitudes (sitting, kneeling, standing) are assumed? Where in space is the speech-act performed? The celebrations of the baptismal liturgy we have outlined imply a number of speakers and actors. Besides the priest or deacon, parents and sponsors take part, as well as the rest of the congregation. Reception into the community and entrance into the church are carried out through actions of community members, who participate as part of the "communion of saints." Expressive sign-actions accompany the spoken words, and these are indispensable for interpretation because they contribute to the overall action of the liturgy. Liturgy accomplishes what it promises. The binding of the baptizand to Christ is accomplished through signing with the cross on the forehead. Extending the hand while praying for liberation symbolizes the function of blessing and protection from evil that is asked of God on behalf of the baptizand. In the anointing with oil, the response to the prayer for strengthening with the power of Christ is experienced in a sign-action. The fact that this part of the liturgy is not performed at the place of baptism underscores its catechumenal character. Its function in the overall ritual is that of preparation for the baptismal event itself. Thus the characteristics of the various anointings associated with baptism can be explained within the broader liturgical context.

Liturgical speech-acts in extra-liturgical context

The social and ecclesial surroundings play their part in shaping liturgy. The ongoing history of society and worldview, of religion and devotion, of social and pastoral realities in the present influence how liturgy is celebrated. In what cultural surroundings, for example, does infant baptism find its place? In a society shaped by a common church culture the baptism of children is a matter of course; the supportive church milieu makes the integration of the newly baptized quite simple. In a secularized society, or one strongly shaped by an absence of any distinct confessional majority, it can happen that infant baptism becomes less normative and gives way to the baptism of adults. In a society in which religious traditions are present it may be easier for people to participate in and understand traditional liturgical formulas with their own linguistic style and imagery than is the case in cultures in which people are no longer familiar with such traditions. The study of liturgies in the past and in the present must take such qualifications into account.

The same is true of the conditions in theology and devotion within which liturgical celebration takes place. The rediscovery of adult initiation in the late twentieth century, given impetus by Vatican II among other things, casts a new light on the whole field of initiation. Very different forms of the one baptism (infant baptism, integration of children of school age, adult initiation) were practiced alongside one another and exercised mutual influence. On the other hand, changes in theology and devotional practice could render rites obsolete. Individual elements could be found problematic or unacceptable by the participants, with consequences for the liturgical celebration: one example is the ancient baptismal exorcism, the prayer for liberation from evil, at the baptism of infants. Thus in order to be able to understand such factors that shape liturgy and its common celebration in essential ways it is necessary to describe the context within which the particular liturgy is celebrated, something that is materially affected by the communicative situation.

The liturgical-theological significance of speech-acts

In a further step we must ask about the meaning of the text, noting its structure, conceptuality, grammar, style, rhetoric, etc. We will observe very different structures in a biblical reading (pericope), an antiphon, a hymn, or an oration, and these are important for the sense of the text itself. We can clarify this with an example, namely, the prayer for liberation from evil in the baptismal liturgy. One of the available texts reads:

Celebrant: Almighty and ever-living God, you sent your only Son into the world to cast out the power of Satan, spirit of evil, to rescue man from the kingdom of darkness, and bring him into the splendor of your kingdom of light. We pray for these children: set them free from original sin, make them temples of your glory, and send your Holy Spirit to dwell within them. (We ask this) through Christ our Lord. *All*: Amen.[142]

The text reveals a clear structure: it begins with an address recalling God's action in salvation history. This is followed by an extended petition directed to God through Christ. The prayer concludes with a formulaic acclamation by the congregation. The address is in the perfect tense, while the petition uses present and future tenses. Thus the prayer takes place on different linguistic levels in time and in this way also incorporates different times in salvation history: God's actions in the past, present, and future. Neither the sequence of structural elements—first praise and thanksgiving, then petition—nor the use of temporal forms is irrelevant. A faith-event is articulated by use of linguistic forms. The second part of the prayer is clearly marked by its introductory "We pray." The three petitions are formulated in parallel language; their content establishes a climax. We can recognize various levels of speech that indicate the faith-event: the celebrant addresses the prayer to God, but the congregation must assent in the closing acclamation; this is a prayer of the community ("we"-form). The formula "through Christ" indicates that Christ is the mediator of the prayer. At the same time, prayer for others, here the immature children, is expressed. The acting subject is God, who is asked to bring human beings enthralled by sin to freedom through Christ. The prayer is an expression of the church's accompaniment of human beings.

There are very few descriptions of the methodology and procedures of liturgics. Wintersig's guidelines[143] for the scholarly and ascetic interpretation of Mass formularies are still worth reading.

---

[142] Rite of Baptism for Children. English translation approved by the National Conference of Catholic Bishops and confirmed by the Apostolic See (Collegeville, MN: Liturgical Press, 2002), 28.

[143] Athanasius Wintersig, "Methodisches zur Erklärung von Messformularen," *Jahrbuch für Liturgiewissenschaft* 4 (1924): 135–52.

An overview of newer English, Italian, and German scholarly approaches, apart from our own work, with illustrative examples, can be found in DeZan.[144] Reinhard Messner has collected references to important types of sources and their evaluation.[145]

[144] Renato De Zan, "Criticism and Interpretation of Liturgical Texts," in *Handbook for Liturgical Studies*, vol. 1: *Introduction to the Liturgy*, ed. Ansgar J. Chupungco (Collegeville, MN: Liturgical Press, 1997), 331–65.

[145] Reinhard Messner, *Einführung in die Liturgiewissenschaft* (see n. 101 above), 35–54.

CHAPTER 3

Historical Sketch of the Roman Liturgy

3.1 Study of the History of Liturgy as a Central Task of Liturgics

Limitations of a purely historical-critical approach

The preceding chapter sketched the historical roots of liturgics. In the course of that presentation the problems involved in a historical outline of the liturgy came to light indirectly. The problems arise from the fact that there is no such thing as *"the"* liturgy; rather, there are any number of forms of celebration and institutions within different ecclesial and local-church traditions. The attempt at a systematic approach quickly collides with its limits. A historical-critical view that reconstructs the individual stages of a liturgy's development can—if it is made an absolute—give the impression that the full-grown Roman liturgy is a "heap of rubble." In the case of the Roman Canon (Eucharistic Prayer I), that has been explicitly asserted—wrongly, as we now know.[1] Such an approach already suffers from reducing the parameters to be established, although those are only adequate to the object when they are mutually enhancing: liturgy is not exhausted in the form of the words used; rather, it lives in the context of celebration, which is in turn embedded in an overall cultural context. Hence sources that attest to the history of thought-patterns and devotion[2] are essential to the writing of the history of liturgy today.

---

[1] Josef Schmitz, "Canon Romanus," in *Prex Eucharistica*, 3/1, *Studia*, "Ecclesia antiqua et occidentalis," ed. Albert Gerhards, Heinzgerd Brakmann, and Martin Klöckener, Spicilegium Friburgense 42 (Fribourg: Academic Press, 2005), 281–310.
[2] Friedrich Lurz, *Erlebte Liturgie. Autobiografische Schriften als liturgiewissenschaftliche Quellen*, Ästhetik–Theologie–Liturgik 28 (Münster: LIT, 2003).

There has probably never been an era so interested in history as the present. Every conceivable anniversary or jubilee is celebrated at great expense. Quantity often trumps quality. This "postmodern tendency," comparable to nineteenth-century historicism, is probably due to the fact that contemporary revolutions in the natural sciences call radically into question the things that constitute the identity of such historical constants as the individual and society. It is true that this way of dealing with the past has a somewhat random character. The old is valued only because it is old, and there is scarcely any effort to try to understand it in its own context.

The current exaltation of the old is in large part a reaction to the disdain in the postwar period for everything traditional. It was a time when people deliberately distanced themselves from the past in every aspect of life. In Germany the suppression of the most recent past during the time of rebuilding may have played a part in that development; it was only external circumstances in the course of the 1970s that put the brakes on the tendency.

Dealing with tradition

The liturgical reform following Vatican II was contemporary with this "second Enlightenment." Two hundred years late, the Roman Catholic Church for the first time adopted some of the positions of the European Enlightenment, at the very moment when "enlightenment" as such was falling into disrepute.[3] Pope John XXIII, with his slogan *aggiornamento*, which could be translated as openness of the church to the world in the sense of a new inculturation, gave an impetus that, while often misunderstood, was nevertheless decisive. One misunderstanding was the opinion, widespread at the time, that the church could and should adopt a new orientation completely independent of its past. History was regarded as dead weight to be thrown overboard. Study of history was at that time legitimated, in part, as presenting a negative foil in contrast to which the new church (and/or the new liturgy) could be developed. This idea was often based on the hypothesis of a degeneration in which the "golden age"

[3] Elmar Salmann, *Zwischenzeit. Postmoderne Gedanken zum Christsein heute* (Warendorf: Schnell, 2004), 100–101.

of patristics was followed by the "dark Middle Ages," leading to a "rigid standard liturgy" in the period between Trent and Vatican II. This way of looking at the history of liturgy is being radically called into question today.[4] The liturgical reforms of Vatican II, in contrast to such extreme positions, proceeded on the premise that the liturgy "is made up of unchangeable elements divinely instituted, and of elements subject to change" (SC 21).

Five decades after the issuing of the Constitution on the Liturgy one must certainly question some tendencies in liturgical reform as having been tributary to the dominant spirit of the times (see the monographs on the twenty-fifth and fortieth anniversaries of the Constitution[5]). Discussion often moves between two extremes: on the one side a rationalistic rejection of the historically developed form of the liturgy; on the other the more or less emotionally driven sentimental invocation, often vehemently pressed by conservative groups, of an ideal liturgy that never existed in reality.[6] In contrast to these two extreme positions, liturgics must practice a proper study of liturgy.[7] Only on the basis of a conscientiously developed historical

[4] Arnold Angenendt, *Liturgik und Historik. Gab es eine organische Liturgie-Entwicklung?*, 2nd ed., Quaestiones disputatae 189 (Freiburg: Herder, 2001).

[5] *Gottesdienst, Kirche, Gesellschaft. Interdisziplinäre und ökumenische Standort-bestimmungen nach 25 Jahren Liturgiereform*, ed. Hansjakob Becker, Bernd Jochen Hilberath, and Ulrich Willers, Pietas Liturgica 5 (St. Ottilien: EOS Verlag, 1991); *40 Jahre Liturgiekonstitution. Relecture und Zukunft. Heiliger Dienst 7*, nos. 3–4 (2004); *Liturgiereform. Eine bleibende Aufgabe. 40 Jahre Konzilskonstitution über die heilige Liturgie*, ed. Klemens Richter and Thomas Sternberg (Münster: Aschendorff, 2004); *Die Zukunft der Liturgie. Gottesdienst 40 Jahre nach dem Konzil*, ed. Andreas Redtenbacher (Innsbruck: Tyrolia, 2004); *Gottesdienst in Zeitgenossenschaft. Positionsbestimmungen 40 Jahre nach der Liturgiekonstitution des Zweiten Vatikanischen Konzils*, ed. Martin Klöckener and Benedikt Kranemann (Fribourg: Academic Press, 2006).

[6] Andreas Odenthal, "'Häresie der Formlosigkeit' durch ein 'Konzil der Buchhalter'? Überlegungen zur Kritik an der Liturgiereform nach 40 Jahren 'Sacrosanctum Concilium,'" *Liturgisches Jahrbuch* 53 (2003): 242–57.

[7] *Liturgiereformen. Historische Studien zu einem bleibenden Grundzug des christlichen Gottesdienstes*, vol. 1: *Biblische Modelle und Liturgiereformen von der Frühzeit bis zur Aufklärung*; vol. 2: *Liturgiereformen seit der Mitte des 19. Jahrhunderts bis zur Gegenwart*, ed. Martin Klöckener and Benedikt Kranemann, Liturgiewissenschaftliche Quellen und Forschungen 88 (Münster: Aschendorff, 2002).

account and its legitimate interpretation can we seek an answer to the question of where the borders lie between the indispensable and the changeable aspects of liturgy.

Historicity as an essential dimension of Christian worship

Historicity is by no means a secondary category in Christian worship. Rather, it is an essential feature, described in the word *anamnesis* (Latin *memoria*—memory, remembering). Anamnesis is in the first place a religious–historically constant phenomenon of the cultic sphere. It is the purpose of rites to stand as markers in the lives of individuals and communities. They bring into the present some central mythological events or those important to the history of the tribe or lineage that are constitutive for the community. But unlike other religions, the revealed religion of the Bible does not rest primarily on mythical (pre- or extra-historical) events but on the concrete, irreversible history of God with humanity. According to Christian conviction, that history arrives at its unsurpassable and definitive culmination in the person and life work of Jesus Christ. Encounter with the crucified and risen Lord is the center of every one of the church's actions that render it cultically present. The way in which the liturgy effects that making present was already modeled in Old Testament Judaism, especially the festal tradition of Passover.[8] The celebration of the liturgy not only preserves an external memory; those participating in the celebration enter into history and become "contemporaries of God." Unlike the ceremonies of myth-based religions, Christian liturgy is not a complete abstraction from the present. Because God has entered directly into human history and even made history, God is present at all times with the divine offer of salvation. This gives the believing community a potential for hope in a future with God. It is the mission of the church's liturgy to bring into relationship the present, the past-made-present, and the hoped-for future. Without

---

[8] Clemens Leonhard, "Die Erzählung Ex 12 als Festlegende für das Pesachfest am Jerusalemer Tempel," in *Das Fest: Jenseits des Alltags*, ed. Martin Ebner, Jahrbuch für Biblische Theologie 18 (Neukirchen-Vluyn: Neukirchener Verlag, 2003), 233–60.

doubt, its social character is an essential dimension of Christian liturgy, and that does not contradict its cosmic embeddedness.[9]

Church and culture

In the history of its expansion the church never encountered a culture-free space that it could have filled independently of everything else. Instead, it was confronted with mature cultures that had developed their own religious systems and corresponding ritual expressions. The first encounter, with Hellenistic culture, coincided with the separation from the root and ground of Judaism. This was the first process of assimilation, discernible in the Bible itself, but it would not be the last. Even in later times, for example, in the Franco-Germanic mission the Christian religion did not remain an unchangeable import. Instead, it combined with local forms of culture and religion, and this led to new types of religious expression. Certainly, that principle was not always maintained in the course of church history. In later times Christianization frequently involved the destruction of local cultures. It was only in the course of the twentieth century that the process began to be rethought.

Adaptation, accommodation, inculturation

The following is a conceptual clarification of the various stages or ways in which assimilation or accommodation has taken place.[10]

Adaptation. This includes the acquiring of local elements (e.g., fertility rituals) that are reinterpreted and integrated into the *syntagma* of Christian liturgy. Included are, for example, field processions of ancient pagan provenance or blessings taken from the religious practices of the peoples north of the Alps.

---

[9] Albert Gerhards, "Geschichtskonstruktionen in liturgischen Texten des Judentums und Christentums," in *Kontinuität und Unterbrechung. Gottesdienst und Gebet in Judentum und Christentum*, ed. idem and Stephan Wahle, Studien zu Judentum und Christentum (Paderborn: Schöningh, 2005), 269–85.

[10] Giancarlo Collet, "Inkulturation," *Neues Handbuch Theologischer Grundbegriffe* 2 (1991): 394–407.

Accommodation. This refers to a more external adaptation of Christian liturgy to the mentality of the particular population, as, for example, in the matching of Christian liturgical vestments to the cultural traditions of Africa or Asia.

Inculturation. Finally, "inculturation" describes a new type of assimilation, to be understood as the desirable outcome of the encounter between two equal partners. This demands a more profound intervention in the substance of texts, rites, and symbols, even to the point of discussing the accommodation of the matter of the eucharistic elements to cultural circumstances.[11]

Inculturation as an ongoing task

It is only in Europe that Christianity can be said to be truly inculturated. As far as the Roman Catholic Church is concerned, Vatican II first addressed the possibility of including all authentic local forms of expression (symbols, gestures, dance, music, and song). But we must not regard that process as having taken place once for all and being finished for all time to come. Instead, inculturation is an ongoing task of the whole church in every place, since the transfer of the Christian heritage must happen ever anew and because, as a result of globalization, every culture is experiencing a steadily increasing process of transformation.[12] The task of inculturation is founded in the nature of Christianity itself; Christianity is for the world but not of the world. The tension involved has often been resolved in one direction or the other: flight from the world or accommodation to it; ghettoization or syncretic leveling—these are constant temptations for the church. The following overview will show the ways in which, at different times, the liturgy has sought its own identity within change. It can treat only the Roman Rite, largely setting aside other liturgical

---

[11] Ansgar J. Chupungco, *Liturgical Inculturation: Sacramentals, Religiosity, and Catechesis* (Collegeville, MN: Liturgical Press, 1992); idem, "Liturgy and Inculturation," in *Handbook for Liturgical Studies*, vol. 2: *Fundamental Liturgy*, ed. idem (Collegeville, MN: Liturgical Press, 1998), 337–75.

[12] Hans Bernhard Meyer, "Zur Frage der Inkulturation der Liturgie," *Zeitschrift für Katholische Theologie* 105 (1983): 1–31; Keith Pecklers, ed., *Liturgy in a Postmodern World* (London and New York: Continuum, 2003).

families, especially those of the East. Even for the Roman West, what follows can sketch only a few essential stages in the history of liturgy. Some recent monographs give a broader overview,[13] as do a variety of longer articles in lexicons and handbooks[14] and a compendium that treats the liturgical history of the West under the aspect of liturgical reforms.[15]

3.2 Jewish Liturgy and Earliest Christian Worship

3.2.1 Jewish Worship in Jesus' World

One cannot speak of Christian worship without referring to Old Testament and Jewish worship.[16] The relationship of Jesus and the early church to Jewish worship reveals continuity and discontinuity. First we must briefly sketch the basic elements of Jewish worship.

[13] Hermann A. J. Wegman, *Liturgie in der Geschichte des Christentums* (Regensburg: Pustet, 1994); Marcel Metzger, *Histoire de la liturgie: les grands étapes*, Petite encyclopédie moderne du christianisme (Paris: Desclée de Brouwer, 1994); Keith F. Pecklers, *Liturgy: The Illustrated History* (Mahwah, NJ: Paulist Press, 2012); Frank C. Senn, *The People's Work: A Social History of the Liturgy* (Minneapolis: Augsburg Fortress, 2006); *Liturgy's Imagined Past/s: Methodologies and Materials in the Writing of Liturgical History Today*, ed. Teresa Berger and Bryan D. Spinks (Collegeville, MN: Liturgical Press, 2016).

[14] *The Oxford History of Christian Worship*, ed. Geoffrey Wainwright and Karen B. Westerfield Tucker (Oxford and New York: Oxford University Press, 2006).

[15] *Liturgiereformen* (see n. 7 above).

[16] *Jüdische Liturgie. Geschichte, Struktur, Wesen*, ed. Hans Hermann Henrix, Quaestiones disputatae 86 (Freiburg: Herder, 1979); Leo Trepp, *Der jüdische Gottesdienst. Gestalt und Entwicklung*, 2d ed. (Stuttgart: 2004); Peter Wick, *Die urchristlichen Gottesdienste. Entstehung und Entwicklung im Rahmen der frühjüdischen Tempel-, Synagogen- und Hausfrömmigkeit*, 2nd ed., Beiträge zur Wissenschaft vom Alten und Neuen Testament 150 (Stuttgart: 2003); *Identität durch Gebet. Zur gemeinschaftsbildenden Funktion institutionalisierten Betens in Judentum und Christentum*, ed. Albert Gerhards, Andrea Doeker, and Peter Ebenbauer, Studien zu Judentum und Christentum (Paderborn: Schöningh, 2003); *Dialog oder Monolog? Zur liturgischen Beziehung zwischen Judentum und Christentum*, ed. Albert Gerhards and Hans Hermann Henrix, Quaestiones disputatae 208 (Freiburg: Herder, 2004); *Kontinuität und Unterbrechung* (see n. 9 above).

Elements of Jewish worship

Worship in Jesus' time took place in three different places, with different cultic actions in each. Primary was the temple, with the sacrificial cult performed by the priests. There were a number of developments and prior stages that cannot be explored in detail here. When the temple was rebuilt after the Babylonian exile, the view of worship recorded in the Priestly writing took command; according to this the sacrificial cult was above all a ritual of expiation that culminated in the annual celebration of the Day of Atonement (Yom Kippur; see Lev 16).

In the time of Jesus the synagogue represented a second locus for Jewish worship. The first synagogues arose as a consequence of the centralization of the cult in Jerusalem. They served primarily as places of assembly for Sabbath worship, when the Law was read, the one God was confessed, and prayers were held in common. The Pharisees related the synagogue to the temple and its worship by means of a strict ritualism expressed in Sabbath restrictions and purity laws. Jesus engaged in argument over this legalistic view of things.

The third and most important "cultic location" for Jewish religion is the family, the private sphere of the home. Personal and family prayer shapes the whole of life: the course of the day (three times for prayer: morning, midday, and evening) and the common meal, which acquired a ritual character through the father's prayers. The Sabbath and the Passover meal were intensively shaped by ritual. The household did not exist in isolation from the other cultic locations: the Sabbath meal and the paschal meal were connected with the synagogue and temple. Hence in the chronology of Jesus' passion the hour when the paschal lambs were slaughtered in the temple plays an important role in John's account (John 19:14).

Jesus' relationship to the Jewish cult: Continuity . . .

Jesus' attitude toward the worship of his era was at first that of a believing member of the people Israel. The infancy narratives give a clear outline of his origins: he fulfilled all the requirements of the law (circumcision, Luke 2:21; presentation in the temple, Luke 2:22-24). Elements of continuity appear also in Jesus' later behavior; thus the Fourth Gospel reports four times that he went up to the temple. Pilgrimage to Jerusalem played a central role in Jesus' life, from the infancy stories to those of the passion.

Synagogue worship was highly important for Jesus. He not only participated but assumed the right of a Jewish man to read from Scripture and interpret it (Mark 1:21, 39; 6:2; Matt 9:35; Luke 4:15; John 6:59). But here we can already see the beginnings of a critique and a deviation from common Jewish cultic usage and traditional interpretations of Scripture (Luke 4:28-29).

In private also, it seems that Jesus largely adhered to the lines of Jewish tradition. Certainly he incorporated certain practices, such as almsgiving, prayer, and fasting into his relationship with God. He was radically critical of such practices when they served the purpose of self-justification (Mark 6:2-3).

. . . and new initiatives

It was precisely against the background of this primary continuity that Jesus' new initiatives and the radicality of the changes he made in certain elements became clear. Ultimately, the radicality of the new was grounded in Jesus' claim that in him the promises of the Old Covenant were fulfilled, that with him the reign of God had broken into human history. This eliminated certain elements of the framework derived from Jewish religious history. The first thing we should mention is the radical separation of clean and unclean in Jewish religion. The command "you shall be holy, for I am holy" (Lev 11:45) was understood to be fulfilled through sacrifices and the adherence to particular requirements. It was tied to priestly activity and culminated in the great day of atonement, Yom Kippur. Jesus eliminated this distinction (Mark 7:1). In doing so, he in essence erased the line of separation, generally accepted in antiquity, between sacred and profane. This is expressed in the miracle stories when Jesus not only heals the sick but also forgives sins. Accordingly, he overrides the cultic laws, such as keeping the Sabbath. He is "lord even of the Sabbath" (Mark 2:28).

Jesus' attitude toward the temple

Jesus' attitude toward worship was expressed in singular fashion in his relationship to the temple. His saying about the destruction and rebuilding of the temple points to a spiritualizing of the idea of temple. His driving the merchants out of the temple, described in all four gospels, should be interpreted as a sign-action: in the time of eschatological fulfillment the temple should remain only as a place of adoration. The prophetic word about the destruction of the temple is to be seen in the same light, as is the depiction of the tearing of the curtain of the temple at the hour of Jesus' death (Mark 15:38). Jesus' self-offering supercedes all substitutionary sacrifices; atonement has been accomplished once for all and is effective through faith (Rom 3:25). The "cult" is now no longer tied to a particular place but happens wherever two or three are gathered in his name (cf. Matt 18:20).

Early Christian worship

In what has been said we can recognize a few features of early Christian worship. First of all we should probably mention the Our Father (Matt 6:9-13): its content is altogether Jewish, and at the same time the plea for the coming of the reign of God was a primary concern of Christian prayer.[17] This eschatological feature can be regarded as characteristic of the early church as a whole and was expressed above all in early Christian meals (eucharistic celebrations), which should be regarded in this perspective as Jesus' new liturgical institution. Nevertheless, the church's eucharistic celebration did not represent a "repetition" of the Last Supper, the exact ritual course of which we do not know. For a theological understanding of the Christian Eucharist we need to include Jesus' other meals as well: those with toll collectors and sinners; the miraculous feedings. The latter, with their prayer of thanksgiving and ritual distribution, clearly bear liturgical features already (Mark 6:39). Afterward Jesus dismisses the crowd and thus shows that he is their host. Jesus bestows community; the limited time of the earthly celebration is a pointer to the uniquely given, unlimited table community in the reign of God to come.

---

[17] Karlheinz Müller, "Das Vater-Unser als jüdisches Gebet," in *Identität durch Gebet* (see n. 16 above), 159–204.

3.2.2 The Beginnings of Christian Worship

Models for the relationship between Jewish and Christian liturgy

The relationship between Jewish and Christian liturgy cannot be reduced to a simple formula. In general we should assume that both Jewish and Christian liturgies, in the forms in which we have received them, are new constructions that were created from older materials—partly independent of each other, partly subject to mutual influence or negative separation. We may discuss the subject using the paradigm of antithesis, the mother-daughter model, or even that of "twin brothers."[18] Recent research tends toward the third model, the "Jacob-Esau paradigm," though that proposal is by no means undisputed. It does have the advantage of being able to include ambivalences within the fundamental perspective of what is common to both. The relationship between Jewish and Christian liturgy is far more complex than was previously supposed. Certainly it is beyond question that most Christian traditions have Jewish roots, but it is often uncertain which individual Jewish traditions influenced Christian liturgy, and when it happened. In addition, we should assume that the liturgical forms in Christianity and rabbinic Judaism developed at roughly the same time, and frequently out of common biblical and post-biblical (Jewish) roots. Moreover, received forms were subject to a constant process of development, the course of which may have implied mutual reactions and interactions. "For example, it is clear that an anti-Jewish tendency was perceptible in the way particular Christian groups shaped an originally Jewish tradition. But on the other hand we cannot exclude the possibility that the reverse was sometimes the case. It is not impossible that certain Jewish ritual forms were created in reaction to or against particular developments in Christianity."[19]

---

[18] Albert Gerhards, "Kraft aus der Wurzel. Zum Verhältnis christlicher Liturgie gegenüber dem Jüdischen: Fortschreibung oder struktureller Neubeginn?," *Kirche und Israel* 16 (2001): 25–44; *Dialog oder Monolog?* (see n. 16 above).

[19] Gerhard Rouwhorst, "Identität durch Gebet. Gebetstexte als Zeugen eines jahrhundertelangen Ringens um Kontinuität und Differenz zwischen Judentum und Christentum," in *Identität durch Gebet* (see n. 16 above), 37–55, at 44.

Limits of mutuality

The obvious incorporation of the Old Testament and Jewish heritage makes it easy to overlook the discontinuity of Christian worship with that of Judaism. To begin with, the Christians continued what they had learned as Jews: they went on reading and rereading the Scriptures, but now those were interpreted christologically. They sensed hidden indicators in the Old Testament writings that paracletically (that is, through the inspiration of the Holy Spirit) interpreted their experience with Jesus of Nazareth. But the worship assembly did not imply withdrawal into a sacred sphere; rather, in the early Christians' eschatological horizon the whole world has been sanctified. The letter to the Hebrews reflects this completely new situation in the time after Christ.

The catechetical effect of the service of the Word (cf. 1 Cor 14) was especially emphasized in Gentile Christianity, alongside its anamnetic and paracletic character. This seems natural when we consider that here the traditional context familiar to Jews was lacking. But common to all Christians, whether Jewish or Gentile, was the anamnetic celebration of Jesus' resurrection in the Sunday Eucharist. It presumes the encounter with Christ in the Word (see the Emmaus narrative in Luke 24:13-35) but conveys an experience that the Word alone cannot give: that of sacramental encounter.

Regular participation in the daily and Sunday worship assemblies was preceded by the fundamental "enlightenment" experienced in baptism. (Enlightenment, φωτισμός, is the Greek church's name for this sacrament.) Here also the sacramental action did not take place without a suitable prior instruction; this is clearly portrayed in Acts in the narrative of the baptism of the Ethiopian chamberlain (Acts 8:26-40). The sacramental encounter is both climax and turning point. Much as, in the Emmaus story, Christ vanishes from the eyes of the disciples, so here the apostle disappears from the view of the newly baptized.

Worship formulae in the New Testament

The New Testament contains an abundance of worship formulae. It speaks repeatedly of singing psalms, hymns, and odes (1 Cor 14:26; Eph 5:12; Col 3:16). We may regard that as reference to a fundamentally charismatic style of early Christians. As for prayers, their wording was not fixed at that time; they probably corresponded to the particular origins of those praying.

Specifically Christian forms of prayer

Forms of prayer peculiar to Christianity, differing from those of Judaism, developed gradually. As far as the addressee was concerned, the Christians certainly retained the direction of Jewish prayer, but now they prayed in the name of Jesus and through Christ. Certainly we also find indications in the New Testament that they appealed to Jesus; the adoration of the Lamb attested in Revelation marks the culmination of the development within the New Testament: the heavenly liturgy, first directed to God alone, has become a liturgy celebrating God and the Lamb (Rev 4–5). As subsequent centuries would show, it was above all in the realm of hymnody that a special christocentrism in Christian prayer developed.

3.2.3 Jewish and Christian Worship

Thus we cannot speak of a "devolution"[20] from Jewish to Christian liturgy. The destruction of the Jerusalem temple must have been as momentous an event for Jewish communities as was the death of Jesus for his group of followers. The result in both cases was a set of new structures that affected all the ancient institutions. There are elements of Jewish liturgy from before the year 70 with which both later Jewish and Christian traditions are in continuity.

Sacred Scripture in worship

The church took over the reading of Sacred Scripture from the synagogue as an essential element of its worship. The *graphai* were at first—how could it have been otherwise?—the Scriptures of the Hebrew Bible and the Septuagint. In time the apostolic letters and the gospels were added. The church never abandoned the Scriptures of the First Testament, even though regionally and from time to time they were accorded very different value.

[20] Gerhards, "Kraft aus der Wurzel" (see n. 18 above).

The biblical books were the textual basis not only for reading but also for hymnody. There was probably a dialectic throughout history between biblicism and free composition. The Christ-hymns, already present in the New Testament and rapidly increasing in number in the postbiblical period, and of which Pliny's letter already speaks, were repeatedly suppressed in the early period as a defense against Gnosticism; the same happened during the Catholic Reformation as a result of centralizing efforts. Old Testament texts, especially the Psalms, are not only the basic component of the Liturgy of the Hours (which at one time was the prayer of everyone, in the manner of the Jewish tradition of prayer!) but were used for antiphonal singing at Mass, which dominated the acoustic code of the sung Mass purely in terms of time but aesthetically as well.

Parallels between Jewish and Christian prayer

In the wake of the liturgical reform after Vatican II, people recognized the original similarity, both in content and structure, between Christian and Jewish prayer and attempted, as part of the reform, to restore that similarity. This was true especially of the heart of liturgical prayer, the Eucharistic Prayer, and its parallels and derivatives in practically every sacramental celebration (both sacraments and blessings). The threefold or twofold structure (praise/thanksgiving and petition) is relevant not so much for structural as for content reasons. This is illustrated by an important parallel: the Jewish *birkat ha-mazon*, the thanksgiving after a meal. One of the numerous versions reads:

Praise: "Blessed are You, L-rd our Gd, King of the universe, Who, in His goodness, provides sustenance for the entire world with grace, with kindness, and with mercy. He gives food to all flesh, for His kindness is everlasting. Through His great goodness to us continuously we do not lack [food], and may we never lack food, for the sake of His great Name. For He, benevolent Gd, provides nourishment and sustenance for all, does good to all, and prepares food for all His creatures whom He has created, as it is said: You open Your hand and satisfy the desire of every living thing. Blessed are You, L-rd, Who provides food for all.

Thanksgiving: We offer thanks to You, L-rd our Gd, for having given as a heritage to our ancestors a precious, good and spacious land; for having brought us out, L-rd our Gd, from the land of Egypt, and redeemed us from the house of bondage; for Your covenant which You have sealed in our flesh; for Your Torah which You have taught us; for Your statutes which You have made known to us; for the life, favor, and kindness which You have graciously bestowed upon us; and for the food we eat with which You constantly nourish and sustain us every day, at all times, and at every hour.

Petition: Have mercy, L-rd our Gd, upon Israel Your people, upon Jerusalem Your city, upon Zion the abode of Your glory, upon the kingship of the house of David Your anointed, and upon the great and holy House over which Your Name was proclaimed. And rebuild Jerusalem the holy city speedily in our days. Blessed are You, L-rd, Who in His mercy rebuilds Jerusalem. Amen.[21]

Jewish (and also Christian) prayer is about renewal of the covenant. God's saving actions in history are made present in praise (it is God who gives nourishment); this is followed by a petition for continuation of the divine engagement until the eschatological fulfillment (table fellowship in the reign of God). In the Eucharist a special passage—the account of the Last Supper and the anamnesis of the death and resurrection of Jesus, reference to the foundational event—adopts a literary *topos* that has its predecessors and parallels in Old Testament and Jewish prayers. It remains an open question whether, and in what way, the Jewish festal tradition of Passover and the forms of celebration of the Passover and Sabbath meals exercised influence on the form of the Christian eucharistic celebration. It is possible that there are parallels to the *todah*, the confessional sacrificial meal, but recent research is very reticent about asserting any dependency.

Parallel symbolic actions

The other central sign-action, baptism, also has (besides the baptism of John, Matt 3:13-17 *parr*.) a counterpart, though only a vague one, in the immersion of proselytes as practiced in Judaism. Here also we should point to the different meaning assigned to baptism by Christian theology since Paul.

---

[21] Text at http://www.chabad.org/library/article_cdo/aid/135366/jewish /English.htm.

94

Finally, we find an analogous form of nearly every Christian liturgical sign-action in Judaism. This is true of anointings and imposition of hands, sprinkling (*asperges*), and the symbolism of light, which was adopted—again with a christological reinterpretation—from Jewish usage into Christian evening worship and from there into the Easter Vigil.

Assembly

The fundamental dimension of Christian worship rooted in Judaism is that of assembly. The Pentecost narrative expresses this clearly. It is true that Christianity did not adopt the strict regulation requiring a minimum of ten men (!), but it has always held fast—at least in theory—to the necessity of the assembly. We may point to the semantic relationship between *synagogē* and *ekklēsia*: both are derived from Greek concepts with the meaning "to assemble."

Structure of the liturgical year

Another important parallel is found in the macrostructure of the liturgical year as it developed, sometimes by adoption, sometimes by deliberate distancing from Judaism. Besides the continued week of seven days and the sequence of Sabbath and Sunday, we should point especially to the Passover-Easter tradition.[22] The Christian celebration of Easter without reference to the exodus event is unthinkable; it shapes the Christian liturgies of Good Friday and Easter in every stage of their development. Certainly it is true in this case also that Christian tradition—where it is a living one—has led to new assimilations and syntheses that have sometimes made the connection with Judaism nearly unrecognizable.

3.2.4 Early Christian Liturgy as Attested by Selected Sources

Time of assembly

Direct liturgical sources for the early period are rare; hence a picture of this very complex epoch in liturgical history can be acquired

---

[22] Hansjörg auf der Maur, *Die Osterfeier in der alten Kirche. Aus dem Nachlass*, ed. Reinhard Messner and Wolfgang G. Schöpf, with a contribution by Clemens Leonhard, Liturgica Oenipontana 2 (Münster: LIT, 2003).

only with difficulty.[23] But we find a series of hints embedded in the writings of the Church Fathers and also in documents from outside Christianity. For example, the letter of Pliny the governor is such a document; it was written to Emperor Trajan in the year 112: "They [the Christians who had been arrested] asserted . . . that the sum and substance of their fault or error had been that they were accustomed to meet on a fixed day before dawn and sing responsively a hymn to Christ as to a god. . . . When this was over, it was their custom to depart and to assemble again to partake of food—but ordinary and innocent food." This brief notice inaugurated a never-ending discussion as to the nature of the assemblies alluded to here: a morning service of the Word and an evening eucharistic celebration, or a morning Eucharist and an evening *agapē*? What is interesting is the assembling in mornings and evenings. That was certainly connected with socio-cultural circumstances on the one hand, but on the other hand the timing contains an inherent symbolism that was applied accordingly by the Christians. This is clear also from the *Phos hilaron*, a light hymn from the time of the martyr church that is still sung today in the Eastern churches and those of the Anglican Communion:

> O gracious Light,
> pure brightness of the everliving Father in heaven,
> O Jesus Christ, holy and blessed!
> Now as we come to the setting of the sun,
> and our eyes behold the vesper light,
> we sing your praises, O God: Father, Son, and Holy Spirit.
> You are worthy at all times to be praised by happy voices,
> O Son of God, O Giver of life,
> and to be glorified through all the worlds.[24]

---

[23] Reinhard Messner, "Der Gottesdienst in der vornizänischen Kirche," in *Die Zeit des Anfangs (bis 250)*, ed. Luce Pietri, Die Geschichte des Christentums 1 (Freiburg: Herder, 2003), 340–441.

[24] From *The Book of Common Prayer and Administration of the Sacraments and Other Rites and Ceremonies of the Church, together with The Psalter or Psalms of David, According to the use of The Episcopal Church* (New York: Church Publishing, 1979), 118.

Light symbolism

The hymn to light is doubly based on light symbolism: the "natural" light of the setting sun and the "artificial" light of the lamps brought in as darkness descends.[25] The hymn quoted here is a part of daily Christian prayer. Besides this daily rhythm, a second crucial rhythm established itself from the beginning: the weekly celebration of the mystery of redemption in the Eucharist.

The Didachē*: A meal celebration without an account of institution*

The eucharistic celebration is a fixed element in the oldest surviving church order, the *Didachē*, the "Teaching of the Twelve Apostles," dating from around the year 100. The time of composition thus corresponds to that of the late New Testament writings. As a church order, the *Didachē* contains a number of directions for liturgy, from baptism through weekly fasting, daily prayer, confession and reconciliation, to Eucharist. However, it is a matter of dispute whether the eucharistic prayers it contains belong to a eucharistic celebration in the strict sense, or only to religiously oriented community meals in Jewish-Christian circles (*agapē*). In any case, these texts lack reference to the institution of the Eucharist at the Last Supper and to the passion, which might possibly be interpreted as indicating a plurality of early Christian liturgical usages.[26] The structure corresponds to that of Jewish meal customs: a prayer of praise over bread and another over wine, and a concluding petition (*Did.* 9), as well as a three-part thanksgiving after the meal, similar to the Jewish thanksgiving prayer (*Did.* 10).

> 1. (And) concerning the eucharist, eucharistize thus: 2. First, concerning the cup: We give you thanks, our Father, for the holy vine of your servant David which you revealed to us through your servant

[25] Peter Plank, *Phos hilaron. Christushymnus und Lichtdanksagung der frühen Christenheit*, Hereditas 20 (Bonn: Borengässer, 2001).

[26] Reinhard Messner, "Grundlinien der Entwicklung des eucharistischen Gebets in der Frühen Kirche," in *Prex Eucharistica* 3/1 (see n. 1 above), 3–41; Peter Ebenbauer, "Eingekehrt in Gottes Zeit. Gebetstheologische Beobachtungen zu Lobpreis und Danksagung in biblischen und nachbiblischen Kontexten," in *Kontinuität und Unterbrechung* (see n. 9 above), 63–106.

Jesus. To you [is] the glory forever. 3. And concerning the broken [loaf]: We give you thanks, our Father, for the life and knowledge which you revealed to us through your servant Jesus. To you [is] the glory forever. 4. Just as this broken [loaf] was scattered over the hills [as grain], and, having been gathered together, became one; in like fashion, may your church be gathered together from the ends of the earth into your kingdom. Because yours is the glory and the power through Jesus Christ forever. 5. (And) let no one eat or drink from your eucharist except those baptized in the name of [the] Lord, for the Lord has likewise said concerning this: "Do not give what is holy to the dogs."[27]

Eucharistic celebration

The basic structures of the eucharistic celebration were established at the latest by the middle of the second century. Around the year 150, Justin described the Eucharist in his First Apology (chap. 65). He reports that the newly baptized were led from the font into the assembly of the faithful, where a common prayer was followed by the kiss of peace. Then bread and wine, together with water, were brought to the presider.

> And he taking them sends up praise and glory to the Father of the Universe through the name of the Son and of the Holy Spirit, and offers thanksgiving at some length for our being accounted worthy to receive these things from Him. When he has concluded the prayers and the thanksgiving, all the people present assent by saying, Amen. . . . And when the Ruler has given thanks and all the people have assented, those who are called by us deacons give to each of those present a portion of the eucharistized bread and wine and water, and they carry it away to those who are absent.[28]

In the next chapter Justin emphasizes the special character of this meal. In accordance with the Last Supper accounts in the gospels it is

[27] Aaron Milavec, *The Didache: Text, Translation, Analysis, and Commentary* (Collegeville MN: Liturgical Press 2003).

[28] Justin, *Apol. 1*, 65, in *St. Justin Martyr: The First and Second Apologies*, trans. Leslie William Barnard, Ancient Christian Writers 56 (New York and Mahwah, NJ: Paulist Press 1997), 70.

traced to Jesus' institution; there is mention of the words of institution as well. It is possible that at this date they were not yet included in the thanksgiving prayer of the celebration itself, as a number of liturgical witnesses suggest (*Didachē*, East Syrian Apostolic Anaphora).[29] The Eucharist is understood as an action carried out in the Holy Spirit, in eschatological hope for the Lord's return. There is also the *anamnesis* of Christ shaped by Paul, which became the dominant motif.[30] The beginnings of developing hierarchical structures still contrast with the charismatic element, as in the permission for non-ordained prophets to celebrate the Eucharist in the *Didachē* (*Did.* 10.7). Here, as with Justin, the exclusion of the unbaptized is an important point. There is still a relatively broad freedom within the community of believers; thus the presider at the liturgical celebration could improvise prayers.[31]

In contrast to comparable documents, the *Apostolic Tradition* (*Traditio Apostolica*; *TA*) is distinguished by an abundance of prayer texts and a detailed description of the various worship services and their content.[32] The uniqueness of this document probably consists above all in the fact that it stands on the threshold between euchological freedom and the establishment of specified texts for liturgical prayer. At a later time, when Christianity began to expand out of the central cities and extend more and more to the countryside, the tendency to specification of liturgical texts and orientation to liturgical centers grew.

The history of influence in the sphere of the Eastern churches is to all intents and purposes unique. This applies, for example, to the structure of the eucharistic prayers, which reveal far greater similarities to the text found in the *Apostolic Tradition* than does the later Roman Canon.

---

[29] Reinhard Messner and Martin Lang, "Die Freiheit zum Lobpreis des Namens. Identitätsstiftung im eucharistischen Hochgebet und in verwandten jüdischen Gebeten," in *Identität durch Gebet* (see n. 16 above), 371–411.

[30] Messner, "Grundlinien" (see n. 26 above).

[31] Achim Budde, "Improvisation im Hochgebet. Zur Technik freien Betens in der Alten Kirche," *Jahrbuch für Antike und Christentum* 44 (2001): 127–41.

[32] For the state of research see *Comparative Liturgy. Fifty Years after Anton Baumstark (1872–1948): Acts of the International Congress, Rome, 25–29 September 1998,* ed. Robert F. Taft and Gabriele Winkler, Orientalia Christiana Analecta 265 (Rome: Pontificio Istituto Orientale, 2001), 583–622.

Rites of initiation

The *Apostolic Tradition* reveals an internal liturgical structure that was already quite developed, though it still contains hints of the openness and spontaneity of the beginnings. The basic cycles of the day (Liturgy of the Hours), the week (eucharistic celebration), and year (Easter celebration) have already been shaped. This framework, still relatively open, would be filled in later. Christian initiation had special significance because of the fact that Christianity had to distinguish itself from a great many external influences. Initiation came at the end of a time of preparation lasting about three years (the catechumenate), made up of a multitude of instructions as well as assemblies for worship with a variety of rituals (examinations, exorcisms with imposition of hands). A rather lengthy first phase, to which subjects were admitted only after being examined for suitability, was followed by a second phase of immediate preparation for initiation; it included a probationary examination, exorcisms, a cleansing bath, and the baptismal fast. The celebration of initiation (*TA* 21, apparently not yet associated with the Easter Vigil) included three ritual foci: (1) the baptismal immersion with anointing at the font before and afterward; (2) imposition of hands and anointing of the forehead in the church by the bishop; (3) baptismal eucharist (*TA* 21.1-37; cf. also the schemata for the catechumenate in *TA* 20). After the baptism there could be a more profound catechesis by the bishop—possibly an indication of the mystagogical phase later attested.

3.3 Origins of the Roman Rite

3.3.1 *Liturgical Language from Greek to Latin*

The identity of the Roman Rite, which developed parallel to numerous rites in East and West, was closely connected with the fact that in Rome, in the period up to the second half of the fourth century, the language of liturgy moved in stages from Greek to Latin (see chap. 5.3). The inculturation in a new way of thinking that accompanied the shift in liturgical language was expressed in the Roman liturgy, for example, in the structure of the canon. If we lay the anaphora of the *Apostolic Tradition* alongside the Roman Canon we can see major differences. The anaphora of the *TA*, besides its severe brevity, bears the marks of internal and formal unity. The text is conceptually clear in its formulation and follows the plan of address handed down in Old Testament prayer formulas: praise, thanksgiving, and petition. The Roman Canon, in contrast—though the earliest form of the text known to us, certainly, comes from the late sixth century—shows clear traces of redaction and reveals a different psychological approach to prayer. The individual parts of the Canon (i.e., the prayers following the Preface and *Sanctus*) are symmetrically arranged around the center, the *verba testamenti* (anamnesis of the Last Supper), and are grammatically attached to the preceding epiclesis through relative constructions. In this perspective the frequently repeated petition for acceptance of the sacrifice is key. In spite of its special features, the Roman Canon corresponds, in its original expression, to the eucharistic tradition common to the whole church.[33]

The uniqueness of the language of Roman liturgy appears especially in the form of the collects, that is, the Roman prayer of the presider. Statements of faith are expressed with the greatest conciseness. The rhetorical flourishes derive in part from Roman legal rhetoric, though biblical references surface more frequently than at first appears (see chap. 5.2, 5.3).

3.3.2 Sources of Early Roman Liturgy

The old Roman liturgy took shape in the period between the end of the fourth century and the beginning of the seventh. Most significant as creators of liturgical forms were popes Leo the Great (440–461) and Gelasius I (492–496). Gregory the Great (590–604) was probably less important as a creator and reformer of the liturgy than his reputation makes one believe.[34] Gregorian chant is named for him because

---

[33] Reinhard Messner, "Unterschiedliche Konzeptionen des Messopfers im Spiegel von Bedeutung und Deutung der Interzession des römischen Canon missae," in *Das Opfer. Biblischer Anspruch und liturgische Gestalt*, ed. Albert Gerhards and Klemens Richter, Quaestiones disputatae 186 (Freiburg: Herder, 2000), 128–84; Josef Schmitz, "Canon Romanus," in *Prex Eucharistica* 3/1 (see n. 1 above), 281–310.

[34] Andreas Heinz, "Papst Gregor der Grosse und die römische Liturgie. Zum Gregorius-Gedenkjahr 1400 Jahre nach seinem Tod († 604)," *Liturgisches Jahrbuch* 54 (2004): 69–84.

he regulated church music, but here again without being active as a composer.

Liturgy before Gregory the Great

It is very difficult to get a picture of liturgy before Gregory the Great. There were no official editions as we know them today. The oldest form of written specification of prayer formulae was found in the so-called *libelli*, collections of pages preserved in the archives of the Bishop of Rome.

Sacramentarium Veronense

A set of these was put together according to a very incomplete monthly plan that has come to be known as the *Sacramentarium Leonianum*. It is true that the book has no direct connection to Leo the Great; consequently a renaming for the location of the library, in Verona, has prevailed, and it is now called the *Sacramentarium Veronense*. The compiler did not assemble the material for Rome, but he did work almost solely with Roman formularies, and for that reason the collection represents a valuable documentation of the liturgy of the city of Rome. A series of these formulae goes back to Pope Vigilius (537–555), as well as to the already-mentioned popes, Leo the Great and Gelasius; consequently, the collection must be dated to the time after Vigilius.

Sacramentaries

Of course, the *Sacramentarium Veronense* was not yet a genuine sacramentary; that term describes a book in which the unvarying ("canonical") official liturgical prayers and those that change according to the day are recorded—chiefly for the eucharistic celebration, but also for other acts of worship. It represents the "list of roles" for those carrying out the worship service; additional books were needed for the full carrying out of the Mass, including the lectionary (for the readings from biblical books other than the gospels), gospel book (for readings from the gospels), and antiphonary (for texts for antiphonal singing, usually consisting of psalm verses). With the establishment of "private Masses" (i.e., celebration of Mass without direct participation by a congregation) in the High Middle Ages, a plenary missal was fashioned out of all these books; it contained all the texts necessary for celebrating Mass.

Sacramentarium Gregorianum

The so-called *Sacramentarium Gregorianum* was a sacramentary in the sense described. Its original form is no longer extant, but it can be approximately reconstructed from its later descendants. It may have been created at the beginning of Gregory the Great's pontificate, and it was retained because of the fact that Charlemagne requested Pope Hadrian I to send him a revision of the *Sacramentarium Gregorianum* from the time of Gregory II (715–731): the so-called "Aachener Urexemplar." Additions were made to it in accordance with the changed requirements of the Frankish imperial church.

Sacramentarium Gelasianum

The form of sacramentary most disputed among scholars is the so-called *Sacramentarium Gelasianum*. It is presumed that the *Gregorianum* is not the oldest Roman sacramentary. The *Sacramentarium Gelasianum Vetus*, surviving in a copy from 750, is regarded as its predecessor. Despite its name, the formulary does not go back to Gelasius I, as is evident from the fact that it contains many non-Roman elements. According to the results of recent research the *Gelasianum* was a sacramentary for the presbyterial (i.e., parish) liturgy, introduced in the Roman titulary churches (i.e., parish churches) in the mid-seventh century. It was an addition alongside the Gregorian tradition of sacramentaries, which represented the papal liturgy (that of the Bishop of Rome) and consequently contained only a limited number of Mass formularies. Later versions of the *Gelasianum*— so-called "mixed types"—combining Roman and Gallican liturgical materials were widely used.

Worship texts and books of rubrics

Certainly the textual component of liturgy as retained in the sacramentaries and other books constituted only one part of the whole. Where do we learn about the ritual enactments? In fact, the earliest

Roman liturgical books contained nothing but texts, with scarcely any rubrics. As the originally simple ceremonies were more and more richly embellished in the course of development of the church year and sacramental rites, but especially as the Roman liturgy began to be adopted in the Carolingian empire, a codification of the customs that until then had been only orally transmitted became necessary. Now collections of ritual actions (*Ordines*) were prepared, some of them containing elements from lands north of the Alps. So sacramentaries and *ordines* have to be read in parallel if we are to get a picture of the form of the Mass celebration that was susceptible to literary recording. In fact, this state of separate parallel books existed only for a while. The two basic types, text books and rubrics, were shaped over time into new liturgical books, now differentiated according to the type of worship service. The first of these was the Roman-German Pontifical (*Pontificale romano-germanicum*), originating in Mainz around 950 and developed from the *ordines*, which the Ottonians brought to Rome, where it became the basis for the later *Pontificale Romanum*. It contained episcopal ceremonies and the texts belonging to them. Alongside it was developed the *Caeremoniale Episcoporum*, a book that described only the course of the rituals. A ritual book for priestly liturgies was prepared, containing descriptions of sacramental actions and the corresponding prayers. Books for scriptural readings were at first conceived for the different roles: the epistolary or lectionary with biblical readings other than the gospels for the lector, the gospel book (*evangeliar* or *evangelistar*) for the deacon. In the course of the High Middle Ages the texts of the Mass liturgy were gathered from sacramentaries, *ordines*, books of readings, and books of sung texts to form a single book, the Plenary Missal. The same is true for the later breviary, which combined the order of days and hours with the texts contained in the sacramentary, the lectionaries, and the antiphonals.

Musical texts

The books for singing (antiphonaries, cantatories) at first contained only texts; the methods of cantillation and the melodies were at first transmitted orally. Only in the ninth and tenth centuries did manuscripts with neums appear; these, however, did not reflect the exact melodies but only regulated the accentuation of the oral performance.

Other secondary books to be mentioned are the martyrology, with hagiographical texts; the *calendarium* with the festal calendars, differing from place to place; and the benedictional, which, unlike the ritual books, contained no sacramental ceremonies but only blessings (benedictions).

From these processes of development we can see that the liturgy grew from a rather simple basic form into a complicated structure. The same is true of the other components, e.g., vestments and the courses of actions within ceremonies. The foundation for the change in the overall picture was already laid down between 312 and 337 during the reign of Emperor Constantine.

Adoption of symbols from imperial court ceremonial

Constantine's laws, which accorded privileges to church officials, led over time to an adoption of imperial court ceremony within Christian worship. The liturgy became a stage of the hierarchically structured church. Much as in the Orthodox church in Byzantium, the imperial symbols and rituals were adopted and reinterpreted as imaging the ceremonies before the heavenly throne. Correspondingly, insignia and badges of office appeared, things that influence liturgical vestments and the staging especially of episcopal services to this day. In this the Bishop of Rome was accorded a special place, recognizable, for example, in the description of the city worship at Rome, a typically Roman form of organization composed of processions and multiple liturgical memorials incorporating not only the microstructure of the individual ecclesial spaces but also the macrostructure of the ecclesiastical city.[35]

3.3.3 The Roman Bishop's Mass around 700

The Ordo number one in Michel Andrieu's edition of the above-mentioned *Ordines Romani* is a detailed description of the

---

[35] Angelus A. Häussling, *Mönchskonvent und Eucharistiefeier. Eine Studie über die Messe in der abendländischen Klosterliturgie des frühen Mittelalters und zur Geschichte der Messhäufigkeit*, Liturgiewissenschaftliche Quellen und Forschungen 58 (Münster: Aschendorff, 1973).

papal Mass around the year 700. This description illustrates how the liturgy that had fully developed over time now appeared.[36]

Location

Early in the morning the pope and his train rode from his residence in the Lateran to the church of the day, the so-called *statio*, which had been designated in the ongoing calendar of celebrations as the place of the next papal Mass. These station churches are indicated in the Roman Missal even today, a relic of the Roman origins of this liturgy. The festal procession bore with it the necessary books, vessels, instruments, and cloths for the liturgy. Participants in the celebration were already assembled at the station church before the pope's arrival.

In the apse, on the benches to the right and left of the papal throne, sat the bishops and presbyters. The *schola cantorum* had taken its place in its choir stalls in front of the apse. Before the choir stalls stood the crucifers with the seven station crosses, carried before the faithful from various parts of the city. In the transept and the forward section of the nave the monks, nuns, and members of the Roman nobility all had their designated places. The Christian people were in the other parts of the nave, separated according to gender. The faithful had brought their offerings of bread and wine with them in order to hand them to the bishop and clergy at the offertory.

Sequence of a papal Mass

When the festal procession arrives at the station church, the person responsible for this house of God welcomes the pope, who, assisted by a deacon, enters the sacristy in the narthex area. Next, in an elaborate Byzantine ceremony, the pope's outer garments are taken from

[36] Michel Andrieu, *Les Ordines Romani du haut moyen âge*, vol. 2, *Les textes* (*Ordines I–XIII*), SSL 23 (Louvain: Spicilegium sacrum lovaniense, 1948); *Gottesdienst der Kirche. Handbuch der Liturgiewissenschaft*, ed. Hans Bernhard Meyer, et al. (Regensburg: Pustet, 1983–), vol. 4, Hans Bernard Meyer, *Eucharistie. Geschichte, Theologie, Pastoral*, with a contribution by Irmgard Pahl (1989), 196–99 (with schema on 198); Theodor Klauser, *A Short History of the Western Liturgy: An Account and Some Reflections*, trans. John Halliburton (Oxford and New York: Oxford University Press, 1979).

him and he dons the pontifical liturgical vestments that have been carried in the procession: alb with cincture, stole, a short inner and a second outer dalmatic, and the chasuble (*planeta*). Last, a deacon lays the pallium around his neck, over the chasuble, and fastens it with brooches or cloak pins. After a series of preparatory rituals, the signal is given to begin: the lighting of seven lamps borne by seven acolytes. Then the schola begins the entrance antiphon.

The entrance ceremony contains an interesting intermezzo: two acolytes bring a small box containing pieces of the bread consecrated at the last previous papal Mass. The pope bows to these fragments (*fermentum*) and decides how many of them he will use at the Eucharist. They will be placed in the eucharistic chalice to document the connection between the celebrations separated in time. To affirm that the various local worship services throughout the city are all united, before communion a fragment of the bread consecrated by the pope is carried to each of the district churches in Rome, where the serving presbyters will use it in the same way at a Eucharist.

After the introit psalm the pope takes his place in the apse where, facing east, he joins in the singing of the *Kyrie eleison* litany. At that time the number of petitions was not yet established; the litany ended when the pope gave the sign. Then he began the *Gloria in excelsis*. The Liturgy of the Word consisted of an epistle, response, and proclamation of the gospel, before which the appointed deacon kissed the pope's feet and received the blessing (as is still done today). Then he proceeded in a solemn procession to the ambo, from which he proclaimed the gospel. With a reverence to the gospel book, the Liturgy of the Word concluded. This description says nothing of a homily or petitions. The latter had vanished from the Roman Mass two centuries earlier. The *Credo*, on the other hand, was not yet part of the liturgy; it was first introduced in the eleventh century.

The eucharistic portion of the Mass began with the offertory procession. The clergy collected the gifts brought by the individual groups of believers; significantly, the pope himself received the gifts of the aristocracy. This action was accompanied by the schola's singing and concluded with the pope's prayer over the gifts. Now the clergy entered the sanctuary and took their places. The congregation was already excluded from active participation in the papal liturgy by this time. Only the clergy joined in singing the *Sanctus*. Likewise, the Eucharistic Prayer was no longer spoken so loudly that it could be understood everywhere; it would have been audible only in the choir.

The breaking of the bread before communion took a considerable time because in this period ordinary bread was still used. Communion was distributed in a strict hierarchical order: first the pope, then the clergy, and finally the congregation, who ordinarily received communion at their places. Hence there was no longer a real communion procession of the faithful, in much the same way as the procession with the gifts had been reduced, as described above.

3.3.4 Essential Features of the Roman Liturgy

The papal liturgy represents the most richly developed ritual liturgical form in the city of Rome. Mass was celebrated more simply in the parish churches, but the further development of the Roman Rite shows that there was a great desire to imitate the form of the papal Mass, to the point of copying it as exactly as possible (e.g., in Fulda). Even the presbyteral Masses, about whose original form we know essentially nothing, acquired features from the liturgy described above. The fundamental features of the Roman-Latin Mass were already established.

Fundamental features of the Roman-Latin Mass

1. Emphasis on hierarchical order, established by insignia, ritual acts (processions), and signs of reverence

2. Added solemnity of the official priestly prayers (the three collects, the Eucharistic Prayer)

3. Juridical style of the prayers and overall abandonment of poetic elements

4. Fading of the dimension of proclamation (reduction of readings, ritualizing of the reading, abandonment of the homily)

5. Gradual reduction of the role of the faithful (*Schola Cantorum* as space within space, abandonment of the prayer of the people, elimination of the people's procession with the gifts, decline in communion of the faithful, and prohibition of lay participation in communion from the chalice)

Over the course of history these basic features have been viewed with some ambivalence. Even today a festive Mass generally makes use of the forms stemming from the Roman-Byzantine papal court ceremonial. The forms of popular piety developed in later times (e.g., hymns, litanies, processions) were scarcely or not at all integrated into the "official" liturgy. On the other hand, the clear strictness and high spiritual demands of the Roman liturgy are impressive. The web of texts, singing, symbols, and rituals represents a "total work of art" that calls for emulation.

3.4 Liturgical Centers in Late Antiquity

3.4.1 The Jerusalem Liturgy

Significance of Jerusalem and the holy places

The true root and ground of Christian liturgy lay not in Rome but in Jerusalem. Here was the place of origin, even though it declined in rank under the five patriarchs in Antioch and later in Constantinople/Byzantium, and Alexandria and Rome achieved much greater influence. In terms of church politics, certainly, Jerusalem was only an honorary patriarchy, but in the history of liturgy and devotion it was ahead of the other centers in one respect: it possessed the holy places. These continued to shape the liturgy in East and West as these latter adapted Jerusalem's topography and ritual organization.

The crucial impetus to the mutual exchange came from pilgrimages to the Holy Land, which increased by leaps and bounds after Constantine and are attested in writing by any number of pilgrims' accounts. The most important of these for liturgics is that of a Spanish nun named Egeria. Its first part describes her itinerary; its second contains an extensive description of the liturgy, especially of Holy Week, in the years 383 and 384.[37]

---

[37] *Egeria: Diary of a Pilgrimage*, trans. George E. Gingras, Ancient Christian Writers 38 (New York and Mahwah, NJ: Newman Press, 1968).

Historicizing reenactment

The changing idea of liturgy is revealed especially in the Holy Week liturgy, which, beginning in Jerusalem, shaped the ceremonies in all the liturgical realms in East and West. It changed dramatically in the period of the great press of pilgrims. The originally symbolic salvation-historical celebration of the Easter Vigil developed into a "Drama of Redemption" in the sense of a historicizing reenactment[38]—essentially a consequence of the development of the church of the martyrs into a church of the masses. Thus the organization of the liturgy reacted to the changing conditions of the time: liturgy, catechesis, and popular piety shaped a synthesis whose tone was set by the dramaturgy of the gospels and the topography of the holy places.

Pilgrimage to Israel and the church year

The consolidation of pilgrimage and the development of the church year did in fact happen during the same period of time. Egeria attests to this in her two-part account. Interconnections point to the affinity between pilgrimage and the church year—for example, the processions on the feast of the Epiphany, on Palm Sunday, and throughout Holy Week. The genuinely Christian pilgrim motif is the *anamnesis* of the mysteries of Christ. The theological foundation derives from the incarnation of the *logos*. The coincidence between the institution of pilgrimages to the Holy Land and the church year, which the feasts of Christ now shaped as a "pilgrimage to the holy places of faith," was accordingly not accidental.

Pilgrimage and the Liturgy of the Word

There are also indications of a religiously motivated planning of the route for ancient pilgrimages, making the experience of the journey a unified existential-religious event. Egeria's itinerary provides some pointers and contains important liturgical elements, for example, a "meditation" attested at many stations along the pilgrim-

---

[38] Martin Klöckener, "Die 'Feier vom Leiden und Sterben Jesu Christi' am Karfreitag. Gewordene Liturgie vor dem Anspruch der Gegenwart," *Liturgisches Jahrbuch* 41 (1991): 210–51, at 218.

110

age route, consisting of prayer, reading, psalm, and prayer.[39] This is the classic structure of the Liturgy of the Word as Josef A. Jungmann described its formal plan (though without an opening prayer): reading, hymn, prayer as the ideal model for a katabatic (descending), diabatic (transforming), and anabatic (rising) dynamic of the Liturgy of the Word.[40]

Beyond this, initiation played an important role in connection with the pilgrimage stations. It seems as if the pilgrim journey represented a kind of special catechumenate, a compressed mystagogy. In any case, the period of preparation and deepening was notably shortened at the place of pilgrimage, in contrast to the normal course. Moreover, in those places no one was bound to the fixed dates for baptism.

3.4.2 The Liturgies of the Eastern Patriarchates

Antioch, Eastern Syria, Constantinople

The crucial influences in the eastern part of the Roman Empire came from two centers: Antioch (later replaced by Constantinople/Byzantium) and Alexandria. Antioch was at first influenced by Jerusalem, whose Eucharistic Prayer (the Anaphora of James) it adopted. Its language was Greek, but it had a Semitic hinterland, which influenced the East Syrian entrance prayer. It was in that region, in the fifth century, that a separate, so-called Nestorian church appeared. Its central Eucharistic Prayer, the Anaphora of the Apostles Addai and Mari, is characterized by the fact that it contains no words of institution.[41] West Syria was soon dominated by Byzantium, but there were cultural forces that pressed toward re-orientalization (for example, Jacob Baradaeus, bishop of Edessa 543–578). Constantinople

---

[39] See, e.g., *Egeria*, chap. 14, pp. 71–72.

[40] Josef A. Jungmann, *The Liturgy of the Word*, trans. from the 4th rev. ed. by H. E. Winstone (London: Burns & Oates, 1966).

[41] Reinhard Messner and Martin Lang, "Die Freiheit zum Lobpreis des Namens" (see n. 29 above); Albert Gerhards, "*In persona Christi in nomine Ecclesiae.* Zum Rollenbild des priesterlichen Dienstes nach dem Zeugnis orientalischer Anaphoren," in *Priester und Liturgie. Manfred Probst zum 65. Geburtstag*, ed. George Augustin, et al. (Paderborn: Bonifatius, 2005), 59–73.

(Byzantium) was given pride of place at the Council of Chalcedon in 451, and its sphere of influence steadily spread. Originally, Constantinople was influenced by Antioch, and in the Middle Ages some Jerusalem traditions reemerged within the Liturgy of the Hours.

Armenia, Georgia

The liturgy of Armenia is related to the Byzantine form; its Christian origins go back to the early fourth century. But Armenia's liturgy also contains elements of Syrian provenance. The Armenian lectionary of Jerusalem (fifth century) is an outstanding liturgical resource, especially for the ordering of the scriptural readings in worship services. We should also mention the liturgy of Georgia on account of its age and relative independence. At the time of the mission to the Slavs and the establishment of new Orthodox churches in the lands of Eastern Europe the form of the Byzantine liturgy was largely fixed as regards its texts, rituals, and structures. There were further developments at a later time, primarily in the realm of liturgical music.

Alexandria

Alexandria in turn had its own independent tradition. Originally also Greek, the language of the liturgy shifted to Coptic. After the separation from the imperial church (451), a parallel Melkite (Byzantine) hierarchy was created. The Alexandrine tradition contains many striking parallels with that of Rome. The church in Ethiopia was also dependent on this Egyptian tradition, but it created its own, partly by incorporating Jewish elements.

3.4.3 Non-Roman Western Liturgies

Africa

Given the dominant position of Rome in the western empire, the ancient western liturgical families were scarcely taken into account, even though they had grown quite independently, especially since they were to a great extent things of the past.[42] There was a genuine

---

[42] For the eucharistic prayers see *Prex Eucharistica* (n. 1 above).

Latin tradition in Africa, its best-known exponent being St. Augustine, but now we can more clearly trace the development of the Eucharistic Prayer in the patristic period from Tertullian and Cyprian to Fulgentius.[43] Now as in the past the connections between African liturgies and the East (Alexandria) and West (Rome/Milan, Spain, and Gaul) remain questionable.

Gaul

The Old Gallican liturgy was at first an independent tradition. Many of its elements (e.g., in the Liturgy of the Hours) were "imported" from the East (John Cassian). Caesarius of Arles and Gregory of Tours report some details from the late patristic period. Most of the surviving liturgical sources since about the eighth century (e.g., the *Missale Gothicum* and the *Missale Gallicanum Vetus*) already contain Roman material. The Old Gallican liturgy succumbed to the Carolingian Reformation, though some of it was revived in the Neo-Gallican liturgical books of the seventeenth and eighteenth centuries.

Spain

In contrast, thanks to the initiative of Cardinal Ximenes (ca. 1500), the ancient Spanish (Mozarabic) liturgy has survived to this day, at least in one chapel of the cathedral at Toledo. Here the Eastern influence is more evident than in the Gallican liturgy. The eloquence of the prayer texts distinguishes them clearly from the succinctness of the corresponding Roman formularies.

Milan

The only non-Roman Western liturgy still surviving is that of the church of Milan. While it is certainly related to the Roman liturgy, not least through later accommodations, it has retained genuine traditions of its own, for example, in the Eucharistic Prayer.[44] Here, too, Eastern influence was stronger than it was at Rome.

---

[43] Martin Klöckener, "Das Eucharistische Hochgebet in der nordafrikanischen Liturgie der christlichen Spätantike," in *Prex Eucharistica* (see n. 1 above), 43–128.

[44] Achille Maria Triacca, "Le preghiere eucaristiche ambrosiane," in *Prex Eucharistica* (see n. 1 above), 145–202.

Celtic (British) liturgy

Finally, we should mention the Celtic (British) liturgy, though only traces of it survive (Stowe Missal). The liturgical language, at least in part, was Celtic. Many of the divergences in the Anglo-Saxon rite, much of which has survived in Anglican liturgy, should nevertheless be explained by the multitude of diocesan usages, just as was the case in the Roman Rite.

3.5 Adaptation of Roman Liturgy North of the Alps

3.5.1 *Backgrounds in the History of Dogma: Defense against Arianism*

It seems that for a long time the Roman liturgy was able to develop independently of the upheavals taking place north and south of the Alps, due to the barbarian invasions and their consequences, but over time it was not spared from external influences. To understand the profound changes at a later time we have to begin with the developments in dogma that formed the preconditions for the unique character of non-Roman liturgy and spirituality.

Doxology as a mark of confessional allegiance

The fundamental reasons for the consequential development in the West lie in the church of the East: in the conflicts over Arianism, which were the occasion for the development of dogma in the fourth and fifth centuries. While in the East the unity of faith was preserved, at least within the empire, by establishing terminology and the corresponding combating of contrary views, in the West, around the middle of the fourth century, the Goths from Byzantium adopted Arian belief. Its core was the statement that the Son is only similar to the Father and so of lesser divine dignity. The Spirit was placed even lower. The doxology, the trinitarian praise at the end of prayers, played a not insignificant role in the Arian conflicts. Into the fourth century the so-called doxology of the economy of salvation was common: "Glory be to the Father through the Son in the Holy Spirit." As Basil remarks in writing about the Holy Spirit, the other doxology, which orders the three Persons as equals, had existed from ancient times. This is the one most common today: "Glory be to the Father and to the Son and to the Holy Spirit." Both formulae could certainly be used alongside one another, as long as they were understood to be doxologies and not dogmatic-argumentative forms of rhetoric. Still, the Arians relied on the economic formula as a basis for asserting the subordination of the Son and Spirit to the Father. On the other side, the Orthodox appealed to the other formula because, understood in Orthodox fashion, it could serve as an argument for the equal essence of all three divine Persons. In time the formula became a mark of one's allegiance: the Arians continued to use the formula of the economy of salvation while the Orthodox or Catholics used the rediscovered and reintroduced equality formula.[45]

Consequences of the Arianism debate for the image of Christ

The Arianism adopted in the Gothic realm was maintained in Spain until near the end of the sixth century. From the point of view of religious psychology the deviations from orthodox teaching are altogether comprehensible. Arianism can be interpreted as an attempt to defend Christ's humanity against the all-too-powerful divine components of his being. It is true that the dogma of incarnation was denied, and yet it is easier to imagine if the *logos* (the Son) stands on a level below that of the Father. On the other side there was a tendency simply to identify Christ with God. But in the West it seems that it was not so much theological speculation that incited such developments; it was more a matter of catechetical simplification.

3.5.2 Changing Images of Christ and Consequences for Devotion in Relation to Liturgical Prayer and Festal Cycles

Shift in the addressee of liturgical prayer

The christological and trinitarian theological developments we have described led, over time, to a profound transformation of the image of Christ. Until the fourth century interest was focused not on the person but on the saving actions inseparable from the person.

---

[45] Josef A. Jungmann, *Pastoral Liturgy*, trans. Francis Brunner, with an introduction by John F. Baldovin (Notre Dame, IN: Ave Maria Press, 2014).

The image of Christ corresponded to the Easter kerygma, that is, the proclamation that Christ overcame sin and death in his Easter victory. Those baptized into Christ felt themselves incorporated into his new life. On the basis of this solidarity of Christ with humanity, Christians were thus inseparably bound to their Lord. The exaltation of Christ's humanity was associated with the exaltation of the whole human race. This Easter context was part of the basis for the Roman liturgical formulas.[46] But outside the immediate area of the Roman liturgy's influence a change was taking place. Because the Arians emphasized the subordination of the Son to the Father, the anti-Arian opposition exalted Christ so much that he had very little in common with humanity. Much as in the doxological formulas of the Eastern church, here also Christ was seen primarily as God. In this perspective he was no longer the way, that is, the mediator from humanity to God and from God to humanity, but became entirely an object of worship. As Josef A. Jungmann showed, this was expressed, among other ways, in a change in the addressee of liturgical prayer:

> This particular cultivation of the trinitarian theme in connexion with the anti-Arian attitude automatically implies a closer attention to the divinity in Christ, while the position of Mediator, appropriate to him in his humanity, was in practice allowed to fall more and more into the background.[47]

In terms of the history of devotion, the development was expressed in a view of Christ as a fearsome ruler. Accordingly, there were a growing number of prayers that stressed the sinfulness of those celebrating the liturgy (apologies). The idea of twofold ontological likeness (one being with the Father; one being with us humans) was increasingly lost. The tie between Christ and believers was regarded as only a moral one.[48] From the early Middle Ages the central

---

[46] Winfried Haunerland, *Die Eucharistie und ihre Wirkungen im Spiegel der Euchologie des Missale Romanum*, Liturgiewissenschaftliche Quellen und Forschungen 71 (Münster: Aschendorff, 1989).

[47] Josef A. Jungmann, *The Place of Christ in Liturgical Prayer* (Staten Island: Alba House, 1965), 220; see Albert Gerhards, "Zu wem beten? Die These Josef Andreas Jungmanns [d. 1975] über den Adressaten des Eucharistischen Hochgebets im Licht der neueren Forschung," *Liturgisches Jahrbuch* 32 (1982): 219–30.

[48] On this see Arnold Angenendt, *Das Frühmittelalter. Die abendländische Christenheit von 400 bis 900*, 3rd ed. (Stuttgart: Kohlhammer, 2001); idem, "Missa

point of reference for Christian identity was no longer the existential community with the Crucified and Risen One created through initiation, as it had been in the ancient church, but repentance.

Celebration of the incarnation isolated from the paschal event

The emphasis on Jesus' divinity corresponded, on the other hand, to an increased interest in the mystery of the incarnation. The dogma that Mary is the Mother of God, proclaimed at the Council of Ephesus in 431, was in no way intended to minimize Jesus' humanity, but *de facto* it led to a downplaying of the humanity in favor of the divinity to the extent that now it was the miraculous circumstances of Jesus' birth that were emphasized and celebrated. In this way the incarnation was no longer related to the paschal event but was seen more and more in isolation. In terms of liturgical history this was expressed in the development of a separate Christmas cycle parallel to the Easter cycle.[49] So the feast of the Epiphany became a second date for baptism and acquired a forty-day period of penance. The remnant of that is the enumeration of the Sundays after Epiphany (in the Roman Catholic Church until the liturgical reforms of Vatican II). In analogy to the Christmas cycle, a separate Pentecost cycle also emerged. The three principal feasts of the church year, originally christological in nature, were now given a trinitarian interpretation.

Exaltation of individual events in the life of Jesus

The reduction in status of the paschal mystery and the emphasis on other content served to promote separate attention to individual mysteries in the life of Jesus. The individual events were no longer interpreted from the center but instead had their own weight. This was certainly based on an effort to protect the substance of Jesus'

---

specialis. Zugleich ein Beitrag zur Entstehung der Privatmessen," in idem, *Liturgie im Mittelalter. Ausgewählte Aufsätze zum 70. Geburtstag*, ed. Thomas Flammer and Daniel Meyer, Ästhetik–Theologie–Liturgik 35 (Münster: LIT Verlag, 2004), 111–90 (first publication 1978/79).

[49] *Gottesdienst der Kirche. Handbuch der Liturgiewissenschaft*, ed. Hans Bernhard Meyer, et al. (Regensburg: Pustet, 1983–), vol. 5, Hansjörg auf der Maur, *Feiern im Rhythmus der Zeit I. Herrenfeste in Woche und Jahr* (Regensburg: Pustet, 1983), 154–85.

humanity, but now the events were seen in isolation and lost their significance for salvation, which can be seen only in connection with the divine incarnation. What remained was the idea of example, something that expanded in similar fashion in the veneration of saints. This, too, lost its original relationship to the paschal mystery, which had still been obvious in the first centuries in the church of the martyrs. Now a moralistic doctrine of virtues replaced the theme of death and life and the biblical idea of discipleship (ἀκολυθία; *sequela*) became only imitation (μίμησις; *imitatio*).

Inculturation

This shift in devotional practice cannot be seen simply as a degeneration of an original superior form. Rather, it was the consequence of a process of inculturation. The fact that this occurred in connection with the Arian conflicts explains much of the deformation. One overall positive feature of this piety is the greater presence to life's concrete questions. The sacramental thought underlying the Roman liturgy remained abstract in many ways. The Franco-German mentality sought to make the statements of Scripture and liturgy concrete. In the process much of the theological and salvation-historical breadth of the patristic period was lost, but at the same time a new synthesis was achieved, one with sufficient power to integrate the Roman liturgical heritage and preserve it beyond the eventual fall of the city of Rome.

3.5.3 Endurance of the Roman Liturgy

*Significance of the Carolingians for the preservation
of the Roman liturgy*

After Gregory the Great there was a pause in the development of the Roman liturgy. Only a few elements were added, primarily from the East. There was an absence of a formative impulse that would have completed the cycle of the liturgical year after Pentecost. The same is true of the sacramental liturgies, which, with the exception of baptism, showed little development. In contrast, especially in Celtic liturgy, there had been an abundance of rites, often inspired from the East. In the Carolingian period there was a remarkable amalgamation, called the Bonifatian-Carolingian reform because it was closely associated with the missionary activity of St. Boniface.[50] On the occasion of his coronation in 754, King Pepin wanted to introduce the Gregorian liturgy of Rome into his kingdom. But as the empire expanded it was impossible, under existing conditions, to provide all the churches with the necessary books. So they went on using the old books, only occasionally augmented by Roman elements. The political idea was to eliminate the coexistence of Old Gallican and Roman usages and to strengthen the unity of the empire through a common liturgy. Charlemagne, who wanted to carry on his father's policies, asked Rome for new books. He was sent a handsome but already out-of-date and thus incomplete copy of the *Sacramentarium Gregorianum* (the "Aachener Urexemplar" mentioned above), which contained only the papal stational services. In Aix/Aachen the situation was probably recognized quite quickly. Besides, it was desired to alter the Roman liturgy to accommodate the traditions of the Franks, for example, by inclusion of other blessing rituals and feastdays. Now the formularies available in the still-extant mixed sacramentaries from Pepin's time that did not exist in the Roman model text were added in an appendix. The result was no longer a compilation of purely Roman formulae but a book that, because of the mixed types of exemplars, contained elements of the older Gallican liturgy.

In the subsequent period the ecclesial and liturgical life in the "eternal city" withered. So ultimately we owe it to the Carolingians' political calculation that the liturgy of the city of Rome survived, at least in its essential elements. But it was not treated as a relic; it was subjected, not least because of its political significance, to a creative transformation.

Further development of Roman elements

The contribution of Franco-German liturgy consisted less in what it retained than in the further development of the liturgy of the city of Rome. At least in their developed form the most impressive ceremonies

[50] Andreas Odenthal, *Liturgie vom Frühen Mittelalter zum Zeitalter der Konfessionalisierung*, Studien zur Geschichte des Gottesdienstes. Spätmittelalter, Humanismus, Reformation 62 (Tübingen: Mohr Siebeck, 2011), 164–69.

of today's liturgy—Holy Week, the consecration of a church, and ordinations—are not of Roman but of Franco-German origin. Their ability to integrate was developed by combining Roman elements with the syntheses of Eastern and local elements already achieved. The formulaic and static liturgy of Rome was thus dramatized in a number of ways. For example, the palm procession on the Sunday before Easter was taken from Jerusalem models,[51] but these were not simply copied; instead they were enriched—for example, by the composition of new hymns. Whereas the Roman liturgy was made up almost completely of biblical elements, now freely composed hymns (which, of course, were often based on biblical texts) achieved increasing importance.

The *genera* of these could be very different. For example, the *Improperia* for Good Friday drew on Eastern models.[52] Other dramaturgical elements of the period are the litanies on rising notes, such as the *Ecce lignum* at the veneration of the cross and the *Lumen Christi* at the Easter Vigil. This tendency to dramatization based on Jerusalem models apparently responded to the need for visible presentation, which was foreign to the Roman liturgy itself. By the adoption of the Roman liturgy, certainly, they had bound themselves in a tight corset that left little room for adaptation, and yet they found themselves in a living process of liturgical expansion. Hence the closed form of the Roman liturgy, impressive in its conciseness, burst open. This came about through expansions—for example, the insertion of texts—in the existing framework (troping). The alternation of biblical (e.g., Psalms) and free poetic elements often yielded an exciting, dramatic form. Another means of expanding the original Roman liturgy was the incorporation of extra elements: here we should refer especially to the Sequence, which was added to the existing sung elements

[51] Sabine Felbecker, *Die Prozession. Historische und systematische Untersuchungen zu einer liturgischen Ausdruckshandlung*, Münsteraner theologische Abhandlungen 39 (Altenberge: Oros, 1995); Albert Gerhards, art. "Prozession II. In der Kirchengeschichte," *Theologische Realenzyklopädie* 27 (1997): 593–97; Andreas Odenthal, "Die Palmsonntagsfeier in Köln im Mittelalter. Zu ihrer Genese anhand liturgischer Quellen des Domstiftes und des Gereonstiftes," *Kölner Domblatt* 62 (1997): 275–92.

[52] Albert Gerhards, art. "Improperia," *Reallexikon für Antike und Christentum* 17 (1996): 1198–1212.

between the readings (sequence = what follows, namely, following the Alleluia). The best known of these is probably the familiar Easter sequence, which already represented an advanced stage of liturgical dramatization. This combines a hymn of praise to the Paschal Lamb with the Easter play, the *visitatio sepulchri*, which gave occasion for further scenic development.[53]

3.5.4 Continuity and Change in the "Roman" Liturgy

Why theology and liturgy went their separate ways

The determinative paradigm shift can be interpreted theologically as follows: in terms of its origins, liturgy claims to be the realization of what it portrays. The reality is not behind things but is necessarily expressed in the things themselves. Only when the church celebrates, and inasmuch as it celebrates, can the work of redemption be present here and now. That is the reason why the Christians of the age of martyrs assigned such high importance to their Sunday eucharistic gatherings. Theologians in the West (especially Ambrose) put this unique truth into words in so-called mystagogical catecheses. Terminologically speaking, of course, the thing represented (sacramental grace) and the representation (liturgy) had to be kept separate. In fact, this led to a distinction between "essential" and "inessential" elements in the liturgical celebration. Increasingly, the liturgical action validly carried out by the priest was seen as essential. The assembly (that is, the physical presence of the other participants) was no longer regarded as necessary. This led, from an early date in the Gallican monasteries, to the practice of private Masses as the normal form.[54] The solemn Mass with an assembly could add nothing qualitatively to it. The plus (that is, the ceremonial, which was not regarded as necessary for the thing itself to happen) was only quantitative. Ceremonial became merely a form of presentation, more and more

---

[53] Albert Gerhards, "Theologische und sozio-kulturelle Bedingungen religiöser Konflikte mit dem Judentum. Beispiele aus der katholischen Liturgie und ihrer Wirkungsgeschichte," in *Kontinuität und Unterbrechung* (see n. 9 above), 269–85.

[54] Arnold Angenendt, "Missa specialis" (see n. 48 above).

divorced from the content of what was presented. This is one reason for the increasingly common allegorical explanations of the liturgy and its separation from theology. It is within the broader context of this development in the early Middle Ages, completed in the High Middle Ages, that we should see the changes in dogma to which we have referred: a turn from salvation-historical conceptions toward an ontological-static one.[55]

Shifting accents in architecture

The liturgical findings only sketched here were matched by a revolution in architecture. The layout of the basilica, originally oriented to the high altar, developed in the course of the Middle Ages into a space with a number of distinct areas and an abundance of individual memorial altars. This completed the shift in accent: the altar is not a holy place because of the Mass that is celebrated there; as a holy place in itself, it draws the honor of the daily Mass to itself.

City liturgy and substitute para-liturgical forms

Medieval sources also report complex organizations that, in the course of the church year, made monastic and conventual churches in a city into loci for official liturgies representing the whole cosmos of Christian faith. This was accompanied by a twofold inversion: the clericalization of the monasteries and the monasticizing of the secular clergy. The sources, it is true, also report how difficult it was to maintain the claims of the "official" church. On the part of the faithful the result was the rise of so-called para-liturgies, popular "substitutes" in which authentic religious emotion could be expressed. In particular these took the form of numerous processions and devotions, with a variety of vernacular elements, that no longer had much in common with the community spirit of the old Roman liturgy. What followed was a period of religiosity focused entirely on the individual, one that also read the ancient forms of the traditional Roman liturgy in that same light.

---

[55] Arnold Angenendt, "Religiösität und Theologie. Ein spannungsreiches Verhältnis im Mittelalter," in *Liturgie im Mittelalter* (see n. 48 above), 3–33.

3.6 Basic Features of the Liturgy in the High and Late Middle Ages; the Liturgy of the City of Cologne as an Example

Medieval liturgy, with its complex history and multiple branches, cannot be described in a brief compass. Consequently we will sketch the liturgical history of the early, high, and late Middle Ages in terms of a single example, that of the city, or archbishopric, of Cologne.[56] The "Cologne liturgy" is in many respects paradigmatic for medieval liturgy as a whole: it embodies a respectable tradition of its own that (unlike the liturgy of Milan) remained within the Roman Rite but maintained itself far beyond the Tridentine reform and well into the nineteenth century.

As already described, the Roman liturgy gained high political significance for imperial policy. This applied not only to the texts, rituals, and chants but also to the church building, prominent examples of which were built on Roman models. Thus the western section of the ancient Cologne cathedral, the Choir of St. Peter, imitated the *confessio* of the ancient church of St. Peter in Rome. However, there were borrowings from the great models both in Rome and in the Holy Land independent of the Carolingian imperial reform.

Monastic and municipal liturgy

Of interest here are the driving forces behind the development of what is called the "Cologne liturgy." For example, we should mention Benedictine monasticism, which aided the success of the Carolingian reform. However, clerical communities living under canonical rules as well as women's monasteries contributed to the survival of an active liturgy. In the early Middle Ages the city was a common liturgical space, and the individual churches, with their congregations, made up a church family. Again the orientation to Rome, already the driving force behind the Carolingian reform, played a major role, something that continued in the Ottonian period.

---

[56] On this see *Kölnische Liturgie und ihre Geschichte. Studien zur interdisziplinären Erforschung des Gottesdienstes im Erzbistum Köln*, ed. Albert Gerhards and Andreas Odenthal, Liturgiewissenschaftliche Quellen und Forschungen 87 (Münster: Aschendorff, 2000).

Cathedral liturgy and Roman orientation of the celebration

The Roman Curia developed its own ceremonial, which became a model for the liturgy of the universal church, but this happened somewhat later, especially through the work of the Franciscans. The Cologne cathedral developed a splendid cathedral liturgy, not least because it enjoyed special privileges. As in Rome, there were for a time three classes of cardinals: in Cologne these were cardinal priests, cardinal deacons, and cardinal subdeacons. One peculiarity was the "orientation of celebration toward Rome," across the altar eastward through the nave (*versus populum*), as in the western Choir of St. Peter in the ancient Cologne cathedral, reflecting the situation in the ancient Roman cathedral of St. Peter. This "Roman celebration" was so important to the people of Cologne that it was retained for the bishop into the sixteenth century, even in the new cathedral at the high altar in the eastern apse.[57]

Orientation toward Rome and Jerusalem: The stational churches

The orientation toward Rome was expressed especially in the stational liturgies, as in that of Christmas, when the Church of St. Maria im Kapitol in Cologne played a prominent role. Originally Santa Maria Maggiore, St. Anastasia, and St. Peter were the intended places for the papal ceremonial stational liturgies in Rome, designated for midnight, dawn, and day, respectively. In the twelfth century in Cologne, Christmas Eve began with Matins in the cathedral. During its course the archbishop stepped into a palanquin and was borne to St. Maria im Kapitol. That church, with its trefoil choir, was built

---

[57] Albert Gerhards, "'Blickt nach Osten!' Die Ausrichtung von Priester und Gemeinde bei der Eucharistie—eine kritische Reflexion nachkonziliarer Liturgiereform vor dem Hintergrund der Geschichte des Kirchenbaus," in *Liturgia et Unitas. Liturgiewissenschaftliche und ökumenische Studien zur Eucharistie und zum gottesdienstlichen Leben in der Schweiz. Études liturgiques et oecuméniques sur l'Eucharistie et la vie liturgique en Suisse. In honorem Bruno Bürki*, ed. Martin Klöckener and Arnaud Join-Lambert (Fribourg: Universitätsverlag; Geneva: Labor et Fides, 2001), 197–217; Uwe Michael Lang, *Conversi ad Dominum. Zu Geschichte und Theologie der christlichen Gebetsrichtung*, Neue Kriterien 5 (Einsiedeln: Johannesverlag, 2003).

in the eleventh century as an approximate copy of the Church of the Nativity in Bethlehem. There the archbishop celebrated the Christmas midnight Mass.

After the conclusion of the Mass, the abbess of St. Maria im Kapitol brought him a white mule; on this the archbishop rode, accompanied by the clergy and people, to the church of St. Cecilia to celebrate the *missa in aurora*. There he received a gray horse on which he rode to the cathedral for the third Mass of Christmas. As many of the Cologne clergy as possible would have been assembled to greet him there. At the end of Mass the gospel for Epiphany was read; from 1164 onward this was especially impressive as the reading took place in the presence of the relics of the "three kings." This explains why the third Mass of Christmas was called the "royal Mass," while the other two were the "Mass of the Angels" and the "shepherds' Mass," respectively.[58]

The processions

Rhinelanders were always familiar with the significance of the procession as a cohesive, sense-satisfying event. Most of the great churches were processional churches, and in them it was not merely the West-East axis that was important. In the basilica of St. Maria im Kapitol the side aisles were laid out as processional access routes around the trifoliate choir, enabling some impressive processions. The Cologne cathedral offered an abundance of processional routes, as the ancient sources attest, even though some of them could be developed only after the completion of the nave. The indoor processions were closely associated with the memorials, the *patrocinia*; the processions not only ended at those places but brought them into a meaningful and perceptible relationship with the whole complex of the church building and the other city churches as well.

---

[58] *Das Lob Gottes im Rheinland. Mittelalterliche Handschriften und alte Drucke zur Geschichte von Liturgie und Volksfrömmigkeit im Erzbistum Köln. Eine Ausstellung der Diözesan- und Dombibliothek Köln (7. März bis 25. April 2002)*, ed. Heinz Finger, Libelli Rhenani 1 (Cologne: Erzbischöfliche Diözesan- und Dombibliothek, 2002), 28–29.

Processions shaped the city's spiritual life mainly in the spring and summer. Of note are the rogation processions: the *litania maior* on the feast of St. Mark (25 April) and the *litaniae minores* on Monday, Tuesday, and Wednesday of Rogation Week (before Corpus Christi). The Corpus Christi procession began in 1264, though in Cologne it competed for a long time with the Cologne city procession on the second Friday after Easter; it was only after the Enlightenment and secularization in the period of the Restoration that the Cologne Corpus Christi procession developed fully. Cologne was home to such an abundance of theophoric processions (that is, those that included the processing of the consecrated Host) that it was felt necessary to set a limit to them by official order.[59]

The Palm Sunday celebration is an especially eloquent example. The organization of the Gallican festival goes back to usages at Jerusalem in late antiquity that mimicked Jesus' triumphal entry into Jerusalem; it was also linked to the Roman passion-centered anamnetic Mass to form the bipolar celebration we know today. The station was St. Gereon. The sources show that in Cologne a special feature was the bishop's sermon in the Maria-Ablass [Mary Full of Grace] chapel of the basilica of St. Ursula. Another unique aspect was the carrying in procession of St. Peter's staff, a priceless relic. For that reason a group of antiphons from the St. Peter *patrocinium* of the cathedral were added to the processional chants. The apostolic claims of the cathedral *patrocinium* manifest in the relic were thus extended beyond the cathedral itself to the whole city. Andreas Odenthal summarizes: "The inclusion of the antiphons in honor of St. Peter shows that the Cologne cathedral church now influenced and shaped the liturgy through its ownership of this relic, the Staff of St. Peter, which emphasized its link to Rome."[60] A special favorite in

[59] Wilhelm-Josef Schlierf, "Die Stadtkölnische Gottestracht und die Fronleichnamsprozession in Köln im Lichte ihrer Geschichte," *Kölner Domblatt* 62 (1997): 293–334; Norbert Trippen, "Gottesdienst und Volksfrömmigkeit im Kölner Dom während des 19. Jahrhunderts," in *Der Kölner Dom im Jahrhundert seiner Vollendung 2. Essays zur Ausstellung der Historischen Museen in der Josef-Haubrich-Kunsthalle Köln*, ed. Hugo Borger (Cologne: Historische Museen der Stadt Köln, 1980), 182–98.

[60] Andreas Odenthal, "Die Palmsonntagsfeier" (see n. 51 above), 292.

the Cologne archdiocese was the *statio ad crucem*, which outlasted the Tridentine reform and endured until it fell victim to nineteenth-century tendencies to centralization.

Cult of relics

The cult of relics was especially important in the Cologne-Rhineland liturgy. It was an inseparable component of the pilgrimages that were here a common occurrence, as in the past. In St. Maria im Kapitol from 1304 onward a *crux miraculosa* was venerated on the central Cross Altar; the breast of the figure contained a reliquary. Here cultic image and devotional image coincided. The choir screen also served as an emblem of the rich collection of relics.[61]

Continuation of medieval traditions

It is by no means merely the buildings, the outer shells, that remain as witnesses to medieval customs; remnants of the stational liturgies can be found even today. Thus the "Römerfahrt," a modern adaptation of the pilgrimage to the seven churches, is still practiced in the Rhineland. (In Cologne it is held on Palm Sunday or during Holy Week and includes the churches of St. Maria im Kapitol, St. Severin, St. Pantaleon, St. Aposteln, St. Gereon, and St. Kunibert.) There the "Gottestracht" (processions), as well as the Corpus Christi procession, first held in Cologne, still play a major role. In connection with the cathedral jubilee in 1998 the pilgrimage around the cathedral choir was revived. One genre characteristic of Cologne liturgy is that of hymns, for example, the Easter processional hymn *Salve festa dies*,[62] and sequences such as that for the transfer of the relics of the Three Kings, *Maiestati sacrosanctae*.[63] Processions and the singing of hymns are regarded as a heritage from the period of the Gallican liturgy.

With secularization, the community Office largely disappeared, to the extent that it was not taken up by monastic communities. The

---

[61] See also Anton Legner, *Kölner Heilige und Heiligtümer. Ein Jahrtausend europäischer Reliquienkultur* (Cologne: Greven, 2003), 134.

[62] See *Das Lob Gottes im Rheinland* (n. 58 above), 131–32.

[63] Ibid., 137–38.

richness of the community Office in the High Middle Ages has been described, using the example of the collegiate church of the Holy Apostles (St. Aposteln). Here, too, the liturgy is oriented to the Roman structure as codified by Amalar of Metz (ca. 775–ca. 850), but in detail it is shaped by the local situation.[64]

3.7 Liturgy in the Period of the Reformation and the Catholic Reform

3.7.1 The Medieval Heritage

Divergence of theology and popular piety

Amalar spent 813 to 814 in Byzantium, where he learned the allegorical interpretation of the Mass, probably from the writings of Pseudo-Dionysius.[65] He saw this as an opportunity to spread the Roman liturgy, foreign in itself, throughout the Carolingian Empire. Whereas previously theologians had tried to convey the content of the liturgy, the allegorese of the Mass that was now developed took no heed of its actual content. Remarkably enough, the great medieval theologians did not oppose it, apparently because the content of the liturgy was not a subject of theological reflection.[66] The liturgy served merely as the depiction of the salvation that was the subject of belief. In principle this took place independently of liturgical action. Liturgy became increasingly a spiritual panorama in which believers participated only from without and whose fruits they tasted only in spirit. In this way the drama of the sacrifice of the Mass and the act

---

[64] Andreas Odenthal, *Der älteste Liber Ordinarius der Stiftskirche St. Aposteln in Köln. Untersuchungen zur Liturgie eines mittelalterlichen kölnischen Stifts*, Studien zur Kölner Kirchengeschichte 28 (Siegburg: F. Schmitt, 1994).

[65] See esp. Alexander Golitzin, *Et introibo ad altare Dei: The Mystagogy of Dionysius Areopagita: With Special Reference to Its Predecessors in the Eastern Christian Tradition* (Thessalonikē: Patriarchikon Idruma Paterikōn Meletōn, 1994); see also Dionysius the Areopagite, *Works*, trans. John Parker (London: James Parker, 1897–1899), available at http://www.ccel.org/ccel/dionysius/works.pdf.

[66] Julia Knop, *Ecclesia orans. Liturgie als Herausforderung für die Dogmatik* (Freiburg: Herder, 2012).

of communicating could be regarded quite independently of one another. Liturgy, with its claim to affect people both intellectually and emotionally and to draw them into active participation in the event, fell by the wayside. While in the mystical view of Pseudo-Dionysius there was still the claim to a possible comprehension of the whole reality of the mystery in which one believed, in the Middle Ages that mystery was separated into a categorial reality comprehensible by the intellect and an emotionality designed for mystical immersion. The classic liturgy was unsuitable for either. While more or less outside the ken of scholastic theology, it represented for mysticism merely a kind of frame to be filled with new elements. The new spirituality no longer looked to the spoken words of, for example, the (softly uttered) Eucharistic Prayer but to the visible form of the elevated host. Here new forms of emotional piety could develop; the theological content of the liturgical tradition remained largely fallow.

Turn to the earthly figure of Jesus

The Middle Ages were powerfully affected by the mendicant orders. Veneration of the Christmas crib and a special love for the Crucified are associated with Francis of Assisi. The turn to the earthly figure of Jesus was ultimately motivated by the spiritualistic tendencies of heretical groups, against which a powerful creation theology was mustered, such as that expressed in Francis's "Hymn to the Sun." The object was to defend the dogma of the incarnation, but that could no longer be accomplished through a symbolic synopsis of the mutually contradictory statements, such as had been achieved in antiquity and even in the early Middle Ages. Instead, one now immersed oneself in an emotional contemplation of the individual circumstances of the earthly life of Jesus, but in order to express his divinity the age elevated Jesus, and in a subsequent period Mary as well, to a superhuman level.

The literary expression of this spiritual attitude, which spread in the Gothic period, was an individualistic style in poetry. This expressed itself in the Latin, and sometimes vernacular, *cantiones*, edifying songs that promoted an emotional view and had little or no theological relevance. By this time the separation between theology and popular piety was complete. The consequences of that development are unmistakable. On the one hand they can be identified in terms of the history of liturgy: The people and the clergy were more and more sharply separated. Only the ritual of the Canon could be explained to the laity, not the content. Accordingly, in this period there developed a specifically lay spirituality as well as separate forms of community worship alongside the official liturgy: for example, preaching services and communion celebrations, processions, and devotions. The claims of the liturgy itself were no longer fulfilled in the form of the Mass itself. Instead, they were shifted to other forms, especially the architecture of the Gothic cathedrals with their imagery. However, the function of the cathedral itself was no longer clear; it was dissipated in a multitude of individual spaces (e.g., side chapels, ambulatories, separate altar spaces). The symbol of the building itself still expressed unity, but the worship services celebrated within it scarcely approached that claim any longer.

3.7.2 The Century before the Reformation

Innovation in the realm of the visual

The phases between the reforms ordered by the church authorities are often described as hostile to innovation. But it would be a mistake to view the pre-Reformation century solely under the aspect of decline. In the perspective of liturgical history this period is regarded as decadent because the texts, especially for priestly actions, are taken as parameters; indeed, on the eve of the Reformation they were urgently in need of revamping. But from a newer perspective the pre-Reformation century was highly productive and innovative in its own way, though not so much in regard to the auditory as to the visual aspects. This is evident, for example, in the vast numbers of images, figures, and triptych altarpieces endowed not by the rich but by relatively poor people.[67] Undoubtedly there was a tendency to externalization in this period. This can be seen in the ecclesiastical culture of the late Gothic period, which placed more and more emphasis on decorative and ostentatious features. Counter-tendencies, widely represented, bore only individualistic features. For many, the demand of the hour

[67] Arnold Angenendt, *Liturgik und Historik* (see n. 4 above).

was not for efforts at reform of church structures but for withdrawal into subjectivity. The *devotio moderna* included some agnostic features such as we can find, for example, in Thomas à Kempis's *Imitation of Christ*. Against this background we might suppose that the period would not have been able to produce any reforming efforts, because those require the exertion of influence, especially from positions of authority, if a reforming impulse is to succeed politically. Still, we can show that there were indeed attempts of that kind in this period, though they were unsuccessful. In what follows, by way of example, we will describe one such attempt at reform promoted by two Italian Benedictine monks.[68]

3.7.3 A Reforming Project on the Eve of the Reformation: The Libellus ad Leonem X (1513)

The two authors of the *Libellus ad Leonem X* of 1513, Paolo Giustiniani (1476–1528) and Vincenzo Quirini (1479–1514), were Camaldolese, members of a reforming group founded out of the Benedictine Order and named for Camaldoli. It sought to combine coenobitic (common) and eremitic (hermit) monasticism. The life context of the two authors was Italy's urban-influenced Renaissance culture between Venice and Rome. Their extensive document was addressed to the newly elected Medici Pope Leo X (1513–1521). His ascent to office brought with it great expectations, especially regarding the Lateran Council, summoned in 1512, which, it was hoped, would effect a longed-for reform of the church. Those hopes were not fulfilled because the papacy was at that time more or less a pawn in the hands of the great European powers.

Education and knowledge of Sacred Scripture

One essential goal of the proposers of reform was to try to advance Christians' knowledge of their faith. First of all, in order to improve the quality of preaching, a better theological and especially a biblical

---

[68] Albert Gerhards, "Ein Reformprojekt am Vorabend der Reformation: der *Libellus ad Leonem X* (1513)," in *Frömmigkeitsformen in Mittelalter und Renaissance*, ed. Johannes Laudage, Studia humaniora 37 (Düsseldorf: Droste, 2004), 391–408.

education should be provided for the clergy. Knowledge of Sacred Scripture must be promoted on a broad basis, and for that purpose the pope should open his libraries to all believers.

Translations into the vernacular

One problem at the beginning of the Modern Era was the exclusive use of Latin in scholarship and church. These authors, however, explained that even the priests no longer had a command of Latin. Therefore they urged that the Scriptures should be translated into the vernacular.

Concern for ethics and divine praise

If the liturgy were celebrated in the vernacular—so the authors believed—it would advance knowledge of divine instruction and of morality among the people. The two Benedictines were concerned not solely with education and edification but also for a pure praise of God in the various vernacular tongues. The experience of ritual multiplicity in the Church of the Holy Sepulchre at Jerusalem, which appeared to have a positive reception, was their model for the greatest possible variety throughout the worldwide Roman Church. The idea of modernity that speaks throughout the *Libellus* lies in the discovery of the significance of the word, behind the phonetic and syntactical structures of language. Apparently this represented a countercurrent to medieval "lust for seeing," which in the meantime had degenerated into superficiality. The particularity, individual arbitrariness, and overall subjectivism associated with it was regarded as a danger. However, the countermeasure was not an objectivism of linguistic identity but a central direction of biblical translations and a standardization of rituals. The authors saw verbal proclamation and prayer as an opportunity for instruction, in which vernacular usage is more than pure information. This was expressed in their emphasis on divine praise, which, according to the Rule of Benedict, should take precedence over everything else.[69] The number of special

---

[69] *The Rule of Benedict*, various editions; see esp. Terrence G. Kardong, *Benedict's Rule: A Translation and Commentary* (Collegeville, MN: Liturgical Press, 1996), 43.3, "Therefore nothing should be put ahead of the Work of God" (p. 351).

rites so popular at the time, especially those of the different Orders, should be diminished. This was a real possibility at the beginning of the sixteenth century, in the wake of the invention of printing. This centralizing proposal, not even advocated with such rigidity by the Council of Trent—the multiple rites were not suppressed—stood in dramatic contrast to the demand to introduce the vernacular. But it was not a real contradiction. The two Camaldolese were concerned with spiritual nourishment from the sources of faith, primarily the Bible, but also the liturgy, which in turn is biblically centered. Giustiniani himself later translated the Bible into Italian. The *Libellus* emerged as part of the reform of the Orders and introduced elements of monastic spirituality into a reforming program for the church as a whole. In this instance "reform" meant efforts toward a more strict observance.

The reforming proposals in this document were children of their time and were in many respects—for example, with regard to the relationship of the Roman church to the other churches and religions—highly questionable. With such an ascetic program the *Libellus* could not have offered a successful concept for the universal church. It remained largely inconsequential, but it represents an important link in the chain of reforming attempts between the Middle Ages and Vatican II.

3.7.4 The Reformers' Liturgical Reforms, with the Liturgy of the Lord's Supper as an Example

One of the most striking features of the Reformation liturgies was the use of the vernacular. Still, Latin was retained for a long time, mainly in liturgies employing a mixture of languages (e.g., the readings, sermon, prayers, and community singing in the vernacular, the choral chants in Latin).

Two Lutheran orders for the Lord's Supper

The varied landscape of the Lutheran liturgical orders was a result of the way in which the Reformation developed, being enforced by the secular authorities against the will of the bishops. The forms of church order corresponding to secular territories often depended on chance factors. In general, the Lutheran liturgies for the Lord's

Supper can be divided into two major groups.[70] The first was based on the existing form of the Latin Mass as developed in the particular region. The second, which was no longer called the "Mass," followed the pattern of the so-called "preaching service" that had arisen especially in the southwestern German cities. Since before the Reformation the Mass was usually celebrated without a sermon, a vernacular preaching service was created separate from the Mass. Its elements also included the recovered common prayer (prayer of the people). In parallel to this extra-liturgical form of Liturgy of the Word there also emerged a likewise simple, popular form of common communion. The latter was more catechetically conceived, and it in turn influenced a number of Lutheran liturgies for the Lord's Supper. This fact gives us a clue to the remarkable parallels between the clerical and lay liturgies on the eve of the Reformation. Where the form of the Roman Mass served as the basis for the orders of the Lord's Supper it was used without alteration. Here also the basic principle was: no Mass without a sermon. This led to the introduction of a new element in the Ordinary of the Mass: the admonition before the Lord's Supper. This was a fixed formula for a Lord's Supper homily and paraenesis, similar to the model addresses common in the ordination liturgies since the pontificate of Pope Durandus in the thirteenth century. However, in the new orders for the Lord's Supper the admonition before the Supper, together with the common prayer, largely took over the function of the Canon, the Eucharistic Prayer. A second basic principle of the Reformation was: no Mass without congregational communion, and under both species.

[70] Irmgard Pahl, *Coena Domini I. Die Abendmahlsliturgie der Reformationskirchen im 16./17. Jahrhundert*, Spicilegium Friburgense 29 (Fribourg: Universitätsverlag, 1983); eadem, *Coena Domini II. Die Abendmahlsliturgie der Reformationskirchen vom 18. bis zum frühen 20. Jahrhundert*, Spicilegium Friburgense 43 (Fribourg: Universitätsverlag, 2005); eadem, "Die Feier des Abendmahls in den Kirchen der Reformation," in Hans Bernhard Meyer, *Eucharistie. Geschichte, Theologie, Pastoral* (see n. 36 above), 393–440; Friedrich Lurz, *Die Feier des Abendmahls nach der Kurpfälzischen Kirchenordnung von 1563. Ein Beitrag zu einer ökumenischen Liturgiewissenschaft*, Praktische Theologie heute 38 (Stuttgart: Kohlhammer, 1998); *Handbuch der Liturgik. Liturgiewissenschaft in Theologie und Praxis der Kirche*, ed. Hans-Christoph Schmidt-Lauber, Michael Meyer-Blanck, and Karl-Heinrich Bieritz, 3rd. rev. and exp. ed. (Göttingen: Vandenhoeck & Ruprecht, 2003).

Concerns of the Reformation liturgies

The Reformers' crucial alterations primarily affected the Canon. From their point of view the Canon, together with the Offertory, emphasized the church's sacrificial action and thus human good works and gave too prominent a role to the priest. Often all that remained were the words of institution, because of their biblical origin; these were now interpreted as a promise to be fulfilled by Christ and not by the priest as consecrator. The Preface, together with the *Sanctus*, was largely retained because it constituted praise. In the perspective of the times these were not part of the Eucharistic Prayer but represented an introduction to it. On the whole there was an effort to carry out the eucharistic celebration in line with its origin. Initial efforts to reshape the whole Canon in line with Lutheran belief were ultimately abandoned nearly everywhere in favor of its complete abolition. Some of its functions were assigned to other elements, such as the admonition just described, the common prayer, the Our Father, and community chants including the *Sanctus* and *Agnus Dei*. This was true especially of the type of service that followed the order of the Mass. The result was a Lutheran Lord's Supper liturgy with biblical aspects reduced to the most elementary, making it understandable for the whole congregation. By contrast the upper German orders, those not oriented to the Mass, incorporated essential elements like thanksgiving and confessional praise in different ways, for example, in the prayer introducing the Lord's Supper, in an especially expansive prayer of praise at the end, or in an inserted *Credo*.

Proprium *of the Lutheran concept of the Lord's Supper*

It is impossible to give a precise orientation of these two types of service to the Lutheran or Reformed creeds (although the laical type of Lord's Supper is closer to the Reformed) because both developed out of models in the medieval church. One common feature was the forgiveness of sins, received as a gift in the Lord's Supper. This resulted in an emphatic expansion of the preparatory parts of the service and common confession in the context of the Lord's Supper, including explicit confession of sins and public admission of guilt. The Lord's Supper itself thus came to be understood as a seal on forgiveness for the individual. Because for Luther the forgiveness of sins and justification became equivalent concepts, we can see the accent on the theology of justification as the *proprium* of the Lutheran understanding of the Lord's Supper, something also expressed in its liturgies. Other aspects, such as *communio*, the Easter character, or the eschatological sense receded into the background. Abandonment of the dimension of celebration in favor of the motif of justification ultimately lent a rather somber coloring to the Lutheran liturgy of the Lord's Supper. Thus the admonition before the Supper was expanded by use of Paul's warning to a worthy reception of the Lord's Supper (1 Cor 10:11) and sometimes became an extended penitential prayer, which may well have had a deterrent effect. On the other hand, the community aspect of sin was much clearer than in the comparable medieval prayers, and with it the way in which the meal itself imposed an obligation.

A diachronic view of a single Lord's Supper tradition, for example, the Anglican, reveals certain constants. Thus there was a change first in the language, then in the structure. Martin Luther's orders for the Lord's Supper yield a similar finding. The Latin *Formula Missae* of 1523 is still strongly dependent on the *Ordo Missae*. Two years later Luther wrote the German Mass, a simple worship form that seemed necessary "for the sake of the simple laity." Here the Preface is replaced by a paraphrase of the Our Father, which also assumes the function of the Canon petitions. The paraphrase of the Our Father continues into an anamnetically shaded admonition to the Lord's Supper. The words of institution and the communion are combined. The *verba testamenti* are recited in the Gospel Tone and—now completely separated from the prayer context—take on the character of proclamation. During the distribution of communion the German *Sanctus* is sung, together with other thanksgiving chants that clearly express Luther's biblicism. The celebration closes with a prayer of thanksgiving and a blessing.

Regularity of Reformation liturgical reform

A number of regular features of Reformation liturgical reform can be derived from these observations. One is the dominance of proclamation; this brought with it the use of the vernacular and verbal forms. A second basic feature was the liturgical expression of the Reformation idea of justification, which meant avoiding any kind of appearance of works-righteousness such as the Catholic idea of sacrifice. All the "suspect" elements of the Roman Mass were accordingly eliminated. On the whole, one may observe two contrary movements: while on the one hand the intent was to bring the worship service closer to the people—hence also the adoption of basic para-liturgical forms—on the other hand the theological accent led to an alienation. Abolition of popular elements of the celebration brought with it an austerity that seemed unacceptable to many. This was only partly alleviated through the inclusion of popular features such as hymnody.

3.7.5 The Catholic Reform's Understanding of the Liturgy

The Reformation and the resulting establishment of different confessions put an end to the fruitful initiatives toward an inculturation of the Roman liturgy.[71] Those initiatives had consisted only of the incorporation of vernacular chants at certain points in the Mass.

First reforming initiatives

Thus on major feasts extra strophes (tropes) were inserted in the sequences (e.g., the hymn "Christ ist erstanden" ["Christ the Lord is risen again"][72] as trope to the Easter sequence *Victimae paschale laudes*, as well as singing after the sermon and after the consecration). Following on these usages, individuals like the dean of the cathedral at Bautzen, Johann Leisentrit (1527–1586), and Georg Witzel in Mainz (1501–1573) tried to put into practice some additional ideas for use of the vernacular in the liturgy of the Catholic Mass. But as a result of the heightening confessional tendencies toward differentiation this soon became impossible.

---

[71] Winfried Haunerland, "Einheitlichkeit als Weg der Erneuerung. Das Konzil von Trient und die nachtridentinische Reform der Liturgie," in *Liturgiereformen* (see n. 7 above), 1:436–65; Albert Gerhards, "Die liturgische Entwicklung zwischen 1600 und 1800," in *Hirt und Herde. Religiosität und Frömmigkeit im Rheinland des 18. Jahrhunderts*, ed. Frank Günter Zehnder, Der Riss im Himmel 5 (Köln: DuMont, 2000), 19–36.

[72] Published in *Geistliche Lieder* (1533) with words by Michael Weisse (1480–1534). The tune appears, with Catherine Winkworth's translation of the words, as "Christ the Lord is risen again!" as no. 184 in *The Hymnal 1982, according to the use of The Episcopal Church* (New York: Church Hymnal Corporation, 1982).

The Council of Trent and the Baroque

The Council of Trent (1545–1563) held fast to the completely Latin Mass, though special regional customs from the pre-Reformation period could be maintained.

In the baroque era we find a colorful array of possibilities for liturgies more or less close to the people. For example, there was the full development of the splendor of baroque pontifical or feast celebrations, spectacles nearly on the scale of an opera. But the same period saw the shaping of forms of popular worship, for example, the richly adorned Corpus Christi processions of the time. On the whole there was a need to articulate festal joy. This occurred in the eucharistic celebration itself and in vespers with specialists, choir singers, and instrumental music. There was a problem when none of these was available. A poorly sung choral office could not satisfy the need for festive expression. Above all in remote areas where there was competition from Lutherans and Reformed, the Catholics were pulled back and forth. It was common in those places to fulfill the desire for musical expression by substituting community hymns.

Church hymnody

It was not for reasons of principle but because of insight into pastoral needs that in the course of the seventeenth century the strict rules regarding the use of the vernacular in worship were relaxed. The *Mainzer Cantual* of 1605 represented a milestone; it was one of the most popular hymnals of the era. The foreword tells how a great many laypersons were very interested in singing at Mass rather than simply contemplating Christ's passion in silence or praying the rosary. So it was permitted, at least in the poorer congregations, that at various points the choir's performance could be replaced by hymns sung by the congregation itself.

Characteristics of Counter-Reformation liturgical reform

We should distinguish different directions in Counter-Reformation liturgical reform. Countering the Reformers' denial of the sacrificial character of the Mass, all the elements that promoted that character were emphasized. This included an elevation of the separate priesthood. The content of the Canon was to remain secret from the laity. Accordingly, no real participation of the faithful in the Mass itself was considered necessary. This centralist and clerical view of the liturgy stood counter to other tendencies shaped above all by pastoral insights from the Counter-Reformation mission. These sought to offer Catholic counterparts to the Lutheran forms that brought the liturgy close to the people. Links were made to special traditions from the pre-Reformation period that had survived, thanks to the relatively tolerant decrees of Trent. They were expanded in the direction of a German Mass, something that was permitted in certain districts toward the end of the baroque era. Certainly, even there it was still largely a matter of the priest and the laity worshiping in parallel. While the congregation sang a more or less suitable German hymn, the priest spoke the prescribed Latin Mass text. This kind of celebration continued into the period of the Enlightenment and was embodied, for example, in Franz Schubert's "German Mass." If we add the other so-called para-liturgical forms of worship we can say that overall the Catholic Reform succeeded in finding a liturgical expression appropriate for the times, one that satisfied the people's desire to participate and still preserved dogmatic integrity as demanded by Trent.

Besides the opportunities for active participation by the faithful thus described—which, of course, did not exist everywhere—we should mention the optical dimension of worship. After the upheaval caused by the Thirty Years' War there was a great longing for visual representation and opulence. The baroque churches accommodated that desire, offering the people something that otherwise was only available to the upper classes. So participation could be realized visually, no longer hampered by choir screens or rood screens—though such participation was more or less passive. Active participation was possible in the numerous devotions, processions, and pilgrimages.

3.8 Initiatives toward Liturgical Reform during the Enlightenment

One important precondition for the reforming initiatives in the Enlightenment period was the creation of modern liturgics with its systematic research and the publication of ancient liturgical sources.

Under the pressure of the sometimes destructive critique of Enlightenment liturgics, it was too often the case that extreme and moderate initiatives were thrown into the same pot. In fact, the outstanding proponents had to be protected from the accusation that they developed liturgy solely on a human basis while neglecting to build it on what is divine. In accordance with the spirit of the times, many liturgists lacked any theology of liturgy that could have enabled them to join the external and internal elements in organic fashion. This divergence of the visible side and the reality believed to be hidden within it was ultimately due to the external opulence of the baroque displays of splendor. The Enlightenment drew its own conclusions by dismantling those displays, but without always moving to the true dimension of the symbol.

3.8.1 Goals and Content of Liturgical Reform in the Enlightenment Era

Places of renewal

Extensive reforms and renewals of the liturgy took place between 1750 and 1850 under the influence of the Enlightenment, both in the Catholic Church and in the churches of the Reformation. The centers of reform were, for Catholicism, the archbishoprics of Breslau, Constance, and Mainz. Individual bishops and vicars general took responsibility for and initiated the reforms, which were almost exclusively promoted by the clergy. An additional aspect of the reform was a more intensive education for the priesthood and continuing education as well. Even now, the broad scope of the associated literature gives us a feeling for its extent and intensity. The most important forums for information about and discussion of the liturgy were periodicals such as the *Diöcesanblatt für den Clerus der Fürstbischöflich Breslauer Diöces* (1803–1820); the *Archiv für die Pastoralkonferenzen in den Landkapiteln des Bisthums Konstanz* (1804–1827), with its predecessor, the *Geistlichen Monatschrift mit besonderer Rücksicht auf das Bisthum Constanz* (1802/1803); or the *Theologisch-Praktische Monathschrift zunächst für Seelsorger* (1802–1811), published in Linz.[73]

[73] [*Diocesan Paper for the Clergy of the Prince-Bishopric of Breslau; Archive for the Pastoral Conferences in the State Capitals of the Diocese of Constance; Spiritual*

Objectives of the Reform

The goal of the reform was primarily the creation of a liturgy that would instruct believers in the meaning of their faith and lead them to truth and virtue. Encouragement to love of God and neighbor as well as the enrichment of religious knowledge were seen as the purposes of a liturgy that, altogether in the spirit of the Enlightenment, should bring people to a higher level of virtue and morality. But an external participation in worship was insufficient for such purposes; rather, the faithful must have a share in the internal treasure of the liturgy.

In the second place, a liturgy conceived in this fashion must have an appeal to the senses or, in the terminology of the time, it must be uplifting. An uplifting liturgy ought to address people with reason and sensibility and thus intensify its effects.

A third concept that appears repeatedly is "purposefulness." The liturgy must be shaped to accomplish its goal. Its founding by Christ must be evident; dignity, harmony, and solemnity are required. A distinction was drawn between what is unchangeable in the worship service—elements traced to Christ and the apostles and to church law—and what is changeable and temporary.

The liturgy proclaims that whoever follows Christ the Savior— Christ is regarded also as a model human being and teacher—will achieve blessedness. People trust in God because virtuousness and blessedness are fulfilled in God.

Monthly, especially for the Diocese of Constance; Theological-Practical Monthly, primarily for Pastors.] See the overview in *Aufklärungskatholizismus und Liturgie. Reformentwürfe für die Feier von Taufe, Firmung, Busse, Trauung und Krankensalbung,* ed. Franz Kohlschein, Pietas Liturgica, Studia 6 (St. Ottilien: EOS Verlag, 1989); Franz Kohlschein, "Liturgiereform und deutscher Aufklärungskatholizismus," in *Liturgiereformen* (see n. 7 above), 1:511–33; Benedikt Kranemann, "Zwischen Tradition und Zeitgeist. Programm und Durchführung der Liturgiereform in der deutschen katholischen Aufklärung," *Jaarboek voor liturgieonderzoek* 20 (2004): 25–47; Ulrich L. Lehner, *The Catholic Enlightenment: The Forgotten History of a Global Movement* (New York: Oxford University Press, 2016).

The reform of the liturgy primarily affected ritual[74] as well as hymnals and prayerbooks,[75] less so breviaries,[76] and evidently not the Missal as a whole. One innovation was a firm emphasis on community Vespers.[77] The Enlightenment liturgists demanded regular preaching on Sundays and hoped to concentrate liturgical life in the parishes. Pilgrimages and processions were sharply reduced in favor of congregational worship. Something similar was true of Benedictions, which were suspected of expressing superstitious beliefs. The revised or newly developed liturgical books for the most part followed diocesan traditions. The Latin texts were almost all translated into German—a crucial feature of this reform. There was a particular interest in the liturgical signs and symbols and a desire to make them clearer. Textual variants, especially in address and response, were offered for different pastoral situations and different participants in the liturgy. Here we can perceive a broader purpose of this reform: if the goal of liturgy is to be attained, the faithful must be able to participate in it knowledgeably. The use of the vernacular and

[74] See most recently Klaus Keller, *Die Liturgie der Eheschliessung in der katholischen Aufklärung. Eine Untersuchung der Reformentwürfe im deutschen Sprachraum*, Münchener Theologische Studien, Systematische Abteilung 51 (St. Ottilien: EOS Verlag, 1996).

[75] *"Der grosse Sänger David: euer Muster." Studien zu den ersten diözesanen Gesang- und Gebetbüchern der katholischen Aufklärung*, ed. Franz Kohlschein and Kurt Küpper, Liturgiewissenschaftliche Quellen und Forschungen 73 (Münster: Aschendorff, 1993).

[76] Liobgid Koch, "Ein deutsches Brevier der Aufklärungszeit. Thaddäus Dereser und sein Deutsches Brevier für Stiftsdamen, Klosterfrauen und jeden guten Christen," *Archiv für Liturgiewissenschaft* 17/18 (1975–76): 80–144; Philipp Gahn, "Joseph Thomas von Haiden und das Reformbrevier von St. Stephan zu Augsburg. Einige Anmerkungen zum Aufsatz von Liobgid Koch, 'Ein deutsches Brevier der Aufklärungszeit,'" *Archiv für Liturgiewissenschaft* 42 (2000): 84–96.

[77] Friedrich Popp, "Die deutsche Vesper im Zeitalter der Aufklärung unter besonderer Berücksichtigung des Bistums Konstanz," in idem, *Studien zu liturgischen Reformbemühungen im Zeitalter der Aufklärung. Die Lateinisch-deutsche Messliturgie Strassers in Göttingen; die Entstehungsgeschichte des Konstanzer Gesangbuches von 1812; die deutsche Vesper im Zeitalter der Aufklärung unter besonderer Berückschtigung des Bistums Konstanz*, Freiburger Diözesan-Archiv 87 (Freiburg: Herder, 1967), 87–495; Franz Kohlschein, "Die Tagzeitenliturgie als 'Gebet der Gemeinde' in der Geschichte," *Heiliger Dienst* 41 (1987): 12–40.

opportunities for variation offered by liturgical books worked toward that end. But when this shifted to a relationship between priests as teachers of religion and the faithful as students, the hierarchical and authoritative relationship familiar as an aspect of Enlightenment absolutism in other parts of society became part of the liturgy as well. On the other hand, insofar as liturgical books made it possible for laypersons to understand the liturgy and join in the priest's prayer, we might call this an emancipation of the laity.

It is part of the liturgical history of the period that the faithful resisted the reforms; at times the changes had to be introduced by force. The liturgy of the Enlightenment was never uncontroversial; it was heavily criticized even later. Only in the course of the twentieth century did liturgics arrive at a more nuanced view.

3.8.2 Intellectual and Spiritual Background and Reforming Program: The Synod of Pistoia as an Example

Backgrounds

One notable example of liturgical reform in the spirit of the Enlightenment was the Synod of Pistoia in 1786. The religious-historical background for the Synod can be seen in the influence of French Jansenism in eighteenth-century Italy.[78] Jansenism was in some sense a late effect of the suppression of the Reformation in France. Dogmatically speaking, it represented an attempt to revive Augustinianism, especially in regard to the doctrine of grace and predestination. The practical-ethical consequence was a moral rigorism, in the face of which dogmatic and speculative interests in Italy clearly took a back seat. Moral rigorism was especially well suited for accomplishing a general reform of the church, something that at the time seemed overdue.

The Josephinian Reforms in Austria[79] provided the model for efforts at reform in Tuscany. Leopold II gave it impetus. He was the son of

---

[78] Albert Gerhards, "Die Synode von Pistoia 1786 und ihre Reform des Gottesdienstes," in *Liturgiereformen* (see n. 7 above), 1:16–51.

[79] Hans Hollerweger, *Die Reform des Gottesdienstes zur Zeit des Josephinismus in Österreich*, Studien zur Pastoralliturgie 1 (Regensburg: Pustet, 1976).

Maria Theresa of Austria and ruled in Florence for nearly a quarter century before ascending the imperial throne in Vienna in 1790. Leopold's church partner in the reform program was Bishop Cipione de' Ricci (1741–1819), who had absorbed the Jansenist spirit during his studies in Rome. In 1780, Ricci was made bishop of Pistoia and Prato. Starting from there, a comprehensive program of church reform was to be applied throughout Tuscany.

Objectives

Leopold of Tuscany attempted to reorder the relationship between state and church in the spirit of the Josephinian Reforms. This included strengthening the conciliar principle against curial centralism, especially through regular synods at different levels. To get the reforms underway, Leopold sent the bishops in Tuscany a framework for reform, the *Punti Ecclesiastici*, dated 26 January 1786. This document treated nearly every element of worship: Mass, Liturgy of the Hours, administration of the sacraments, devotions, processions, and other usages. Thus, for example, it was said to be necessary to revise public prayers if they contained statements contrary to church teaching. One of the principal tasks of the synod was to be reform of the breviary and missals, eliminating false and erroneous statements and taking care that the whole of Sacred Scripture be read in the course of the year. In particular, Leopold urged a thorough reform of the system of stipends and indulgences. A particular feature of Enlightenment reform was the elimination of the numerous feastdays, whose frequency had in fact become a social problem. Other reform initiatives touched the veneration of relics and the saints as well as detailed instructions about the adornment of churches. All sacred actions are said to be for the purpose of leading the people to true and enlightened devotion.

The territorial prince's *Punti Ecclesiastici* were certainly welcomed by the bishop of Pistoia and Prato as an opportunity to do something serious about the reform of the whole of church life he had long sought. So he called a diocesan synod; it met in Pistoia from 18 to 28 September 1786. Its final decree on prayer contained a great many statements about the liturgy, the foremost of which are listed in the next section.

Pistoia: Central Pronouncements

- *Orientation to the patristic era*: As in the ancient church, a solemn baptismal liturgy with participation of the faithful was to be held on Easter and Pentecost. Overall, there was an attempt to reduce an excessive eucharistic piety to the standard of ancient Christian veneration of the Eucharist.

- *Participation of the faithful in the liturgy*: A fundamental statement of the synod is that the faithful are co-offerers of the Mass; the liturgy is a common action of priest and people. This led to a number of conclusions that seem obvious today: the liturgical rites should be simplified; the liturgy should always be spoken aloud and in the language of the people; in addition, books containing the *Ordo Missae* in the vernacular should be made available for the people to read. A further consequence of the principle of participation by the faithful in the liturgy was the distribution of communion to the participants in every Mass.

- *Liturgical space*: Regarding the arrangement of liturgical space, it was provided that there should be only one altar in a church and no images or relics should be placed on it. These latter are only to be interpreted as symbols of the future resurrection. Certainly, the relationship to the content remained purely external. For this synod, images were nothing but a substitute for books provided for the illiterate, intended to recall certain events in salvation history. Accordingly, only instructive and uplifting imagery was to be permitted.

- *Revision of liturgical books*: The synod took up the demands of the *Punti Ecclesiastici* regarding the revision of the breviary and missal. The "lies" and other imperfections were to be removed. The readings in the breviary were to be arranged in such a way that in the course of a year the whole Bible would be read. The overall reform of the church's public prayer served the purpose of placing in the hands of the people the means necessary to enable them to join their voices with that of the whole church.

Overall tendency

On the whole, the reform program of Pistoia contains some notable initiatives that could be regarded as harbingers of the twentieth-century liturgical renewal. In fact, in the wake of baroque excesses—for example, the excessive numbers of saints' days, novenas, octaves, pilgrimages, processions, etc.—reform was urgently needed. Abuses of indulgences, benefices, and stipends were obvious. It was a question of concentrating on essentials: Sunday was to be restored as the central Christian feastday. The center of Christian community should be the parish; this represented an opposition to individualistic notions of salvation. Thus the synod emphasized that the liturgy should stand in balanced and mutual relationship with life in general.

Reasons for failure

This ambitious program of reform was shattered by internal and external factors. We may accept the judgment of many historians that the reforming initiative of Pistoia remained only an episode, and yet many of its demands coincided with those of the later Liturgical Movement: for example, the significance of the communion of the faithful at Mass, the value of the vernacular, and "active participation" in the sacrifice. Alongside demands conditioned by their own time, the Enlightenment reformers articulated older concerns of the Middle Ages and especially the Reformation period. The failure of the reforming initiatives of Pistoia had biographical and historical grounds: these were probably the wrong protagonists, and the time was not ripe for a genuine liturgical renewal. Further conditions were required, and we will speak of those in what follows.

3.9 Liturgical Currents in the Age of the Restoration

The Enlightenment and the Romantic Era

The simultaneity of very different spiritual and intellectual currents makes a unified assessment of the period at the beginning of the nineteenth century extremely difficult. We must consider especially secularization and its consequences (e.g., the end of monastic liturgies, the elimination of spiritual rulers and their musical culture), as well as the later consequences of the French Revolution and the Napoleonic upheavals. Countercurrents in spiritual and intellectual history are already visible. Still, individual objectives of the Enlightenment remained in view: better education and instruction for clergy and people, authoritative rules for works of art and the practice of the arts, and emphasis on the authority of local bishops. Alongside these, Romantic tendencies were beginning to spread: the inclination to historicism and the restoration of an idealized Middle Ages, embrace of nationalistic images, and the rise of ecumenical ideas with the goal of national church unity.

Countertendencies

Ultimately, however, anti-Reform tendencies emerged: a centralized organization of the Roman Catholic Church in Rome, increased solidification of confessional divides, and a radical divorce of the church from a world felt to be hostile to the church and faith.

The tendencies summarized here give a hint of the enormous tensions in that century. In what follows we will consider in particular the effects on church music as affected by the times, since it was especially in this field that renewal was possible.[80] In contrast, after the reforming efforts of the Enlightenment the texts and rites were no longer subject to debate. They were fixed "for all time" by the Tridentine reform, now fully applied for the first time. Likewise, the church space changed hardly at all; while historicism recovered medieval language about forms and sometimes created impressive spatial ensembles, the building program remained essentially that of the Catholic Reform.

3.9.1 Church Music as "Sacred Art"

Removal of church music from the liturgy

In the early nineteenth century, church music was faced with a double danger: on the one hand that of secularization, on the other

---

[80] Albert Gerhards, "Der liturgische Hintergrund der Palestrina-Renaissance im 19. Jahrhundert," in *Palestrina und die Idee der klassischen Vokalpolyphonie im 19. Jahrhundert. Zur Geschichte eines kirchenmusikalischen Stilideals*, ed. Winfried Kirsch, Palestrina und die Kirchenmusik im 19. Jahrhundert 1 (Regensburg: Bosse, 1989), 181–94; Jakob Johannes Koch, *Traditionelle mehrstimmige Messen in erneuerter Liturgie—ein Widerspruch?* (Regensburg: Pustet, 2002); Eckhard Jaschinski, *Kleine Geschichte der Kirchenmusik* (Freiburg: Herder, 2004).

that of spiritual and artistic impoverishment, insofar as church music was changed along radical-enlightened lines. In general there was an attempt to counter these dangers with formal and stylistic reforms and the demand for an "art of sacred music." This was associated with an idealization of ancient music. In contrast, contemporary music was regarded as theatrically degenerate, worldly, and lascivious. The search for a pure church music style concealed a drama whose consequences are felt even today: the complete separation between the secular and the spiritual. The Romantics' moral-ascetic religious feeling in fact did not allow for any musical development in the liturgy. Something similar was true for both Catholics and Protestants. So a new style of spiritual music performances developed in the city concert halls; we can locate the beginning with the renewed performance of Felix Mendelssohn-Bartholdy's *St. Matthew Passion*. Works like Johannes Brahms's *German Requiem* were written only for the concert hall and were no longer rooted in the liturgy. A genuine renewal of church music could not come from that side—at least according to the perspective of the time. It presupposed a reflection on the bases of Christian faith.

Johann Michael Sailer

One of the most important pioneer thinkers in that direction was Johann Michael Sailer (1751–1832). Sailer's influence, especially through his great circle of students, had an enduring effect on the whole nineteenth-century reform. The ideas he promoted rested on a liturgical-theological basis that was indebted on the one hand to the Catholic Enlightenment and on the other hand contained the basic directions of the later Restoration. In his opinion all true religion must be twofold: internal and external. Therefore true religion had to express itself in art, that is, worship. In turn, all true and sacred art, like every liturgy, must be both a revelation of God and a revelation of faith. Art and liturgy are therefore necessary consequences of religion as revelation. In addition, it is the task of art to enliven the inner person. Revealing and enlivening are for Sailer the basic functions of all liturgy and of true religion itself.

From these general ideas Sailer drew conclusions about the shape of worship, which for him was the action of the whole church. Therefore congregational song was also liturgically relevant. Of course, this did not mean for him that the choir could not assume the role of singers on festive occasions. As much as he advocated the use of the vernacular in the liturgy, he did not make it an absolute. That kind of balance is characteristic of Sailer. So he showed some reserve in face of the excessive demands of the Enlightenment types for simplicity; it must not decline into plainness. Sailer's views on such subjects reveal an integrative idea of liturgy, the kind that would develop only some hundred years later in the wake of the Liturgical Movement. Still, Sailer's suggestions were not wholly unsuccessful—though that success was ambivalent.

3.9.2 Development of Church Music in the Nineteenth Century

Quest for "pure music"

After Sailers was appointed to the cathedral chapter at Regensburg in 1821 that place became a center for liturgical renewal. Sailers's ideas were adopted by the Silesian physician and gifted lover of music Carl Proske, whom Sailers appointed in 1830 to an unpaid office as director of the cathedral's music. After Sailers's death Proske traveled to Italy twice to collect genuine liturgical music; he thought that would be the place to find it intact. King Ludwig I and the government in Munich supported the musical reform program initiated by Proske, which had to counter resistance from the cathedral chapter. This was the time when the cathedral at Regensburg and other medieval cathedral structures were being completed. It was desired that a similarly pure music would develop within these new buildings, though that was mistakenly equated with the Gothic. So people thought that simple chorales—at most accompanied by the organ—were most appropriate for the Gothic cathedral.

Further developments reveal that the efforts at reform of church music in the nineteenth century were motivated by liturgical theology and influenced by Franz Xaver Schmid (d. 1871), a liturgist and student of Sailers, who published a two-volume book on liturgics in 1832; it was avidly studied by the Regensburg group and applied as a foundation for reforms. In it Schmid distinguished ceremonies in the narrower sense, which the celebrant was required to perform according to instructions from the church, and worship acts by the faithful, which only required the church's permission. Especially in the second edition (1840) the new initiatives were pressed further toward centralistic and clergy-centered ideas and a juridicizing of the liturgy.

Music as part of liturgy

Liturgically speaking, this laid the foundation for the later authoritarian reforms imposed by the Allgemeine Cäcilien-Verband. Schmid's approach certainly advocated for valid knowledge of the nature of church music and liturgy corresponding to the ancient Roman tradition. According to him, church music not only performs a service function but constitutes an integrative part of the liturgy as a whole. The human voice in particular is a living organ of Christian worship. Therefore its use is demanded by the *mysterium* of the liturgy itself and is not merely for its ornamentation.

Restorative tendencies and juridicizing of the concept of liturgy

However, around mid-century, as part of the general resistance to liberal anti-church attacks from various sides, a combative Catholic consciousness developed, and there was a demand for renewal of the Roman Catholic Church in restorative directions. As regards liturgy and church music the reference point was the reform in Regensburg. One cannot overlook the increasing juridicizing of the concept of liturgy, according to which liturgy consists essentially of ceremonies defined and determined by rubrics (understood as liturgical laws).

Franz Xaver Witt: Liturgy as priestly action

These basic ideas were programmatically and organizationally applied by Franz Xaver Witt (1834–1888), the founder and first president of the Allgemeine Cäcilien-Verband (ACV), and were implemented for future use. Like Proske, Witt was also primarily interested in the renewal of the liturgy and the reintegration of church music within it. Witt drew a firm line between the external form and the internal nature of the celebration, the sacrifice of Christ. The priest's action constituted the bridge between the internal essence and the external performance. Liturgy is therefore an action of the priest. But Witt did not understand that in the sense of the priesthood of all the baptized; he thought of it only in terms of the ordained priesthood; only the ordained were able to celebrate. Consequently Witt, like all Cecilians, wanted to allow only men (clergy if possible) and boys to sing at worship. In this concept the faithful have no influence on the worship event. They are attendees, but the choir participates. The choir does not take the role of the people, because the people can play no part in worship. This led to a distinction between "liturgical and non-liturgical worship services." Only in "Masses" not appropriate for singing, that is, the priest's so-called private Masses, was it permissible to have congregational singing in the vernacular.

3.9.3 The Cecilia Movement and Increased Centralization

Centralizing tendencies

Franz Xaver Witt brought attention to the spiritual transformation in nineteenth-century Catholic Germany. He sharpened centralizing tendencies by denying the bishops the right to regulate the liturgy. Accordingly, the ACV became an organ for supervising the maintenance of Rome's regulations for liturgy and church music. For that purpose the regulations, heretofore unsystematically organized, were to be collected in a legal code for church music. According to a private but widely read handbook, *Die Kirchenmusik nach dem Willen der Kirche* [Church Music as the Church Wills to Have It] by Paul Krutschek, the people's singing at liturgy was not only to be opposed but should be eliminated altogether. True divine praise consisted not in musical form but in meticulously following the rules.

Gregorian chant

On close inspection, what we see here is a cancellation of every process of inculturation that had ever happened since the transfer or adoption of Roman liturgy in other countries. Thus Gregorian chant was seen as liturgical singing in the strict sense. But the Cecilians were not concerned about the question of authenticity, the issue being addressed above all by the centers of monastic studies, especially in France. It was simply about a Roman-authorized edition of the chant;

that alone could claim liturgical status. But, in fact, the high status accorded to chant was merely formal. In artistic terms polyphonic works—especially the special compositions of the Cecilians themselves, which are sometimes questionable—were more highly valued.

Liturgical education and church choirs

However, it would be wrong to assert that the Cecilian movement was not interested in liturgical education. On the contrary: the movement desired to improve the situation of liturgy and church music, which was, in fact, largely deficient. In terms of organization this was done through the establishment of centers for church music and the widespread introduction of the ACV. This reforming project was successful. Church choirs were founded everywhere. In general, the level of church music was elevated, including that of congregational singing.

3.9.4 From Restoration to Liturgical Movement

The development of church music in the nineteenth century is a good example of how reforms are the children of their times. The scarlet thread was the awareness that church music, church singing, is an integrating factor in festal liturgy, inasmuch as it can be properly and fully developed only in sung form. The verdict on church music in every case depended on the definition of liturgy. The early Cecilians were concerned to remove church music from its independent and secularized status and reintroduce it into the liturgy. Since liturgy meant the worship of the whole church, thus including the faithful, community singing at worship was altogether desirable, and in festal celebrations the choir was merely representative of the whole. At the end of the development, after the establishment of the Cecilian movement, church music was restored as part of the liturgy. However, the juridicizing and exclusive singling out of the priestly actions necessarily led to a clericalization of the choir, with the fatal consequence that, in line with the contemporary mind-set, women no longer had any opportunity to participate. This position was adopted by Pope Pius X's instruction on church music in 1903. Remarkably enough, it was precisely that pope who at first embodied the centralization and juridicizing of liturgy and church music and at the same time represented the turning point for the fundamental liturgical renewal of the twentieth century.

3.10 The Liturgical Movement and Renewal

3.10.1 *Personalities and Centers of the Liturgical Movement*

Roots of the Liturgical Movement

The liturgical movement is one of the most complex phenomena in the history of the church in the twentieth century. This is evident at the outset when we try to determine when it began. In spite of ourselves we push farther and farther back into history in the attempt to discover its roots. Those can be found partly in the sixteenth century, the era of the Reformation and the Catholic Reform. Important impulses also came from the period of the Enlightenment. Certainly the real predecessors of the Liturgical Movement are to be found in the last two-thirds of the nineteenth century. As we have shown, it was precisely centralization and the orientation to Rome that led to a new interest in the ancient liturgy. In France and Germany the Missal was translated. Remarkably, the breakthrough in the twentieth century was also a fruit of the restorative tendencies in the nineteenth. Important centers of that restoration were French and Belgian Benedictine monasteries that delved into their own tradition for the sake of a true renewal of church music and thus of the whole liturgy.

Tra le sollecitudini

The instruction (*motu proprio*) on music titled *Tra le sollecitudini* [Among the cares], issued by Pope Pius X on 22 November 1903, shortly after his entry into office, was completely a prisoner of that spirit. The significance of this writing was that it granted church music a liturgical value of its own. The pope recognized the spiritual and thus overall religious significance of church music as an essential element of the liturgy. If church life were to be renewed there must, in his opinion, first be a renewal of worship.

Filled as We are with a most ardent desire to see the true Christian spirit flourish in every respect and be preserved by all the faithful, We deem it necessary to provide before anything else for the sanctity and dignity of the temple, in which the faithful assemble for no other object than that of acquiring this spirit from its foremost and indispensable font, which is the active participation in the most holy mysteries and in the public and solemn prayer of the Church.[81]

It would scarcely be possible to overvalue this statement: after a long time, at last a papal document again acknowledged worship as the source of faith. It is not merely a mass of ceremonials by which the celebration is to be carried out according to law; it is the place of believers' immediate encounter with the Lord. Vatican II would adopt the reference to active participation and make it one of the key concepts of liturgical renewal.

The Mechelen Congress

This instruction on church music gave official status to what theretofore had been mainly private attempts to acquaint the faithful with the liturgy, but most people were still unaware of the significance of the statement. The breakthrough to the Liturgical Movement came with the so-called Mechelen Event of 23 September 1909, and its key figure was a young professor of dogmatic theology from the abbey of Mont César, Dom Lambert Beauduin.[82] Beauduin was asked to present his concept of liturgy and pastoral work at a conference in Belgium, the Congrès National des Oeuvres Catholiques. He noticed that liturgy was located on the program not within the topic of "upbringing in and realization of the faith" but as part of "art." Behind this was the idea that liturgy was nothing but a pious ceremony. In spite of these bad omens, Beauduin was able to propagate his ideas at the congress through the voice of another, the historian Gottfried Kurth, who held a major discourse whose complete wording has not survived. He said, among other things:

[81] Pope St. Pius X, *Tra le sollecitudini* (Instruction on Sacred Music), 22 Nov. 1903, introduction. See http://www.adoremus.org/MotuProprio.html.
[82] Balthasar Fischer, "Das 'Mechelner Ereignis' vom 23. September 1909," *Liturgisches Jahrbuch* 9 (1959): 203–19.

The church also teaches us the language in which we must speak with God. We encounter the whole glory of the divine Word in the liturgy. Liturgy is the summit of all human poesy and thought. It utters before God the needs and endless misery of human existence. If there is an explanation for why so many Christians are fleeing the church, it is most certainly the inadequacy of the prayers that have taken the place of the beautiful, ancient, traditional liturgy. On the day when the sacred book on the altar ceases to be for the many an incomprehensible book with seven seals—on the day when all find in it once more the key to what the priests are saying at the altar of God—on that day a great number of those who have abandoned the houses of God will return.[83]

The Mechelen Event proved to be a kind of sluice that opened the way to fruitful pastoral-liturgical work in Belgium and Germany. It is no surprise that the Liturgical Movement began with other inner- and extra-ecclesial breakthroughs at much the same time. The background was the positive expectation that people could be led to the good through appropriate enlightenment and instruction—an expectation that, certainly, was severely dampened by the First World War.

Three wings of the Liturgical Movement

The Mechelen Event marked, for the moment, only a single, somewhat formal idea of what constituted the Liturgical Movement, which in fact is as varied and sophisticated as its protagonists. We can distinguish at least three wings:[84]

- the Benedictine orientation (led by the Belgian monasteries of Mont César and Maredsous and the German cloisters of Beuron and Maria Laach)
- the parallel Liturgical Movement that was part of the youth movement (Romano Guardini, the Burg Rothenfels, and Haus Altenberg)

[83] Ibid., 207–8.
[84] Burkhard Neunheuser, "Die klassische Liturgische Bewegung (1909–1963) und die nachkonziliare Liturgiereform. Vergleich und Versuch einer Würdigung," in *Mélanges liturgiques. Offerts au R. P. Dom Bernard Botte O.S.B.* (Louvain: Abbaye du Mont César, 1972), 401–16.

- the popular liturgical movement initiated primarily in Austria and centered in parishes (Pius Parsch in Klosterneuburg; the Leipzig Oratory)

Four phases of the Liturgical Movement (according to Guardini)

Romano Guardini distinguished four phases of the Liturgical Movement:[85]

- An initial phase, in the nineteenth century, was interested in recovering the material from patristic times and the High Middle Ages, still perceptible in the liturgical books.

- A second phase took place in an academic and Benedictine milieu and concerned itself with a kind of restoration, the construction of an ideal liturgy to which the laity would have no access.

- Thus there came a third phase, the work of centers of the popular liturgical apostolate and the youth movement. This was about applying the new knowledge to parish practice. Here the problem of the vernacular played a central role, so that we might speak of a first form of inculturation.

- According to Guardini a fourth phase began with the Second Vatican Council. In it such questions must be addressed as: "How is a genuine liturgical action shaped—in distinction from other religious actions, both individual and freely shaped community activities such as 'popular devotions'? How is the underlying basic action structured? What forms does it take? What false directions threaten it? What relationship does it bear to the structure, and to the sensibilities of people today? What must happen if they are to learn it in a correct and honest way?"[86] In this famous essay at the beginning of the liturgical reform Guardini again posed the question of the liturgical capacity of

[85] Arno Schilson, "Romano Guardini: Wegbereiter und Wegbegleiter der liturgischen Erneuerung," *Liturgisches Jahrbuch* 36 (1986): 3–27.

[86] Romano Guardini, "Der Kultakt und die gegenwärtige Aufgabe der Liturgie," in idem, *Liturgie und liturgische Bildung* (Würzburg: Werkbund-Verlag, 1966), 9–18, at 15.

modern people that he had laid out at the beginning of the Liturgical Movement.[87]

Preconditions for the liturgical reform of Vatican II

The following impulses from the Liturgical Movement were among the conditions for Vatican II's liturgical reforms (see also chap. 2, "History, Outline, and Methods of Liturgics," and chap. 4, "Theology of the Liturgy"):

- The discovery of the spiritual riches of the liturgy (Solesmes). This was connected with the revival and strengthening of Benedictine life, first in Francophone and later also in German-speaking abbeys. In France inspiration also came from the (anti-Gallican) orientation to Rome and the associated discovery of the ancient sources of Roman liturgy.

- The discovery of the role of the faithful (Pius X, Lambert Beauduin). No longer was only the valid and licit action at the center; instead, the fruitful, intelligent participation of believers was to advance the church's spiritual life.

- The discovery of the presence of mystery (Odo Casel). Against one-sided and thus inadequate theological concepts of sacrificial and sacramental theology, the mystery theology of Odo Casel, Benedictine of Maria Laach, enjoyed a successful triumph. This created the preconditions for a theology of the liturgy that understands it as a celebratory making-present.

- The discovery of the church as *mysterium* (Romano Guardini). The overcoming of a purely juridical understanding of the church brought the image of the "mystical body" of the church into perspective. The liturgy is to give tangible expression to this invisible reality, as was practiced, for example, at Burg Rothenfels.

[87] Albert Gerhards, "Romano Guardini als Prophet des Liturgischen. Eine Rückbesinnung in postmoderner Zeit," in *Guardini weiterdenken*, ed. Hermann Josef Schuster, Schriftenreihe des Forum Guardini 1 (Berlin: Dreieck, 1993), 140–53.

- The discovery of the parish as the primary place in which the church is realized (Athanasius Wintersig; Pius Parsch; Leipzig Oratory). This was about a renewal of the church in the spirit of the liturgy. Any number of parish centers, many of them with notable church architecture, conveyed to others a new community experience of church.

- The discovery of Easter as the center of the whole liturgy (Pius XII). The whole of the liturgy, with all its facets, finds its central meaning in the paschal mystery of the crucified and risen Christ. This principle, made transparent in today's liturgy, was called to mind by Pope Pius XII.

3.10.2 Principles and Results of the Liturgical Reform at Vatican II

This is not the place to elucidate the whole program of liturgical reform.[88] In what follows we will focus on one important question: what is the image of the church that underlies the reforms, and how is it expressed in today's liturgy? The Liturgical Movement accomplished a qualitative advance from a juridical to an organic view of the church, something that was officially ratified by Pius XII's encyclicals *Mystici Corporis Christi* (1943) and *Mediator Dei* (1947). The Liturgical Movement received a new stimulus from these writings, as well as from the reform of Holy Week by the same pope in the 1950s, and that led directly to the preparations for Vatican II.

The conciliar document that is constitutive for the postconciliar liturgical reform is the Liturgy Constitution, *Sacrosanctum Concilium* (see the commentary literature in appendix 4). It was adopted on 4 December 1963, with 2,147 "yes" votes and only four "no" votes, as the first document of the council.

In the preparatory phase before the council, the world church was asked for suggestions and requests for what the council's deliberations should touch on, with a view to renewal of the church. The Fulda bishops' conference suggested, among other things, a revision of the calendar and the church year in order that its center, the Christ

---

[88] See Albert Gerhards, *Erneuerung kirchlichen Lebens aus dem Gottesdienst. Beiträge zur Reform der Liturgie*, Praktische Theologie heute 120 (Stuttgart: Kohlhammer, 2012).

mystery, might emerge more clearly once again. The order of pericopes should be revised, the prayer of the people renewed, and communion in the chalice should be made available to the laity on certain
occasions. The celebration of Mass *versus populum* was addressed. The
breviary should be accommodated to the demands of pastoral life,
the rites for the baptism of adults and children reformed, and positive
experiences with the vernacular should be taken into account in a
renewal of the liturgy.[89] Similar concerns appear in a document issued
by Cardinal Julius Döpfner of Berlin for Christians in East Germany.
He pointed to the situation of Germans in the Eastern diaspora: their
spiritual life was dependent on active participation in the liturgy. In
the immediate preparation for and during the council the constitution
underwent a complicated and sometimes tense process of discussion.

Structure of the Constitution on the Liturgy

The liturgy constitution is structured as follows (cf. also the overview in appendix 4): a foreword (articles 1–4) is followed by a first,
fundamental chapter, "General Principles for the Restoration and
Progress of the Sacred Liturgy" (articles 5–46); this takes up one-third
of the Constitution. The remaining chapters treat the Eucharist, the
other sacraments and sacramentals, the Liturgy of the Hours, the
liturgical year, church music, sacred art, liturgical vessels and vestments. An appendix with a conciliar declaration on calendar reform
concludes the document.

Theological concerns

The Constitution contains some important new theological accents.[90] Its starting point is the idea that the liturgy should be the
source of faith and Christian life. This corresponds to the dialogical
understanding of the liturgy, with its katabatic, diabatic, and anabatic
character (see *SC* 5; 7) and the centering of all liturgy in Christ's

[89] Johannes Wagner, *Mein Weg zur Liturgiereform 1936–1986. Erinnerungen*
(Freiburg: Herder, 1993), 50.
[90] Albert Gerhards, "Gipfelpunkt und Quelle. Intention und Rezeption der
Liturgiekonstitution *Sacrosanctum Concilium*," in *Erinnerung an die Zukunft. Das
Zweite Vatikanische Konzil*, ed. Jan Heiner Tück (Freiburg: Herder, 2012), 107–26.

paschal mystery (see *SC* 5, and frequently elsewhere). The liturgy constitution, with its concept of "active participation," introduced a new intensity and new forms for the faithful's cooperative celebration of the liturgy. Liturgy is described as the celebration of the whole church and all believers. The document gives a new weight to the role of Sacred Scripture in the liturgy (see *SC* 24), provides more space for the vernacular (see *SC* 36), but also calls for a renewal of the liturgical symbols. The Constitution accords great significance to liturgical instruction and education in liturgics. Acculturation and inculturation, including explicit processes of exchange between liturgy and culture, are enabled. Finally, *SC* 25 demands an immediate revision of the liturgical books and thus the practical implementation of the Liturgy Constitution. This was quickly taken up after the council, as some important books reveal: in 1969 the *Ordo baptismi parvulorum* was published, followed in 1970 by the *Missale Romanum*, and in 1971–1972 by the four-volume *Liturgia horarum*. Vernacular versions appeared at irregular intervals. German versions of the liturgy for infant baptism (1971), the Missal (1975), already preceded by a study edition, and the three-volume Liturgy of the Hours (1978) quickly followed. In the United States the new Missal was put into effect in 1973; the Liturgy of the Hours preceded it in 1970, and the rite for infant baptism followed in 1974.

Participatio actuosa *and the image of the church*

Some of the council's theological accents need to be discussed in more depth. We have already spoken about the principle of "active participation" (*participatio actuosa*) by the faithful in the liturgy. The liturgy constitution expanded it to a new dimension, grounded in an image of the church no longer "christomonistic" but "pneumatological," as developed by Vatican II. The pneumatological image placed emphasis on the Pentecostal community of the faithful with their multiple charisms. In contrast, the christomonistic image emphasized the institutional aspect, the hierarchy and church structures; it sees the church primarily as a continuation of Christ's incarnation.

In the Western church the christomonistic interpretation has dominated, at the expense of the pneumatological. One consequence among others was that worship increasingly became a specialized action performed by the clergy. The people's opportunities for religious expression were shoved to the margins or located entirely outside the liturgy itself. In its Constitution on the Church and the documents that built on it, Vatican II achieved a fundamental change in perspective that was prepared for but not yet fully developed in the Constitution on the Liturgy. Starting with the Constitution on the Church (*Lumen Gentium*), when the council speaks of the church itself it no longer begins with the hierarchy but with the entirety of the people of God (*LG* 2). Thus the subject of the church's actions is no longer the hierarchy exclusively. This is especially true of the church's liturgy. When a community celebrates the liturgy, the subject of the act of worship is not the abstract church as a whole but the congregation assembled in that place, which is an expression of the church as worldwide *communio*. This eucharistic ecclesiology is explicitly adopted in *Lumen Gentium* 26.

Regarding the principle of "active participation" this means that it is no longer a matter of participation in an alien event but of taking part individually in a reality of which one is oneself a part, to which one belongs. It is true that, in a catholic understanding, the assembly is and remains hierarchically organized, but the clergy are no longer a group set above the people; they are part of the people and have their parts to play, just as do others.

Danger of overemphasis on the incarnational principle

The structure of liturgical celebrations in the period before Vatican II reveals another serious consequence of overemphasis on the incarnational principle. To put it simply, liturgy was simply a function, an event for the distribution of grace. But in the understanding of the ancient church that reality is primarily the gift of God in the Holy Spirit and thus can be experienced only in a context of praise, thanksgiving, and petition. Praise and thanksgiving, however, had vanished in part or altogether from the prayers of the Western liturgy, in particular the celebration of the sacraments. It was even true of the Eucharistic Prayer: the thanksgiving expressed in the Preface was for a long time nothing but an introduction to the prayer itself. In the context of petition, the words of institution (now called "the consecration"), couched in the indicative, stood out in isolation. The decline of the dimension of proclamation corresponded to this kind of sacramentalistic thinking. The church no longer gathered to proclaim and praise the saving work of God, because it believed it was in possession of that salvation. The loss of the dimension of assembly also meant a loss of connection to the present. The natural circumstances of the human and the world were not taken seriously and therefore could not be made transparent toward God.

Attempt at correction

The liturgical reform after Vatican II attempted a cautious correction of these developments: greater value was now assigned to the assembly aspect, and the proclamation of the word was given higher status everywhere. Relationship to the present time and the creation motif took on a more substantial place in the Eucharistic Prayer and elsewhere. On the whole, the liturgy offers space for the expression of the current experiences of the assembled group or congregation in varied ways.

Effects on liturgical space

The renewal of liturgical theology can be illustrated, by way of example, in the effects it had on the space for liturgy:[91]

- Concentration on a single, freestanding altar and elimination of side or subordinate altars (made possible by the introduction of concelebration): This corresponds to the interest in a "christocentric church art" on the part of the Liturgical Movement, according to which the congregation assembles around an altar that symbolizes Christ.
- Separation between altar and place for reservation of the Eucharist (tabernacle), which now may be placed in a separate chapel:

---

[91] Albert Gerhards, "Spaces for Active Participation. Theological and Liturgical Perspectives on Catholic Church Architecture," in *Europäischer Kirchenbau 1950–2000 / European Church Architecture 1950–2000*, ed. Wolfgang Jean Stock (Munich: Prestel, 2002), 16–51; idem, "'. . . zu immer vollerer Einheit mit Gott und untereinander gelangen' (SC 48): Die Neuordnung der Kirchenräume durch die Liturgiereform," in *Liturgiereform* (see n. 5 above), 126–43.

Celebration of the Eucharist and eucharistic piety outside the Mass are more sharply distinguished, especially because the faithful are to receive communion from the species consecrated at the Mass they are attending.

- Introduction of a fixed place for proclamation of the Word (ambo) near the altar, making the pulpit obsolete: The elevation of the proclamation of the Word is to receive visible expression in the reintroduction of the ambo. In most cases the pulpit, used outside the liturgy, seemed inappropriate for the purpose. At the same time, spaces were created also for the placement of the book of the gospels (or lectionary or Bible).

- Introduction of a fixed seat for the priest as worship leader: This gives visible expression to the shape of the liturgical celebration as a structured assembly.

- Changes in the communion rite (communion procession), whereby the altar rails became nonfunctional; at the same time, their original function of fencing off the chancel likewise seemed unnecessary: The altar space and that reserved for the congregation are to be different but not separated. Reception of communion in processional form is meant to emphasize the community aspect; however, it was not always received as intended.

- Alteration of the function of the baptismal font insofar as it was desired that water be blessed at every celebration except in Eastertide. Associated with this was the shifting of the place of baptism from the entry area to a location visible to the congregation: Because baptism was again regarded as a celebration, the place of baptism had a new value, especially where the baptism of adults was celebrated. Likewise desirable in this connection was a place for reservation of the blessed oils.

- Change in confessional practice, introduction of confessional rooms, and the reduction in number of confessionals: The introduction of penitential services was accompanied by a decline in individual confessions. A more welcoming confessional room was seen as an appropriate replacement for the confessional, which had become common only since the baroque period. A corresponding symbolic presentation of the sacrament of reconciliation is a largely unfulfilled endeavor.

3.10.3 Limits of Reform and Future Prospects

The coincidence of liturgical reform and social reform in Germany

The causes of an erosion in traditional piety were seeded in the 1950s. When liturgical reform began, the development of pluralism and individualization as well as the weakening of faith traditions and decline in Mass attendance were already observable. In West Germany the reform—simultaneous with the student revolts of the 1960s—fell upon a society in turmoil. The questioning of authority also colored the church's internal life. Skepticism and disinclination to rituals felt to be traditional and authoritarian affected the church, and particularly liturgical rites as well. Overemphasis on the verbal, rejection of solemnity, and a very freewheeling attitude toward "officially" prescribed liturgical texts have been regarded as trends in the liturgical life of the early 1970s.[92] In East Germany the liturgical reform encountered an authoritarian political regime that limited and posed obstacles to a free development of faith communities. It appears that individual elements of the postconciliar liturgy (e.g., the full number of readings in the Liturgy of the Word at Mass and the procession with the gifts at Eucharist) were better implemented in what are now the eastern states of the German Federal Republic.

Stages of postconciliar liturgical history

1. Liturgy as a place for creativity . . .

If we take a systematic look at the history of postconciliar liturgy we can perceive a number of stages, despite all sorts of regional differences.[93] The first stage, in the period immediately after the council,

---

[92] Balthasar Fischer, "Zehn Jahre danach. Zur gottesdienstlichen Situation in Deutschland zehn Jahre nach Erscheinen der Liturgie-Konstitution" (1963), in idem, et al., *Kult in der säkularisierten Welt* (Regensburg: Pustet, 1974), 117–27, at 122–24.

[93] Benedikt Kranemann, "Die Liturgiereform im Bistum Münster nach dem II Vatikanum. Eine Skizze," in *Kirche, Staat und Gesellschaft nach 1945. Konfessionelle Prägungen und sozialer Wandel*, ed. Bernd Hey, Beiträge zur Westfälischen Kirchengeschichte 21 (Bielefeld: Luther Verlag, 2001), 67–85; idem, "Gottesdienstformen und die Rezeption der Liturgiereform des Zweiten Vatikanischen Konzils in

was marked by experiments with the new liturgy. New hymns and texts were created, as well as new eucharistic prayers and collects that were used alongside the officially proposed liturgical books; liturgical spaces began to be reshaped and liturgical education intensified. What is so remarkable is the rapid shift in thinking: the liturgy, which shortly before was still strictly regulated by rubrics, became a place for creativity and reshaping. The roles of laypersons in worship, including women, changed. Concerning the changed view of individual roles we might ask whether it was through the liturgy itself that Catholics' own perspective on roles in general underwent a change. From a theological viewpoint, all the baptized developed a new self-concept through the liturgy.

. . . but also for rejection of liturgical reforms

Also part of the postconciliar history of liturgy was the rise of groups that rejected the renewal of worship, along with Vatican II itself. They advocated (and still advocate) especially that the so-called Tridentine Mass should continue to be celebrated.

2. Publication of texts and new requirements

A second phase of reform is associated with the introduction of the new liturgical books.[94] By being put into print the reform process acquired a new authority and a much stronger influence in the world church. In Germany this was the time of the Würzburg Synod of the West German dioceses (1975), which produced a consensus document on worship.[95] The Pastoral Synod of the Catholic Churches in

---

Deutschland," in *Katholiken in den USA und Deutschland. Kirche, Gesellschaft und Politik*, ed. Wilhelm Damberg and Antonius Liedhegener (Münster: Aschendorff, 2006), 62–72.

[94] Martin Klöckener, *Die liturgischen Bücher im deutschen Sprachgebiet. Verzeichnis für die pastoralliturgische Arbeit, die liturgische Bildung und das liturgiewissenschaftliche Studium* [as of 1 October 1995], Pastoralliturgische Hilfen 9 (Trier: Deutsches Liturgisches Institut, 1995).

[95] "Gottesdienst. Beschluss," in *Gemeinsame Synode der Bistümer in der Bundesrepublik Deutschland. Beschlüsse der Vollversammlung. Offizielle Gesamtausgabe 1,*" edited by order of the Presidium of the General Synod by Ludwig Bertsch, et al. (Freiburg: Herder, 1976), 196–225.

East Germany[96] in the same year did not produce its own statement on liturgy but spoke of it in a number of other documents. We can observe regional differences in the reception of liturgical reform as well as clear commonalities that can be described as a tendency to a differentiation in religious and liturgical life: there are different ways of participating in the liturgy. Believers take differing views of the obligatory nature of worship and its regulations, and there is an upheaval in the ways of handing on the faith.

3. Revision of postconciliar liturgical books

A third stage is associated with the reworking and revision of the postconciliar liturgical books, which were intended to reflect experiences from the postconciliar reform. They are a sign that the process of revisions and reforms within the church has not ended. The revised marriage rite, whose second edition was published in 1992, is a clear indication of the fact that in Germany at the end of the twentieth century the liturgy was less and less often celebrated in a pastoral context. The book now contains texts for marriage to an unbaptized partner who believes in God as well as others for marriage to a nonbelieving partner, with corresponding provisions for unbaptized and unbelieving persons in the liturgy.[97] However, toward the end of the century the tensions within the church with regard to liturgy grew sharper. On the one hand we can see centralizing Roman tendencies at the expense of the local churches and new stringencies in ecclesiastical regulations; on the other hand, insuperable problems in pastoral liturgy made church regulations of worship less and less acceptable, and alternative texts and rules for worship were applied. Examples from the Liturgy of the Hours show how the progress of reform could be meaningfully pursued by means also of new forms of worship. The diocese of Munich-Freising developed new books

---

[96] See *Konzil und Diaspora. Die Beschlüsse der Pastoralsynode der katholischen Kirche in der DDR* (Berlin: Morus Verlag, 1977).

[97] *Die Feier der Trauung in den katholischen Bistümern des deutschen Sprachgebietes*, 2nd ed., by order of the Bishops' Conferences of Germany, Austria, and Switzerland, as well as the (arch)bishops of Bozen-Brixen, Lüttich [Liege, Belgium], Luxemburg, and Strassburg (Zürich, Freiburg, Regensburg, Salzburg, and Linz: Benziger, Herder, Pustet, St. Peter, Veritas: 1992), 30–31; 79–111.

for congregational liturgy, combining the traditional order of prayer with new, freer forms and texts.[98]

4. Missionary interpretation:
opening the liturgy for those indifferent to religion

A fourth stage began with the rediscovery of the church's missionary self-concept.[99] The religious possibilities in the public sphere were taken more to heart, and the same was true of the church's liturgy and more public forms of celebration. In those latter also, the church should be open to all as an invitation to faith. There was a search for forms of worship appropriate even for groups indifferent to religion but at the same time refusing to deny that the paschal mystery is the center of Christian worship.[100] Such new forms of religious ritual were linked with ecclesiological options: does the church see itself as a tiny isolated remnant, or does it wish to be church in the midst of society and in dialogue with it?

At the same time, because of the shrinkage of financial means, there arose the problem of maintaining existing church buildings. More and more dioceses and church bodies have been preoccupied since the turn of the century with the question of expanding the spectrum of uses for their buildings, repurposing them, or even tearing them down. Will it be possible to maintain an effective presence of Christianity in the public sphere? Will the opportunities offered by church buildings for a more intense dialogical presence of Christians in a plural society be recognized and exploited?

Problems in dealing with liturgy

No one would assert that the liturgy reforms of Vatican II have produced an ideal situation. Quite the contrary: problems with the

---

[98] *Morgenlob / Abendlob. Mit der Gemeinde feiern* [Service Book], ed. Paul Ringseisen, 3 vols. (Planegg: promultis, 2000, 2004); Paul Ringseisen, *Morgen- und Abendlob mit der Gemeinde. Geistliche Erschliessung, Erfahrungen und Modelle. Mit einem Beitrag von Martin Klöckener*, new ed. (Freiburg: Herder, 2002).

[99] "'Zeit zur Aussaat.' Missionarisch Kirche sein," 26 November 2000, Die Deutschen Bischöfe 68 (Bonn: Sekretariat der Deutschen Bischofskonferenz, 2000).

[100] *Gott feiern in nachchristlicher Gesellschaft. Die missionarische Dimension der Liturgie*, ed. Benedikt Kranemann, Klemens Richter, and Franz-Peter Tebartz-van Elst (Stuttgart: Katholisches Bibelwerk, 2000; first publication 1988–1989).

liturgy seem instead to have expanded. Besides the social conditions we have described, this is also connected, within the church, with the fact that we have not yet discovered an integrative image of the church that relates charism and office harmoniously to one another. Most of the difficulties in the parishes (e.g., with church buildings) can be traced to this tense situation. The revived discussion of re-arranging church spaces and celebration *versus populum* is an indicator of this.[101] But the path broken by the council represents such an epochal change that it could scarcely be completed in the course of one or even two generations.

The apostolic letter Summorum Pontificum *(2007)*

The document *Summorum Pontificum*[102] produced fresh tensions. Now the Mass may be celebrated according to the *Missale Romanum* of 1962 and the other sacraments according to the "older rituals," that is, the older Pontificals, and the Roman breviary of 1962 may also be used. The "extraordinary" preconciliar form stands alongside the "ordinary" form, the postconciliar liturgy; both are parts of a single rite. Subsequent documents regulate the details. Any number of theological questions arise:[103] What is the relationship of the two "forms" to one another? Given the obvious theological differences, can they be regarded as expressions of the same rite? Critics say that the situation thus created is not in accord with the theology and instructions of the Constitution on the Liturgy.[104]

---

[101] *Communio-Räume. Auf der Suche nach der angemessenen Raumgestalt katholischer Liturgie*, ed. Albert Gerhards, Thomas Sternberg, and Walter Zahner, Bild, Raum, Feier, Studien zu Kirche und Kunst 2 (Regensburg: Pustet, 2003); Klemens Richter, *Kirchenräume und Kirchenträume. Die Bedeutung des Kirchenraums für eine lebendige Gemeinde*, 2nd ed. (Freiburg: Herder, 1999).

[102] Pope Benedict XVI, motu proprio *Summorum Pontificum* (On the Use of the Roman Liturgy Prior to the Reform of 1970), available at http://w2.vatican .va/content/benedict-xvi/en/motu_proprio/documents/hf_ben-xvi_motu -proprio_20070707_summorum-pontificum.html.

[103] See *Ein Ritus, zwei Formen. Die Richtlinie Papst Benedikts XVI. zur Liturgie*, ed. Albert Gerhards, Theologie kontrovers (Freiburg: Herder, 2008).

[104] Martin Klöckener, "Wie Liturgie verstehen? Anfragen an das Motu proprio 'Summorum Pontificum' Papst Benedikts XVI," *Archiv für Liturgiewissenschaft* 50 (2008): 268–305.

CHAPTER 4

Theology of the Liturgy

Liturgy articulates Christian faith convictions and communicates them in ritual form. It is a celebratory event in which the church's faith is on display. This is indicated by the axiom *Lex orandi, lex credendi* (see chap. 2.2.7.2). At the same time it requires a continually renewed theological reflection if it is not to lose its meaningful center in the thicket of the multiple interpretations applied to it. That is the task of the theology of liturgy, which this chapter addresses. Its starting point is the celebration of liturgy as a human assembly that knows itself called by God and subject to some very specific preconditions (4.1). It works out the liturgy's dynamic image of God, corresponding to worship as an event of encounter between God and the human (4.2). The liturgy is interpreted as a celebration of Christ's paschal mystery (4.3), one of the central statements of today's liturgical theology, and as an event that is always effected by the Spirit (4.4). Hence the theology, Christology, and pneumatology of worship celebrations must be addressed. The liturgy's participation in the divine economy of salvation (4.5) and the relationship between earthly and heavenly liturgy (4.6) will be presented. Liturgy is glorifying God, but at the same time it is also the healing of the human being. Therefore the liturgy's image of the human is also a subject of liturgical theology (4.7). Finally, we must inquire into the relationship between liturgy and the Christian life (4.8).

4.1 Liturgy as Assembly in the Presence of God

4.1.1 Assembly as an Anthropological Phenomenon

Religious assemblies in general

The basic event of Christian liturgy is described in the anthropological phenomenon of "assembly," which is understood first of all as the coming together of human beings for a particular purpose. Such an assembly will have different compositions, depending on group, occasion, and purpose. It acts according to certain rules; that is, it is standardized and repeatable. It is characterized by an order of roles and forms. Finally, it is necessary as a communicative action of the group and thus points beyond what is immediately evident. Religious assemblies in particular frequently reveal stereotypical features of speech and symbol, signs of formalization. We may mention the possibility of repetition, the use of fixed linguistic expressions and formulae and established symbols and actions, among other things.[1] A community assembly is possible only if there is a basic set of rules for the course of action and a known purpose. Religious assemblies necessarily tend toward ritualization; they are repeatable, and in their repetition they may represent and enable particular content on the basis of a recurring ritual involving participation, in some form, on the part of the particular group.

Special character of the Christian liturgical assembly

This gives us a basis for explaining the distribution of liturgical roles, the assignment of texts, symbols, and actions to those playing particular parts, the constitution of church community through the liturgical celebration, and the communication of social relationships and a specific worldview through the liturgical assembly. However, essential features of the Christian liturgy—for example, that God is its initiator, that Christ is active as subject of the assembly, and that human beings experience transformation through the liturgy—cannot be derived altogether from anthropology; they require a theological basis, as we will show. It will become clear that in the liturgical assembly, in which persons know themselves to be called by God through Christ and in which they respond to God's call with and through Christ, anthropology and theology work hand in hand.

---

[1] Bernhard Lang, "Ritual/Ritus," *Handbuch religionswissenschaftlicher Grundbegriffe* 4 (1998): 442–58.

4.1.2 Liturgy as an Assembly Summoned by God

Relationship to Christ

We encounter assemblies with the character of worship in the Old and New Testaments. Thus the latter gives frequent accounts of gatherings for prayer and worship (Acts 4:5; 12:12; 1 Cor 5:4; 14:23) and especially for Eucharist (Acts 20:7-8; 1 Cor 11:17-18, 33; 14:26). The nature, place of assembly, and situation may vary, but one thing remains recognizably the same: these assemblies are always oriented to Christ. This is especially evident in the Eucharist, which is celebrated in awareness of Christ's presence, something that is narrated with great emphasis in the Emmaus pericope (Luke 24:13-35). The assurance of Christ's presence is a background to the various gatherings: "where two or three are gathered in my name, I am there among them" (Matt 18:20). When it is said of baptism that it takes place in the name of Jesus (Acts 10:47) and thus unfolds its purifying effect (1 Cor 6:11), the association with Christ is obvious. According to the New Testament, liturgy always takes place in the name of Jesus Christ, the Son of God. The value of what happens in the liturgical actions is measured against God's revelation in Jesus Christ. This connection is very clear in 1 Corinthians 11:27 regarding the Lord's Supper. Anyone who eats the bread and drinks the cup of the Lord unworthily becomes guilty of the body and blood of Christ and thus of the Christ who gave himself on the cross. Hence liturgical assembly cannot be separated from the Christ-event. Gathering in the name of Jesus, as well as constant praise and prayer, is constitutive for the *ekklēsia* of Christians.[2]

Assemblies in the Old Testament: God's initiative

The Christian assembly thus falls in line with assemblies described in the Old Testament (קְהַל יהוה), which God calls; this is especially clear in God's order to Moses according to Deuteronomy 4:10: "Assemble

---

[2] Helmut Hucke and Heinrich Rennings, *Die gottesdienstlichen Versammlungen der Gemeinde*, Pastorale 2 (Mainz: Matthias-Grünewald, 1973); Klaus Berger, "Volksversammlung und Gemeinde Gottes. Zu den Anfängen der christlichen Verwendung von 'ekklesia,'" *Zeitschrift für Theologie und Kirche* 73 (1976): 167–207.

the people for me." Exodus 19:7 tells how the elders of the people came together at God's command. The people themselves assembled at the command of God, conveyed through Moses, to hear God's word. Similarly, in Deuteronomy 5:1 Moses calls the people together so that he may give them the commandments God had handed him. According to Nehemiah 8:3 the assembled people listen to God's law proclaimed by Ezra. Here, then, we find a kind of assembly that follows the usual pattern of human gatherings with regard to its form, the distribution of roles, ritualization, etc., but whose specific characteristic is the divine initiative.

New Testament: the presence of Christ and his saving action

This strand of traditional assembly for worship continues in the New Testament, but now it is Christ at whose command the people assemble (see 1 Cor 11:24-25), or Christ's name that marks each assembly and its actions. Still more: according to Matthew 18:20, Christ himself is present in this assembly (see also Matt 28:20). That alone gives it its proper quality: the presence of Christ means the presence of the Risen One and his saving action. This names the reason and content as well as the primary subject of the act of worship. What happens at worship, in its particulars as well, happens as an actualization of the suffering, death, resurrection, and exaltation of Christ. We can see how close the connection between liturgy and assembly is from the fact that as late as the early Middle Ages the Eucharist was still called σύναξις (assembly).[3] That concept reappears in two documents of Vatican II: the dogmatic constitution *Lumen Gentium* (*LG* 28) and the decree on the ministry and life of priests, *Presbyterorum Ordinis* (*PO* 5).

Continuing Christ's saving work

The Liturgy Constitution says that the church has never ceased to gather for the celebration of the paschal mystery (*SC* 6). This assembly is interpreted as the continuation of Christ's saving work, rooted in

---

[3] Hans Bernhard Meyer, *Eucharistie. Geschichte, Theologie, Pastoral*, with an introduction by Irmgard Pahl, vol. 4 in *Gottesdienst der Kirche. Handbuch der Liturgiewissenschaft*, ed. Hans Bernhard Meyer, et al. (Regensburg: Pustet, 1989), 39.

the sending of the Son by the Father—that is, having its origins in God. The proclamation of the Good News and the accomplishment of God's saving work "through sacrifice and sacrament" have their place in the assembly. Like Pius XII's 1947 encyclical *Mediator Dei* (par. 20) on questions regarding the liturgy, the Constitution points to the presence of Christ in the assembly (*SC* 7) and describes liturgy as the work of Christ and his body. The baptized assemble for liturgy as the source and summit of the church's action (*SC* 10; *LG* 11).

Liturgy as dialogue: at the beginning of worship . . .

Along these lines, for example, we find the opening elements and corresponding rubrics of a number of today's liturgical celebrations, which interpret the actions to follow and the assembly itself in the opening words and actions of the celebration. The Missal regards the gathering of the congregation, the entry of the priest and his assistants, with accompanying song, and the honoring of the altar (as symbol of Christ) as symbolic actions. Already here there is a realization that people are gathering around Christ. The sign of the cross that follows then expresses this in word and gesture. All those present join in making this sign, which, with its accompanying words, "In the name of the Father and of the Son and of the Holy Spirit," recalls the baptismal formula, and as they join in the celebration they place themselves under the sign of Christ.

The shortest of the prescribed greeting formulae, spoken by the priest with arms outstretched in a gesture of welcome and responded to by the congregation, is "The Lord be with you . . . and with your spirit." Other such formulae are "Grace and peace from God our Father and the Lord Jesus Christ be with you," or "The grace of our Lord Jesus Christ be with you" (see John 20:21, 26, etc., as well as 1 Cor 1:3, etc.). The greeting and response express the action involving God/Christ and the people that constitute this assembly.

. . . and in the Liturgy of the Hours

Something similar can be said, in different ways, of other liturgical celebrations, for example, the Liturgy of the Hours. On the level of actions, the coming together and assembling of people for liturgy has a sign-character, but the sequence of prayers that opens this liturgy also indicates that this is an assembly in the presence of God. The first Hour begins with the invitatory from Psalm 51(50):17: "O Lord, open my lips . . . that my mouth may proclaim your praise." Those who begin the day with this verse consider themselves and their lives in the presence of God, make present to themselves their own distance from God, and affirm that they are dependent on God's grace. Even though the opening elements of the Liturgy of the Hours differ from those of the Mass, they have a common purpose: to orient the assembly toward God.[4]

4.1.3 Celebration of Liturgy in a Structured Assembly

Participatio *and hierarchical structure*

In the New Testament sources the liturgical assembly is described as a familial gathering, and yet it is structured according to duties and ministries.[5] However, the ministry of leadership and an action of the believers present are by no means exclusive, since the umbrella for everything is assembly in the name of Jesus Christ. Christ himself accomplishes his saving work for the people and celebrates with the congregation. The people who act in the liturgy participate in the work of Jesus Christ. This participation can take very different forms, but it must always be located within the mission of Christ and legitimated by it. This is true especially of the ministry of liturgical leadership, which the New Testament associates with a leading role in the congregation: the action is done for and with the congregation.[6]

---

[4] Angelus A. Häussling, "Wie beginnt Gottesdienst? Beobachtungen an den Horen der Tagzeitenliturgie" (1991), in idem, *Christliche Identität aus der Liturgie. Theologische und historische Studien zum Gottesdienst der Kirche*, ed. Martin Klöckener, Benedikt Kranemann, and Michael B. Merz, Liturgiewissenschaftliche Quellen und Forschungen 79 (Münster: Aschendorff, 1997), 257–70.

[5] Walter Kirchschläger, "Die liturgische Versammlung. Eine neutestament-liche Bestandsaufnahme," *Heiliger Dienst* 52 (1998): 11–24; Martin Klöckener and Klemens Richter, eds., *Wie weit trägt das gemeinsame Priestertum? Liturgischer Leitungsdienst zwischen Ordination und Beauftragung*, Quaestiones disputatae 171 (Freiburg: Herder, 1998).

[6] Walter Kirchschläger, "Begründung und Formen des liturgischen Leitungs-dienstes in den Schriften des Neuen Testaments," in *Wie weit trägt das gemeinsame Priestertum?*, 20–45.

By contrast, within the congregation celebrating liturgy, more precisely in the celebration of the sacraments, a distinction is made today between the leadership role in the congregation, the liturgical ministries, and the remaining members of the congregation. The basis for full and complete participation in the liturgy is initiation. The liturgical actions are "celebrations of the church which is 'the sacrament of unity,' namely, the holy people united and organized under their bishops" (SC 26). Every believer is "called into service," with her or his charisms; ordination, assignment of duties, and cooperation in the celebration are different ways in which, and with what degree of obligation, the various charisms are called for. At the same time, SC 26 opens up the possibility that laypersons may carry out liturgical actions without a priest, as exemplified by the Liturgy of the Hours (SC 84; 100), sacramentals (SC 79), and the Liturgy of the Word (SC 35.4). It is true of every liturgical celebration, whether led by the ordained or by laity, that "all taking part in liturgical celebrations, whether ministers or members of the congregation, should do all that pertains to them, and no more, taking into account the rite and the liturgical norms" (SC 28).

4.1.4 Listening and Responding as Fundamental Human Actions in the Liturgical Assembly

While the initiative for the liturgical assembly comes from God, the human participants are called to listen and respond to what God has promised. Thus the human person (initiated by baptism) is included in the liturgy as an active subject. The liturgical assembly neither exists for itself nor is concentrated on itself; it is directed to God, who has revealed himself in Jesus Christ. Therefore listening and responding are basic human actions in the liturgical assembly. The Sunday Eucharist, as a form of liturgy, makes clear in its opening what is to be central to it. The introduction is followed—after the confession of sin—by the *Kyrie*, *Gloria*, and collect of the day. The *Kyrie* and *Gloria* are closely connected: they are an expression of the glorification of *Kyrios Christos*, made audible and visible in, among other things, the congregation's standing and singing. These are some of the first things that bring the whole congregation into action in this liturgy. The fact that this takes place formally, in part, in the liturgy should not obscure the personal event that underlies it. Formulaic expression, which remains more general and rises farther above the individual than do freely formulated texts, can even make individual participation and personal reception easier because these are not tied to something concrete.

In the liturgy the human being encounters God in her or his whole existence and personally receives God's promise of salvation. This can take place, for example, in the collect, the prayer of the day. After the introduction ("Let us pray"), according to ancient tradition, there should be a space for the silent prayer of the faithful; then, with the *collecta*, the summary and therefore brief prayer, the priest closes the act of praying. However, this connection between common and individual prayer is not very often evident in today's liturgical practice.

The response of the congregation can take as great a variety of forms as the liturgical assemblies themselves. Besides thanksgiving and praise there are also petition and lament, so that account is taken of the lived realities of the assemblies in the form of acclamation and petition as well.

Encounter between God and the human person

It is an indispensable aspect of all liturgical actions and speech-acts that the dimension of communication between God and the human be recognizable and available to be experienced in the liturgical action itself. Therefore, for theological reasons, the levels of communication in the prayer-action, in terms of style and address, must be maintained, not for formal reasons, but for the sake of the liturgical event itself. The form and meaning of the celebration must correspond. In particular a mystagogical liturgy, that is, one that unfolds in the action itself and largely speaks for itself, must be coherent. In view of the fact that the liturgy is a community event, such clarity of form and execution is important so that the core of the event may not be lost to view.

This aspect of assembly is also indispensable to the various liturgical celebrations, as the Liturgy of the Hours attests. Speech and nonspeech elements form the opening. The praying community constitutes itself in assembling; in the opening acclamations it already makes itself known as the community that has gathered around the Lord and announced its presence, so that its praise and thus also its assembly in the presence of God are made possible. In some monastic communities it is customary to hold a *statio* before the Liturgy of the Hours, a gathering in the cloister, for example, whereby the different aspects of liturgical assembly are made visible.

> People assemble because they have something to do together; but because what they have to do is praying and listening, each individual comes with and in the community to a common service. . . . The gathering is followed by a procession to the place for the Liturgy of the Hours. . . . Only then, after they have acknowledged each other and come to mutual agreement, can the common turning toward God take place in the opening dialogue of the call to prayer.[7]

4.1.5 Gathering of the Community—Gathering of the Church

Ecclesial dimension of the liturgical assembly

Liturgical assembly always signifies more than this individual gathering here and now. It possesses an ecclesial dimension insofar as the church is built on it (congregation, local church, universal church). This, too, places its own conditions on the liturgical assembly: on the one hand to articulate this ecclesial relationship, and on the other hand to be able to bring its own contribution to it. At the same time the church, because of its apostolicity, preserves the enduring saving event for the liturgy. The ecclesiality of the liturgical assembly, that is, celebration within the church's order of prayer, is indispensable for such an assembly.

Initiation as reception into the people of God

The celebrations of initiation do not signify reception into a particular congregation, even though they are celebrated in a congregational context and the congregation is the primary place in which church is experienced. Rather, they incorporate the baptizand into the people of God and thus have a primarily ecclesiological significance, since the church as a whole is affected by each initiation. We

---

[7] Häussling, "Wie beginnt Gottesdienst?" (see n. 4 above), 263–64.

come to the same conclusion when we emphasize the christological aspect of baptism, the incorporation into Christ, for Christ no longer lives apart from his body, the church (see 1 Cor 12:12-13; Eph 5:23). In addition, we should not overlook the fact, and this especially in regard to baptism, that the church lives from it. The Rite of Baptism for Children says that baptism "is a sacramental bond of unity linking all who have been signed by it."

Eucharist as celebration of the whole church

In the same way we can show with regard to the Eucharist that those celebrating know themselves to be united, beyond the individual congregation, with the local and universal church; still more, it is out of the *communio* of celebrating congregations that the church is built up, and church is realized in the congregations celebrating Eucharist. The intercessions (from Latin *intercedere* = intercede, present petitions) in the Eucharistic Prayer express this mutual relationship: "Be pleased to confirm in faith and charity your pilgrim Church on earth, with your servant N. our Pope and N. our Bishop, the Order of Bishops, all the clergy, and the entire people you have gained for your own."[8] The Christians assembled in the particular place know themselves to be gathered for Eucharist with the pope, bishops, and all believers. The intercessions are a representation of the whole church in each individual eucharistic celebration.

The Liturgy Constitution underscores the unity of liturgical life in the diocese, with the bishop at its center. Church is especially visible when the whole people participates fully and actively in the liturgy, "in the same liturgical celebrations, especially in the same Eucharist, in one prayer, at one altar, at which the bishop presides, surrounded by his college of priests and by his ministers" (SC 41).

Eucharistic ecclesiology, the impulse for which comes especially from Orthodox theology,[9] expresses this ecclesial positioning of the Eucharist as well as the importance of the individual, celebrating con-

---

[8] *The Roman Missal, Third Edition* (Collegeville, MN: Liturgical Press, 2011), 654.
[9] Karl Christian Felmy, *Einführung in die orthodoxe Theologie der Gegenwart*, Lehr- und Studienbücher zur Theologie 5 (Münster: LIT, 2011).

gregations.[10] The church is built up in the Eucharist. Christ himself, in the Holy Spirit, here creates the church as his body. Therefore the definition of church derives from the eucharistic celebration. Church becomes reality in eucharistic community; in that community the church is constituted. "One bread, one body" (1 Cor 10:17) is the primary theological idea behind this ecclesiology, which indeed is not limited to Eucharist but should also be realized in the lives of Christians.

Eucharistic ecclesiology also found a reception in the documents of Vatican II, as attested by *LG* 3:

> As often as the sacrifice of the cross by which "Christ our Pasch is sacrificed" (1 Cor 5:7) is celebrated on the altar, the work of our redemption is carried out. Likewise, in the sacrament of the Eucharistic bread, the unity of believers, who form one body in Christ (see 1 Cor 10:17), is both expressed and achieved. All are called to this union with Christ, who is the light of the world, from whom we come, through whom we live, and towards whom we direct our lives.[11]

The ecclesiological dimension is constitutive not only for baptism and Eucharist, but for every liturgical celebration. These obtain their form not only from the prayer elements, especially those in which the local or universal church is named, but also from the leaders who serve by authority of the church, the church's order of prayer, etc.

4.1.6 The Making-Present of Salvation History in the Symbolic Actions of Liturgy

Relationship of liturgy to the end-time

Liturgy as an event of assembly in the sense just described can be spoken of only on the level of symbols. Liturgical celebration is

---

[10] Anton Thaler, *Gemeinde und Eucharistie. Grundlegung einer eucharistischen Ekklesiologie*, Praktische Theologie im Dialog 2 (Fribourg: Universitätsverlag, 1988).

[11] For further theological consequences see the so-called Munich Document, "Das Mysterium der Kirche und der Eucharistie im Licht des Mysteriums der Heiligen Dreieinigkeit."

symbolic action that represents what is celebrated and enables participation in it. Similarly, "dialogue" and "communication" take place only in the mode of symbol. Like symbols, the liturgy is characterized by its ability to enable participation in what it represents, even though that in which it participates ultimately remains apart, as a whole and in its ultimate nature. Like a symbol, the liturgy thus has a fragmentary and splintered character. If we relate the symbolic action to the aesthetics of faith we can speak of participation in the event being celebrated, and accordingly of nearness to God, but we must also mention the preliminary character of what lies in a symbol, because the symbol gives only a share in the divine reality and not that reality itself. Thus what happens in the liturgical assembly is a community around Christ and God; as such it is to be filled with a living, personal character by the people present. But the ultimate realization of that community is reserved for the heavenly liturgy. In the symbolic event the liturgical assembly already has a share in that saving reality (see Heb 12:22-24). "This relationship with the eschatological liturgy is indispensable for the liturgical assembly, yet participation in the full sense is something only hoped for in the future."[12] The eschatological tension involved has to mark every liturgical assembly that finds itself on the way and trusting in fulfillment. The assembly itself becomes a symbol of the heavenly festal gathering. In the liturgy the hope for salvation becomes a "promised reality."[13]

The *Gloria* and *Sanctus* make all this clear. The heavenly liturgy echoes in the quotation of the angels according to Luke 2:14 with which the ancient hymn begins, as with Isaiah 6:3 and Revelation 4:8 in the acclamation that closes the Preface, or, more precisely, the earthly liturgy joins itself to the angels' praise. The biblical quotations that are inserted mark the interweaving of the two liturgies (see chap. 4.6.1). The singing of the *Gloria* and *Sanctus* becomes a symbolic

---

[12] Claus-Peter März, "Das 'Wort vom Kult' und der 'Kult des Wortes.' Der Hebräerbrief und die rechte Feier des Gottesdienstes," in *Wie das Wort Gottes feiern? Der Wortgottesdienst als theologische Herausforderung*, ed. Benedikt Kranemann and Thomas Sternberg, Quaestiones disputatae 194 (Freiburg: Herder, 2002), 82–98, at 94.

[13] Franz Joseph Schierse, *Verheissung und Heilsvollendung. Zur theologischen Grundfrage des Hebräerbriefes*, Münchener Theologische Studien. Historische Abteilung 9 (Munich: Karl Zink, 1955), 203.

action that opens the special character of this liturgical assembly to experience.

4.2 Theo-logy

Multiplicity in communication with God

Because of space limitations we can here mention only a few aspects of the theology of the liturgy, that is, the way the liturgy celebrates God and thus gives witness to God.[14] Besides, what we find in the liturgy is not a unified, systematically developed theology; rather, in word and action it enables participation in the event of salvation through a multifaceted ritual event. The liturgy is meant to facilitate communication not *about* God but *with* God. The multitude of possibilities, especially in poetic forms and sign-actions, for proclaiming God in the liturgical celebration and finding assurance of God's presence is a sign of the multifacetedness of God about which the liturgical celebrations speak and in which they lend a share— depending on one's life situation, the time within the church year, etc. Here the liturgy shapes its own language. It does not define or systematize; it is by no means to be understood as "prayed dogma"; rather, it enables ever-new approaches and thus a completely personal access to the mystery of God.

4.2.1 Encounter with the Personal God

God's nearness and withdrawal

Liturgy is something that happens between God and the human being, currently described in terms of dialogue, communication, or encounter. The way this takes place in the course of a liturgy shows us that the liturgy presupposes God's personhood, as is evident above all when God is addressed as a partner, as "you/thou."[15] This personal

---

[14] Julie Kirchberg, *Theo-logie in der Anrede als Weg zur Verständigung zwischen Juden und Christen*, Innsbrucker theologische Studien 31 (Innsbruck: Tyrolia, 1991): "speaking to God in speaking about God."

[15] Robert Le Gall, "Die Namen Gottes in der Liturgie," *Internationale katholische Zeitschrift Communio* 22 (1993): 63–77.

address presumes the presence of the speaker and the one spoken to. The "I" and the "thou" are bound together in this dialogue, bringing with them their whole history. God's personhood is spoken of in the liturgy in a number of ways, for example, in attributes such as "benevolent," "almighty," "merciful," "faithful," "all-knowing," "ruler of all," "gracious," "exalted," or in predicates such as "God of mercy," "God, our creator and redeemer," "Father in heaven," "God, light of the nations," "Father of all the faithful," "unchanging power, eternal light," but also in appeals such as "come," "be near to us," "help us," "grant us," or "stir up our hearts" (all examples from orations in the Missal). The statements that appear in address to God mark important theological differences, above all when attributes such as "holy," "heavenly," "invisible," or "eternal" are added. They attest to closeness when God is described as benevolent, gracious, and merciful; they express the dynamics of the relationship and its purposefulness. But, without calling into question that God is attentive to human beings, they also reveal God's withdrawnness when they call God "holy," "heavenly," or "invisible." Thus what is unique about the relationship to God is expressed in liturgical language in the attributes associated with God: in the liturgy, human persons entrust themselves to a God who is near and simultaneously distant. The appeals we have cited express the intensity and trust of the relationship. This tension, with its fragility as well as the attitude of expectation, must be taken into consideration in speaking of the image of God and the relationship to God in the liturgy. Finally, the special character of the God-human relationship may not be overlooked: the liturgy is about an encounter between Creator and creature that is markedly different from intra-human communication. Therefore the liturgy should always be regarded as an analogous speech-act on the way toward its true identity.

4.2.2 Doxological Address to God

Extension of biblical prayer-language

The forms of address to God in the liturgy are doxologically formulated (from Greek δόξα, honor, glory, magnificence) or at least doxologically influenced. They express praise to God in a wide range of forms. This is a continuation and extension of biblical prayer language and is marked by conciseness, hymnic character, formality, and the like. Essential aspects of the relationship to God and central characteristics of God are named; here we find an echo of the salvation history that lies behind the language. Doxological speech—which should be distinguished from the prayer-element called "doxology" (see chap. 5.2.5.3)—reflects human faith in God and experience of God. Doxology is the liturgical language appropriate to God; more precisely, it is the expression of the adoration and glorification due to God.

The prayer appeals cited above express expectation and hope toward God and convey something of the tension, as well as the conflicts, that can be addressed in the liturgy. Prayer and liturgy are also confronted with God's absence. They can be the space in which the human being can make a free decision before God. But those celebrating may also experience God's absence as a contradiction between, on the one hand, the promise of salvation and the hope of sharing in it already within the liturgy and, on the other hand, concrete experience of the world and life's experiences. Appeals, petitions, and even lament articulate that in the liturgy. They must be taken seriously as experiences of faith; they presuppose that what has been described is a reliable image of God, one that makes these experiences of contrast possible and encourages us to struggle toward nearness with God.

Doxology is expressed not only in prayer but also in other acts of divine worship in the liturgy, including the readings, confession, hymns, and play.

Physical expression

The doxological dimension of liturgy would be attenuated if we were to limit it to verbal expressions. The human being as a whole person is engaged in communication with God, including all her or his expressive abilities: postures and attitudes at prayer such as standing or kneeling, extending the arms or folding the hands (see chap. 5.2.6) give palpable form to the worship of God and are, indeed, shaped by the physical expression of the doxology itself.

4.2.3 The God of History

God's power in history

The prayer-event shows God to be the one who is experienced as acting within human history. The liturgical texts confess God as powerful in time. Attributions such as fidelity, mercy, and graciousness and also prayers for God's coming and for assistance point to experiences that are interpreted and attested as actions of God. The liturgy, as an event between the personal God and the congregation, rests on the experience of faith, that God shows God's self to humans in their history as present and attentive to them. It expresses that experience in pictorially rich language and so is open to a varied reception that can (also) interpret new experiences in light of traditional prayer. The liturgy itself is experienced as a place in which God acts within human history and in which the human being stands worshipfully before God.

Fourth Eucharistic Prayer

Eucharistic Prayer IV gives especially emphatic expression to this salvation-historical dimension of the image of God in the liturgy. Thus the Preface reads: "yet you, who alone are good, the source of life, have made all that is, so that you might fill your creatures with blessings and bring joy to many of them by the glory of your light."[16] Important in this image of God is the distinction of stages in time that play a role: creation as the originating event, God's blessing as enduring present. God acts in history, which this Eucharistic Prayer describes as salvation history. A passage after the *Sanctus* describes the fragility of that history in the transition from Preface to epiclesis: human beings have indeed lost God's friendship through their misdeeds—an expression filled with ardent intensity—but God did not let them be lost; God helped them to seek and find God.[17] The potential for hope associated with the encounter with God in the liturgy is evident here.

[16] *The Roman Missal* (see n. 8 above), 656.

[17] "And when through disobedience he had lost your friendship, you did not abandon him to the domain of death. For you came in mercy to the aid of all, so that those who seek might find you" (ibid., 657).

This Eucharistic Prayer also makes concrete what salvation history means in Christian liturgy. The Post-*Sanctus* begins by praising God for all God's works, then names the creation of humans in the image of God, God's kindness toward them, turning to them again in Jesus Christ, even in their sinfulness, and ends by speaking of the Holy Spirit, who continues and perfects the work of Christ.[18] This is about "praising the working of God in history until its completion."[19] Thus the liturgy, in recalling God's work in history, celebrates all time from creation to fulfillment. It interprets it, as we will show, within the hermeneutical perspective of the Christ-event (see chap. 4.3.2). God's saving work precedes that of humans in the liturgy, which not only points toward God but is a place in which God is sought with the greatest urgency and implored to be present as the Lord of history.

4.2.4 God Images in Liturgy

Images of God are central and dominant in the liturgy: the Creator, the Self-Revealer, the Savior. These appear in the sacraments, in the Liturgy of the Hours, in the feasts of the church year, and also in liturgies of the word and benedictions.

God the Creator

God is celebrated as creator. Eucharistic Prayer IV, just cited, expresses this in the Eucharist, that is, at the center of Christian liturgy;[20] the pertinent biblical readings from Genesis 1 and 2 proclaim the

[18] "For you came in mercy to the aid of all, so that those who seek might find you. Time and again you offered them covenants and through the prophets taught them to look forward to salvation. And you so loved the world, Father most holy, that in the fullness of time you sent your only Begotten son to be our savior. . . . And that we might live no longer for ourselves but for him who died and rose again for us, he sent the Holy Spirit from you, Father, as the first fruits for those who believe, so that, bringing to perfection his work in the world, he might sanctify creation to the full" (ibid.).

[19] Heinzgerd Brakmann, "*Foedera pluries hominibus*. Anmerkungen zur Revision des Eucharistischen Hochgebets IV," *Liturgisches Jahrbuch* 50 (2000): 211–34.

[20] Manfred Probst, "Das Schöpfungsmotiv im Eucharistischen Hochgebet," *Liturgisches Jahrbuch* 31 (1981): 129–44.

event of creation at different points in the liturgy but are especially central at the Easter Vigil; elevated forms of prayer such as the address and praise to God over the water (blessing of baptismal water), and individual collects, as well as psalms, hymns, etc., recall the event of creation. Alongside thanksgiving to the Creator we find, as in every text praising God, a tribute to God—in this case as Creator. Thanksgiving and praise are combined with affirmation of created reality, which must also be understood as an assignment to care for and preserve that creation. But in the liturgy, history does not exist as past event; instead, in the liturgical memory that makes present, it becomes the "now" of the people. Creation is part of human history; those celebrating know that they are dependent on God as their Creator. This touches them in their being as persons because in praising the Creator they recall their own dignity as image of God. Finally, the liturgy also uses concepts of creation theology to express the eschatological new creation in Christ. Thus in the collect after the reading from Genesis 1:1–2:2 at the Easter Vigil it says: "may those you have redeemed understand that there exists nothing more marvelous than the world's creation in the beginning except that, at the end of the ages, Christ our Passover has been sacrificed."[21]

The self-revealing God

The second image we should name is that of God who is self-revealed in Jesus Christ. It shapes the Christian liturgy and finds its most compact expression in the celebration of the paschal mystery. In the life, suffering, death, resurrection, and exaltation of Jesus, God is revealed. In him God reveals the special degree of divine closeness to human beings; Jesus is God's self-interpretation. This, too, is explicit, for example, in Eucharistic Prayer IV: "To accomplish your plan, he gave himself up to death."[22]

In the context of the revelation in Christ the ideas of time already mentioned, the interweaving of salvation history and present salvation, are projected further in terms of the completion of salvation. Thus the Son "sent the Holy Spirit from you, Father, as the first fruits

[21] *The Roman Missal*, 365.
[22] Ibid., 657.

for those who believe, so that, bringing to perfection his work in the world, he might sanctify creation to the full."[23] When the prayer continues with "[t]herefore, O Lord, we pray: may this same Holy Spirit graciously sanctify these offerings,"[24] it is clear that those who believe in Christ already share in eschatological salvation.

God the Redeemer

The third God-image is that of God as redeemer. Eucharistic Prayer IV speaks of very different ways in which this redeeming action of God is experienced: in the aid we are given so that we may seek and find God, in the sending of the Son as savior, in his resurrection from the dead, in the gift of the Spirit. If we understand redemption as liberation of persons from the contexts of evil that oppress them and obstruct their development as human beings, then we discover in the liturgy a multitude of biblical experiences of redemption that tell of it. Different literary genera and sign-actions such as anointings, layings-on of hands, blessings, etc., remind us of it and address God's redeeming action. God is venerated as the one who brings redemption. But the hope for a sharing in the event of redemption is still more clearly expressed. Remembering God's action brings about the reality that here and now people are part of the history of redemption, of the history of salvation and the eschatological fulfillment. It is also true that the doxology of God as redeemer applies to those who speak that doxology and are thereby enabled to experience themselves as redeemed. In Christian liturgy the praise of the redeeming God is connected to the confession of Christ. In Jesus Christ and his life the divine work of redemption is incarnated: "To the poor he proclaimed the good news of salvation, to prisoners, freedom, and to the sorrowful of heart, joy."[25]

Sunday as the bringing together of all three images of God

Sunday and its liturgical celebrations bring all three images of God together in exemplary fashion, without that necessarily being

[23] Ibid.
[24] Ibid., 658.
[25] Ibid., 657.

said explicitly in individual texts. Sunday is the time in which to experience God as the Creator, as the one who is self-revealed in Jesus Christ, and as redeemer. This occurs, among other ways, in the many names given to this day over a long period of tradition. It is connected with creation and new creation in Christ (the first day); it celebrates the revelation of the power of God in Christ, the paschal mystery (the Day of the Lord); finally, on this day God's redemptive action is central (the eighth day as the beginning of eschatological time). Sunday is an example of how the image of God and the event of liturgical action work together in such a way that the former is experienced in the latter. It offers a "space" for that experience.

Blessing: praise of God and gift of God

Benedictions as well, with their biblically grounded theology of creation, soteriology, and ecclesiology,[26] create an aesthetic space in which to experience God: the Creator, who in Christ is the God of redemption, is proclaimed in a form accessible to the senses.[27] The blessing given to the person derives from the salvation-creating action of God. Blessings apply to a great many situations in human life; in the benediction God is proclaimed as the one who is present in the life of the human person. The liturgy is shaped by a dynamic picture of God, who is the origin and guarantor of blessing. Corresponding to this, praise and thanksgiving toward God are at the forefront; thus they are likewise blessing of God (objective genitive).[28] Here the two-fold meaning of Hebrew ברך, Greek εὐλογεῖν, and Latin *benedicere* finds expression: blessing means both praise of God (objective genitive) and God's blessing (subjective genitive) for human beings. Blessing gives thanks for the salvation God has already given to human beings, but at the same time it expresses eschatological expectation of

[26] Ulrich Heckel, "Segnung und Salbung. Theologische und praktische Über-legungen zur Einführung einer neuen Gottesdienstform," *Kerygma und Dogma* 47 (2001): 126–55, at 129.

[27] Reiner Kaczynski, "Die Benediktionen," in Bruno Kleinheyer, et al., *Sakramentliche Feiern*, vol. 2, Gottesdienst der Kirche 8 (Regensburg: Pustet, 1984), 233–74, at 242–43.

[28] Florian Kluger, *Benediktionen. Studium zur kirchlichen Segensfeiern*, Studien zur Pastoralliturgie 31 (Regensburg: Pustet, 2011).

the fulfillment of the salvation that has dawned in Christ. Blessing is given to human beings by God through Jesus Christ.[29]

Example: the blessing of the fruits of the harvest

This is illustrated very well in the Book of Blessings, for example, in the "blessing on the occasion of thanksgiving for the harvest," which first thanks the Creator for the fertility of nature, then asks that God may cause people to praise God unceasingly and at the same time strive toward the blessings of the world to come, closing with a doxology that links both praise and petition with the Christ-event:

> God our Creator, who never cease to bestow your bounteous fruits from the rains of the heavens and the riches of the soil, we thank your loving majesty for this year's harvest. Through these blessings of your generosity you have fulfilled the hopes of your children. Grant that together they may praise your mercy without end and in their life amid the good things of this world strive also after the blessings of the world to come. We ask this through Christ our Lord. Amen.[30]

This blessing (which includes other prayer elements and texts from Scripture) and the actions that accompany it show that the liturgy does not treat God discursively but attempts to open through presentative symbolism a space in which God can be experienced.

4.3 Christology

Celebration of the singular Christ event

At the center of Christian liturgy stands the Christ-event: the life, suffering, death, resurrection, and exaltation of Jesus Christ. This shapes every Christian worship service and determines its identity. The liturgy places various accents and recalls individual events in the life of Jesus, depending on the season of the church year and the reason for the particular liturgical celebration. It confesses Christ as

---

[29] Heckel, "Segnung und Salbung."
[30] *The Book of Blessings* (Collegeville MN: Liturgical Press, 1992), 358–59.

the servant of God, the sacrificial lamb, the high priest, but despite all differences it always celebrates the one Christ-event.

Light symbolism of the Easter Vigil

In this liturgy the confession of Christ is especially impressive; here the history of salvation accepted in faith is displayed in an aesthetics of text, symbol, and symbolic action that seizes all the believers' senses. Thus the Easter Vigil does not explain in discursive symbolism that Christ is the salvation of humanity but stages it in a presentative symbolism combining the darkness of the night and the light of the Easter candle, the scent of incense, the chanted recollection of the history of salvation in the *Exsultet* and other prayers (see chap. 4.7.4 below). The thing being celebrated takes hold of those present. Incarnation, proclamation, death, and resurrection are experienced as a saving event. The Christ-event is recalled in such a way that its meaning for the present becomes obvious. In the liturgical celebration the faithful receive a share in it.

Transformation and repentance

Encountering the Christ-event in the liturgy involves human transformation. The diabatic dimension of liturgy, that is, the transforming bridge,[31] contributes to the human person's becoming new. At worship this is repeatedly asked of God, and at the same time believers "are called to become like Christ. Liturgical action means acting with the mind and in the power of Christ" and ultimately signifies repentance and transformation.[32]

Christian liturgy is also the anticipation of Christ's return. It is governed by the conviction that salvation history is not yet complete, as the community acclamation in the Eucharistic Prayer acknowledges: "We proclaim your death, O Lord, and profess your resurrection, until you come again." The ancient church's liturgical

---

[31] Werner Hahne, *Gottes Volksversammlung. Die Liturgie als Ort lebendiger Erfahrung* (Freiburg: Herder, 1999); idem, *De arte celebrandi oder Von der Kunst, Gottesdienst zu feiern. Entwurf einer Fundamentalliturgik*, 2nd ed. (Freiburg: Herder, 1991).

[32] Hahne, *Gottes Volksversammlung*, 235.

acclamation, "Maranatha," "Come, Lord Jesus" (see 1 Cor 16:22; Rev 22:20), expresses that anticipation. Fulfillment is not yet. That, too, is part of the faith-aesthetics of liturgy as we experience it in the course of the church year. Good Friday and Holy Saturday must be endured as times when decay and death, as corollaries of creation, are starkly present.[33] The expectation that the promises will only be fulfilled with the return of Christ, the experience of the yet-to-come, is part of the Christian potential in hope. Soteriology and eschatology, praise and petition therefore form a unity in the liturgy and are close companions.

4.3.1 Liturgical Prayer "to Christ" (ad Christum)— "through Christ" (per Christum)

Prayer to God the Father

Behind what happens in the liturgy "it is necessary, ultimately, that the Father should appear as the one who effects it all."[34] In the presidential prayers, that is, those of the presider, it is already clear that the faithful turn with and through Christ to God.[35] These prayers have a special status in the liturgical celebration, something that should also be expressed in carefully crafted theological formulations. Prayers that promote tri-theistic ideas and could obscure the clarity of the monotheistic confession, in the eyes of Jews and Muslims as well, are out of the question in general, but especially here. Therefore it is required that in the celebration of Mass the Eucharistic Prayer and the orations must be directed to God by the praying community gathered around

---

[33] Hans-Ulrich Wiese, *Karsamstagsexistenz. Auseinandersetzung mit dem Karsamstag in Liturgie und moderner Kunst*, Bild, Raum, Feier. Studien zu Kirche und Kunst 1 (Regensburg: Schnell & Steiner, 2002).

[34] Irmgard Pahl, "Die Stellung Christi in den Präsidialgebeten der Eucharistiefeier. Textbefund des heutigen Messbuchs und Anforderungen an eine Revision," in *Christologie der Liturgie. Der Gottesdienst der Kirche: Christusbekenntnis und Sinaibund*, ed. Klemens Richter and Benedikt Kranemann, Quaestiones disputatae 159 (Freiburg: Herder, 1995), 243–57, at 256.

[35] For the historical implications of this see Josef A. Jungmann, *The Place of Christ in Liturgical Prayer* (Staten Island, NY: Alba House, 1965), 125–278.

Christ.[36] The conclusion to the collect of the day makes it clear that it is directed through Christ (*per Christum*) to the Father: "the collect prayer is usually addressed to God the Father, through Christ, in the Holy Spirit, and is concluded with a trinitarian ending."[37]

Christ as mediator of prayer

Christ, who lives with God in the unity of the Holy Spirit, is the mediator of prayer. That role is set within the framework of the confession of the triune God. Likewise, the few prayers that are directed to Christ maintain this theology: "Who live and reign with God the Father in the unity of the Holy Spirit, one God, for ever and ever."[38]

"Mediator" says something about Christ that, although there are few traces of it in official statements, is central to Christology.[39] Christ is the mediator between God and the human, since he is truly God and truly human: in Christ, God is with the human race, and at the same time human persons are with God.[40] According to 1 Timothy 2:5 there is one "mediator between God and humankind, Christ Jesus, himself human." According to Hebrews 8:6; 9:15, he is the mediator of a new covenant. Accordingly, the order of Christian prayer traces revelation in a reverse and responsive order: through Christ, in him, and with him.[41] With the attribute "mediator," then, we are not only at the center of Christology but at the heart of the liturgy.

[36] *GIRM* 54
[37] Ibid.
[38] Ibid.
[39] Heinz-Günther Schöttler, "'Per Christum . . .' Christus als Weg. In memoriam Friedrich-Wilhelm Marquardt (d. 25 Mai 2002)," *Bibel und Liturgie* 76 (2003): 4–15.
[40] Philipp Harnoncourt, "Die Gegenwart des Mysteriums Christi in den Sakramenten. Entwurf eines Modells zur Sakramententheologie," in *Die Feier der Sakramente in der gemeinde. Festschrift für Heinrich Rennings*, ed. Martin Klöckener and Winfried Glade (Kevelaer: Butzon & Bercker, 1986), 31–46.
[41] Josef Wohlmuth, "Trinitarische Aspekte des Gebetes," in *Beten: Sprache des Glaubens, Seele des Gottesdienstes. Fundamentaltheologische und liturgiewissenschaftliche Aspekte*, ed. Ulrich Willers, Pietas Liturgica 15 (Tübingen and Basel: Francke, 2000), 83–101, at 94.

According to these theological considerations and by order of the church, the addressee, at least in the central prayers of Christian liturgy, is always the Father, even when it is evident that the prayer is first directed to the Son. This is either expressed directly or the Father is indirectly glorified in the Son. The confession is always of one God in three persons.

The prayer texts and conclusions in the *General Instruction for the Liturgy of the Hours* (*GILH*) are no different from those in the Missal. This instruction speaks even more clearly about Christ's mediatory role in prayer:

> Prayer directed to God must be linked with Christ, the Lord of all, the one Mediator through whom alone we have access to God. He unites to himself the whole human community in such a way that there is an intimate bond between the prayer of Christ and the prayer of all humanity. In Christ and in Christ alone human worship of God receives its redemptive value and attains its goal.[42]

Christian prayer without reference to Christ is impossible; in fact, it is only the connection with Christ that makes it possible in the first place. The mediator gives access to the Father for those who pray. The direction in *GILH* speaks of the prayer of Christ and that of human beings, which must necessarily be connected so that the praise of God in Christ may attain its supreme meaning.

The orations in the liturgical books largely maintain this theology of prayer, although in regard to other strands of tradition, such as that represented by the Greek anaphora of Gregory, we should not overlook the fact that prayer *ad Christum* had and still has its place especially in hymns and in psalm-prayers interpreted as referring to Christ, in acclamations, and of course in private prayer. Thus we may say of Christian prayer that prayer to Christ is indispensable, as long as we keep in mind that it must be in accord with the requirement that prayer be trinitarian.[43]

---

[42] *GILH* 6.

[43] Albert Gerhards, "Zur Frage der Gebetsanrede im Zeitalter des jüdisch-christlichen Dialogs," *Trierer Theologische Zeitschrift* 102 (1993): 245–57, at 250.

4.3.2 Liturgy as Celebration of the Paschal Mystery

The concept of the "paschal mystery"[44] sums up the whole saving event in Jesus Christ, which the liturgy recalls, celebrates as present, and for whose fulfillment it hopes.[45]

The "paschal" concept

The "paschal" idea must be understood, first of all, in terms of the Old Testament "Pasch" or Passover. It is the sign of God's saving action in Israel at the exodus that, in ritualized form, became an element of cultural memory and in fact took on an identifying character for Israel. In reflecting on it and celebrating it in Christian liturgy we must keep in mind that this tradition continues in Judaism today. At the same time, we should understand "Pascha" in light of the Christ-event, which is also celebrated in liturgically ritualized form as the evidence of the inbreaking of the reign of God. The lamb of the Old Testament Pascha is interpreted in terms of Christ and his self-gift on the cross.[46] The paschal lamb of the Old Testament people of God is understood by Christians as a type of the saving action of Jesus Christ, but in that they proclaim Christ, the new paschal lamb, as also Son of God, the hermeneutics of the Old Testament covenant are surpassed.

Old Testament Passover and Christian reading

In light of the facts that the Old Testament is indispensable to Christians as Sacred Scripture and that Judaism continues to celebrate Passover and keeps the paschal tradition alive, we must ask what can be the relationship of the Christian reading of the Pascha to that of the Old Testament and its reception in Judaism.

---

[44] Winfried Haunerland, "*Mysterium paschale*. Schlüsselbegriff liturgietheologischer Erneuerung," in *Liturgie als Mitte des christlichen Lebens*, ed. George Augustin and Kurt Kardinal Koch, Theologie im Dialog 7 (Freiburg: Herder, 2012), 189–209.

[45] See *SC* 5.

[46] For the very different interpretations of "pasch" in the ancient church see Hansjörg Auf der Maur, *Feiern im Rhythmus der Zeit I. Herrenfeste in Woche und Jahr*, vol. 5 of *Gottesdienst der Kirche. Handbuch der Liturgiewissenschaft*, ed. Hans Bernhard Meyer, et al. (Regensburg: Pustet, 1983), 69.

For the systematic theologian Josef Wohlmuth, the Christian liturgy, which celebrates the new and eternal covenant, incorporates the memory of suffering and resurrection "into the covenant at Sinai and the prophetic renewals of its promise by internalizing the Torah and the radical forgiveness of sins" (see Jer 31:31-33). According to Wohlmuth, Eucharist thus comprehends not only "the time between Jesus' birth and the Last Day"; the Christian confession of salvation must be expanded "to include the covenantal election and its promises, indeed the creation and fulfillment as well."[47]

Jürgen Werbick, also a systematician, emphasizes that the Old Testament is not made superfluous by the celebration of the Christian "paschal mystery." In celebrating the paschal mystery the church cannot ignore the broader context of Israel's experience, for the understanding of the Christ-event depends on that context of tradition. Understanding Christ's Pascha in light of Israel's experience of God means acknowledging that the experience of God's faithfulness in Jesus cannot be detached from the experience of God's faithfulness to Israel.[48]

Albert Gerhards points to the Good Friday petition that speaks of the fidelity of the Jews to their covenant with God. It regards as indispensable that Christians speak of a renewal of the one, unabrogated covenant with God in Christ. He sees the church and Israel as companions on the way, traveling "toward the eschatological gathering in the realm to come."[49]

Daniela Kranemann, thinking against this background about the dramaturgy of the celebration of the paschal mystery, concludes that "Israel . . . is no longer regarded at dramaturgically important points in the liturgy as a silent witness to a past now illuminated by the Christ-event but as the first and living participant in God's

[47] Josef Wohlmuth, "Eucharistie: Feier des neuen Bundes," in *Christologie der Liturgie. Der Gottesdienst der Kirche: Christusbekenntnis und Sinaibund*, ed. Klemens Richter and Benedikt Kranemann, Quaestiones disputatae 159 (Freiburg: Herder, 1995), 187–206, at 205.

[48] Jürgen Werbick, "Bibel Jesu und Evangelium Jesu Christi. Systematisch-theologische Perspektiven," *Bibel und Liturgie* 70 (1997): 213–18, at 217.

[49] Albert Gerhards, "Kraft aus der Wurzel. Zum Verhältnis christlicher Liturgie gegenüber dem Jüdischen: Fortschreibung oder struktureller Neubeginn?," *Kirche und Israel* 16 (2001): 25–44, at 35.

great drama of salvation that had its beginning in the act of creation, entered its second grand act in the election of Israel at Sinai, and ultimately opens out to the world of the nations in the person and work of Jesus Christ, so that henceforth Christians and Jews may hope for and await together its salvific outcome."[50] That summary may also be seen as a theological criterion for today's liturgy.

Liturgy as celebration of the "mystery"

The liturgy is the celebration of "mystery." That concept is used only reservedly in the Old Testament because of its pagan sacral origins. We find it in Daniel 2:28-29, 47 and in early Jewish apocalyptic texts in the sense of a secret revealed by God, communicating "what will happen at the end of days" (Dan 2:28). *Mysterium* here has eschatological significance and points to the coming of the reign of God. The New Testament uses μυστήριον to speak of the Christ-event. Thus in Mark 4:11 and its parallels the term refers to the inbreaking of the reign of God in Jesus' work. Similarly, Paul writes about "God's wisdom, secret and hidden" (1 Cor 2:7) that has been revealed in history in the Crucified. Colossians 2:2 understands μυστήριον as the saving event in Christ ("the knowledge of God's mystery, that is, Christ himself"; see also Col 1:27; Eph 3:4-5; 5:32). In him the saving will of God is manifest. So *mysterium* refers to a reality that surpasses human thought and is irrevocably bound up with revelation. It is a gracious gift of God. Jesus Christ is the mystery of God into which believers are drawn for their salvation. It is present in the community in which it is proclaimed. This is a clearer concept than *sacramentum*[51] for expressing the salvation-historical dimension of the liturgical celebration. *Mysterium* thus points to both the present and the eschatological dimensions of Christian liturgy as well as to the faith that in the celebration of the liturgy one participates in the divine saving action in Christ.[52]

---

[50] Daniela Kranemann, "Mehr als eine Statistenrolle! Israel in der Dramaturgie der christlichen Liturgie," *Bibel und Liturgie* 76 (2003): 16–27, at 25.

[51] Latin *sacramentum* originally meant the oath sworn by soldiers on their banners: see Eva-Maria Faber, *Einführung in die katholische Sakramentenlehre*, 3rd ed. (Darmstadt: Wissenschaftliche Buchgesellschaft, 2011), 33.

[52] Ibid., 26–28; see above, chap. 1.2.

Celebration of the whole reality of salvation

Inasmuch as the suffering, death, resurrection, and exaltation of Jesus Christ are described in the one concept of "paschal mystery," it expresses that the liturgy as a whole celebrates the one saving mystery of Christ. Thus the liturgy cannot set aside either Jesus' life or his suffering and cross or his resurrection if it is to proclaim Christ personally in his entire saving reality and make it possible for people in their brokenness to come to a personal encounter with Christ. In terms of the paschal mystery, the liturgy contains a fundamental tension between mortality and resurrection, one whose eschatological overcoming may be hoped for on the basis of the Christ-event.

Mysterium paschale is one of the guiding concepts in the Constitution on the Liturgy and may be regarded as expressing a "short form" of postconciliar theology.[53] A program is here evident: "It is not (any longer) the incarnation that is to be regarded and proclaimed as the all-determining (because apparently 'already' concluded) saving action, but the 'paschal mystery.'"[54] Ultimately, the one salvation is celebrated in both, but while in the incarnation we emphasize a static Christology of Christ's preexistence and exaltation (with Christmas the most notable example), the celebration of the paschal mystery (exemplified by the Easter Triduum) expresses a Christology of exaltation, thus a dynamic one focused on salvation history.[55] The central event of Christian faith with its dynamic extension to the lives of Christians, the participation through baptism in the saving event of Christ, and the expectation of eschatological fulfillment: all that is in view in the paschal mystery.

The paschal mystery as guiding concept of the Constitution on the Liturgy

The Constitution on the Liturgy refers repeatedly to the paschal mystery. Romans 6:4 says that by baptism men and women are

---

[53] Angelus A. Häussling, "'Pascha-Mysterium.' Kritisches zu einem Beitrag in der dritten Auflage des 'Lexikon für Theologie und Kirche,'" *Archiv für Liturgiewissenschaft* 41 (1999): 157–65.

[54] Ibid., 164.

[55] Rupert Berger, "Ostern und Weihnachten. Zum Grundgefüge des Kirchenjahres," *Archiv für Liturgiewissenschaft* 8 (1963): 1–20.

implanted in the paschal mystery of Christ (*SC* 6), that is, taken up entirely in that saving event ("spirit of adoption"). This theology was expressed, among other ways, in some aspects of the ancient church's baptismal liturgy, in which the baptizands' passage through the baptismal font and immersion in it ritually imaged their dying and rising with Christ. An effort is being made to incorporate similarly expressive sign-actions in today's rite of baptism.

The celebration of Mass, with proclamation of the word, Eucharist, adoration (*adorare*), and thanksgiving (*gratias agere*), is interpreted as a coming together to celebrate Christ's paschal mystery (*SC* 6). The paschal mystery is the center of the liturgy from which all sacraments and sacramentals derive their power (*SC* 61).

Emphasis is placed on Sunday as the original feast day on which believers should assemble to celebrate the paschal mystery. It is the "foundation and kernel of the entire liturgical year" (*SC* 106), which is thus set in its entirety within the horizon of the *mysterium paschale*. It has a centering function for the spirituality and thus the lives of the faithful (*SC* 107).

The paschal mystery is also central to the various parts of the Liturgy of the Hours, and it is the hermeneutical focus of the recited texts from Scripture (see chap. 5.1 below). Christ is celebrated as present in his pro-existence, that is, his self-surrender on behalf of human beings. This liturgy in particular is repeatedly interpreted as the church's cooperation in Christ's prayer to the Father (*vox Christi ad Patrem*), as well as prayer directed to Christ (*vox ecclesiae ad Christum*).[56]

The numerous examples in the liturgy show, as does *SC*—also followed by liturgical theology—how the paschal mystery applies to the liturgy as a whole and names within it the salvation-historical event celebrated by the great variety of liturgical forms, in which they all participate. Questioning this theological centering and seeing the paschal mystery only in the Eucharist would, for one thing, imperil the mutual relationship of the various liturgical celebrations, all of

---

[56] Balthasar Fischer, *Die Psalmen als Stimme der Kirche. Gesammelte Studien zur christlichen Psalmenfrömmigkeit*, ed. Andreas Heinz (Trier: Paulinus-Verlag, 1982), 86–89; for the paschal mystery's shaping of the various forms of celebration see Irmgard Pahl, "Das Paschamysterium in seiner zentralen Bedeutung für die Gestalt christlicher Liturgie," *Liturgisches Jahrbuch* 46 (1996): 71–93.

which share in the one saving event; besides, it would not be evident that even lesser and simpler forms of celebration enable participation in the one mystery of Christ.

4.3.3 *Presence of Christ in the Liturgy*

Throughout its tradition the church has held fast to the faith conviction that Christ is present in the celebration of the Eucharist. This is expressed in the form of the celebration, for example, in the solemn treatment of the gospel book or the eucharistic species. The background is the promise that Christ will be present to the church (Matt 28:20: "I am with you always, to the end of the age"), which echoes in the confession of the young Christian assembly (Col 1:27: "Christ in you, the hope of glory"). The key New Testament passage in Matthew 18:20 has been interpreted by recent Roman Catholic documents on liturgy entirely in terms of worship,[57] though broader interpretations are possible. In any case, the presence of Christ is closely linked with the liturgy as a basic function of the church.[58]

Christ's presence in the liturgy is a real, dynamic, and personal presence. To take a biblical example, the Emmaus pericope (Luke 24:13-35) makes this very clear. The disciples encounter the risen Christ on the road to Emmaus; he interprets himself for them in light of Scripture; they recognize him as the Risen One when he breaks bread for them. Christ is experienced as personal in the interpretation of Scripture ("Were not our hearts burning within us while he was talking to us on the road, while he was opening the scriptures to us?" [Luke 24:32]) and in the breaking of the bread ("Then their eyes were opened, and they recognized him" [Luke 24:31]).

In the church's tradition the presence of Christ promised to the disciples has been associated especially with the liturgy. The personal nature of that presence is stated expressively in certain liturgical forms. In the Eucharist it is presence under the forms of bread and wine,

---

[57] *Mediator Dei* 20; *SC* 7; for the whole history of interpretation see Ulrich Luz, *Matthew 8–20: A Commentary*, Hermeneia (Minneapolis: Fortress Press, 2001), 459–61.

[58] Franziskus Eisenbach, *Die Gegenwart Jesu Christi im Gottesdienst. Systematische Studien zur Liturgiekonstitution des II. Vatikanischen Konzils* (Mainz: Matthias-Grünewald, 1982).

combined with the words of interpretation: "This is my Body," "This is the chalice of my Blood, the Blood of the new and everlasting covenant." Here Christ's total self-surrender is experienced as present. "Externally perceptible earthly living presence" and "the most concrete inner life-force" of Christ are encountered in the Eucharist.[59]

The presence of Christ in the proclamation of the word

Christ's presence in the word, familiar in early tradition,[60] is interpreted by SC 33 to mean that Christ himself proclaims the Good News in the liturgy. Presence in the word means "self-proclamation." In the communication event of the liturgy the proclamation of the word is "divine proclamation in terms of the life-histories of those who speak and hear."[61] Correspondingly, the treatment of the word constitutes a complex ritual event. The place of proclamation (the ambo), the announcement of the reading, the closing formula, and the response of the congregation, as well as the responsory (in the Liturgy of the Word at Mass) or the response after the readings in the Liturgy of the Hours, the design of the book containing the biblical texts, and not least the person who reads the texts express the special dignity of what is presented as the word of God.[62]

. . . and in the assembled community

Besides these, tradition and present interpretation recognize the presence of Christ in the assembled community, something that is visibly and audibly expressed in the liturgical texts and actions. Christ

---

[59] Michael Welker, *Was geht vor beim Abendmahl?* (Stuttgart: Quell, 2004).

[60] Otto Nussbaum, "Von der Gegenwart Gottes im Wort," in *Gott feiern. Theologische Anregung und geistliche Vertiefung zur Feier von Messe und Stundengebet*, ed. Josef G. Plöger (Freiburg: Herder, 1980), 116–32.

[61] Dorothea Sattler, "Gegenwart Gottes im Wort. Systematisch-theologische Aspekte," in *Wie das Wort Gottes feiern?*, 123–43, at 140.

[62] Benedikt Kranemann, "Wort–Buch–Verkündigungsort. Zur Ästhetik der Wortverkündigung im Gottesdienst," in *Liturgia et Unitas. Liturgiewissenschaftliche und ökumenische Studien zur Eucharistie und zum gottesdienstlichen Leben in der Schweiz. Études liturgiques et oecuméniques sur l'Eucharistie et la vie liturgique en Suisse. In honorem Bruno Bürki*, ed. Martin Klöckener and Arnaud Join-Lambert (Fribourg: Universitätsverlag; Geneva: Labor et Fides: 2001), 57–72.

himself, who is present in the Eucharist, is active in the congregation's praise. A liturgy with dialogical and communicative forms of proclamation of the word and in the community meal corresponds to that truth.

Presence and absence

The liturgy is about the liturgically remembered earthly reality of Jesus and the heavenly reality of the Risen One as something we can experience. In addition, as regards the presence of Christ we need to keep in mind the eschatological "already and not yet," that is, the simultaneity of nearness, personal presence, and communion with Christ on the one hand, and absence, distance, and removal on the other. Such a consideration is necessary for a right understanding of what is meant by "personal presence."

Actual presence

An attempt has been made to sum up the different aspects of this "presence" in theological terms. The concept of "actual presence" (from *actio*, the presence of act and deed) is supposed to express the sacramental mediation of Christ's presence. His presence is effectively conveyed through persons, symbols, and signs. We speak of dynamic symbols in which the presence of Christ in the liturgy takes place. At the same time, actual presence designates the presence of Christ mediated by the Holy Spirit. The Spirit unlocks and conveys the presence of Christ to the faithful.

Actual presence is more precisely described as a commemorative actual presence. Christ is present today. That presence of Christ is independent of human subjectivity; however, it is pneumatically conveyed. In liturgical commemoration, the anamnesis, there occurs a personal encounter with the Risen and Exalted One.

Proleptic final presence

Proleptic final presence describes the anticipation of fulfillment in the liturgy. Here the Parousia, the return of Christ in the end time, is celebrated in anticipation, and a share is given in that saving event. This combines hope for Christ's return and hope for the promised inheritance.

Real memorial, re-presentation

The salvation-historical personal understanding of the presence of Christ that is fundamental to liturgical theology today was rediscovered in the twentieth century. The decisive studies on the subject are those of Odo Casel (see chaps. 2.2.5.2 and 3.10.1). Casel emphasizes the real memorial, that is, the actual presence of the saving action in the liturgical celebration, not only as a memory of that saving event. In the liturgy, and especially in the Eucharist, what happens is not a repetition of the saving action but its re-presentation. The cultic mystery is

> not something that stands alongside faith and a religious-moral life . . . something that would mediate the gifts of grace or have a community-building function within the visible community of the church. Certainly, that is also its task, but in the first place the cultic mystery is the objective and necessary presentation and making-present of Christ's saving work. It therefore, to that degree, stands at the center of Christian existence, so that faith itself achieves a symbolic, generally identifiable expression and religious life derives its strength and obligation from it. In the cultic mystery the Christ mystery becomes visible and effective; it is therefore a kind of continuation and further unfolding of the *oikonomia Christi*, which without the cultic mystery could not communicate itself to all the peoples of the community of salvation, expanding in time and space.[63]

Casel sees the sacraments as ritual symbolic acts in which the saving plan of God that was fulfilled in Christ is shown and realized. The Christ mystery is present in the liturgy as a cultic mystery in the form of memorial. This saving memorial is, for Casel, at the same time the core of Christian liturgy. It is a really effective, objective memorial of the paschal mystery. Christ and his saving action are made present. The liturgy enacts the Christ mystery in ritual form. It is intended to make present God's saving deeds in symbols; the faithful then participate in its saving power.

Those celebrating liturgy as "contemporaries of God's saving deeds"

Angelus Häussling continued this theological line in the context of the outgoing twentieth century. According to him, liturgy is the

---

[63] Odo Casel, "Glaube, Gnosis und Mysterium," *Jahrbuch für Liturgiewissenschaft* 15 (1935): 155–305, at 194.

"memorial of something past and yet liberation in the present." The person celebrating liturgy here and now is a "contemporary of God's saving deeds." Through Christ's saving action such a one experiences transformation, becomes different, and can live accordingly. In the demonstrative actions of the liturgy, for example, in praying the Our Father, the *Benedictus*, or the *Magnificat*, but also in sign-actions such as baptism with water, anointing, etc., the one celebrating liturgy clarifies her or his own role by identifying, beyond the individual situation, with the guiding figures of salvation history. Thus someone who sings the *Magnificat* enters into the story of Mary associated with it, interprets his or her life in those terms, and knows himself or herself, like Mary, to be in relationship with God and God's saving work.[64]

This new liturgical-theological orientation, which draws its criteria above all from an engagement with the ancient church, first shaped the encyclical *Mediator Dei* of 1947, which in article 20 speaks of the presence of Christ "at the august sacrifice of the altar both in the person of His minister and above all under the eucharistic species" as well as "in the sacraments" and "in prayer of praise and petition we direct to God." This was also reflected, along with thoughts derived from the Liturgical Movement, in the documents of Vatican II and in the postconciliar period. *Sacrosanctum Concilium* 7 speaks of the presence of Christ in the church in general, but then especially in the celebration of the liturgy. It names the sacrifice of the Mass, the person of the priest, and the eucharistic species. Ideas from the Liturgical Movement are included, for example, when the document speaks of presence in the Word and in the community assembly.

Presence of Christ

Important postconciliar documents such as the *General Introduction to the Roman Missal* (*GIRM*) or the eucharistic instruction published in 1967 have a different order, especially as regards the naming of the presence of Christ in the community. *GIRM* 27 says: "For in the

---

[64] Angelus A. Häussling, "Liturgie: Gedächtnis eines Vergangenen und doch Befreiung in der Gegenwart" (1991), in idem, *Christliche Identität aus der Liturgie. Theologische und historische Studien zum Gottesdienst der Kirche*, ed. Martin Klöckener, Benedikt Kranemann, and Michael B. Merz, Liturgiewissenschaftliche Quellen und Forschungen 79 (Freiburg: Herder, 1997), 2–10.

celebration of Mass . . . Christ is really present in the very liturgical assembly gathered in his name, in the person of the minister, in his word, and indeed substantially and uninterruptedly under the Eucharistic species."[65]

The eucharistic instruction *Eucharisticum Mysterium* adds this quotation from Pope Paul VI's encyclical *Mysterium Fidei* (1965): "This presence [of Christ] is called 'real' not to exclude the idea that the others are 'real' too, but rather to indicate presence *par excellence*" (*MF* 39). This refines the Liturgy Constitution's statement about the types of liturgical presence: it is a matter of the Lord's one and active presence in the liturgy.

Christ as subject of the liturgical celebration

Christ is the subject of liturgical celebration. He celebrates together with his church, the body of Christ. The celebrating church is the visible form of Christ personally present; it is taken into Christ's subjectivity. But "church" includes all believers. The *participatio actuosa* (active participation) of the baptized is indispensable for the celebration of the Eucharist because only in that way can the church, as the body of Christ, be the expression and place of the presence of Christ and make visible the present Christ.

4.4 Pneumatology

4.4.1 Liturgy as an Event Effected by the Spirit

Prayer for the gift of the Holy Spirit

Western theology—unlike that of the East—has paid too little attention to the pneumatological dimension of the liturgy.[66] And yet prayer for the gift of the Holy Spirit is one of the elementary aspects of every liturgy: pneumatology is an essential foundation of liturgical

---

[65] See Edward Foley, et al., *A Commentary on the General Instruction of the Roman Missal* (Collegeville, MN: Liturgical Press, 2007).

[66] Felmy, *Einführung in die orthodoxe Theologie der Gegenwart* (see n. 9 above).

theology.[67] That is indicated, to begin with, by the fact that *SC* 6, the article of the Constitution on the Liturgy whose subject is the paschal mystery and its celebration, concludes with the assertion (which does seem something like an afterthought) that all this takes place in the power of the Holy Spirit. The presence of the saving work and saving deeds is mediated by the Spirit. This constitutes a program for postconciliar liturgy that we have not yet fully addressed.

The liturgy's pneumatology rests on the New Testament witness; the dimension of experience of the Spirit is already present in the Old Testament, but it was also profoundly shaped by experiences of the Spirit after Easter.

The Risen One is present in the community in the Holy Spirit for the sake of its salvation. Confession of Christ is made through the Holy Spirit (1 Cor 12:3). The life of those baptized into Christ is life in the Holy Spirit (1 Cor 6:11; 12:3, 13), despite the fact that Paul frequently speaks of living "in Christ" and "in the Spirit" alongside one another (see, e.g., Rom 8:1-11). People experience themselves as a new creation in the Holy Spirit and know themselves to be indebted to their Creator. Receiving the Spirit obligates one to a corresponding way of life (Gal 3:1-5), which is interpreted as the fruit of the Spirit (Gal 5:19-26).

According to Romans 8:15 the basis of all the liturgy's pneumatology is the gift of the Spirit to Christians in baptism. As the apostles could begin their mission only after Pentecost, and so after receiving the gift of the Spirit, so this is the "Spirit of adoption" that allows Christians to join in crying "Abba, Father!" (Rom 8:15; Gal 4:6). This last is a prayer acclamation; whether it is liturgical in its form must remain an open question.

Liturgy as Spirit-event

The Spirit of God enables people for worship. Liturgy is therefore essentially a Spirit-event. The gathering of people for liturgy and the upbuilding of that assembly into a church is likewise a pneumatic event.

---

[67] Philipp Harnoncourt, "Vom Beten im Heiligen Geist," in *Gott feiern* (1980), 100–115; Christian Schütz, *Einführung in die Pneumatologie* (Darmstadt: Wissenschaftliche Buchgesellschaft, 1985).

Of course, those who pray know what they hope for and what they ask of God, but so that they may know how to pray and to express what they hope for, the Spirit they have received in baptism (Rom 8:23) must intercede for them (Rom 8:26-27). Human beings, as part of perishable creation, can only pray adequately to God in the power of the Holy Spirit.

The gift of the Spirit is indeed a gift (1 Thess 4:8; 1 Cor 12:7; 2 Cor 5:5; Rom 5:5); it is something received (Rom 8:15; 1 Cor 2:12; 2 Cor 11:4; Gal 3:2). Those who have received the Spirit "who comes from God" can arrive at the knowledge of what the grace of God has given (see 1 Cor 2:12-13). A new reality is opened to them, one different from the spirit of the world. This is key to the character of liturgy as an event effected by the Spirit: the fundamental event is gift. The presence of Christ and the turning of people toward Christ, and through Christ to God, all happens in the Holy Spirit.

4.4.2 Doxology, Epiclesis, Invocation

Two prayer elements in which the working of the Spirit in the liturgy are expressed with special emphasis are the doxology and the epiclesis (see also chap. 5.2 below).

Little doxologies

Doxology here means praise in trinitarian form, for example:

- to conclude the collect at Mass and in the Liturgy of the Hours: for example, "we ask this through [him], Our Lord Jesus Christ, your Son, who lives and reigns with you in the unity of the Holy Spirit, one God, for ever and ever . . ."

- as a conclusion to the Eucharistic Prayer: "Through him, and with him, and in him, O God, almighty Father, in the unity of the Holy Spirit, all honor and glory is yours, for ever and ever," or

- at the end of the psalms and biblical canticles in the Liturgy of the Hours: "Glory be to the Father and to the Son and to the Holy Spirit, as it was in the beginning, is now, and ever shall be, world without end."

These prayer formulae ("little doxologies") took their present form in the wake of the christological struggles in the ancient church. They reveal the attempt, within the church, to express the relationship of the three Persons in adequate theological language (see chap. 3.5.1 above). The equality of the Persons within the Trinity is not to be called into question.[68]

In the unity of the Holy Spirit

Consequently, the Holy Spirit is named in central liturgical prayers. The allusion to the "unity [*unitas*] of the Holy Spirit" is more than a nod to the triune God; it puts the economy of salvation and therefore God's actions for human beings into words. The Spirit is visible as the life-principle of the church, which sees itself unified in its praise of God and thus in the liturgy through the Holy Spirit. In the Eucharistic Prayer the doxology expresses the unity of Christ and church, but also the unity of the faithful in the church, which, too, is the work of the Spirit. The doxology that concludes the collects, besides glorifying the triune God, offers praise to the Father for the saving action performed through Christ in the Holy Spirit. At the same time the formula brings to realization the fact that the church prays through Christ in the Holy Spirit.

Such liturgical formulas are couched in a standardized language that expresses central statements about faith and the reality that is constituted in the prayer, all in very few words. Therefore the congregation must be able to assent to what is said with "amen," thus "ratifying" the prayer and making it their own.

"Amen" as the congregation's approval of the epiclesis

The epiclesis ("calling on" or "calling down") is the element in eucharistic prayers and prayers of dedication, also found in some collects, in which God is explicitly called on to act in the Holy Spirit. In the eucharistic prayers it is separated into an epiclesis over the gifts and a communion epiclesis after the words of institution; these are also found in the appeal to and praise of God over the baptismal

---

[68] Jungmann, *The Place of Christ in Liturgical Prayer* (see n. 35 above), 172–90.

water, in the words of consecration at ordinations, in the blessing of couples, and so on. In each case this is the central prayer-action of the respective liturgy. The epiclesis is a part of prayers to which a consecratory meaning is assigned. The fact that in them the Holy Spirit is named as the gift requested of God underscores the significance of pneumatology for the liturgy.

It is especially the epicleses that express the work of the Spirit, often quite pictorially and thereby emphatically; they make it known that the human being is dependent on the gift of the Spirit. The Eucharistic Prayer first asks that the gifts of bread and wine be sanctified, "that they may become the Body and Blood of your Son our Lord Jesus Christ."[69] Those celebrating are to participate in Christ's table fellowship, obviously here and now but also in the eschatological fulfillment with God. The epiclesis reveals a present eschatology. The communion epiclesis asks that those celebrating, filled with the Holy Spirit, "may become one body, one spirit in Christ."[70] Thus it asks that the faithful may be transformed and find unity in the Spirit; church comes from Eucharist.

The blessing of the baptismal water (first formula; see appendix 1.2) prays for the descent of the power of the Spirit into the water, making it a sign of the Spirit. The preceding catalogue of paradigms from the Old and New Testaments makes clear what "power of the Spirit" means here; it describes how throughout salvation history God has worked through the sign of water.

Liturgy and salvation history

When we now pray for the gift of the Spirit we include salvation history: the waters of creation, which possessed sanctifying power; the destruction of the old and bringing forth of the new humanity in the Flood; the liberation from slavery experienced by Israel in its transit through the Reed Sea; the baptism of Jesus, in which the sins of humanity were washed away; blood and water from Jesus' side on the cross, the origin and life of the church; the command to the disciples to baptize.

[69] *The Roman Missal* (see n. 8 above), Eucharistic Prayer III, p. 650.
[70] Ibid., 653.

The gift of the Spirit is bound up with the hope that the human being, as image of God, will become a new creation through baptism in water and the gift of the Spirit. The epiclesis formulates the petition that "all who are buried with Christ in the death of baptism rise also with him to newness of life."[71] The vitality of the pneumatological event that changes the very reality of life is expressed especially well in these paradigms: everything is destroyed and something new comes to be; structures of oppression are cast down and freedom is given; human beings are washed clean of their entanglement in sin; from the crucifixion and thus the Easter event the church arises and stands subject to Jesus' missionary command, that is, to preach, baptize, and hand on the story of salvation. Destruction and new creation are named together and make the ambivalence of the Spirit's work fully clear. Finally, the Eucharistic Prayer petitions for resurrection to eternal life through being buried with Christ and describes baptism as a *transitus* event fulfilled in the power of the Holy Spirit.

The first blessing-prayer over the bridal couple is similarly formulated; it recalls the creation of man and woman and then implores the gift of the Holy Spirit for this marriage: "Send down on them the grace of the Holy Spirit and pour your love into their hearts, that they may remain faithful in the Marriage covenant."[72]

The prayer of consecration for priests, again similarly structured, makes it clear that the Holy Spirit is the principle of the church's life. In light of Old and New Testament paradigms it asks for the new priests, among other things, the grace of the Holy Spirit for the work of preaching. The authority to do so is conveyed through the gift of the Spirit.[73]

Examples of appeals to the Spirit

The Roman Catholic liturgy contains appeals to the Spirit in the form of hymns, sequences, as well as acclamations, antiphons, and responsories in which the Holy Spirit is called upon *in persona* and asked to come, but there are no collects addressed directly to the Holy

---

[71] *Rite of Baptism for Children* (Collegeville, MN: Liturgical Press, 2002), 35.

[72] *Order of Celebrating Matrimony* (Collegeville, MN: Liturgical Press, 2016), 22.

[73] See *The Roman Missal*, "For the Ordination of a Bishop," 1140; "For the Ordination of Priests," 1153.

Spirit. One example of the great variety of appeals is found in the liturgy for Pentecost. The dynamic of the Spirit event is emphatically expressed in the first antiphon for the *Magnificat* at First Vespers. It speaks of the twofold meaning of the Pentecost feast: the outpouring of the Spirit and, as a consequence, the assembly of the eschatological people of God: "Come, Holy Spirit, fill the hearts of all believers and set them on fire with your love. Though they spoke many different languages, you united the nations in professing the same faith, alleluia."[74] Other antiphons sing of the work of the Spirit in the church and their being enabled to preach ("All were filled with the Holy Spirit, and they began to speak, alleluia"[75]), and of the forgiveness of sins, which is given in the Spirit ("Receive the Holy Spirit; the sins of those you forgive shall be forgiven, alleluia"[76]).

4.4.3 *Laying-on of Hands and Anointing as Demonstrative Actions*

Significance of the hand in sign-actions

The laying-on of hands and anointing are sign-actions that express the petition for the Spirit and the Spirit's work. This is not obvious in and of itself; an interpretation through prayer or accompanying text is necessary if these signs are to be understood as actions demonstrating the Spirit-dimension of the liturgy. It is not accidental that both involve gestures made with the hand. This can on the one hand indicate the transfer of power; on the other hand, both anthropologically and theologically, it can indicate care, protection, healing, and encouragement but also taking possession or identification. The hand represents the opening of contact between human persons; here it images the communication between God and the human.

Laying-on and extending of hands

Laying-on of hands as conveying the Spirit is found as early as Deuteronomy 34:9, where Joshua is filled with the spirit of wisdom because Moses has laid hands on him. The New Testament witnesses to a

---

[74] *The Liturgy of the Hours*, vol. 2 (New York: Catholic Book Publishing, 1976), 1015.

[75] Ibid., 1036.

[76] *Benedictus* antiphon, ibid., 1029.

corresponding practice in some communities for initiation (Acts 8:14-18; 19:3-7), for entrusting someone with an office (Acts 6:1-7; 13:1-3; 14:23; 1 Tim 4:14; 2 Tim 1:6), and for healing through the gift of the Spirit (Acts 9:12-17), which then also makes proclamation possible.

A variety of liturgical celebrations include the laying-on or extension of hands as a sign for the working of the Spirit. This practice is also found in Orthodoxy, in the churches of the Reformation, and among Anglicans. It is true that theological interpretations may vary, but we may call laying-on of hands an ecumenical symbol of the first order. In sacramental celebrations of the Roman Catholic Church the laying-on and extension of the hands have special significance as representations of the working of the Spirit; this is clear in the Eucharistic Prayer, in the imposition of hands at confirmation, in the sacrament of reconciliation, at ordinations, in the blessing of a married couple (at the epiclesis), and in the blessing of chrism. In the first formula for blessing baptismal water (see appendix 1.2) the water is also touched at the epiclesis as a sign of the sending of the Spirit that is occurring. The laying-on of hands signals to all those participating in the celebration that God's saving work for human beings in the power of the Spirit is ongoing. It represents the working of the Spirit and is a promise of its effectiveness.

Anointing

The case of anointing is similar. Anointings are among the central liturgical-ecclesial sign-actions. They express God's care for human beings and thus the personal dimension of what is being celebrated. These, too, are symbols of the working of the Spirit, as we can see in baptism and confirmation as elements of initiation, or at the ordination of bishops and priests. The confirmation liturgy speaks of sealing with the gift of the Spirit, thus making the person entirely subject to the effective power of the Spirit and bestowing it as life principle. Likewise, the anointing with chrism at baptism can be interpreted as incorporation into the people of God and into Christ, who is priest, king, and prophet. Anointing, as a pneumatic event, effects "the constituting of the new human being."[77] On this basis the

---

[77] Reinhard Messner, *Einführung in die Liturgiewissenschaft*, 2nd ed., UTB 2173 (Paderborn: Schöningh, 2009), 125; see ibid., 126–27 on the *munera Christi* and their significance for the baptized.

anointings in other liturgies may be interpreted as developing what
has been promised in the post-baptismal anointing.

Representative action as symbolic action

Both of these sign-actions illustrate something that is specific
to the liturgy's pneumatology: the liturgy's representative actions
(language- and sign-events) are communications that attest to the
working of the Spirit, the Bible, and the liturgy. Representative action is a symbolic event that is understood in liturgy as something
made possible and carried out by God. When the liturgy speaks of
the working of the Spirit it is as a performative event for the sake of
believers, one that is essentially carried out in a form perceptible to
the senses.

4.4.4 The Holy Spirit in the Liturgy's Poetic Texts

The prayers and sign-actions of the liturgy make perceptible the
fullness of the effects attributed to the Spirit: creation and enabling of
life, bestowal of freedom and peace, the gifts of unity and community
(in the church), strengthening for witness in proclamation and life,
making possible both prayer and liturgy, and bestowal of a sharing
in eschatological salvation.

Through the centuries it is especially poetic texts used in a wide
variety of forms of church music that have most clearly expressed
what both individual Christians and the church as a whole associate
with the working of the Spirit of God. Thus there are a great many
hymns that implore the coming of the Spirit. One outstanding example is the sequence *Veni, sancte Spiritus* by Stephen Langton of
Canterbury (1150/55–1228):

Veni, Sancte Spiritus

Veni, Sancte Spiritus	Come, Holy Spirit,
Et emitte caelitus	from heaven shine forth
Lucis tuae radium.	with your glorious light.
Veni, pater pauperum,	Come, Father of the poor,

Veni, dator munerum,	come, generous Spirit,
Veni, lumen cordium.	come, light of our hearts.
Consolator optime,	You are our best comforter,
Dulcis hospes animae,	Peace of the soul,
Dulce refrigerium.	in the heat you shade us.
In labore requies,	In our labor you refresh us,
In aestu temperies,	in the noonday heat you cool us,
In fletu solatium.	and in trouble you are our strength.
O lux beatissima,	Most kindly warming light!
Reple cordis intima	Enter the inmost depths of our hearts,
Tuorum fidelium.	for we are faithful to you.
Sine tuo numine,	Without your presence
Nihil est in homine,	we have nothing worthy,
Nihil est innoxium.	nothing pure.
Lava quod est sordidum,	Wash what is filthy,
Riga quod est aridum,	moisten what is arid,
Sana quod est saucium.	heal what is wounded.
Flecte quod est rigidum,	Bend the rigid
Fove quod est frigidum,	warm the chill,
Rege quod est devium.	straighten the bent.
Da tuis fidelibus,	On all who receive you in faith,
In te confidentibus,	who trust in you,
Sacrum septenarium.	bestow the sevenfold gift of grace.
Da virtutis meritum,	Grant that they may grow in you
Da salutis exitum,	and persevere to the end.
Da perenne gaudium.	Give them lasting joy!

Literary analysis

The sequence is artistically composed. Every Latin verse consists of seven syllables, a reference to the sevenfold gift of the Holy Spirit. Every third verse ends with –ium. The sequence has a consistent literary structure and lyrical beauty. This is evident, among other things, in that the word spiritus is played on repeatedly throughout the lyric. The quality of the composition shows that we are at a central point in the liturgical event.

Content analysis

In its content as well, the text follows a clear plan. First it speaks of the Pentecost event. The petition for "your glorious light" alludes both to the tongues of fire at Pentecost and to the "light of our hearts." Strophes 3 and 4, echoing John 14–16, paint what "best comforter/counselor" means. It is the strength of the sequence that it is able to integrate the working of the Spirit with everyday human life: the Spirit of God gives rest in work, cooling in the heat, consolation to those who weep. The liturgy's pneumatology most certainly has a human *Sitz im Leben*; it is situated within human life.

The next two strophes lyricize how the Spirit works in human beings. The light motif from the first two strophes reappears, underscoring that human persons are entirely dependent on the Spirit's guidance or will (*numen*). In *nihil* (nothing) we can read an allusion to creation theology. There is an echo of creation from nothing as well as of the emptiness in the human as a consequence of primal sin. Strophes 7 and 8 again run through the things effected for us by the Spirit of God: *lava, riga, sana, flecte, fove, rege*. This is a very different vocabulary from that of a dogmatic discourse. The liturgy expresses in images the works that are implored of the Holy Spirit. The final two strophes turn our attention again to the *communio fidelium*, who are the singers of the hymn. With Isaiah 11:2-3 they pray for the sevenfold gifts of the Spirit; the Isaiah text says of the "Spirit of the Lord" that it is "the spirit of wisdom and understanding, the spirit of counsel and might, the spirit of knowledge and the fear of the Lord." God's presence in the Holy Spirit is the life principle of the Christian as it is of the church and its liturgy. The sequence expresses this with liturgical tools, thus in its own way enriching theological reflection on the Holy Spirit. As a testimony to the history of devotion, the sequence shows above all that we are not dealing with a marginal theme in liturgy and Christian existence but with what is central.

Over and over in the history of hymnody we find examples of how the subject of the Holy Spirit and the Pentecost event are approached with naturalism and sensual joy. This is very evident in Paul Gerhardt's "Pentecost Song" (1653):

Paul Gerhardt, "Pentecost Song"

O enter, Lord, Thy temple,
Be Thou my spirit's Guest,
Who gavest me, the earth-born,
A second birth more blest.
Thou in the Godhead, Lord,
Though here to dwell Thou deignest,
For ever equal reignest,
Art equally adored.
Thou, Holy Spirit, teachest
The soul to pray aright;
Thy songs have sweetest music,
Thy prayers have wondrous might.
Unheard they cannot fall,
They pierce the highest heaven
Till He His help hath given
Who surely helpeth all.
Thy gift is joy, O Spirit,
Thou wouldst not have us pine;
In darkest hours Thy comfort
Doth ever brightly shine.
And, O how oft Thy voice
Hath shed its sweetness o'er me,
And opened heav'n before me
And bid my heart rejoice![78]

Effects of poetic language

Poetic language, in comparison to other liturgical texts such as collects, achieves a higher level of emotion. It therefore comes closer to the heart and offers space and latitude for varied interpretations and receptions. As does Umberto Eco in his *The Open Work*, we may say that the effect of such poetic texts in the liturgy is to "encourage

[78] English version by Catherine Winkworth, available at http://www.hymnary .org/text/o_enter_lord_thy_temple.

'acts of conscious freedom' on the part of the performer and place him at the focal point of a network of limitless interrelations."[79]

Spirit metaphors in new language

In contrast to the reserve of Western theology, the metaphors, sound patterns, etc., in pneumatology, especially in hymns to the Spirit, succeed in describing the work of the Spirit in a highly personal way. The same is true even today, as shown by a hymn published in 1986 by Marijke Koijck-deBruijn, "De Geest van God waait als een wind." She uses traditional metaphors in a new form of language and brings home the dynamic of the Spirit in a vital way.

> The Spirit of God moves like the wind,
> It comes on peaceful wings.
> Like breath that gives the creature life
> It wakes unrest within us
> That often dares to be a storm
> Deriding force and evil.
> It cools like breezes fresh.
>
> And Spirit's like a fire, too
> Its flaming arms' outburst
> Stifles all that serves the wrong
> And still with mercy glows.
> It is the spark of hope that winks,
> A light that waits and beckons,
> A gleam in eyes and hearts.
>
> God's Spirit acts in silent hours,
> Impels with tender powers,
> Our wisest mother, guiding us,
> The source of all good strength.
> She gives us courage forth to go,

[79] Umberto Eco, *The Open Work* (Cambridge, MA: Harvard University Press, 1989), 4.

Bestows new understanding,
And spreads her cloak to shelter.[80]

The Spirit, described in feminine metaphors, works in the singing community ("guiding us," "she gives us courage") and protects
it ("spreads her cloak to shelter"). It sings of the Spirit's lifegiving
power and the encouragement it offers people ("impels with tender
powers"), as well as its action ("gives us courage forth to go"). The
metaphors open up the reality of the Spirit of God.

Feminine depictions of the Spirit

Feminine portrayals of the Spirit receive very little appreciation in
the various Christian liturgies. In this hymn they echo in the image of
the mother, inspired by feminine images of God in the Old Testament
(the Spirit as *ruach* [fem.]), in apocryphal texts, and certain features
of various languages (Spirit/wind as a feminine noun in Semitic
languages). Thus sources from the early Syrian and Armenian liturgy describe the Holy Spirit as mother; Armenian baptismal hymns
even call her the birthing mother. There is growing interest in these
poetic-theological phenomena in early Christian liturgy as we seek
a more expansive image of God that corresponds to the multifaceted
biblical image (see Deut 32:11, 18; Isa 42:14; Luke 13:24).[81]

[80] Translation by Linda M. Maloney. From the German in Cornelia Müller,
"Der Gottesgeist weht wie ein Wind," in *Kirchenlied im Kirchenjahr. Fünfzig neue
und alte Lieder zu den christlichen Festen*, ed. Ansgar Franz, Mainzer hymnologische
Studien 8 (Tübingen and Basel: Francke, 2002), 517–23.

[81] Gabriele Winkler, "Überlegungen zum Gottesgeist als mütterlichem Prinzip
und zur Bedeutung der Androgynie in einigen frühchristlichen Quellen," in
*Liturgie und Frauenfrage. Ein Beitrag zur Frauenforschung aus liturgiewissenschaftli-
cher Sicht*, ed. Teresa Berger and Albert Gerhards, Pietas Liturgica 7 (St. Ottilien:
EOS Verlag, 1990), 7–29.

4.5 Liturgy and the Economy of Salvation

4.5.1 Temporal Modes of Liturgy and Participation in the Divine Economy of Salvation

Significance of temporal modes

If, in preparation for a liturgical celebration, one investigates the time-focus of what is being celebrated, one encounters a melding of various temporal modes whereby something fundamental to the liturgy—participation in the divine economy of salvation—is indicated and made real. This can be seen in the speech- and sign-actions but also, for example, in the spaces within which the celebration takes place as well as in the iconography of the liturgical locations and other instances of the plastic arts. In the performative actions of the liturgy the present time of the celebrating community (today), the past (salvation history), and the fulfillment of salvation (the future) coalesce. But in the liturgy these temporal modi are not a series of chronological sections; they are the expression of human-temporal existence in face of the eternity of God. In the temporal modi of the liturgy God allows the celebrating community to participate in the divine fullness of being. This sharing is a pneumatic event that is carried out in the symbolic action of liturgy.

First example: the collect for January 6

The collect for the great feast of the Epiphany of the Lord (January 6) can make this clear. It reads:

> O God, who on this day revealed your Only Begotten Son to the nations by the guidance of a star, grant in your mercy, that we, who know you already by faith, may be brought to behold the beauty of your sublime glory. Through our Lord Jesus Christ, your Son, who lives and reigns with you in the unity of the Holy Spirit, one God, for ever and ever.[82]

Here we can distinguish three levels: the Magi, as the gospel pericope, Matthew 2:1-12, proclaims, followed the star: Christ is revealed to the

---

[82] *The Roman Missal* (see n. 8 above), 185.

nations. This is first recalled as an event in the past, but—and here something specific to the liturgy's temporal character appears—it is at the same time about the present: the revelation happens "on this day." The community gathered for liturgy is drawn into God's revealing work and participates in it, as the biblical text about the Magi announces. The community interprets what happens today not only in terms of the past; it sees itself as contemporary with the revelatory event. The collect approaches the limits of what can be uttered in speech: "on this day you revealed . . . by the guidance of a star." The fact that *hodierna dies* does not refer to a date in the historical calendar is made even more clear later in the Mass by the Preface, with the words: "for today you have revealed the mystery of our salvation in Christ as a light for the nations."[83] What is worth noting here is the attitude of the faithful, who are not merely onlookers at this event but participants because, like the Magi, they too have come to knowledge in faith. This is also to name the hermeneutical perspective for perceiving the melding of times in the liturgy: faith.

Finally, a wider temporal dimension is in view when the collect speaks of the unobstructed vision of divine glory. Faith already gives knowledge of God, but God's glory remains obscured. There is an obvious tension: we have knowledge, but only in preliminary form. Unveiled seeing remains—we may add—a part of eschatological fulfillment. Again the faithful gain a share in this future salvation in the liturgical symbolic event: "we . . . know you already by faith, may [we] be brought to behold the beauty of your sublime glory."

The three temporal modes come together in God's eternity, as is clear in the form of address included in the German version of the collect: "God, ruler of all." The temporal modes are encompassed by God's reality. Their intercalation originates in God. The liturgy represents that.

The degree to which these modi are interwoven in the liturgy is illustrated for example in the Easter hymn "At the Lamb's high feast we sing." The text, in its Latin version, *Ad cenam agni providi*, comes from the fifth/sixth century and has been recited as part of the Liturgy of the Hours since the early Middle Ages. It is located in

---

[83] Ibid., 544.

the Vespers of Easter and the Sundays of the Easter season. The text has been revised over the centuries; the hymn celebrates the Christ-event as a story of liberation and interprets it in terms of both Old and New Testaments.

Second Example: "At the Lamb's High Feast We Sing"

At the Lamb's high feast we sing
praise to our victorious King,
who has washed us in the tide
flowing from his wounded side;
Praise the Lord, whose love divine
gives his sacred blood for wine,
gives his body for the feast,
Christ the victim, Christ the priest.

Where the Paschal blood is poured,
death's dark angel sheathes the sword;
Israel's hosts in triumph go
through the waves that drown the foe.
Christ the Lamb whose blood was shed,
Paschal victim, Paschal bread;
let us with a fervent love
taste the manna from above!

Mighty victim from on high,
pow'rs of hell now vanquished lie;
sin is conquered in the fight:
you have brought us life and light;
your resplendent banners wave,
you have risen from the grave;
Christ has opened Paradise,
and in him we all shall rise.

Easter triumph, Easter joy,
sin alone can this destroy;
souls from sin and death set free
glory in their liberty.
Hymns of glory, hymns of praise

Father, unto you we raise;
Risen Lord, for joy we sing:
let our hymns through heaven ring.[84]

The combining of temporal levels is quite obvious here. We sing here and now "at the Lamb's high feast," praise the "victorious King," and at the same time sing of him "who has washed us in the tide / flowing from his wounded side." Past, present, and future are expressed. The hymn includes the various temporal modes, and the people who sing it participate in this coalescing of times in the subsequent verses.

The combination of temporal modes is as subtle in individual verses. For example, in the second verse the Old and New Testament Passovers are brought together as one in recollected salvation history. At the same time, a sharing in this history is opened for participants in the present: "Let us with a fervent love / taste the manna from above." The human being is drawn into God's saving history with humanity and becomes a "contemporary" of that history.[85]

The succeeding verses speak of the significance of participation in the salvation that is coming to be: this is an event that bestows freedom and is celebrated especially in scenes from Exodus as an explicit history of liberation, and in scenes from the death and resurrection of Christ as an event that touches all human existence. Christ appears as the victor, while the powers associated with the suppression of life and freedom are destroyed ("Pow'rs of hell now vanquished lie; / sin is conquered in the fight"). Participation in the modes of liturgical time promises the people a sharing in the salvation-historical event and at the same time points them to a new role because they are now among "the first liberated creatures."[86]

[84] Translation by Robert Campbell (1814–1868); alt. *Liturgy of the Hours* II (see n. 74 above), 540–41.

[85] See Angelus A. Häussling, "Liturgy: Memorial of the Past and Liberation in the Present," in *The Meaning of the Liturgy*, ed. idem (Collegeville, MN: Liturgical Press, 1994), 107–18.

[86] Jürgen Moltmann, "The First Liberated Men in Creation" (orig.: "Die ersten Freigelassenen"), trans. Reinhard Ulrich, in idem, et al., *Theology of Play* (London: SCM, 1973), 26–90. (Translator's note: "Die ersten Freigelassenen" is gender neutral; "men" is not an appropriate English rendering in the twenty-first century, nor would Moltmann approve!)

What does this collapsing of the ages signify?

By making salvation history present today, the liturgy proposes to change the hopes and perspectives of the faithful in light of divine activity. New perspectives on life as well as new options for action are opened as the faithful are bound up in the past history of salvation as well as its future. The associated tension between "already" and "not yet" is expressed in a great many texts and actions. This is indispensable to the liturgy because the tension here expressed is appropriate to the faith-event as well as the realities of this life.

Light symbolism

The liturgy's temporal performance is realized not only in words but also in signs and symbolic actions. Thus the *Lucernarium*, the light ceremony at Vespers, like that of the Easter Vigil, symbolizes Christ as the one present in the liturgical assembly, calls him to mind in the sign of light as the one who has brought light (see the hymn *Phos hilaron*, cited in chap. 3.2.4), and glorifies him as the one who will return in the eschaton. This is expressed compactly in the symbol of light and the various ways in which it is incorporated in the liturgy: bearing the paschal candle into the church as a symbol of Christ in the darkness of the space; the passing of the light to the faithful; the placing of the candle in a prominent place within the church. Particularly with regard to the symbol of light we should note that at crucial stages in the biography of Christians' faith and the corresponding rituals (initiation, with baptism and first communion: baptismal candle and first communion candle; marriage: wedding candle; death: candle for the dying) light is repeatedly a sign of participation in the economy of salvation.

4.5.2 The Dimension of Memory in the Liturgy

God's effective power in history becomes humanly present in the liturgy and is expressed in the dimension of memory.

Communicative and cultural memory

In modern theories of memory[87] a distinction is drawn between communicative and cultural memory. Communicative memory has its place in everyday discourse. Memories related to the recent past are its content, which is communicated through present recollection, experience, and hearsay.[88] Cultural memory, on the other hand, secures the memory of the original event that is the source of the particular community's existence. It refers to the absolute past and the primal history handed on in myth. Its media include word, image, dance, symbolic coding, and staging. History in the mode of cultural memory possesses normative and formative power.[89] What is in play here is an essential dimension of human life insofar as limitation to the here and now is called into question and the "simultaneity" of the everyday is confronted with non-simultaneity in time.[90] To that extent remembering serves to liberate and is, to quote Herbert Marcuse, "air blowing from another planet."[91]

Liturgy as a memory-event in symbolic form

Against this background, liturgy can be described as a memory-event and -locus described in symbolic form in which the incorporation of the celebrating community into God's historical acts of salvation is given expression.[92] Consideration of mnemotechniques can illuminate this aspect of the liturgy, but it leaves the excess of theological meaning unexplained. In the liturgy people experience

---

[87] See Maurice Halbwachs, *On Collective Memory*, trans. Lewis A. Coser (Chicago: University of Chicago Press, 1992); Jan Assmann, *Cultural Memory and Early Civilization: Writing, Remembrance, and Political Imagination* (Cambridge: Cambridge University Press, 2011).

[88] Assmann, *Cultural Memory*, 35.

[89] Ibid., 38.

[90] This is its "contrapresent" function; see ibid., 62.

[91] As quoted in ibid., 69.

[92] Diana Güntner, *Das Gedenken des Erhöhten im Neuen Testament. Zur ekklesialen Bedeutung des Gedenkens am Modell des Psalms 110*, Benediktbeurer Studien 6 (Munich: Don Bosco, 1998); Gunda Brüske, "Die Liturgie als Ort des kulturellen Gedächtnisses. Anregungen für ein Gespräch zwischen Kulturwissenschaften und Liturgiewissenschaft," *Liturgisches Jahrbuch* 51 (2001): 151–71.

themselves as participants in salvific events of the past in a personal-dynamic way, that is, in a form that affects them anew in their person-hood. God himself acts in Christ. The things that are remembered, as well as the remembering, issue in God. Liturgical anamnesis as a medium of remembering in liturgy is a pneumatic act and must not be understood as a human means of controlling God, in the sense of magic. The connection between anamnesis and epiclesis makes it clear that God acts personally, through the working of the Spirit, in the minds and memories of those celebrating. Because of human limitation to space and time, the ritually imitative act must ultimately be made possible by God. God is the center of this event. Creation, the covenant with Israel, incarnation, Christ's Passover—God is self-revealed to human beings as Creator and Redeemer and so makes human thought and memory possible. A making-present can arise out of God's personal and dynamic relationship to human beings. Accordingly, in the liturgical celebration the community always exists in a different time dimension: this present, but another as well.

Anamnesis

In the anamnesis the community brings to mind God's history with humanity—in the hope that God will also act in the present time for the sake of human salvation. Hence the anamnesis is implicitly a petition to God to be self-revealed as the God of salvation history in the present time also. Anamnesis does not involve an anachronistic retroversion to a different historical situation and its events. It is about remembering salvation history in the hope of participating in the same divine reality today.

Forms of memory involving the senses

This anamnesis happens in the liturgy by use of a multitude of forms of remembering in which the senses participate.[93] In the same way, the dimension of memory is expressed in the various forms of

[93] See, for example, Dietmar Thönnes, "Das textile Gedächtnis der Kirche. Mnemotechniken und anamnetische Aspekte liturgischer Kleidung," *Liturgisches Jahrbuch* 47 (1997): 78–88, on the anamnetic function of liturgical vestments.

epiclesis, petition, and intercession. All these presuppose a memory of God's salvation history.

Lament and memory

We can even see lament as a dimension of memory. In Catholic liturgy it is expressed almost exclusively in the words of biblical texts, especially the lament psalms. Lament, as an expression of faith in God, points to God's mighty deeds in the past and confronts them with the miserable present. It grows out of the contradiction between what is remembered and what is happening now.[94]

4.5.3 The Dimension of Expectation in the Liturgy

Today's liturgy extends its reach not only into the past but also into the future. It participates in the eschatological salvation that has announced itself in Christ and anticipates its final fulfillment. In symbolic acts the liturgy gives a holistic share in the salvation already in progress, but at the same time it hopes for the final fulfillment of God's reign and so stands under an eschatological reservation. This dimension of expectation is indispensable to liturgy.[95]

Present eschatology

Liturgy is shaped by present eschatology. It stands under the influence of what is still hoped for, that is, what awaits its fulfillment. It has an anticipatory character. Symbols, texts, and actions express the truth that, despite its preliminary character in the words and signs of the liturgy, ultimate salvation has been promised.[96] Liturgy

[94] For lament see Gotthard Fuchs, ed., *Angesichts des Leids an Gott glauben? Zur Theologie der Klage* (Frankfurt: J. Knecht, 1996); Georg Steins, ed., *Schweigen wäre gotteslästerlich. Die heilende Kraft der Klage* (Würzburg: Echter Verlag, 2000).

[95] For the significance of memory and expectation see Richard Schaeffler, "Kultisches Handeln. Die Frage nach Proben seiner Bewährung und nach Kriterien seiner Legitimation," in idem and Peter Hünermann, *Ankunft Gottes und Handeln des Menschen. Thesen über Kult und Sakrament*, Quaestiones disputatae 77 (Freiburg: Herder, 1977), 9–50.

[96] Emil Joseph Lengeling, "Von der Erwartung des Kommenden," in *Gott feiern* (1980), 193–238.

joins present and future before God. It therefore exists in a theologically productive tension with regard to both the kerygma and its forms of expression in which salvation history is celebrated under the conditions of the present.

Examples

Expectation of the promised future is also expressed in the epiclesis, that is, in the invocation of the name of God and the gift of the Spirit. So the epiclesis of the consecratory prayer over the baptismal water asks that those who are buried with Christ in baptism may rise with him to everlasting life. Baptism gives a share in the promised salvation.

The proleptic dimension of the liturgy is also expressed in petitions and intercessions. Thus one of the solemn blessings at the end of the Mass reads, "And may you, who have already risen with Christ in Baptism through faith, by living in a right manner on this earth, be united with him in the homeland of heaven."[97] This blessing brings together the present and the eschatological fulfillment.

Even lament articulates future hope before God. It gives vehement expression to present experiences of suffering and deprivation and expresses the hope that God, who has been shown throughout history to hold human beings beloved, may also continue to work for their salvation. Lament above all testifies to human hopes and expectations in relationship with God.

4.6 Community Liturgy and Heavenly Liturgy

4.6.1 Heavenly Liturgy as Glorifying God

Isaiah 6:1-4

Divine praise is not restricted to the actions of the earthly liturgy and the gathered community. Rather, biblical and church traditions speak of a heavenly liturgy: praise of God offered by the angels, according to Isaiah 6:1-4. There the prophet speaks in metaphorical language of this worship performed in the presence of God.

---

[97] *The Roman Missal* (see n. 8 above), 677.

This heavenly liturgy is about praising God. The actors are the angels; according to Revelation 4–5 these are the heavenly beings whose worship sounds forth "day and night" (Rev 4:8), that is, unceasingly. Revelation 19:1-2 also tells us that "hallelujah" is sung before God in the heavenly liturgy: "Hallelujah! Salvation and glory and power to our God, for his judgments are true and just."

Revelation 5:1-6

According to Revelation 5:1-2, the Lamb stands "between the throne and the four living creatures and among the elders" (Rev 5:6) as mediator before the divine throne, whose transcendence is maintained. The Lamb is then worshiped and a "new song" is sung.

Obviously these are very central passages for the self-concept of the liturgy of Christian communities. How else could we explain the fact that, for example, the song of the angels in Isaiah 6 and Revelation 4:8, the *Sanctus*, is part of every Mass? When the congregation sings it, they join the heavenly chorus of praise. Earthly and heavenly liturgy harmonize, as is proclaimed at the end of the Preface to the Eucharistic Prayer: "and so, with the Angels and all the Saints we declare your glory, as with one voice we acclaim . . ."[98]

4.6.2 The Earthly Liturgy's Participation in the Eschatological Heavenly Liturgy

Liturgy as a cosmic whole

The congregation gathered around Christ is already participating in the promised eschatological liturgy in which history finds its fulfillment.[99] "The singing of the angels would never be permitted to disappear from the Church's worship, for that is what first gives the

---

[98] Ibid., 645.

[99] Peter Brunner, "Zur Lehre vom Gottesdienst der im Namen Jesu versammelten Gemeinde," in *Geschichte und Lehre des evangelischen Gottesdienstes*, ed. Karl Fredinand Müller and Walter Blankenburg, Leiturgia 1 (Kassel: Stauda, 1954), 83–364, at 168–80; Michael Kunzler, *Die Liturgie der Kirche*, AMATECA 10 (Paderborn: Bonifatius, 1995), 43–49.

Church's praise the depth and transcendence that are called for by the character of the Christian revelation."[100] The church's worship must be transcended by a higher order of being, the angels; it is only a supplement to that worship. "That tells us that in the liturgy, humanity is seen only in a total cosmic context, and that humanity's praising is concerned specifically with this cosmic totality."[101]

A great many other examples show this supplementary character: prayers and hymnody (e.g., the *Gloria*), signs and actions, but also, for instance, the shaping of the church space (paintings in the apse and on the arch over the altar, statues of angels and saints near the altar, etc.; outstanding examples are Hagia Sophia in Istanbul, St. Apollinare in Ravenna, or St. Paul Outside the Walls in Rome).

Biblical point of contact: the letter to the Hebrews

The letter to the Hebrews reveals the fundamental theological conviction that the celebration of liturgy brings together heaven and earth, because there is "[one] great high priest . . . Jesus, the Son of God" (Heb 4:14). Through the "blood of Jesus," that is, the saving work of Jesus Christ, the congregation enters into God's sanctuary, treading "the new and living way that he opened for us through the curtain (that is, through his flesh)" (Heb 10:19-20).

Hebrews 12:22-24, which is part of a New Testament reading that may be chosen for, among other occasions, the dedication of a church, speaks of approaching Mount Zion as the heavenly Jerusalem, "the city of the living God," for the festal gathering of "innumerable angels" and the firstborn, and "Jesus, the mediator of a new covenant."

Hebrews' horizon of experience

The thoroughly christological form of the Mass makes it possible to relate the liturgy of the heavenly Jerusalem to the earthly lit-

---

[100] Erik Peterson, *Das Buch von den Engeln. Stellung und Bedeutung der heiligen Engel im Kultus* (Leipzig: J. Hegner, 1935), 53–54. English: "The Angels and the Liturgy: Their Place and Meaning in the Liturgy," in *Theological Tractates*, ed. and trans. Michael J. Hollerich (Stanford: Stanford University Press, 2011), 106–42, at 122 .

[101] Ibid., 122.

urgy and to clarify the truth that the congregation participates in the heavenly liturgy through its confession of the Crucified and Risen One. For a liturgical theology today, the horizon of experience that underlies Hebrews is worth noting: the withdrawal of members of the community from worship (Heb 10:25) is interpreted as a crisis of faith. Christians see themselves being forced to the borders of society (Heb 10:32-36), and their own liturgical celebration is no longer regarded as the place where salvation is experienced and mediated (Heb 13:7-17). The letter to the Hebrews addresses this situation, places worship within its larger soteriological and eschatological context, and thus is able to weigh and proclaim its significance for Christian life: it is an event that takes place between God and the human. The interpretation of the community's liturgy in relation to the heavenly liturgy is intended to give it a new persuasive power and vitality. Above all it is evident that worship is not something marginal for Christians but a fundamental faith event.[102]

What the Liturgy Constitution says

The Constitution on the Liturgy also deals with this interaction, interpreting the earthly liturgy as an anticipatory participation, a foretaste of the heavenly liturgy. It sees the Christian community as a pilgrim on the way to "where Christ is sitting at the right hand of God, minister of the sanctuary and of the true tabernacle" (SC 8). Thus there is no assertion of an identity between the two liturgies; rather, it is a question of the earthly worship participating in (not imitating!) the heavenly liturgy. This includes the fact that the liturgy already joins in the heavenly song of praise: "With all the hosts of heaven we sing a hymn of glory to the Lord; venerating the memory of the saints, we hope to share their company; we eagerly await the Saviour, Our Lord Jesus Christ, until he our life shall appear and we too will appear with him in glory" (SC 8).

[102] Claus-Peter März, "Das 'Wort vom Kult' und der 'Kult des Wortes'" (see n. 12 above).

4.6.3 Earthly Liturgy in Eschatological Tension

The difference between heavenly and earthly liturgy must not be obscured

Certainly we cannot overlook the difficulties that come with such statements and formulations. SC 9 points out that faith and conversion must precede the celebration of liturgy and makes clear the necessity of being led to faith.[103] Faith is the foundation from which to seek and find an understanding of what "heavenly liturgy" means. In spite of all the exaggerations that are possible here, the salvation-historical thread that links earthly to heavenly liturgy must be preserved in order to express the faith event of worship and its dignity.

In this connection SC 8 speaks of hope that we may "share the company" of the saints, and also for the return of the Savior, Jesus Christ, thus emphasizing the eschatological tension in the liturgy. Eliminating that would mean introducing a triumphalism into the liturgy that is unjustifiable, either anthropologically or theologically. A liturgy that did not maintain the distinction between earthly and heavenly worship would not take seriously the reality of human life with all its limitations and experiences of suffering, doubt, and seeking, nor could those be meaningfully articulated in the liturgy. At the same time the expectation of Christ's return and thus all theological eschatology would be carried *ad absurdum*. Liturgy, as a symbolic event, represents the heavenly liturgy on the one hand but without on the other hand needing to erase the everyday human reality and its experiences.[104]

At the same time a liturgy that includes people and their lives here and now as constitutive of the celebratory event must make it clear that in its fundamental reality the liturgy is not a human production but an entry into a divine reality. This has consequences for the evaluation of the dignity and value of both the liturgy and the human person.

---

[103] Angelus A. Häussling, "Liturgiereform und Liturgiefähigkeit," *Archiv für Liturgiewissenschaft* 38/39 (1996/1997): 1–24, at 5.

[104] Andreas Odenthal, *Liturgie als Ritual. Theologische und psychoanalytische Überlegungen zu einer praktisch-theologischen Theorie des Gottesdienstes als Symbolgeschehen*, Praktische Theologie heute 60 (Stuttgart: Kohlhammer, 2002), 47–77.

Finally, a liturgy that joins in the hymn of the heavenly liturgy that in turn reflects God's glory involves a theological-aesthetic challenge to strive for forms appropriate to the solemn event.

4.7 The Person in the Liturgy

Liturgy has been described as an event of encounter between God and the human, unfolding through Christ in the Holy Spirit and carried out in a human assembly. Thus the human person is a constitutive part of the liturgy; her or his action, as response to God's turning toward us, is indispensable for worship. Liturgy presupposes that when God turns to humans (making them holy) they will accept and respond (glorification). Both *katabasis* and *anabasis* touch the human self. Therefore the role of human persons in the liturgy and its image of humanity are an object of liturgical theology.[105]

4.7.1 Sanctification of the Human Person in the Liturgy

Image of the human in the liturgy

The claims of Christian liturgy encompass and saturate human life and, to put it in simple terms, place it under divine blessing. This is true from birth to death, for essential decisions in life and faith, for days, weeks, and years. The liturgical symbolic event celebrates that human beings, through the sanctification that comes to them from God, are placed in the presence of God. Consequently the liturgy shows that human beings may rely on God's nearness in the widest variety of life situations. It regards them as destined to live their new creation in Christ. That shapes the liturgy's image of the

---

[105] Crispino Valenziano, "Liturgy and Anthropology: The Meaning of the Question and the Method for Answering It," in *Handbook for Liturgical Studies*, vol. 2: *Fundamental Liturgy*, ed. Ansgar J. Chupungco (Collegeville, MN: Liturgical Press, 1998), 189–225; Werner Hahne, *De arte celebrandi; oder Von der Kunst, Gottesdienst zu feiern: Entwurf einer Fundamentalliturgik* (Freiburg: Herder, 1991); Karl-Heinrich Bieritz, "Anthropologische Grundlegung," in *Handbuch der Liturgik. Liturgiewissenschaft in Theologie und Praxis der Kirche*, ed. Hans-Christoph Schmidt-Lauber, Michael Meyer-Blanck, and Karl-Heinrich Bieritz, 3rd. rev. and exp. ed. (Göttingen: Vandenhoeck & Ruprecht, 2003), 95–128.

human. According to the liturgy's statement, human beings achieve fulfillment when they allow themselves to be drawn into Christ's paschal mystery and thus into the mystery of God.

We can see this in the celebrations of initiation and of reconciliation ("O God, author of true freedom, whose will it is to shape all men and women into a single people released from slavery, grant to your Church, we pray, that, as she receives new growth in freedom, she may appear more clearly to the world as the universal sacrament of salvation, manifesting and making present the mystery of your love for all"[106]), and of marriage as well, when the communion of husband and wife is seen as an image of the covenant renewed in Christ, and also in the burial liturgy (death as transition to the ultimate life with Christ), etc. The liturgy expresses the goal and ultimate meaning of the human being and of human life. Through Christ, God reveals to humans the truth of their lives. In the liturgy, in its texts and symbols, that is expressed and celebrated. This takes place above all in the anamnesis and the prolepsis, statements of the origin and goal of human life. The saving work proclaimed to them in the liturgy therefore touches persons at the core of their existence.

Relationship between God and the human in the liturgy

The actions of the liturgy offer human persons an orientation and convey a sense of meaning. Therefore Sacred Scripture, the proclamation of God's history with humanity, is given a special place in worship. That is to say, it is precisely through the relationship between God and the human that is celebrated and takes place in liturgy that human life is revealed to be a being-in-the-presence-of-God. The defects as well as the true purpose of human life, humans in their sins as well as in their hopes for salvation, the human being living in oppression and unfreedom but also called to freedom—all these are made visible. This means also that human beings are touched in their whole personhood by the event of liturgy; they are made to cooperate in worship as it happens; to that extent the reality of the individual is of explicit and implicit significance in worship.[107]

---

[106] *The Roman Missal* (see n. 8 above), 1270.

[107] Albert Gerhards, "Gottesdienst und Menschwerdung. Vom Subjekt liturgischer Feier," in *Markierungen. Theologie in den Zeichen der Zeit*, ed. Mariano

This is observable, for example, in baptism, in which the individual is called by name and that name is pronounced in the act of baptizing; it is to this person that baptismal grace is given. God's care and concern are for the concrete person. Renewal of baptismal vows or the *Credo* spoken in the first-person singular attest something similar, as do the individual sacraments: in each case these are liturgical actions in which the personal "I" and her or his life is participant. If liturgy is understood as an event of encounter, the human "I" that communicates with God is always a part of that event. Human personhood does not end in the presence of liturgy; rather, the celebrations of baptism or Eucharist, the Liturgy of the Hours or a Benediction make real and concrete the participation of the individual in the relationship with God that is being celebrated. Liturgy bestows identity.

This has further consequences for the celebratory shape of liturgy. It takes verbal and nonverbal forms in which both individuals and the community are able to experience God's caring attention and respond to it. The very anthropology of liturgy calls attention to the necessity of liturgical forms of communication; these make possible the dialogical event between God and the human.

Worship services should be characterized by openness to human lives. Liturgy offers a variety of opportunities for *participatio actuosa*: in common prayer the faithful articulate their personal concerns before God within the community liturgy. Silence, as a space for personal prayer that—as in the collects (see chap. 5.2.5.1)—issues in community prayer, makes it clear that the individual, as a person, stands before God as part of a community. Thus the liturgy can integrate individual prayer into the community prayer event. At the same time, however, it contains publicly articulated and more community-centered prayer, for example, in the Prayers of the People.

Liturgy is nourished by the community of individuals

Liturgy is a community event, as is already clear from its ecclesiological significance, but at the same time it always touches the

Delgado and Andreas Lob-Hüdepohl, Schriften der Diözesanakademie Berlin 11 (Berlin: Morus, 1995), 275–92.

individual as a part of that community. The ceremony itself must take that into account. Both individualistic and "closed corporation" ideas about liturgy must be opposed. The liturgy is nourished by the community of individuals. It should make it possible for them to put themselves into words, again and again, in relation to God. At the same time the human person develops as a social being in the liturgical community. Therefore liturgy can be called "a fabric of relationships"[108] both vertically and horizontally.

4.7.2 Alteration of Human Reality

Liturgy claims to make a significant contribution to the creation of human identity and the shaping of lives. Vatican II therefore said of the Eucharist that in its celebration the faithful "should be drawn day by day into ever more perfect union with God and each other, so that finally God may be all in all" (SC 48, following 1 Cor 15:28). Elsewhere it is said of the "effects of the sacraments and sacramentals" that their celebration "sanctifies almost every event" in the lives of the faithful "with the divine grace which flows from the paschal mystery" (see SC 61). Salvation history, recalled and celebrated in the liturgy, in whatever form, accordingly affects human lives. The liturgy itself emerges from a process in which human life is changed by the encounter with God, and union with God and fellow humans is intensified and solidified. This is especially clear in the initiation of adults, which extends over a fairly long period of growth in the life of faith.

Identification with the figures of salvation history

One medium of the liturgy in this regard is situative identification with the figures of salvation history.[109] In that the person celebrating liturgy identifies with persons in the history of salvation and enters into their roles whether through texts or sign-actions, she or he understands her or his life as lying within God's time. These persons thus mark themselves as those who hope to receive God's blessing. At the

[108] Ibid., 288.
[109] Angelus A. Häussling, "Liturgie: Gedächtnis eines Vergangenen" (see n. 14 above).

same time, the reality of their lives is also changed; it is now seen not as random but as qualified by God. The precondition for this identification of roles and the perception that in the liturgy one's own life is given meaning and identity by God is faith in God's working in time. Within this horizon of trust in God the liturgy celebrates that the human being lives out of an origin that is enduring and effective and that, above all, can always renew human life over and over again.

This perspective on liturgy can also be verified in terms of cultural anthropology, out of cultural memory. The perception of human reality is not restricted to the measure of the ordinary, the everyday; instead, what is remembered makes possible a new vision of reality.

Reorientation by God in the liturgy

This model of cultural memory is surpassed in liturgical theology because divine grace is seen as the basis for the process of remembering. What is offered to people with performative effect in the liturgy, that is, the promise of salvation, cannot be achieved by humans; it must be offered by God. Through the liturgy human life experiences a fundamental reorientation insofar as worship celebrates the destiny of the human to be a new creation. The congregation celebrating liturgy is then a community on the way to that goal.

Shaping of the world in which we live

If we can speak here of a qualification of human life in terms of God's salvation history, the liturgy also obligates people to shape their own lives as well as the life of society on the basis of what is celebrated, that is, in the meaning presented by the Gospel. A way of life appropriate to the liturgy is demanded. The liturgy invites people to repentance and thereby develops its effect.[110] Hence human reality is affected by the liturgy, on the one hand, insofar as human life is set

---

[110] Klemens Richter, "Liturgie und Seelsorge in der katholischen Kirche seit Beginn des 20. Jahrhunderts," in *Seelsorge und Diakonie in Berlin. Beiträge zum Verhältnis von Kirche und Grosstadt im 19. und beginnenden 20. Jahrhundert*, ed. Kaspar Elm and Hans-Dietrich Loock (Berlin and New York: de Gruyter, 1990), 585–608; idem, "Soziales Handeln und liturgisches Tun als der eine Gottesdienst des Lebens," *Gemeinsame Arbeitsstelle für gottesdienstliche Fragen*, no. 27 (1996): 15–30.

within a new horizon and participates in the reality proclaimed by the liturgy. On the other hand, individuals as well as the community are encouraged to live from the liturgy. The perspective the liturgy opens is that of human liberation. The human being responds to what is celebrated in the liturgy with a corresponding way of life.

Example: baptism

Every liturgical celebration announces the freedom that has been promised to humanity and is celebrated in the liturgy as already begun. In particular we should expect this from the various celebrations of Christian initiation that, as rituals of transition, celebrate what is promised to Christians: the "freedom only [God's] sons and daughters enjoy."[111] Individual baptismal celebrations are very differently structured and can signify liberation from the power of evil or from primal sin.[112] They also represent sharing in the resurrection,[113] the gift of eternal life,[114] and acceptance as children of God.[115] Hope for human liberation also implies hope for the overcoming of a way of being human that is marked by encounters with injustice, sin, and death, and the opening of a new living space associated with the attribute of being "children of God." But at the same time it makes possible a life in the already promised participation in the "freedom of the children of God."

The liturgy thus opens a horizon for human beings toward which they can shape their lives in the liturgy in different ways. Praise and thanksgiving for success in life, but also petition and lament for life situations in which we cannot yet perceive anything of the promised freedom: all these find their place here. In light of the promises, fragmented human life must be allowed to speak in the liturgy. This corresponds to the celebration of the paschal mystery, including the suffering, death, *and* resurrection and exaltation of Jesus Christ. None of those may be omitted, because otherwise the good news of Christ is truncated and does not do justice to the people who celebrate it.

[111] *Rite of Baptism for Children* (see n. 71 above), 29.
[112] Ibid., 28–29.
[113] Ibid., 35.
[114] Ibid., 45.
[115] Ibid., 44.

4.7.3 "One" in Christ: The Inclusive Image of Humanity

Equal worth despite difference

Galatians 3:28 offers a touchstone for the image of human beings in the liturgy, one that applies to all who have been baptized into Christ: "There is neither Jew nor Greek, there is neither slave nor free person, there is not male and female; for you are all one in Christ Jesus."[116] This verse is part of one suggested reading for celebrations of the reception of adults into the church and for the baptism of children. The celebration itself forbids any kind of exclusivity in the Christian liturgy. No one may be excluded from the celebration or disadvantaged in the liturgy because of gender or origin, social group, or anything else. At the same time, the image of humanity in the liturgy does not recognize any kind of abstract equality. It is evident that everyone may participate in the liturgy in her or his full humanity. Today's liturgy accordingly contains some clear statements: "It is truly right and just to give you thanks . . . for by the word of your Son's Gospel you have brought together one Church from every people, tongue, and nation."[117] Differences of race or culture do not result in exclusion from the church and its liturgy. So: "For though the human race is divided by dissension and discord, yet we know that by testing us you change our hearts to prepare them for reconciliation."[118] Here we find expressed the hope that differences among people may be overcome in God; the liturgy requires it. The theological grounds are compelling: that all people are made in the image of God; the Gospel of Christ that overcomes all boundaries between human beings; reconciliation with and before God.

Throughout its history the liturgy has been very ambivalent in its approach to this principle of a so-called inclusive image of humanity. The ritual instruction for the burial liturgy still has to point out that the service treats poor and rich alike and allows no respect for persons. Only very recently and quite reluctantly was access to

---

[116] Ibid., 136.

[117] *The Roman Missal* (see n. 8 above), Eucharistic Prayer for Use in Masses for Various Needs I: The Church on the Path of Unity, Preface, p. 775.

[118] Ibid., Eucharistic Prayer for Reconciliation II, p. 767.

Catholic liturgy opened to the non-European cultural traditions and forms of expression in churches of the so-called Third World. One familiar example is the Mass of Zaire, which brought about a symbiosis of Catholic eucharistic liturgy and regional cultural celebration in language, song, and symbol.[119] As for the image of the human in the liturgy since Vatican II, it is worth noting that different human cultures of celebration have been accepted as ways of expressing the faith. At the same time, even today there is ongoing strife over a liturgy in which women can be equal participants, one that breaks through narrowly androcentric prayer formulas and integrates expressions of feminine spirituality—despite a number of changes in this direction.[120]

Liturgical proclamation must make use of forms that include all people.

4.7.4 Human Physicality and the Liturgy

An appreciation of the anthropological side of the liturgy requires that we take seriously its engagement of the body and the senses.[121] Both the reception of what is proclaimed and celebrated in worship and the self-expression of the participants happens by way of the senses, that is, as an articulation of the human in its physicality. Humans, as body-spirit beings that communicate with their surroundings through their senses, are dependent on their physical bodies for thinking, feeling, and acting. This of course includes language, but the whole is essentially much more diverse and hence more complex. Human beings participate with all their senses in the event of faith celebrated in liturgy: hearing (the acoustic dimension: words, singing, music, etc.), seeing (the optic dimension: gestures, colors, vestments, vessels, etc.), feeling (the tactile dimension: laying-on of hands, anointing, etc.), smelling (the dimension of odor: incense,

---

[119] Der neue Messritus im Zaire. Ein Beispiel kontextueller Liturgie, ed. Ludwig Bertsch, Theologie der Dritten Welt 18 (Freiburg: Herder, 1993).

[120] Liturgie und Frauenfrage (1990); Teresa Berger, Gender Differences and the Making of a Liturgical History: Lifting a Veil on Liturgy's Past (Farnham, Surrey, and Burlington, VT: Ashgate, 2011).

[121] Emil Joseph Lengeling, "Wort, Bild und Symbol als Elemente der Liturgie," in idem, Liturgie: Dialog zwischen Gott und Mensch, ed. Klemens Richter (Altenberge: Telos, 1988), 91–108.

perfumed oils, etc.), and tasting (the gustatory dimension: bread, wine).[122] They express themselves through posture, gestures, attitude (as a more complex unity of postures and gestures), and sequences of movement.[123] Through their physicality they take part in the event of the liturgy, which surpasses the merely discursive and happens on the plane of what presents itself to all the senses (see chap. 5.2.6 below).

Liturgy is essentially oriented to presentative signs. These speak as a unified structure, communicate nonverbally, and call for corresponding forms of interaction involving the senses. The multiplicity of presentative signs, which are indispensable to worship if the worshipers are to adequately comprehend what is being celebrated, corresponds to the articulation of the human body.[124]

Embodiment of believing attitudes

Physicality is thus not only to be understood as instrumental, so that one acts through the body, but in a symbolic sense as well. Faith is carried out in human physicality so that the physical expression becomes a symbol of the faith-event. Thus human attitudes toward God in faith are embodied in standing, sitting, and kneeling. "The spiritual element [must] transpose itself into material terms because it is vital and essential that it should do so. Thus the body is the natural emblem of the soul, and a spontaneous physical movement will typify a spiritual event."[125] Physicality is thus a symbolizing self-expression.[126] If this important sphere is neglected, an essential

---

[122] This list is taken from Hermann Reifenberg, "Bemühungen um die Zeichen in der Liturgie. Ansatz der Liturgiekonstitution, Ergebnisse, Möglichkeiten," in *Lebt unser Gottesdienst? Die bleibende Aufgabe der Liturgiereform*, ed. Theodor Maas-Ewerd (Freiburg: Herder, 1988), 63–74.

[123] A. Ronald Sequeira, "Gottesdienst als menschliche Ausdruckshandlung," in Rupert Berger, et al., *Gestalt des Gottesdienstes. Sprachliche und nichtsprachliche Ausdrucksformen*, 2nd ed., Gottesdienst der Kirche 3 (Regensburg: Pustet, 1990), 7–39, at 28–29.

[124] Susanne K. Langer, *Philosophy in a New Key: A Study in the Symbolism of Reason, Rite, and Art* (Cambridge, MA: Harvard University Press, 1957).

[125] Romano Guardini, *The Spirit of the Liturgy* (Chicago: Biretta Books, 2015), 34.

[126] Gerard Lukken, "Liturgie und Sinnlichkeit. Über die Bedeutung der Leiblichkeit in der Liturgie," in idem, *Per visibilia ad invisibilia. Anthropological,*

dimension of liturgical anthropology will be absent and the fundamental action of the liturgy will be marred.

Incarnation

Theologically, the importance of physicality can be grounded in the incarnation in Jesus Christ. In 2 Corinthians 4:4 and Colossians 1:15, Christ himself is called the image of the Father. He is the sign of God, the primary sacrament of God. In his existence God's presence is revealed. It can be perceived in Christ, and he already gives us a share in it. Here again it is a question of sense-perception. First Peter 2:3 can speak, with Psalm 34:9, of tasting the goodness of the Lord ("Taste and see how gracious the Lord is," in the words of one of the most ancient communion antiphons). Second Corinthians 2:14 speaks of the "fragrance that comes from knowing [Christ]."

Physicality and pneumatology

Pneumatology is also significant for physicality in the liturgy. Through the working of the Spirit, human physicality becomes a symbol in the event of encounter between God and the human. "Thus in the liturgy it is a matter of human physicality as a reality ensouled with the Spirit of Jesus Christ."[127]

4.8 Liturgy and the Christian Life

4.8.1 Remembered Salvation History and Diaconal Action

Divine mercy as the measure

Christian social engagement is a consequence of the celebration of faith. Liturgy and *diakonia* are closely connected and mutually dependent.[128] The liturgy recalls the paschal mystery as a liberating event

---

Theological, and Semiotic Studies on the Liturgy and the Sacraments, collected and edited by Louis Van Tongeren and Charles Caspers (Kampen: Kok Pharos, 1994), 118–39, at 123.

[127] Ibid., 127.

[128] Richter, "Soziales Handeln und liturgisches Tun als der eine Gottesdienst des Lebens," 15–30.

and applies it, beyond the particular celebration, to daily life. The salvation-event-made-present lives on in the celebrating community. In this sense the liturgy demands consequences for everyday living: the mercy of God toward human beings celebrated in the liturgy, made visible in Jesus Christ, must become the standard for how those celebrating will act. The liturgy enables such diaconal action because, as a symbolic action, it acquires performative power. It does not merely motivate in a subjective sense but really enables.[129] Making salvation history present in its enduring effects is meant to effect changes in the world's reality. Thus the diaconal significance of liturgy is, in the first place, the consequence of the actual presence of salvation history, through which, as claimed, for example, in initiation, people experience a *transitus* and thus a transformation. When creation, incarnation, passion/resurrection, and the sending of the Spirit are celebrated, people give thanks in the liturgy for their creation and the gift of redemption and freedom, and they are emboldened and enabled for a corresponding life and action.

Example: Eucharistic Prayer

Thus, for example, the Eucharistic Prayer for Masses for Various Needs recalls the Christ-event in order then to speak of its relevance for the present: "[Christ] is the way that leads us to you, the truth that sets us free, the life that fills us with gladness. Through your Son you gather men and women, whom you made for the glory of your name, into one family, redeemed by the Blood of his Cross and signed with the seal of the Spirit."[130] The prayer asks that God will aid believers so that, through the liturgical celebration, they may be brought to love of neighbor and responsibility for the world: "Grant that all the faithful of the Church, looking into the signs of the times

---

[129] Richard Schaeffler, "'Darum sind wir eingedenk.' Die Verknüpfung von Erinnerung und Erwartung in der Gegenwart der gottesdienstlichen Feier. Religionsphilosophische Überlegungen zur religiös verstandenen Zeit," in *Vom Sinn der Liturgie. Gedächtnis unserer Erlösung und Lobpreis Gottes*, ed. Angelus A. Häussling, Schriften der Katholischen Akademie in Bayern 140 (Düsseldorf: Patmos, 1991), 16–44, at 40.

[130] *The Roman Missal* (see n. 8 above), Eucharistic Prayer for Masses for Various Needs III, 787–88.

by the light of faith, may constantly devote themselves to the service of the Gospel. Keep us attentive to the needs of all that, sharing their grief and pain, their joy and hope, we may faithfully bring them the good news of salvation and go forward with them along the way of your Kingdom."[131]

Worship as a way of life

The connection between anamnesis and way of life is strengthened by a personal and dynamic understanding of liturgy, one that recalls and celebrates the personal God as the one who acts, from creation to completion, and who as such also comes to believers in the liturgical event of encounter. The Constitution on the Liturgy says, in speaking of the nature of the liturgy and its significance for the church's life, that what is received in faith should be continued in life (SC 10). With regard to the Eucharist, it continues: "The renewal in the Eucharist of the covenant between them and the Lord draws the faithful and sets them aflame with Christ's compelling love." What is crucial here is that this is not about a repurposing and aesthetic reshaping of the liturgy but rather that Christian existence and practice are the consequence of what is celebrated in worship. In "worship as a way of life" people work together and are empowered to act.[132]

In the United States there has been a particular emphasis on the close relationship between liturgy and justice. Social movements and social action are seen as bound up with the doctrine of the Mystical Body of Christ. That teaching has been key to the linking of liturgy and justice, as liturgy has been seen as foundational for the church's social action. The basic idea has been: "liturgical renewal which did not connect to real life was a dead issue"[133] and even that "Liturgical participation that failed to address the needs of the weaker members of the Mystical Body of Christ was no participation at all."[134]

---

[131] Ibid., 790–91.

[132] Bernd Wannenwetsch, *Political Worship: Ethics for Christian Citizens* (Oxford and New York: Oxford University Press, 2004), *passim*, esp. 217.

[133] Keith F. Pecklers, *The Unread Vision: The Liturgical Movement in the United States of America; 1926–1955* (Collegeville, MN: Liturgical Press, 1998), 148.

[134] Ibid.

4.8.2 Liturgical Anticipation of Salvation and Christian Options for Action

Anticipation of reconciled life

But liturgy is also a participation in the future promised by God. The celebration, in its remembering-and-making-present, awaits the return of Christ and consequently looks forward to the promised eschatological salvation. The liturgy celebrates that salvation as already begun in Christ but still anticipated as something yet to be fulfilled. This anticipation through the liturgy should be for Christians a call and an impulse to liberating action. In that liturgy makes it possible to experience the gulf between the prophetic vision of peace being celebrated and the real current situation, there arises a historical potential for the integration of mysticism and politics.[135] In the anticipation of reconciled life in the presentative action of the liturgy the faithful already proclaim future freedom. A new worldview with new options for action can arise out of these experiences of interruption and contrast. In this way daily life plays a role in the liturgy, but at the same time it is transcended toward God.

4.8.3 The Mutual Relationship of Liturgy and Diakonia

Feedback from diakonia in worship

At the same time, the mutual dependency of liturgy and *diakonia* also ties Christians' social engagement back into the liturgy.[136] When the church defines liturgy as its source and summit (*SC* 10), *diakonia* is also in need of being rooted in worship. Otherwise there is a danger that it will lose its own *proprium* and therefore its specific foundation. Hence the diaconal dimension is a criterion for the liturgy, and at the same time the link back to the liturgy is a measure of Christian

---

[135] Edward Schillebeeckx, *Christ: The Christian Experience in the Modern World*, trans. John Bowden, The Collected Works of Edward Schillebeeckx 7 (London: Bloomsbury, 2014), 800–805.

[136] *"Ahme nach, was du vollziehst . . ." Positionsbestimmungen zum Verhältnis von Liturgie und Ethik*, ed. Martin Stuflesser and Stephan Winter, Studien zur Pastoralliturgie 22 (Regensburg: Pustet, 2009).

diakonia.[137] The Lutheran and Roman Catholic churches in Germany spoke of this mutuality in their 1997 document "Für eine Zukunft in Solidarität und Gerechtigkeit":[138]

> The church's life has its center in worship. In worship the church receives God's gift and responds with prayer, confession, and praise. This response is above all one of thanksgiving. Those who live in thanksgiving can understand reality as something for which to be grateful and thus will proceed more confidently in the duties imposed by economic and social action. Christian social action loses its strength if it is no longer bound back into prayer and celebration. In worship, Christians are liberated and commissioned for service to the world.

This intertwining of liturgy and *diakonia* is more or less clearly evident in every liturgical celebration. The liturgy of the Sacred Triduum makes it real by placing life within the horizon of salvation and resurrection while at the same time making palpable the tension between the experience of condemnation and the hope for salvation. Central actions in worship make the paschal mystery efficaciously present and so enable, ever anew, a living relationship with God and attitudes toward Christian *diakonia*: a sense of justice, sensitivity to suffering, readiness to engage on behalf of others and to make decisions based on faith.[139] This is true, for example, of the sharing of bread and wine as a sharing of life and its possibilities, indicated already on Maundy Thursday at the offertory procession and preparation of the gifts with the chant "Where true charity is dwelling, God is present there."[140] The same can be said of the veneration of the cross on Good Friday as a memorial of Christ's suffering, that is, of Christ's "pro-existence," and in the celebration of light that begins the Easter Vigil, when the

---

[137] *Die diakonale Dimension der Liturgie*, ed. Benedikt Kranemann, Thomas Sternberg, and Walter Zahner, Quaestiones disputatae 218 (Freiburg: Herder, 2006).

[138] "[Toward a Future in Solidarity and Justice]," 85, § 256.

[139] Marianne Heimbach-Steins and Georg Steins, "Sehnsucht nach dem umfassenden Heil. Liturgie und Diakonie im österlichen Triduum," *Gottesdienst* 34 (2000): 33–35; Klemens Richter, "Liturgie und Seelsorge"; idem, "Soziales Handeln"; *Die diakonale Dimension der Liturgie*.

[140] *The Roman Missal* (see n. 8 above), 303.

history of redemption and freedom are sung in the *Exsultet*, and finally in the celebration of baptism, in which the *transitus* from death to life takes place and a decision for faith is required.

Prayer and social conscience

We should also mention the Universal Prayer or Prayer of the Faithful at Mass. In the ancient church this was a prayer for the poor and suffering, understood as a prayer for one's neighbor but also an opportunity to approach a way of life corresponding to the message of faith in one's daily life. The prayer was accorded great significance for the social conscience of the communities. The intention of the ancient church continues when, in today's Missal, prayers are offered "for those who govern with authority over us, for those weighed down by various needs, for all humanity, and for the salvation of the whole world."[141]

Preparation of the gifts and collection

Mention should be made of the preparation of the gifts and the collection. Like the Prayer of the Faithful, these are organic elements of the Mass in which its diaconal character is expressed. The ritual practiced in the ancient church whereby other gifts intended for care of the poor were brought along with the bread and wine developed into the practice of bringing money offerings.[142] The underlying intention is that the faithful themselves may place their own lives within the eucharistic sacrifice, and thus in Christ's pro-existence. The relationship to the diaconal dimension of being a Christian is obvious.

What is celebrated in worship must be opened to those joining in the celebration as relevant to themselves and their lives; that is a primary requirement following from the mutual relationship of liturgy and *diakonia*. In addition, God must be proclaimed as the God

---

[141] *GIRM* 69.

[142] For the history see Josef A. Jungmann, *The Mass of the Roman Rite: Its Origins and Development*, trans. Francis Brunner, 2 vols. (New York: Benziger, 1951); one-volume abridged ed. 1959, "Part 4: The Mass Ceremonies in Detail: The Sacrifice," 315–21.

who is decisive for humanity. God's enduring decision for creation, apparent also in the event of the incarnation, is made visible in the creation-theological shape of the liturgy. The liturgy must consistently maintain the eschatological tension and never obscure it, in order that it may be the ground and ultimate motivation for diaconal action.[143]

[143] Benedikt Kranemann, "Feier des Glaubens und soziales Handeln. Überlegungen zu einer vernachlässigten Dimension christlicher Liturgie," *Liturgisches Jahrbuch* 48 (1998): 203–21.

CHAPTER 5

Forms and Methods of Expression in Worship

This chapter treats elements and dimensions that are appropriate to different degrees for every liturgy. It is impossible to write here of every type or form of expression in liturgical celebrations in full detail. This applies, for example, to body-language (imitation, gestures, posture, attitude, movement) or the particular celebrations throughout the liturgical year and in the lives of individuals or of the whole church. But, as in the preceding chapters, these aspects will have their place in the treatment of the individual topics. Thus the sum of the longer sections will illustrate the overall spectrum of the liturgy of the Roman Rite.

5.1 Sacred Scripture in the Liturgy

5.1.1 The Significance of Biblical Texts in Liturgy

Among the texts important for Christian worship, the biblical books have a special prominence.[1] There are a number of reasons for this.

The Bible as the basic document of Christian faith

When biblical texts are read, quoted, or alluded to, the liturgy makes reference to the fundamental documents of Christian faith and so gives voice to the foundation of the community of faith. The Old

---

[1] Renato De Zan, "Bible and Liturgy," in *Handbook for Liturgical Studies*, vol. 1: *Introduction to the Liturgy*, ed. Anscar J. Chupungco (Collegeville, MN: Liturgical Press, 1997), 33–51.

Testament texts of the Torah or the prophets, the gospels and Acts, the New Testament letters, and so on—all these tell the story of God with humanity as handed down in the Bible. The biblical texts of the liturgy give essential expression to the reasons why Christians assemble for liturgy and the hopes they share. They recall the foundational events of salvation. That is why the Old and New Testaments are indispensable to the liturgy! Christian tradition has given a special place of honor to the gospel because of its solid set of traditions about Christ and its special importance for Christian proclamation. The gospels have been and are read in the assurance that we can read *the* Gospel of Christ in the four canonical books. Christianity asserts that Christ himself is present in the gospel.[2]

God is present to human beings, including those of the present day, as the God of revelation, from creation to the consummation of all things. In the New Testament readings the Gospel of Christ is articulated through its reception and affirmation by the early Christians. The texts are themselves proclamations of the Gospel. At the same time they mark the ecclesial context of the *relecture* of the Gospel into which the congregation now celebrating liturgy enters and is incorporated.

The Old Testament also has an essential significance for Christians, not only because the New Testament's confession of Christ and his Gospel would be incomprehensible without the Old Testament, but above all because of the enduring meaning of the history of divine revelation preserved in it.

Old and New Testaments in the current order of readings

Unlike many Christian lectionaries in the past, including that of the Roman Catholic Church before Vatican II, today's lectionary integrates the two-in-one Bible made up of Old and New Testaments.[3]

---

[2] Thomas Söding, "Wort des lebendigen Gottes? Die neutestamentlichen Briefe im Wortgottesdienst der Eucharistiefeier," in *Wie das Wort Gottes feiern? Der Wortgottesdienst als theologische Herausforderung*, ed. Benedikt Kranemann and Thomas Sternberg, Quaestiones disputatae 194 (Freiburg: Herder, 2002), 41–81, at 42.

[3] For the place and dignity of the Old Testament in past lectionaries see Heinzgerd Brakmann, "Der christlichen Bibel erster Teil in den gottesdienstli-

It thus makes possible a dialogue between Old and New Testaments leading to a proclamation that is tension-filled but thereby does justice to the history of revelation. The interplay between Old and New Testaments in the liturgy is regarded as constitutive, for it "takes both into account: the utterly fundamental and in this sense primary meaning of the Old Testament for the *ekklēsia*'s reading of Scripture in worship and the development from Old to New Testament, which . . . can be understood as neither evolutionary nor pedagogical, and also not moral and spiritual, but only as drama of salvation, but therefore constitutive for the *ekklēsia* and its Eucharist."[4]

Intent of scriptural reading in worship

The liturgy recalls the biblical history of salvation, but not as something in the past; it does not read the text simply as an ancient and venerable record. Rather, the proclamation of the word in its many forms is subject to the demand that what is proclaimed from Scripture has a present-day character and is bound up with the hope of a future consummation. What has been said of the temporal modes of the liturgy and its relationship to the divine economy of salvation (see chap. 4.5.1) is also true of the scriptural reading. The church counts the proclamation of Scripture as one of the places in which Christ is present (see chap. 4.3.3). The different ways in which Scripture is used build a bridge between salvation history and those celebrating. Anamnesis by means of biblical reception is part of the liturgy's cultural memory. The reading of Scripture and the memorial character of liturgy are mutually related.

Liturgy as an event of encounter between God and the human takes its life primarily from the proclaimed word of God, which human hearers accept and to which they respond in the celebratory event. This act of hearing and responding is especially obvious in the liturgy when, as at the Easter Vigil, a biblical reading is followed by a

---

chen Traditionen des Ostens und Westens. Liturgiehistorische Anmerkungen zum sog. Stellenwert des Alten/Ersten Testaments im Christentum," in *Streit am Tisch des Wortes? Zur Deutung und Bedeutung des Alten Testaments und seiner Verwendung in der Liturgie*, ed. Ansgar Franz, Pietas Liturgica 8 (St. Ottilien: EOS Verlag, 1997), 565–99.

[4] Söding, "Wort des lebendigen Gottes?" (see n. 2 above), 71.

meditative phase and then a prayer. The prayer makes the meaning of the reading visible: it does not inform, for example, about interesting events in the history of religion; instead it aims at transformation and enrichment of human beings and their lived reality. Transformation is its purpose.[5]

One of the collects that may follow the third reading at the Easter Vigil (Exod 14:15–15:1) refers back to the reading to praise God, whose ancient wonders still shine forth in the present, explains this, and thus clearly proclaims how what is recalled in the biblical text ("formerly") applies to people today and becomes ("now") a liberating event. "O God, whose ancient wonders remain undimmed in splendor even in our day, for what you once bestowed on a single people, freeing them from Pharaoh's persecution by the power of your right hand, now you bring about as the salvation of the nations through the waters of rebirth."[6]

What is made present and recalled in the reading is related to the lives of believers, and vice versa. The significance of reading Sacred Scripture is given prominence in relation to the life stories of those who read and those who listen.[7]

5.1.2 Biblical Books as Sacred Scripture

Word of the living God

For the liturgy, the biblical books have the character of "Sacred Scripture." This is especially evident in the Liturgy of the Word at Mass: after each reading the lector says "The word of the Lord," and the congregation responds, "Thanks be to God," thus affirming that what it heard was a specific communication-event. The priest or deacon introduces the reading of the gospel with words such as "A reading from the holy Gospel according to N." and may end with "The Gospel of the Lord." The personally directed response, "Praise

---

[5] Reinhard Messner, Einführung in die Liturgiewissenschaft, 2nd ed., UTB 2173 (Paderborn: Schöningh, 2009), 185.

[6] The Roman Missal, Third Edition (Collegeville, MN: Liturgical Press, 2011), 366.

[7] Dorothea Sattler, "Gegenwart Gottes im Wort. Systematisch-theologische Aspekte," in Wie das Wort Gottes feiern?, 123–43, at 140.

to you, Lord Jesus Christ," emphasizes that the proclamation of the gospel represents Christ himself. The normativity of the basic testimony of the Bible for the community of faith is expressed particularly in such rituals. The Bible can thus rightly be said to be the most important book for worship.[8]

The Constitution on the Liturgy gives a correspondingly important theological weight to our engagement with these texts with its metaphors: "table of God's word," which provides us richer fare, and "treasures of the Bible," which are to be more lavishly opened (SC 51). Fundamental to this is the certainty in faith that Christ himself proclaims the Good News in the liturgy (SC 33), that is, that Christ is present in the Word.

Signs of the dignity of what is proclaimed

The significance of biblical texts is expressed in the complex ritual of the Liturgy of the Word and its representative symbolism. This is especially emphatic in the Mass for Sundays. The ambo, as the place for reading, is the locus for proclamation and therefore is reserved for the readings and responsory psalm as well as the *Exsultet*, homily, and bidding prayers. The design of the Lectionary and Gospel Book (or a Bible for the readings) has a symbolic character, indicating the status of what is read from them. There are other symbols as well: how the book is treated (processional entry with the Gospel Book), the use of candles and veneration with incense, the acclamations that frame the reading of the texts, and the underlying spiritual event (God's revelation in the word, the presence of Christ). All these are indicators, as are bodily postures such as sitting, which expresses intense listening, or standing as a sign of respect.[9]

[8] Hans Bernhard Meyer, "Liturgie in lebenden Sprachen. Das 2. Vatikanum und die Folgen," in *Die Feier der Sakramente in der Gemeinde. Festschrift für Heinrich Rennings*, ed. Martin Klöckener and Winfried Glade (Kevelaer: Butzon & Bercker, 1986), 331–45, at 339.

[9] Benedikt Kranemann, "Wort–Buch–Verkündigungsort. Zur Ästhetik der Wortverkündigung im Gottesdienst," in *Liturgia et Unitas. Liturgiewissenschaftliche und ökumenische Studien zur Eucharistie und zum gottesdienstlichen Leben in der Schweiz/Études liturgiques et oecuméniques sur l'Eucharistie et la vie liturgique en*

5.1.3 The Use of Biblical Texts in Liturgy

Principles of the current order of readings

In Roman Catholic worship today there is no service in which biblical texts are not read or recited. The course of readings is not unplanned; rather, it follows a number of principles. For the Liturgy of the Word at Mass and in the Liturgy of the Hours a number of distinct orders are followed, structured by particular criteria. For the Mass, the sequence of readings distinguishes between Sundays and weekdays, integrating texts from the Old and New Testaments. In the Liturgy of the Word for Sundays and feast days the Old Testament reading is followed by a psalm and then the New Testament reading; the gospel reading that follows is preceded by an alleluia (replaced during Lent by a Christ-antiphon). In the Easter season the Old Testament reading is replaced by a pericope from the Acts of the Apostles. The three-year lectionary cycle for Sundays and feast days gives prominence to the Gospel of Matthew in Year A, that of Mark in Year B, and that of Luke in Year C. The Gospel of John is reserved for certain festal seasons.[10] The governing principles for the choice of the Old and New Testament readings and the gospels are "thematic correspondence" (for the major festal seasons) and "selective sequence (*lectio continua*)" (only for the New Testament reading and the gospel). A number of basic principles are applied to the combination of texts: there is a desire to include as comprehensive a selection of biblical texts as possible in the course of a year. Particular traditional readings that have embedded themselves in certain feasts and festal seasons are to be considered. That is why, for example, on Christmas and Epiphany and during the Paschal Triduum the same biblical texts are read in all three cycles. In addition, some texts have been combined for thematic coordination, to make them easier to hear and understand. An accommodation and choice of texts is also possible.[11]

Suisse. In honorem Bruno Bürki, ed. Martin Klöckener and Arnaud Join-Lambert (Fribourg: Universitätsverlag; Geneva: Labor et Fides, 2001), 57–72.

[10] Benedikt Kranemann, "'Lesejahr D?' Das Johannesevangelium in der Liturgie," *Bibel und Kirche* 59 (2004): 167–70.

[11] See the overview in Elmar Nübold, *Entstehung und Bewertung der neuen Perikopenordnung des Römischen Ritus für die Messfeier an Sonn- und Festtagen* (Paderborn:

Theology, tradition, and pastoral concern accordingly underlie the order of readings.

The two-year cycle of readings for weekday Masses includes a New Testament reading not taken from the gospels and the gospel itself. The gospel is the same each year (Weeks 1–9, Mark; 10–21, Matthew; 22–34, Luke). The readings are divided into Year 1 (odd-numbered years) and Year 2 (even-numbered years). There are special readings for seasons apart from the common church year ("ordinary time").[12]

Strengths and weaknesses

Certainly among the strengths of the current lectionary is the multitude of biblical texts that are read. This gives a broad foundation to liturgical proclamation. At the same time, the broad inclusion of the Old Testament enhances its worth, though this is a subject that (liturgical) theology is far from having exhausted.

Still, some critical reflections are in order. The division of pericopes (that is, the scope of the texts and their selection) has been challenged. The manner in which the Old Testament is incorporated into the overall scheme of lectionary texts has long been a subject of discussion. Thus the Old Testament reading is coordinated to the gospel, which becomes problematic when the Old Testament text can only be read as a (contrasting) foil for or introduction to the gospel or exclusively as part of the scheme of promise (in the Old Testament) and fulfillment (in the Christ-event proclaimed in the New Testament).

For example, the Old Testament reading on the Sixth Sunday in Year B (Lev 13:1-2, 45-46) is such a snippet of the biblical pericope that it serves only as a contrasting foil for the gospel: both texts are about leprosy. In this case the strict Old Testament regulations regarding lepers are set against Jesus' calm encounter with the sick persons. On

---

Bonifatius, 1986), 385–90; Ansgar Franz, *Wortgottesdienst der Messe und Altes Testament. Katholische und ökumenische Lektionarreform nach dem II. Vatikanum im Spiegel von* Ordo Lectionum Missae, Revised Common Lectionary *und* Four Year Lectionary: *Positionen, Probleme, Perspektiven*, Pietas Liturgica 14 (Tübingen and Basel: Francke, 2002), 72–73.

[12] For the order of readings and its origin see Nübold, *Entstehung und Bewertung*.

the Seventeenth Sunday in Year B the Old Testament reading about Elisha's multiplication of bread (2 Kgs 4:42-44) is coordinated with Jesus' multiplication of the loaves (John 6:1-15). The danger is that the Old Testament pericope will only be read as a preliminary stage anticipating the New Testament event. Likewise, in the Chrism Mass on Maundy Thursday the promise-fulfillment scheme asserts itself when first Isaiah 61:1-3a, 6a, 8b-9 is read and then the gospel passage in Luke 4:16-21 in which the Isaiah text is quoted, ending with the words "today this scripture has been fulfilled in your hearing."

Alternative models

The current order of readings, therefore, does not always do justice to the value of the Old Testament for Christian identity or to the way in which liturgy and the significance of the revelation of God described in the Old Testament shape our understanding of the Christ-event. Alternative models for resolving this problem have been suggested. The liturgist Hansjakob Becker favors an order of readings oriented to the history of salvation, one that would elevate the Old Testament qualitatively and make clearer its fundamental and relational status. The Old Testament is the foundation of the Liturgy of the Word, the gospel its crown. The consequence, for Becker, is that the Old Testament sets the theme; it should be read sequentially, reconstructing the course of salvation history. The New Testament is then a *relecture* of the Old Testament.

In this proposal for an order of readings oriented to salvation history, for example, Jonah 1:1–4:11 would be read on the twenty-third Sunday after Pentecost, and gospels would be related to particular motifs in that text in the different years of the cycle: Mark 4:35-41 (the storm at sea) takes up the motifs of flight and storm; Matt 12:38-41 (sign of Jonah) that of the fish, etc.[13]

The Old Testament scholars Norbert Lohfink and Georg Braulik call for a bipolar order of readings for Old Testament and gospel.

---

[13] Hansjakob Becker, "Wortgottesdienst als Dialog der beiden Testamente. Der Stellenwert des Alten Testaments bei einer Weiterführung der Reform des Ordo Lectionum Missae," in *Streit am Tisch des Wortes? Zur Deutung und Bedeutung des Alten Testaments und seiner Verwendung in der Liturgie*, ed. Ansgar Franz, Pietas Liturgica 8 (St. Ottilien: EOS Verlag, 1997), 659–89, at 676.

They regard the Torah as the guide to the Old Testament; accordingly, it should be recited as a sequential reading. The New Testament is the eschatological counter-pole to "the Law and the prophets" and should be read as such. This calls for the gospel also to be read sequentially, that is, as *lectio continua*. The second reading is reserved for the prophetic and wisdom writings, the New Testament letters and Revelation, that is, as commentary either on the reading from Torah or the gospel. The preacher may choose from among alternative texts in light of the homily. The order of readings should be "oriented to the structure of the biblical canon itself."[14] All of these models are discussed from biblical- and liturgical-theological points of view and in light of pastoral-theological-homiletical perspectives.

Use of the Psalter in the liturgy

The use of the Psalter in the liturgy presents other questions and challenges. In the Liturgy of the Hours the psalms are said or sung in a four-week cycle. A wide variety of criteria for selection have been applied. Some psalms are used at Lauds, Vespers, and Compline because they seem particularly appropriate for the time of day and for community liturgy. Others are assigned to Sunday because they seem to speak so explicitly of the paschal mystery. Some psalms have been chosen with an eye to the church year and the season; a number of those said or sung on major feasts and other festal celebrations have established a tradition that shapes the liturgy for those days.[15]

---

[14] Norbert Lohfink, "Moses Tod, die Tora und die alttestamentliche Sonntagslesung," in *Leseordnung. Altes und Neues Testament in der Liturgie*, ed. Georg Steins, Gottes Volk S/97 (Stuttgart: Katholisches Bibelwerk, 1997), 122–37, at 137; see also Georg Braulik, "Die Tora als Bahnlesung. Zur Hermeneutik einer zukünftigen Auswahl der Sonntagsperikopen," in *Bewahren und Erneuern. Studien zur Messliturgie. Festschrift für Hans Bernhard Meyer, SJ, zum 70. Geburtstag*, ed. Reinhard Messner, Eduard Nagel, and Rudolf Pacik, Innsbrucker theologische Studien 42 (Innsbruck and Vienna: Tyrolia, 1995), 50–76; for discussion of the use of the Old Testament in the Lectionary see Franz, *Wortgottesdienst der Messe* (see n. 11 above).

[15] *GILH* 126–35; see the overview in Vitus Huonder, *Die Psalmen in der Liturgia Horarum*, Studia Friburgensia 74 (Fribourg: Universitätsverlag, 1991).

Dealing with psalms of imprecation

Working with psalms shows quite clearly that reflection on the use of biblical texts in the liturgy remains a task for liturgics. Thus in the choice of psalms in the current Liturgy of the Hours the omission of the psalms of imprecation 58(57), 83(82), and 109(108) as well as some similar verses is regarded as problematic.[16] "The reason for the omission is a certain psychological difficulty, even though the psalms of imprecation are in fact used as prayer in the New Testament, for example, Revelation 6:10, and in no sense to encourage the use of curses."[17] Certainly, Old Testament exegesis can also show that these texts are not about vengeance but about the triumph of God's law and justice in our own day. Those praying them shout out their confusion and despair in the face of unjust suffering, articulating their fear and their situation, which is contrary to God's reality. Ultimately these psalms move powerfully toward a rejection of human violence in favor of God's power to act against injustice. With a thoughtful introduction or a translation that can open up their meaning, they may serve an important function in Christian prayer life.[18]

Rigid christologizing

A kind of reading applied until recently even to the psalms in the liturgy that saw them as witnessing to a lower level of revelation than the Christ-event developed a problematic understanding of these texts and subjected them to a "christologizing" that was often very rigid. The Old Testament text had first to be fitted into a Christology, a process that degraded the worth of the texts themselves and their theological relevance. It is only under the influence of newer exegetical approaches (e.g., "canonical exegesis"), which read the individual psalms philologically within the whole Psalter and so

---

[16] Albert Gerhards, "Die Psalmen in der römischen Liturgie. Eine Bestandsaufnahme des Psalmengebrauchs in Stundengebet und Messfeier," in *Der Psalter in Judentum und Christentum*, ed. Erich Zenger, Herders biblische Studien 18 (Freiburg: Herder, 1998), 355–79.

[17] *GILH* 131.

[18] Erich Zenger, *A God of Vengeance? Understanding the Psalms of Divine Wrath*, trans. Linda M. Maloney (Louisville: Westminster John Knox, 1996).

develop the theology of the eschatological-messianic dimension of the psalms, that a new liturgical-theological hermeneutic of the psalms has emerged. The Old Testament is already a messianically oriented book within whose larger context the individual psalms can be read. This is a point of contact for the reception of the psalms in Christian liturgy.

Those who take these poetic texts seriously can also give new weight to the Psalter as a "book of life" and discover "the fundamental significance of the existential and anthropological dimension of the Psalter in the liturgy."[19] Here very different and even contradictory human situations are given expression before God: joy and suffering, despair and hope. All facets of human life are brought into the liturgy by these texts. Biblical texts, above all, guarantee that Christian worship will remain embedded in life itself.

5.1.4 The Reception of Biblical Texts in Worship

The process of reading and the potential meanings of a text

When liturgics asks about the aesthetics of reception of biblical texts in worship it includes both readers and hearers in its consideration. Its concern is with the dynamic by which the liturgy makes the Bible its own, and consequently with the ever-new actualization of these texts. Gregory the Great's statement that "the divine pronouncements grow with the reader"[20] applies also to the liturgy and its use of Scripture. The individual biblical texts, their motifs and imagery, can be heard anew from one liturgical celebration to another. Thus, for example, the pericope of the Beatitudes (Matt 5:1-12a) is recommended for a great variety of liturgies: for the Fourth Sunday in Ordinary Time in Year A but also as a possible selection for confirmation, anointing of the sick, marriage, and burial. A different beatitude comes to the fore in each type of celebration, making possible a new reading and

---

[19] Harald Buchinger, "Zur Hermeneutik liturgischer Psalmenverwendung. Methodologische Überlegungen im Schnittpunkt von Bibelwissenschaft, Patristik und Liturgiewissenschaft," *Heiliger Dienst* 54 (2000): 193–222, at 221; see also the more developed account of the newer hermeneutical discussion there.

[20] Gregory the Great, *In Ezek.* 22, *CChr.* SL 142, 87.

hearing. According to literary-critical reception theory, the creation of a meaning for the text in the process of reception is the work of the reader and so possesses a certain dynamic.

> For . . . bringing to fruition, the literary text needs the reader's imagination, which gives shape to the interaction of correlatives foreshadowed in structure by the sequence of the sentences. . . . The written part of the text gives us the knowledge, but it is the unwritten part that gives us the opportunity to picture things; indeed without the elements of indeterminacy, the gaps in the text, we should not be able to use our imagination.[21]

Biblical texts also lend themselves to such a multiplicity of meanings. As with other literary texts, what they say is determined by their content, but on the other hand there are "gaps" that make possible a whole series of new interpretations.

Significance of tradition

Thus in the event of reception of a text from the Old or New Testament in the liturgy there is always the possibility that a new vitality will unfold. This is all the more true in the ever-new *relecture* within the tradition of a church community of faith that knows itself to be "in explicit continuity with the communities which gave rise to Scripture and which preserved and handed it on. In the process of actualization, tradition plays a double role: on the one hand, it provides protection against deviant interpretations; on the other hand, it ensures the transmission of the original dynamism."[22]

So, for example, Exodus 14 was read as early as 1 Corinthians 10:1-2 in terms of the Christ-event and baptism, but then it was also broadly received in liturgical tradition in prayer texts, hymns, the literature of preaching, the shape and decoration of baptisteries and other liturgical spaces in the context of baptism. The first prayer over the baptismal water says: "Through the waters of the Red Sea you

[21] Wolfgang Iser, "The Reading Process: A Phenomenological Approach," *New Literary History* 3, no. 2: *On Interpretation: I* (Winter 1972): 279–99, at 282, 288.

[22] Pontifical Biblical Commission, *The Interpretation of the Bible in the Church* (Boston: Pauline Books, 1993), 4.A.1, p. 118.

led Israel out of slavery, to be an image of God's holy people, set free from sin by baptism."[23] The *Exsultet*, the solemn Easter chant, in contrast sings of that night as the night of salvation in which Israel was made to "pass dry-shod through the Red Sea."[24]

Open possibilities for interpretation within the church

The particular biblical text achieves its specific contours by being used in the context of Christian liturgy and thus of a community of faith and its hermeneutic. The possibility for multiple readings thus revealed was summarized by the Pontifical Biblical Commission in its document *The Interpretation of the Bible in the Church* (1993):

> A written text has the capacity to be placed in new circumstances, which will illuminate it in different ways, adding new meanings to the original sense. This capacity of written texts is especially operative in the case of the biblical writings, recognized as the word of God. Indeed, what encouraged the believing community to preserve these texts was the conviction that they would continue to be bearers of light and life for generations of believers to come. The literal sense is, from the start, open to further developments, which are produced through the "rereading" (*relectures*) of texts in new contexts.[25]

Genera of liturgical uses of Scripture

It is not only the very different character of the individual biblical books but also the great variety of ways they are used in the liturgy that has led to the development of different genera of usages. Besides the reading of pericopes taken from Scripture, as the most familiar example, we should mention the psalms (as reading, as prayer, as meditation), biblical hymns (including the *Benedictus* [Luke 1:68–79], *Magnificat* [Luke 1:46-55], and *Nunc dimittis* [Luke 2:29-33]), prayers

---

[23] *Rite of Baptism for Children*. English translation approved by the National Conference of Catholic Bishops and confirmed by the Apostolic See (Collegeville, MN: Liturgical Press, 2002), 34.

[24] *The Roman Missal* (see n. 6 above), 350.

[25] Pontifical Biblical Commission, *The Interpretation of the Bible in the Church*, 2.B.1, p. 84.

(especially the Our Father), biblically influenced poetic forms (such as the *Gloria* or *Te Deum*, but also many hymns, both traditional and modern), reception of Scripture in prayers (through quotations or allusions to motifs), formulae and acclamations ("Amen," "Alleluia," "Hosanna," "Maranatha," and others), in preaching, but also in the furnishing of the liturgical space (altars with retables, statues and pictures, church windows, etc.). Here we encounter the biblical texts as literal quotations, in indirect allusions, or through motifs used as reminders.[26]

Reception of Scripture in Jewish and Christian worship

The *relecture* of biblical texts can lead to different receptions from one congregation or faith community to another. We may use Psalm 92 as an example. It is recited as part of the prayers at the beginning of the Jewish Sabbath. First Psalms 95–99 and 29 are read, then the Sabbath hymn, "Come, my Beloved, to meet the Bride; let us welcome the Shabbat." Then Psalm 92, followed by Psalm 93, is sung as the "Psalm for the Sabbath Day."[27] In the Roman Catholic Liturgy of the Hours, Psalm 92 is used at Lauds on Saturday, that is, the same day as the Jewish Sabbath (in weeks 2 and 4 of the cycle). There the superscription for the psalm in Week 2 reads, "Praise of God the Creator,"[28] and it is preceded by a quotation from St. Athanasius: "Sing in praise of Christ's redeeming work."[29] The antiphon is taken from Psalm 92:3. In the Christian context the Sabbath motif is explicitly denied any role; instead, the reference to Athanasius and the context of the other texts of the hour show that the Christ-event is to be taken as the reference point for Christian appreciation of these texts. This

---

[26] Albert Gerhards, "Schriftgebrauch im Gottesdienst. Zur Bewertung der Rolle des Gottesdienstes in den Überlegungen des Ökumenischen Arbeitskreises evangelischer und katholischer Theologen unter besonderer Berücksichtigung des Alten Testaments," in *Streit am Tisch des Wortes?*, 491–503, at 495.

[27] *Sidur Sefa Emet = Hebrew Prayer Book* (Halberstadt: League of Orthodox Jewish Congregations, 1923).

[28] *The Liturgy of the Hours*, English translation prepared by the International Commission on English in the Liturgy, vol. 3: *Ordinary Time, Weeks 1–17* (New York: Catholic Book Publishing, 1975), 962.

[29] Ibid.

example also indicates the allure of an interreligious interpretation of Scripture for the liturgy, because implicitly Psalm 92 forms a bridge between the two religious communities.

Both interpretations open a possible spiritual sense of the biblical text; the document of the Biblical Commission sees this not as the result of intellectual speculation but as "setting the text in relation to real facts which are not foreign to it."[30] Within the Christian liturgy the text, the paschal mystery celebrated in the liturgy, and the life situation of those celebrating are brought together. Thus biblical text and celebrating community, and thus the church, all participate in the reception of Scripture in worship.

Significance of an order of readings

Interaction with the Bible in the liturgy takes place within the frame of a community of tradition and narration. Therefore, for example, an order of readings that regulates the choice of biblical texts for the Liturgy of the Word at Mass says something about the identity of the church as a community of reception and also about the meaning it assigns to ambiguous biblical texts. Therefore the obligatory nature of the order of readings in the liturgy is all the more necessary; at the same time, it must also remain the object of discussion among theologians and within the church itself.

Four functions of the Bible in the liturgy

At the same time we can recognize four different functions the liturgy assigns to Sacred Scripture:

1. A *didactic* Liturgy of the Word, such as we encounter as early as the ancient church's catechumenal services, serves to convey and deepen knowledge of biblical stories of faith. As a rule, in such services the reading of Scripture is followed by an interpretation.

2. A *kerygmatic* or *anamnetic* Liturgy of the Word uses the biblical reading to recall what is now being celebrated in the liturgy. Such readings are closely related to the other rituals in the particular service.

---

[30] *Interpretation of the Bible in the Church*, 2.B.2, p. 86.

3. A *paracletic* Liturgy of the Word has a pastoral function; the reading is related to the circumstances of the individual and the assembly.

4. Finally, in a *doxological* Liturgy of the Word the proclamation of the Word functions as praise to God. This is the task, for example, of psalmody.[31]

These dimensions of proclamation of the Word of course overlap; they indicate the weight of Sacred Scripture in the liturgy, resulting above all from anamnesis, because they point simultaneously to the core event in the proclamation of the Word and in the liturgy: the encounter with God in the action-event of the liturgy. Therefore it is also said that "liturgical celebration, based primarily on the word of God and sustained by it, becomes a new event and enriches the word itself with new meaning and power."[32]

5.1.5 Intertextuality of Biblical Texts in the Liturgy

What is "intertextuality"?

A further characteristic of liturgical reception of Scripture is described by the word "intertextuality." This term, taken from literary criticism, is here used to express the dialogical nature of liturgy's use of Scripture: the individual biblical text is related within the liturgical celebration to other texts and thus is part of a dialogue that is called "intertextual" and that initiates an additional text, the "macro-text."[33] The biblical text in the liturgy is placed in a changed context; it is transformed into a new text. The introduction of older texts into a new context is extraordinarily important, especially for the liturgy because, by means of the older—here biblical—texts, expression is given to anamnesis and thus participation in salvation history.

---

[31] Paul F. Bradshaw, "The Use of the Bible in Liturgy: Some Historical Perspectives," *Studia Liturgica* 22 (1992): 35–52.

[32] General Introduction 3, in *Lectionary for Mass* (Collegeville, MN: Liturgical Press, 1998).

[33] Alexander Deeg, "Gottesdienst in Israels Gegenwart: Liturgie als intertextuelles Phänomen," *Liturgisches Jahrbuch* 54 (2004): 34–52.

Forms of intertextuality: (1) scriptural texts in mutuality

We can observe different forms of intertextuality in the liturgy. Thus in the Liturgy of the Word in Masses on Sundays and feast days we encounter the sequence of Old Testament reading, psalm, New Testament reading, alleluia, gospel. Such a structure is by no means arbitrary; it brings the texts of the two-in-one Bible into dialogue in the context of the liturgy. The Old and New Testament texts set in relation to one another engage in a mutual interrogation and commentary. The psalm and alleluia open up a particular horizon of understanding. How the biblical texts are heard depends on the particular celebration and those who join in it and varies from service to service.

(2) Dialogue between liturgical and biblical texts

We can also observe a dialogue between biblical and "liturgical" texts when a collect, a Eucharistic Prayer, a hymn, etc., play on the same biblical text, so that text speaks within text, resulting in a new form of the text. The sixteenth-century hymn "Lo, how a Rose e'er blooming" exemplifies this:

> Lo, how a Rose e'er blooming
> from tender stem hath sprung!
> Of Jesse's lineage coming
> as seers of old have sung.
> It came, a blossom bright,
> amid the cold of winter,
> when half spent was the night.

Here Old and New Testament texts are clearly drawn from Isaiah 11:1-2; Luke 1:31-33; and Romans 15:12; these establish the meaning of the hymn. The biblical text is read into a hymn and is received in a new context, usually the liturgies of the Christmas season.[34]

[34] See Hansjakob Becker, "Es ist ein Ros entsprungen," in *Geistliches Wunderhorn. Grosse deutsche Kirchenlieder*, ed. Hansjakob Becker, et al. (Munich: Beck, 2001), 135–45.

(3) Dialogue between different liturgical celebrations

Finally, intertextuality points to the dialogue between different liturgical celebrations that is made possible by biblical texts. For the canticles *Benedictus*, *Magnificat*, and *Nunc dimittis*, as well as the *Gloria* that is sung in the Eucharist (on major feasts, feasts, special celebrations, and Sundays except in Advent and Lent; see *GIRM* 53), Norbert Lohfink has shown that the texts in the Gospel of Luke are closely linked by key words ("selective word relationships") as well as their internal connections, and thereby emphatically and thoroughly express messianic hope. They bring those connections into the Christian liturgy and thereby open up a new, polyphonic meaning: "[F]or those who pray the Liturgy of the Hours the four hymns are set within the course of events in exactly the same way as they are set within the events of the Infancy Narrative. They stop the action. They open horizons. They combine into an interpretation, spanning the whole of salvation history, of the very events that are taking place in each concrete day of each one's life."[35] The theological arc between the texts here saturates the course of the day, through the liturgy.

Typology

A typology of intertextuality developed by the literary-critical scholar Gérard Genette can be applied to the study of liturgy.[36] While Genette applies "intertextual" in the narrower sense only to quotations, plagiarism, and allusions, the quotations or allusions within the biblical texts recited in the liturgy (whether as readings, hymns, or prayers) can also be designated *intertextual*. For when Genette defines "allusion" as "an enunciation whose full meaning presupposes the perception of a relationship between it and another text, to which it necessarily refers by some inflections that would otherwise remain

---

[35] Norbert Lohfink, "The Old Testament and the Course of the Christian's Day: The Songs in Luke's Infancy Narrative," in idem, *In the Shadow of Your Wings: New Readings of Great Texts from the Bible*, trans. Linda M. Maloney (Collegeville, MN: Liturgical Press, 2003), 136–50, at 150.

[36] Gunda Brüske, "Lesen und Wiederkäuen: *Lectio divina*, Liturgie und Intertextualität. Zugleich ein Beitrag zur Hermeneutik liturgischer Texte," *Erbe und Auftrag* 78 (2002): 94–103.

unintelligible,"[37] that can certainly be applied to the complexity of biblical allusions in the liturgy:

- Genette calls the relationship of an individual text to those that frame it or to the whole constituted by the literary work *paratextual* and sees in it "probably one of the privileged fields of operation of the pragmatic dimensions of the work—i.e., of its impact upon the reader."[38] We can observe such a textual relationship, for example, between the psalm and the antiphon, between the readings and the gospel and the texts surrounding them, between reading and sacramental event. Genette's remarks highlight the value of those relationships.

- The transformation or imitation of biblical texts, in hymnody, for example, Genette would call *hypertextual*. A text (hypertext) is derived from a prior text (hypotext), is layered on it, and recalls it, as we can see, for example, in the *Gloria* in relation to Luke 2:14.

- The commentary on a text can be called *metatextual*. This seems to apply very well to the homily in relation to the biblical text, although Genette does not consider quotation or even reference to the original text a necessity.[39]

- Finally, there are generic relationships between texts that can be called *architextual*. "[G]eneric perception is known to guide and determine to a considerable degree the readers' expectations, and thus their reception of the work."[40] The introduction to a reading ("A reading from the book of Deuteronomy" / "from the letter of Paul the apostle to . . .") and to the gospel ("from the holy Gospel according to") points to the "genre" of the text and thus to its significance within the whole of the liturgy; it can influence how the reading is received. The singing of a psalm, even though nothing is said about the genre, steers how the participants in the celebration receive it.

---

[37] Gérard Genette, *Palimpsests: Literature in the Second Degree*, trans. Channa Newman and Claude Doubinsky (Lincoln: University of Nebraska Press, 1997), 2.

[38] Ibid., 3.

[39] Ibid., 4.

[40] Ibid., 5.

Intertextuality, in the broad sense, marks out the particular situation within which biblical texts are read and heard in the liturgy and clarifies their specific and multiple meanings in the context of worship. It points both liturgics and pastoral theology to their duty to make the polyphony of the texts audible in their particular fields. Finally, it reveals what a sensitive and multilayerd process takes place in the use of biblical texts in liturgy. These are fundamental theological and aesthetic processes for the various liturgical celebrations.

5.2 Prayer in the Liturgy

Prayer is distinct in many ways from everyday action. What kind of "dialogue" takes place if one is certain that no direct answer will be received? What are the conditions for an appropriate address to God? What is the relationship between spontaneous prayer and prayer in familiar formulae, or between personal prayer and prayer in community?

5.2.1 Prayer in the Tension between Life Experience and Faith Tradition

The hermeneutical connection between tradition and individual life experiences

In order to be able to answer these questions we must consider the act of praying as such, as well as the content of the prayer. The religious philosopher Richard Schaeffler treats prayer in connection with the tension between life experience and faith. It is always a concrete person who prays, and present individual and community experience enters into the prayer. "But when the one praying uses a 'prayerbook' she or he places her or his current life experience within the context of a tradition that has shaped the prayer of one's ancestors. The tradition of the believing community and the current life experience of the one praying are mutually interpretive." There is even a relationship of "hermeneutical mutuality" between the tradition of faith and the particular current experience of life.[41]

---

[41] Richard Schaeffler, "Das Gebet: Schule des Glaubens und Schule des Lebens im Judentum," in *Lebenserfahrung und Glaube*, ed. Gisbert Kaufmann (Düsseldorf: Patmos, 1983), 73–90, at 74.

Prayer as response

The prayer of the individual is always preceded by a sense of having been affected by the world and other people, past and present. This passive internal state works itself out in a constant process of suffering toward which the person, as an active and free being, must take a position and arrive at some answers. Given these fundamental anthropological constants, prayer is a specific expression of the developing, "self-transcending" person.

Prayer as God's location on earth

The characteristics of prayer in the biblical stories can be defined precisely from the margin of its possibilities, in light of the experience of those who are far from God. Because of its role in the Old and New Testaments, Psalm 22 seems an apt example. It begins with the cry: "My God, my God, why have you forsaken me?" The psalm reflects the experience of the destruction by the Babylonians of the temple and thus of the sacrificial cult, an experience that became permanent after the destruction of the Second Temple. Until that time the temple was seen as *the* place on earth where the name of God dwelt. After its destruction, the question arose: where is God now present; where can we speak to God? The psalm answers in verse 4: "Yet you are holy, enthroned on the praises of Israel." The exegete Frank-Lothar Hossfeld interprets this as follows: "The ancient title of the invisible 'cherubim throne' in Solomon's temple (1 Sam 4:4; 2 Sam 6:2; Pss 80:2; 99:1) is revised and spiritualized."[42] It is a revolutionary idea. God does not live exclusively in one place but is present in every place where God's name is praised, where Israel sings its psalms: "The prayer holds open for the 'God without a temple,' the God without a space, the possibility for ever-new arrival in the world, a place for God's presence. It is now the special calling of the community of the Jewish people, the community of faith, to sing such psalms and to hold open in the world such a place for divine arrival and

---

[42] Frank-Lothar Hossfeld and Erich Zenger, *Die Psalmen*, vol. 1: *Psalm 1–50*, Neue Echter Bibel, Kommentar zum Alten Testament 29 (Würzburg: Echter Verlag, 1993), 149.

presence."[43] So prayer constitutes a place within space-time, the *kairos* of the presence of God in the place and at the time of Israel's singing of the psalms.

Prayer and eschatological anticipation

In Christian understanding the question of the place where God is enthroned has been sharpened still further. Mark and Matthew report Jesus' dying words to have been that same cry of abandonment by God in Psalm 22 (Mark 15:34; Matt 27:46). The ripped curtain of the temple reveals the empty holy of holies (cp. Mark 15:38; Matt 27:51), for the holy of holies is wherever the Son of God breathes forth his Spirit. God's presence is shown in the death of the one abandoned by God: "Truly this man was God's Son!" (Mark 15:39; see Matt 27:54). In the post-Easter interpretation of the event, Jesus Christ is the steadfast place of God's dwelling. Where his disciples gather in his name, he is among them (see Matt 18:20). God's glory, the divine presence first experienced at the cherubim throne (see Isa 6:2) now, after the exaltation of the Crucified to the right hand of God, fills heaven and earth (cp. the *Sanctus* at Mass). So here also we find an anticipation of the eschatological fulfillment at the end of the ages.

Eschatological dimension of the Our Father

The Our Father, the central prayer of Christians, is semantically a Jewish prayer through and through,[44] as by hallowing the name of God it places those praying it in the presence of God. With the petition for the coming of God's reign and that the will of God be done "on earth as it is in heaven" it turns attention to the end time, which, however, has already begun. The Greek text reads "and forgive us our debts, as *forgiven* to our debtors."[45] In the context of the Our Father the

---

[43] Schaeffler, "Das Gebet," 76.

[44] Karlheinz Müller, "Das Vater-Unser als jüdisches Gebet," in *Identität durch Gebet. Zur gemeinschaftsbildenden Funktion institutionalisierten Betens in Judentum und Christentum*, ed. Albert Gerhards, Andrea Doeker, and Peter Ebenbauer, Studien zu Judentum und Christentum (Paderborn: Schöningh, 2003), 159–204.

[45] Joachim Gnilka, *Das Matthäusevangelium 1, Kommentar zu Kap. 1,1–13,58*, Herders Theologischer Kommentar zum Neuen Testament 1.1 (Freiburg: Herder, 1989), 212, 224–27.

readiness and ability to forgive is not a condition for the forgiveness asked of God. It is already a *consequence* of the divine forgiveness experienced in Jesus' death on the cross (Matt 26:28; see the words over the cup in the Eucharistic Prayer: "for the forgiveness of sins").

Institutionalized prayer

In the relationship presented here, in which prayer is oriented to the "unforeseeable past" and the "unimaginable future," individual prayer surpasses the character of a private event. This points to the transition from private to community prayer. The latter is involved in a process of institutionalization. Criteria such as theological integrity, literary quality, oratorical gestures, and a degree of "objectivity"—certainly hard to measure—characterize this transition. For every individual person praying, institutionalized prayer realizes, within a church-community context, an act of personal appropriation (not usurpation!) of a tradition of faith that has been handed down but that also remains a living thing.

5.2.2 Origins of Liturgical Prayer

How does a dialogue take place in liturgical prayer at all? A look at the beginning of the church's daily Liturgy of the Hours gives us a clue in the invitatory to the first hour, "O Lord, open my lips, that my mouth may declare your praise; Glory to the Father . . ." This is taken from Psalm 51(50):17, which also begins Jewish morning prayer. To break it down, in its liturgical context the verse says:

"Lord":

> *Anaclesis*: calling upon the name (*kyrios/dominus*) God has revealed, a precondition for entering into relationship.

"open my lips":

> *Epiclesis*: petition to be enabled to speak and empowered for dialogue, that is, God's action is first required before a human being can act.

"that my mouth may declare your praise":

> *Purpose of the petition*: to be enabled for divine praise/*anamnesis* of God's saving deeds. This is a kind of prophecy: when God acts on me, opening my lips, I will be able to praise God.

> The customary relationship between praise/thanksgiving and petition (see chap. 3.2.3) is here reversed. The petition does not

arise out of praise and thanksgiving but instead precedes them. Whereas in the Eucharistic Prayer, for example, praise and thanks presuppose the already existing religious "I" and "we," here the prayer is about bringing them into existence.

"Glory to the Father . . .":
Doxology: praising the Trinity, something that will be done repeatedly in the course of the Liturgy of the Hours.

Since St. Benedict this has been followed by the invitatory psalm, 95(94). In the prologue to the Rule of St. Benedict this psalm is given as the reason for the basic attitude of monks, and of Christians in general: to listen with "astonished ears" to hear "the divine voice, which daily cries out to us: 'Today, if you hear his voice, do not harden your hearts.'"[46] The psalm continues with a quotation, primarily from Numbers 14, where God responds to Israel's defection during the years in the wilderness with a cursing oath: "They shall not enter into my rest!" To put it in positive terms, those who today listen to God's voice *will* enter into the Promised Land. This "today" is the *kairos* that God offers every day. Each day is thus a day of salvation. Israel's history becomes a warning to Jews and Christians at prayer to take today seriously.[47]

5.2.3 God's "Today" in the Synthesis of Time: Collapsing of Past and Future in the Now

Identification of roles by invocation

The question then is: how shall we bridge the hiatus between past and future in worship? This is an existential act that must be prepared for. It cannot happen through catechetical instruction alone; it already presupposes an act of faith carried out in prayer. But how can that

---

[46] Angelus A. Häussling, "Die Psalmen des Alten Testaments in der Liturgie des Neuen Bundes," in *Christologie der Liturgie. Der Gottesdienst der Kirche: Christusbekenntnis und Sinaibund*, ed. Klemens Richter and Benedikt Kranemann, Quaestiones disputatae 159 (Freiburg: Herder, 1995), 87–102, at 97.

[47] Albert Gerhards, "Geschichtskonstruktionen in liturgischen Texten des Judentums und Christentums," in *Kontinuität und Unterbrechung. Gottesdienst und Gebet in Judentum und Christentum*, ed. idem and Stephan Wahle, Studien zu Judentum und Christentum (Paderborn: Schöningh, 2005), 123–39.

hiatus be overcome in worship? Angelus A. Häussling has introduced the phrase "identification of roles by invocation" into the discussion.[48] Of crucial importance in this context is the way in which the religious "I" and "we" are constituted for the act of worship. According to Richard Schaeffler it requires, on the part of those praying, a synthesis of experience through reflection that enables identification and identity, because participation plays a special role in religious events of identification: in the Christian context it means experiencing participation in Jesus' destiny through a constantly repeated recitation of the events of his life, death, and resurrection. By means of an interpretation of one's own life experience in light of the gospel at worship one experiences "attachment of memory and expectation in the present." Schaeffler explains: "Everything that is said and done in the worship celebration takes its content from remembering in praise what God has already said and done. *Memory thus supplies the content for the religious celebration. But at the same time it must be said that it is the celebration that endows the content of memory with its effective presence.*"[49]

Called by name

The present within which the religious "I" and "we" are constituted out of the joining of remembered past and expected future is accomplished not through abstract thinking or in the pure interiority of imagination but in the language-act of calling on the name "in which the human being enters into correlation with God, in that encounter experiencing the long-ago saving acts of God as present in such a way that God's saving acts that are hoped for in the future appear in signs, but are also anticipated as effective in the present."[50]

---

[48] See Angelus A. Häussling, "Liturgy: Memorial of the Past and Liberation in the Present," in *The Meaning of the Liturgy*, ed. idem (Collegeville, MN: Liturgical Press, 1994), 107–18.

[49] Richard Schaeffler, "'Darum sind wir eingedenk.' Die Verknüpfung von Erinnerung und Erwartung in der Gegenwart der gottesdienstlichen Feier. Religionsphilosophische Überlegungen zur religiös verstandenen Zeit," in *Vom Sinn der Liturgie. Gedächtnis unserer Erlösung und Lobpreis Gottes*, ed. Angelus A. Häussling, Schriften der Katholischen Akademie in Bayern 140 (Düsseldorf: Patmos, 1991), 16–44, at 17.

[50] Ibid., 34.

In this sense an actualized relationship to God is logically prior to the act of worship: knowing that God has called us by name and calling on the Name of God in turn constitute the precondition for interpreting the worship event as dialogue. It consists of an act of eulogizing recall and confident petition. In this way liturgical prayer shows itself to be much more an expression of divine allowing-to-happen than an articulation of personal desires and petitions.

The constitutive act of calling on the name also reveals the linkage between the human and God as two interrelated subjects in prayer. Important for liturgical theology here is the consideration that the different liturgical forms attesting to a synthesis of time in the community's commemorative existence are saturated or "intersected" by the promised pneumatic presence of the risen Crucified One. Therefore in the synthesizing time-consciousness of the faithful, when the congregation remembers Jesus Christ's paschal mystery, his hidden presence in the "now" of the liturgical celebration can be experienced as well.

5.2.4 Fundamental Theological Structures of Jewish-Christian Methods of Prayer

Hearing precedes praying

For a right understanding of the specific method of Jewish and Christian prayer it is important to recognize that hearing precedes prayer. As Schaeffler notes, "Hear, O Israel . . ." (Deut 6:4-9; 11:13-21), the Jewish confession of faith, gives its specific character to all Jewish prayer, life, and thought, but it is not really a prayer: it is not the human person who calls on God but God who calls to the listening people. But when the Jewish faithful have bound those words that call them to listen "on [their] foreheads and in [their] hearts" they are able to speak and to direct their praise and petitions to God.

Praise and petition

Praise and petition, as will be shown, are not mutually exclusive actions but instead condition one another. "Hear, O Israel" is followed, in private and in community prayer in Judaism, by the prayer that is simply called *the* prayer (*ha Tefillah*), or also the Eighteen Benedictions because of its eighteen (later nineteen) petitions, and that is related to the "Our Father" of Christians.[51] These petitions reflect the various kinds of experiences in Jewish life and end with a summary benediction (*berakah*) that begins with a brief act of praise. "The summary benediction calls on God, praising God as the one who has already done and still does what those who pray this prayer expect God will also do now and in the future."[52] Angelus Häussling characterizes biblical as well as Jewish prayer in this way: "Prayer to the God of Israel is always confession of this God who is revealed in acts of salvation and judgment and in the message of the prophets. God is self-revealed and accepts those who are addressed and who listen into a contract of liberating confession sealed with a covenant."[53]

Jewish ways of prayer and Christian prayer

A structure and function analogous to those in Jewish prayer are found also in Christian prayers, not only in the Eucharistic Prayer, but also in the orations typical of the Roman liturgy, the collects (see chaps. 3.3; 4.1.4; 5.2.5.1). The different accents in Jewish and Christian prayer, which exist in spite of all they have in common, are associated primarily with their differing eschatological perspectives. The Old Testament and Jewish texts are overwhelmingly structured so that the petitionary element appears as the organic *verso* of the anamnesis of praise—in light of the open situation of the present and on the basis of the hope for a promised future in accord with God's fidelity and covenant promises. This can be shown in the Eighteen Benedictions, which begin with the invitatory known also in Christian liturgy: "O L-rd, open my lips, and my mouth shall declare your praise." This is followed by a long prayer of praise that says God remembers the devotion of the ancestors. Thus the sixth petition reads: "Forgive us, our Father, for we have sinned; pardon us, our King,

---

[51] See *Identität durch Gebet* (n. 44 above).

[52] Schaeffler, "Das Gebet" (see n. 41 above), 84.

[53] Angelus A. Häussling, "Die Übung der Tagzeiten in der Geschichte der Kirche. Gebet und Bekenntnis," *Heiliger Dienst* 57 (2003): 23–37, at 23; see Peter Ebenbauer, "Eingekehrt in Gottes Zeit. Gebetstheologische Beobachtungen zu Lobpreis und Danksagung in biblischen und nachbiblischen Kontexten," in *Kontinuität und Unterbrechung* (n. 47 above), 63–106, at 65.

for we have transgressed; for You do pardon and forgive. Blessed art thou, O L-rd, who is gracious, and does abundantly forgive."[54] The Jewish community of faith knows itself to be on a path that is open to the future. In praise, thanksgiving, and petition it entrusts itself to God's direction and at the same time, through such prayer, experiences God's blessing. We no longer encounter this attitude as a matter of course in Christian prayer texts. According to Peter Ebenbauer it can be shown that the *thanksgiving* that responds to Jesus and God's eschatological gift and miracle gives priority to Jesus' divine significance and to Davidic-messianic interpretation over praise of God, and that the *epicletic elements* are no longer the natural *verso* of praise and thanks but have acquired a specifically eschatological and ecclesiological focus.[55] Because of Jesus, Christian believers are no longer fundamentally located in a present situation that is part of the imperfect tense of an open history but in the perfect tense of the end-time epiphany of God. The epicletic dimension is concentrated in imploring the ratification of that epiphany throughout this world, especially in those places where the *ekklēsia* is at work (sacramental dimension). We may conclude from this, among other things, that, despite their structural relationships, it is not possible to conclude a linear development of the Eucharistic Prayer from the Jewish *berakah* (see chap. 3.2).

Epiclesis in the Roman liturgical tradition

The concentration on epicletic prayer is characteristic especially of the Roman liturgical tradition. This is true not only of the collects but above all of the Eucharistic Prayer, the Roman Canon, which nevertheless, despite the purely epicletic structure of its discourse (apart from the Preface and *Sanctus*), with anamnetic insertions, preserves the theological integrity of the heritage of the ancient church.[56] Peter Ebenbauer summarizes:

---

[54] https://www.tzion.org/articles/EighteenBenedictions.htm.

[55] Peter Ebenbauer, "Eingekehrt in Gottes Zeit" (see n. 53 above); idem, *Mehr als ein Gespräch. Zur Dialogik von Gebet und Offenbarung in jüdischer und christlicher Liturgie*, Studien zu Judentum und Christentum (Paderborn: Schöningh, 2010).

[56] For the structure of the Eucharistic Prayer see chap. 5.2.5.2.

Praise and thanksgiving, praising-and-blessing the commemoration of God, make up the common theological and cultic-logical foundation of Jewish and Christian worship and prayer. [That foundation] grounds the relationship between time and history that is so peculiar to Jewish and Christian liturgy. . . . Such prayer, in its language-structure, for the most part also results in an epicletic gesture in the broadest sense of the word, that is to say, a corresponding linguistic expression. . . . God's coming and remaining at hand in the figure of the biblically guaranteed witness to the power of his inexpressible Name acquires symbolic effectiveness in the epicletic calling-down and summoning gesture within the anamnetically encompassed euchology of the prayer.[57]

Lament

In particular, the experiences of the Shoah have sensitized us to acknowledging lament—alongside the already-mentioned prayers of praise, thanksgiving, and petition—as an adequate expression of Jewish-Christian relationship to God. Complaint to God is a form of prayer clearly attested in the Bible. Above all, it puts into words the contradiction between the attribution of power and goodness to God in light of conditions in the world. The theological foundation for lament is the Spirit-effected hope of believers, something given to every baptized person as a down payment on the reality of eschatological salvation (see Rom 8:23-25).

5.2.5 Forms and Formulae of Liturgical Prayer

In what follows we will speak, without making any claim to completeness, of some basic forms of liturgical prayer, especially those characteristic of the Roman liturgy: oration (collect), Eucharistic Prayer, doxology, acclamation, and litany.[58]

---

[57] Ebenbauer, "Eingekehrt in Gottes Zeit," 67–68.

[58] See the corresponding chapters in Rupert A. Berger, et al., *Gestalt des Gottesdienstes. Sprachliche und nichtsprachliche Ausdrucksformen*, 2nd rev. ed., Gottesdienst der Kirche 3 (Regensburg: Pustet, 1990).

5.2.5.1 Oration (Collect)

The form of the Roman Mass is essentially determined by the three so-called collects (*collecta* = collection, gathering) at the end of the introductory rite (*oratio*, prayer of the day), at the preparation of the gifts (*super oblata*, previously *secreta*, prayer over the gifts), and after communion (*post communionem*, closing prayer). The prayer of the day, as a rule, also functions as the oration in the various hours of the Liturgy of the Hours. The euchology of the collects largely determines the theology of the Mass.[59]

The current collect for the Easter Vigil reads in Latin:[60]

> *Oremus.*
> *Deus, qui hanc sacratissimam noctem*
> *gloria dominicae resurrectionis illustras,*
> *excita in Ecclesia tua adoptionis spiritum,*
> *ut, corpore et mente renovati,*
> *puram tibi exhibeamus servitutem.*
> *Per Dominum.*

In the translation the oration has the following structure:[61]

Invitation:	Let us pray.
	(silent prayer)
Address (anaclesis):	O God,
Predication (anamnesis):	who make this most sacred night radiant with the glory of the Lord's Resurrection,
Petition (epiclesis):	stir up in your Church a spirit of adoption,
Requested consequence:	so that, renewed in body and mind, we may render you undivided service.

---

[59] Winfried Haunerland, *Die Eucharistie und ihre Wirkungen im Spiegel der Euchologie des Missale Romanum*, Liturgiewissenschaftliche Quellen und Forschungen 71 (Münster: Aschendorff, 1989).

[60] *Missale Romanum ex decreto sacrosancti oecumenici Concilii Vaticani II instauratum auctoritate Pauli PP. VI promulgatum Ioannis Pauli PP. II cura recognitum.* Editio typica tertia (Rome: Typ. Vaticanis 2002), 360.

[61] *The Roman Missal* (see n. 6 above), 368.

Conclusion (doxology):	Through our Lord Jesus Christ, your Son,
	who lives and reigns with you
	in the unity of the Holy Spirit,
	one God, for ever and ever.
Acclamation:	Amen.

The oration has a basic anamnetic/epicletic structure; in the German version the Pauline motif of the "spirit of adoption" is clarified by an anamnetic insertion referring to baptism.

The indicative address, "O God" (without further attributes), is followed by a predication in a relative clause that names God, with praise and thanksgiving, as the one who from the beginning and again and again until today has done the things that are asked of God in the second, deprecative part of the oration. The petition is subdivided into the epiclesis proper and the consequences that are implored. The conclusion, in the tradition of Roman orations, is not an explicit doxology in the sense of praise, even though it exercises that function (obscured in German by the addition of "This we ask" before "through our Lord Jesus Christ").

5.2.5.2 Structure of the Eucharistic Canon

The genre "Great Thanksgiving," which includes other sacramental prayers of dedication and blessing besides the Eucharistic Prayer, also has an anamnetic-epicletic basic structure.[62] The anamnetic section may be divided, depending on the particular nature and provenience of the prayer, into (among others) a section of praise (*eulogia*) and thanksgiving (*eucharistia*).[63] In the Eucharist the account of the meal is inserted into this basic structure: the words of institution in the form of an insertion (embolism), which has a different status depending on the eucharistic tradition and can even be omitted; in every case it connects the institution of the Eucharist by Jesus to the remembering of his death and resurrection.[64] Depending on the

[62] See the text example in appendix 2.2.

[63] See chap. 3.2.

[64] *Anaphora of Addai and Mari*; see Reinhard Messner and Martin Lang, "Die Freiheit zum Lobpreis des Namens. Identitätsstiftung im eucharistischen Hochgebet und in verwandten jüdischen Gebeten," in *Identität durch Gebet*, 371–411.

tradition, the words of institution are referred more directly to the anamnetic (as in the West Syrian tradition) or the epicletic section (as in the Roman tradition). Within the "eucharistic block" there is a shift from remembrance (past) to petition (future): remembering (*memores*) the death and resurrection, we bring the gifts (*offerimus*) and pray (*et petimus*).

Unity of epiclesis and anamnesis

To that extent the Great Thanksgiving can only be divided theoretically into epicletic and anamnetic sections. From a pragmatic point of view of the prayer they constitute, instead, an indissoluble unit, more or less like the two sides of a single coin. The presentation of the gifts and the petition for eschatological completion and fulfillment of the reign of God that has begun in Jesus Christ takes place within the commemoration of Jesus Christ's paschal mystery.

> *Anamnetic section*
> Praise-filled memorial, *eulogia* and/or *eucharistia*
> *Institutio*
> Words of institution and "special anamnesis" with "epiclesis": *memores, offerimus, et petimus*
> *Epicletic section*
> Petition that these things be granted and fulfilled

The Egyptian Anaphora of Basil represents a high point among eucharistic prayers in ecumenical Christianity, from the point of view both of structure and of content. According to Achim Budde[65] it is arranged as follows:

> Praise of creation
> Memorial of salvation
> Account of institution
> Epiclesis
> *Memento*
> Doxology

---

[65] Achim Budde, *Die ägyptische Basilios-Anaphora. Text, Kommentar, Geschichte*, Jerusalemer Theologisches Forum 7 (Münster: Aschendorff, 2004), 206.

The praise of creation (with the *Sanctus*) and the doxology constitute the doxological frame (comparable to the opening and closing *berakah* in the more complex Jewish prayers). The memorial of salvation and the account of institution are assigned to the anamnetic section, the epiclesis and *memento* (intercessions) to the epicletic. The "meal event," with the account of institution and the epiclesis (which includes the "special anamnesis" because of its grammatical dependency) bracket and connect the two parts. The bridge is the present action: "We offer." The fourth Eucharistic Prayer in the Roman Missal is most like this one in its structure because it emulates the Antiochene type of anaphora, although with the insertion of a so-called consecration epiclesis before the account of institution:

Basic structure of Eucharistic Prayer IV
1. Praise of creation (unchangeable Preface, with *Sanctus*)
2. Memorial of salvation
3. "Consecration epiclesis"
4. Account of institution
5. Anamnesis and offering
6. "Communion epiclesis"
7. Intercessions (*memento*)
8. Closing doxology

The second Eucharistic Prayer,[66] which draws on the anaphora of the so-called *traditio apostolica* (see chap. 3.2.4), has a similar structure, but without an expansive memorial of salvation.

It is not only the Eucharistic Prayer that contains this basic structure. Rather, the liturgical tradition includes a great many prayers of consecration and blessing created in accord with the same basic anamnetic-epicletic structure (for example, the blessing of baptismal water, blessing of oils, ordination prayers, dedications of churches and altars).

The Roman Canon, the Eucharistic Prayer of the Roman liturgy that was created between the fourth and seventh centuries,[67] does

---

[66] See appendix 2.2.
[67] Josef Schmitz, "Canon Romanus," in *Prex Eucharistica 3: Studia, Pars prima: Ecclesia antiqua et occidentalis*, ed. Albert Gerhards, Heinzgerd Brakmann, and

have a basic anamnetic-epicletic structure, but it has been subjected to so much redaction that the various prayer forms are grouped symmetrically around the words of institution. According to Johannes H. Emminghaus[68] we find the following structure (here presented very schematically):

	Content and Function	Texts
E[1]	Praise in dialogue: Preface and Sanctus	Dominus vobiscum to Sanctus
D[1]	Transition and First Prayer for Acceptance	Te igitur

C[1]	First intercessions: for Church, Pope, Bishop
	    for the living
	First list of Saints
		In primis
		Memento Domine
		    famulorum
		Communicantes

B[1]	First Formula of Offering First (Consecratory) Epiclesis	Hanc igitur Quam oblationem
A	Double Consecration: Bread Wine (Exclamation and Acclamation) Anamnesis	Qui pridie Simili modo (Mysterium fidei . . .) Unde et memores
B[2]	Second formula of offering Second (Communion) Epiclesis	Supra quae Supplices te rogamus

C[2]	Second Intercessions: for the Deceased
	                for the Participants
	
	Second List of Saints
		Memento etiam
		Nobis quoque
		    peccatoribus
		Et societatem donare
		    digneris

D[2]	Concluding Blessing	Per quem haec omnia
E[2]	Praise of the final doxology	Per ipsum et cum ipso

5.2.5.3 Doxologies

In contrast to Jewish *berakah*, the New Testament and the originary phase of Christian liturgy saw the development of the doxology. Its

---

Martin Klöckener, Spicilegium Friburgense 42 (Fribourg: Universitätsverlag, 2005), 281–310.

[68] Johannes H. Emminghaus, *The Eucharist: Essence, Form, Celebration*, trans. Linda M. Maloney (Collegeville, MN: Liturgical Press, 2005); see appendix 2.

essential features are naming of the recipient, doxological predicate (often only as a noun), formula of eternity, acclamation. The most common is the "little doxology," especially at the end of the psalms in the Liturgy of the Hours, but also in popular prayers (e.g., the Rosary):

Doxological predicate:	Glory (be)
Naming of the recipient:	to the Father and to the Son and to the Holy Spirit
Eternity formula:	as it was in the beginning, is now, and ever shall be, world without end.
Acclamation:	Amen.

The *Gloria* at the beginning of Mass, on the other hand, is called the "great doxology."

The strongly monotheistic direction of prayer is already relaxed in the New Testament. For example, God is called "the Father of our Lord Jesus Christ." The Pauline letters frequently contain the formula "through Christ" (for example, in the Colossians hymn). The doxology can also refer directly to Christ (probably for the first time in Rev 5:13: "To the one seated on the throne *and* to the Lamb be blessing and honor and glory and might forever and ever!"). The next step in the development, following the explication of trinitarian belief, is the paratactic naming of the Holy Spirit, something we find already in triadic form in the New Testament (Matt 28:19). In the wake of the dogmatic developments in the fourth century the parataxis, that is, the placing of Father, Son, and Holy Spirit on the same plane, was given a new significance because it was now desirable to produce arguments from tradition for the equality of the divine being of the three persons (see chap. 3.5). In the first centuries the doxology "glory be to the Father through the Son in the Holy Spirit" dominated.[69] The different prepositions make it clear that the praise is directed to God,

[69] Basil the Great; see Albert Gerhards, "La doxologie, un chapitre défini-tif de l'histoire du dogme?," in *Trinité et liturgie. Conférences Saint-Serge, XXXe semaine d'études liturgiques, Paris, 28 juin–1er juillet 1983*, ed. Achille M. Triacca and Alessandro Pistoia, Bibliotheca 'Ephemerides liturgicae' Subsidia 32 (Rome: C.L.V.-Edizioni liturgiche, 1984), 103–18.

the Father of our Lord Jesus Christ. The Son is the mediator, and the Spirit is like the aura within which the doxological address takes place. The "unity" of the Holy Spirit refers to the nature of God and the church united in the Holy Spirit. So at the end of the Eucharistic Prayer, to this day, the Roman church prays:

Relation:	Through him and with him and in him
Recipient:	O God, almighty Father,
Mode:	in the unity of the Holy Spirit,
Predicate:	all glory and honor is yours,
Eternity formula:	for ever and ever.
Acclamation:	Amen.

5.2.5.4 Acclamations

Acclamations are basic forms of communicative expression that can also be spontaneous and require no special preparation. They represent the original and most fundamental form of "active participation" by the faithful. They exist as independent words or phrases (e.g., the *Kyrie* at the beginning of Mass) or in the context of the presider's prayers. We have already mentioned "Amen" as an affirmation of a prayer. Within the Eucharistic Prayer the various liturgical regions, especially the East, insert a great number of acclamations. They can appear:

1. in the opening dialogue: three-part antiphonal forms (The Lord be with you / and with your spirit. Lift up your hearts / we lift them up to the Lord. Let us give thanks to the Lord our God / it is right and just)
2. at the end of the Preface: the *Sanctus*
3. in the "post-*Sanctus*" (memorial of salvation): *Kyrie* acclamations and/or Amen (sometimes expanded), at the end, for example, of petitions for mercy
4. in the account of institution: ending the words over the bread and cup with "Amen" (sometimes expanded)
5. in the field of the "special anamnesis": anamnetic acclamations at the beginning or end (sometimes transitional to petition)
6. in the epiclesis: conclusion of the petition over bread and cup with "amen" (sometimes expanded)

7. in the *memento* (intercessions): acclaimed with *Kyrie eleison*; sometimes expanded in part; other epicletic acclamations

8. at the end of the concluding doxology: ending with "Amen" (sometimes expanded)

Significance

Acclamations are by no means merely secondary, because they are often an essential part of the linguistic and theological structure (e.g., the *Sanctus*). The acclamations are informative about the community's understanding of its role from a pragmatic point of view:

- response: "and with your spirit"; "we lift them up to the Lord" (first and second responses in the opening dialogue)
- empowering assent: "it is right and just" (third response in the opening dialogue)
- affirmation: Amen (at the end of the Eucharistic Prayer)
- implementation/solemnization: "Holy, holy, holy . . ."; "Christ has died . . ." (*Sanctus* and anamnetic acclamation after the words of institution).

The acclamations to the Eastern churches' anaphoras make the church visible as the subject of the eucharistic action. They call into question the idea of exclusive representation grounded in the Roman Canon and affirmed in the exegesis of that canon, and its further development to the point that the priest is seen as the exclusive representative of Christ.[70]

5.2.5.5 *Litanies*

Litanies are invocations with repeated refrains. In the liturgy the litany of the saints at the blessing of baptismal water in the Easter Vigil and other rites of blessing and consecration plays a significant role. There are numerous other litanies, especially in the realm of popular piety, corresponding to particular devotional traditions (e.g., to the Holy Eucharist, to the Sacred Heart of Jesus). The most important

---

[70] See also Gerhards, "Geschichtskonstruktionen." (see n. 47 above).

of these is probably the Marian or Lauretian Litany, not least because of its connection to the Eastern churches' Akathistos hymn.[71]

Litanies are part of every liturgical ceremony in the Eastern churches. The intentions are presented by the deacon and acclaimed with a petition for mercy, with a closing prayer by the priest at the end. The General Intercessions or Prayers of the People in the Mass also follow this model. They were reintroduced by Vatican II (*SC* 53) and as a rule have the following structure:

> Introduction (priest)
> Intention (deacon or lector)
> *(Silent prayer)*
> Acclamation (cantor/congregation)
> [additional prayer intentions]
> Closing prayer (priest)
> Amen acclamation (congregation)

A contrasting exception is the Great Litany on Good Friday, which has the following structure:

> Intention (deacon): "Let us pray for . . ."
> Instruction to kneel (deacon)
> *(Silent prayer)*
> Instruction to rise (deacon)
> Collect (priest)
> Amen acclamation (congregation)

5.2.6 Prayer in Action: Postures and Gestures

Prayer is, from the human point of view, first of all entering into relationship through an act of gathering, something that takes place when people turn their attention away from themselves and toward someone else, someone who, however, is not visible. This can take place in Christian liturgical prayer through the so-called orientation of prayer, turning to the East.[72]

---

[71] Berger, *Gestalt des Gottesdienstes* (see n. 58 above), 216.
[72] Albert Gerhards, "*Versus orientem, versus populum*. Zum gegenwärtigen Stand einer alten Streitfrage," *Theologische Revue* 98 (2002): 15–22.

Turning to the East

For the most part a general use of this orientation came about relatively late. Its roots are varied. The usage common in pagan religiosity was reinterpreted by Christians: in place of the rising sun, Christian prayer is directed to the *sol salutis*: Christ, who arises in the East, from the Father. The appellation "sun of justice" or "sun of righteousness" (Mal 3:20) was commonly used by theological writers from the second century onward; the first witness to a Christian orientation to the East for prayer goes back to about the year 100. Probably the most powerful expression was found in the turning to Christ during the baptismal liturgy, in the rite of *apotaxis* and *syntaxis*: the baptizands stood facing the West and rejected Satan by spitting (*apotaxis*). Then they turned to the East and accepted Christ (*syntaxis*). The question of positioning for prayer has lately been more discussed in connection with the appropriate expression of the Eucharistic Prayer and the orientation of the church building.[73]

Standing and bowing before God

There is an explicit direction for posture in other community acts of prayer as well: for example, at the beginning of the Eucharistic Prayer when, after the greeting "The Lord be with you," the second exchange is: "Lift up your hearts—We lift them up to the Lord." This, too, is about an explicit direction toward God, in this case clothed in the spatial image of the heaven over us. The deliberate turn toward God corresponds to a particular posture. In all the liturgies of the ancient church the appropriate attitude for prayer is standing before God. God makes the human being a partner who may approach God face-to-face. Of course, we also stand before God as imperfect people, so that bowing is an equally appropriate attitude for prayer. In the Eastern churches there is a whole series of prayers said while bowing.

---

[73] Joseph Ratzinger (Pope Benedict XVI), *Theology of the Liturgy: The Sacramental Foundation of Christian Existence*, trans. Michael J. Miller (San Francisco: Ignatius Press, 2014); see also Albert Gerhards, Thomas Sternberg, and Walter Zahner, eds., *Communio-Räume. Auf der Suche nach der angemessenen Raumgestalt katholischer Liturgie*, Bild, Raum, Feier, Studien zu Kirche und Kunst 2 (Regensburg: Schnell & Steiner, 2003); Gerhards, "La doxologie" (see n. 69 above).

The West is also familiar with bowing, for example, at the *Gloria Patri* or the doxological strophes of the hymns in the Liturgy of the Hours.

Prostration and kneeling

Another prayer posture is prostration, representing an act of subjection that seems appropriate on certain occasions. Such a point in the church year is Good Friday, when, at the beginning of the liturgy, priest and assistants prostrate themselves, as is done once in Jewish liturgy on the Day of Atonement, Yom Kippur. Analogously, there is a prostration in the ordination liturgies and at profession liturgies of religious orders. Otherwise the Western liturgy uses kneeling, which in a sense represents an attenuated form of prostration. Here again it is a matter of deliberately making oneself small. It is significant that in earlier times it was not usual to kneel during the Easter season (compare this with the Akathistos hymn in the East, in which there is no prostration), because it did not seem appropriate to the festive character of the season.

Processions

Prayer can also find a particular expression in forms of movement within space. The procession relates particular spaces to one another, thus creating a space of its own. The people praying are also set in motion together as a result and acquire an identity through their common, perceptible action toward a common goal. In their action the community of believers represent the pilgrim people of God, among whom or at whose head Christ himself (often represented by a cross or other Christ-symbol) travels with them. Public processions and pilgrimages add the element of spectatorship in the sense of an interpretive perception of the world.[74]

Position of the hands

What position should the hands assume during prayer? The older attitudes include the so-called *orans* position (somewhat outstretched

[74] Sabine Felbecker, *Die Prozession. Historische und systematische Untersuchungen zu einer liturgischen Ausdruckshandlung*, Münsteraner theologische Abhandlungen 39 (Altenberge: Oros, 1995).

arms with open hands). Especially in the Mediterranean this was the usual prayer position for all believers; only in the course of time did it become specific to the ordained priesthood. In contrast to this gesture is the "Northern" attitude with closed (folded) hands, expressing a concentration on what is within. Beyond these we find a spectrum of postures for personal prayer (folded arms, covering the face with the hands, etc.) that, similarly to folded hands, support an inward act of prayer.

5.3 The Language of Liturgy

5.3.1 Language as Means of Liturgical Expression

Language is one of the primary means of expression in Christian liturgy. It follows both anthropological and cultural[75] as well as essentially liturgical-theological premises.[76] When we treat of language it is always in light of the specific communicative situation of worship. It is here that encounter between God and the human takes place, but also communication in human community with certain assigned roles.

The task of liturgical language

Liturgical language participates in the celebration of the mystery of divine self-revelation in Jesus Christ, confessed as present in the liturgy; from this comes its plausibility. The task of language in liturgy is neither to inform about the content of the faith nor to comment on the actions. Rather, language is an essential part and agent of liturgical performance.[77]

---

[75] From the perspective of linguistics see Elisabeth Hug, *Reden zu Gott. Überlegungen zur deutschen liturgischen Gebetssprache* (Zürich: Benziger, 1985); Albrecht Greule, "Die liturgischen Text- und Redesorten," *Heiliger Dienst* 56 (2002): 231–39.

[76] Winfried Haunerland, "*Lingua Vernacula*. Zur Sprache der Liturgie nach dem II. Vatikanum," *Liturgisches Jahrbuch* 42 (1992): 219–38; Gunda Brüske, "Plädoyer für liturgische Sprachkompetenz. Thesen zur Sprachlichkeit der Liturgie," *Archiv für Liturgiewissenschaft* 42 (2000): 317–43; see also Josef Schermann, *Die Sprache im Gottesdienst*, Innsbrucker theologische Studien 18 (Innsbruck and Vienna: Tyrolia, 1987).

[77] Stephan Winter, "Am Grund des rituellen Sprachspiels. Notwendige Klärungen zu 'Performance' und 'Performativität' in liturgiewissenschaftlichem Interesse," *Bibel und Liturgie* 84 (2011): 12–27.

Performance

The concept of "performance" is taken from linguistic philosophy, in particular the work of John L. Austin. The speech-act does something: that is, it creates a reality apart from speech itself. For example, when the justice of the peace pronounces a couple married, they are married. An authorized person performs an action on the eligible subject, here a couple, and that action creates a reality. Formulae such as "I promise fidelity to you" or "I love you" or "I forgive you" create a new situation that did not exist before the words were spoken. Liturgical celebrations, especially the sacraments, contain many such performative utterances. In the case of the marriage liturgy the pronouncement that the couple are husband and wife or the nuptial blessing, which is central to the liturgy's doxological event, are such utterances. These are not merely texts to be understood in a linguistic-logical sense, as locutionary in nature; they effect an action (they are illocutionary) and because they bring about a result they are perlocutionary.

When something is spoken in the liturgy, reality is changed. A new thing is created; action takes place in words.[78] The language-event has a dynamic quality. The statement "I baptize you in the name of the Father and of the Son and of the Holy Spirit" not only states that something is happening; it *accomplishes* the baptism (the catechumen becomes a baptized Christian) and thus has performative power. Theologically, what is decisive is the tie to the reality of salvation that is being celebrated.

> Liturgical language . . . makes us capable of adjusting to reality in its several manifestations: to the reality of salvation which comes to us from God by the mediation of Jesus Christ, who is announced in the texts of Scripture and is accomplished in the words of the Canon, and received in the words of the action of grace. All these words prepare the soul to hear what they propose and effect.[79]

[78] Richard Schaeffler, *Kleine Sprachlehre des Gebets*, Sammlung Horizonte 26 (Einsiedeln and Trier: Johannes Verlag, 1988), 18.

[79] Jean Ladrière, "The Performativity of Liturgical Language," trans. John Griffiths, *Concilium* 9, no. 1 (1973): 50–62 (= Herman A. P. Schmidt and David N.

When the Eucharistic Prayer for Maundy Thursday adds "that is today," the language indicates the reality that encounters the people in this celebration.

Significance of language for community

Thus liturgical language serves not only as a vehicle for prayer before and to God but at the same time is a medium of communication within a human community impressed by what is celebrated as well as the special characteristics of the traditional community "church." Language is part of the liturgical *actio* and so is a community act. Language is essential to the fact that community exists and can communicate; therefore such language must be appropriate to that community. At the same time the community of tradition shapes the language of liturgy in a very particular way. Throughout the history of the liturgy such linguistic shapings and formulations, characteristic of worship, have been handed down; in the present they continue to be received and are to an extent being augmented.

Roles and offices

In addition, different roles and offices in worship have been shaped within the church's community of tradition; these are also identified by figures of speech. This is true, for example, of the formulae for greeting and blessing: certain parts are reserved for the presider and others for the congregation. The same is true of the presidential prayers, which are tied to specific roles or offices, and of the readings and the gospel, etc. Consequently, the language of worship is multi-layered and corresponds both to the differentiation within Christian worship and also to the differing life situations within which people come to worship before God. This is reflected especially in the different linguistic forms of the worship service, such as praise, thanksgiving, petition, lament, as well as confession and admonition.

The consequence of participation in the vertical as well as the horizontal dimension of worship is that the language of worship must

---

Power, eds., *Liturgical Experience of Faith* [New York: Herder and Herder, 1973], 50–62, at 58).

be appropriate to the complex reality and communicative situation. This is true also of the linguistic level, that is, grammar and rhetoric. How God approaches those who pray and is experienced by them can be expressed very concretely in forms of speech, even though these are always only approximations.

For example, *Deus, qui nos ad imaginem tuam creasti*[80] uses a relative clause and a predicate to express who God is and how God can be experienced by us. The construction *Deus, qui* ("O God, who") produces an especially close tie between address to God and predication of quality. Vernacular forms express this in different forms: "O God, who have created us in your image."[81]

Recurring linguistic elements

The form of language thus expresses what sustains the prayer as a faith-event and what happens within it. Hence the liturgy makes use also of particular rhetorical elements that frequently recur in standardized form. The collects regularly use the elements of anaclesis, predication, petition, doxology, and community acclamation (see chap. 5.2.5.1). The fundamental dialogical action of the liturgy takes place in the panegyric predication and accompanying petition: *katabasis* and *anabasis* are "put into words." The standardization of linguistic actions also makes it easier for all those present to participate in the liturgy.

Linguistic tools in liturgy

Other rhetorical tools play a role in a vernacular liturgy and should not be overlooked. Thus the liturgy makes use of the following linguistic tools, among others:[82]

---

[80] *Missale Romanum* (see n. 60 above), 828.

[81] *The Roman Missal* (see n. 6 above), 1317.

[82] Benedikt Kranemann, "Funktionswandel der Rhetorik in der katholischen Liturgie. Deutschsprachige Gebetstexte von der Aufklärung des 19. Jahrhunderts bis zur Liturgiereform des späten 20. Jahrhunderts," in *Religion und Rhetorik*, ed. Holt Meyer and Dirk Uffelmann, Religionswissenschaft heute 4 (Stuttgart: Kohlhammer, 2007), 102–21.

Paradox	In the blessing of the baptismal water (first formula) baptism is compared to the flood, thus signifying both destruction and new beginning ("for you have destroyed the old man in order to awaken new life") and expressing the paradox and ultimate incomprehensibility of the faith-event.
Parallelism	This stylistic element can, for example, express the intercalation of stages in time; thus the *Exsultet* says: This is the night, / when once you led our forebears, Israel's children, / from slavery in Egypt / and made them pass dry-shod through the Red Sea. // This is the night / that with a pillar of fire / banished the darkness of sin. // This is the night / that even now, throughout the world, / sets Christian believers apart from worldly vices / and from the gloom of sin, / leading them to grace / and joining them to his holy ones. // This is the night, / when Christ broke the prison-bars of death / and rose victorious from the underworld.[83] The parallel sentence structure relates the different times to one another, underscoring their simultaneity. The next sentence thus emerges all the more prominently: "Our birth would have been no gain, / had we not been redeemed."[84]

---

[83] *The Roman Missal* (see n. 6 above), 354–55.
[84] Ibid., 355.

Pleonasm	Pleonasm works by piling up words with similar meaning that also possess vividness and emphatic character, as in the beginning of the *Exsultet*:
	Exult, let them exult, the hosts of heaven, / exult, let Angel ministers of God exult, / let the trumpet of salvation / sound aloud our mighty King's triumph! / Be glad, let earth be glad, as glory floods her, / ablaze with light from her eternal King, / let all corners of the earth be glad, / knowing an end to gloom and darkness. / Rejoice, let Mother Church also rejoice, / arrayed with the lightning of his glory, / let this holy building shake with joy, / filled with the mighty voices of the peoples.[85]
Quotation	This element possesses a special theological weight and authority because it marks an identification of situations and roles, and hence contemporaneity, as in the blessing of baptismal water (first formula; see appendix 1.2): "After his Resurrection, [he] commanded his disciples: 'Go forth, teach all nations, baptizing them in the name of the Father and of the Son and of the Holy Spirit'" (see Matt 28:19, Vulgate).[86]

This list of rhetorical tools could be extended.

---

[85] Ibid., 353.
[86] Ibid., 377.

5.3.2 History of Language in the Worship of the Catholic Church

The history of the language used in the liturgy is far more complicated than one might suppose in light of the long dominance of Latin in the Roman Catholic Church.[87] The various Christian liturgies made use of a great number of languages; they also changed languages and sometimes used more than one simultaneously. The first communities in Syro-Palestine would have spoken both Aramaic and Greek in their liturgies. Greek, the common language of antiquity in its *koinē* form, very quickly became the language of Christian liturgy in many regions of the western Mediterranean. In polyglot Rome, Greek was the language of liturgy in the first centuries. Besides Greek, but also replacing it, we find in ancient church liturgy and in the transition from antiquity to the Middle Ages such languages as Old Ethiopian (Ge'ez), Armenian, Coptic, Nubian, and Georgian, as well as Syriac, linguistically close to Aramaic. In the Roman province of Africa, by contrast, Latin was used in worship in a cultural context in which Punic was spoken. Here, then, liturgical language was already something set apart.[88]

Liturgical language as artificial

From the second century onward there was increasing use of Latin in Rome for catechumenal rites, initiation, and in the Liturgy of the Word. In the second half of the fourth century, under Pope Damasus, Latin was established as the liturgical language for the Eucharist also, and it was subsequently used in the mission field even though some vernacular elements continued to be employed, for example, in baptism, marriage, and confession; in hymnody; and in preaching. While we can here see a clear break between liturgical and everyday language, the same was true in Rome, because this liturgical Latin was an artificial language clearly separate from that in daily use. The level of the language, neologisms in vocabulary and syntax, a succinct style (*gravitas romana*), rhythm (*cursus*), and the adoption of biblical

---

[87] Keith F. Pecklers, *Dynamic Equivalence: The Living Language of Christian Worship* (Collegeville, MN: Liturgical Press, 2003).

[88] Georg Kretschmar, "Kirchensprache," *Theologische Realenzyklopädie* 19 (1990): 74–92, at 74–80.

and pagan linguistic and stylistic elements marked this liturgical Latin.[89] At the same time new language was developed to express the content of Christian faith. Latin liturgical language was thus from the very beginning a kind of speech that was not generally understood. At the same time, however, the shift to this liturgical language was motivated by the desire to see the opportunity to join in prayer and to understand the liturgy as constitutive for Christian worship.

Tension between appropriateness and intelligibility

Here there are already signs of a tension that has accompanied discussions of liturgical language through the centuries: on the one hand the language ought to be in accord with the sacred event of worship and in a certain sense even veil it; on the other hand there is a demand that the faithful should be able to cooperate in the worship service with understanding and thus also through language. So we can often read contemporary understandings of liturgy in their manner of dealing with language.

Latin acted as a bond between various liturgical families. It was used not only in the Roman but also in the Old Gallican, Mozarabic (Old Spanish), Celtic, and Ambrosian liturgies.

Though we should not overlook cultural-historical factors that served to solidify the use of Latin in the liturgy, political changes (especially the strengthening of Byzantine rule in the sixth century) caused Greek to recover its significance in the liturgy in the sixth/ seventh centuries in Rome and Italy. The creed was recited in both languages, and in the Liturgy of the Word the readings were proclaimed in both Latin and Greek.[90] Until late in the Middle Ages the liturgy of the Catholic Church retained texts and hymns in Greek. Even today, Greek texts such as the *Kyrie eleison* (part of the Roman Mass since 500) and the Trisagion on Good Friday (first attested at the Council of Chalcedon in 451) are sung.

---

[89] Martin Klöckener, "Zeitgemässes Beten. Messorationen als Zeugnisse einer sich wandelnden Kultur und Spiritualität," in *Bewahren und Erneuern* (see n. 14 above), 114–42, at 125.

[90] Leopold Lentner, *Volkssprache und Sakralsprache. Geschichte einer Lebensfrage bis zum Ende des Konzils von Trient*, Wiener Beiträge zur Theologie 5 (Vienna: Herder, 1964), 20.

In subsequent centuries Latin liturgical language was increasingly less understood; explanations became necessary. The eventual result was alienation from the language of worship and so also from participation. The language thus preserved had developed into sacred speech.

Controversies over appropriate liturgical language

Still, subsequent centuries saw repeated conflicts over appropriate liturgical language.[91] In the wake of the Slavic mission in the ninth century the Greek missionaries Constantine (Cyril) and Methodius used Slavic and translated the Roman Mass into the vernacular. They evoked strong criticism because only the languages inscribed on the cross (John 19:20)—Hebrew, Greek, and Latin—were regarded as sacred languages. Pope John VIII (872–882) decided, nevertheless, that it was contrary neither to faith nor to church teaching for the Mass or the Liturgy of the Hours to be sung in Slavic or for the biblical texts to be proclaimed in that language, because God created not only the older languages but all others as well. Even so, subsequent centuries saw repeated conflicts over the question of language.

There was also controversy over liturgical language in connection with the case of the Chinese rite, that is, the question of the extent to which Confucian rites could be adapted to the Catholic liturgy. In 1615, Pope Paul V (1605–1621) authorized the Jesuits to celebrate the Roman liturgy in Mandarin, but Pope Alexander VII (1655–1667) in 1661 forbade all attempts to introduce the vernacular into the liturgy, saying that it was against the dignity of the mysteries to make the texts of the missal accessible to all the faithful.

Trent: Rejection of the vernacular Mass

The Council of Trent spoke out against the use of the vernacular in the Mass. While there was recognition of the significance of liturgy for instruction in the faith, it was said that this should be done not by making the language comprehensible but by explanation.[92] The problems associated with liturgical language are clearly revealed here.

[91] Ibid., 47–53.
[92] See DH 1749, 1759.

Attitude of the Reformers to the vernacular liturgy

The Reformation opened the liturgy to German, although as to the process we need to differentiate among Reformers. Beginning in 1520, congregations that had joined the Reformation celebrated in the vernacular. Martin Luther's "Deutsche Messe und Ordnung Gottis diensts, zu Wittemberg fürgenommen"[93] appeared in 1526. German was used throughout, among other things for the purpose of preaching the Gospel to all. Luther made the vernacular liturgy possible, though cautiously and always with respect for freedom of decision. In 1525 he said in a sermon:

> I have struggled so long with the German Mass because I did not want to give cause for the factious spirits [i.e., Karlstadt and the pietists] who jump in without thinking or considering whether God wants it. But now, since so many from every land have begged me, with so many writings and letters, and the secular power is urging me so strongly, we seemingly cannot excuse ourselves or argue against them, but must attend and see that it is God's will.[94]

So the Latin Mass continued alongside the German.[95] Luther explained the value he still accorded the Latin by saying: "For in no wise would I want to discontinue the service in the Latin language, because the young are my chief concern. . . . I would rather train such youth and folk who could also be of service to Christ in foreign lands and be able to converse with the natives there."[96] Calvin, in contrast, vehemently rejected Latin in the liturgy. For the Reformers the Mass, and worship overall, was predominantly a word-event in which the Word now became the means of grace.[97] The vernacular liturgy is the logical consequence.

---

[93] WA 19:72–113 = LW 53:51–90.

[94] WA 19:50–51 [not in LW].

[95] See the Latin *Formula Missae et Communionis*, 1523 (WA 12:205–20 = LW 53:15–40).

[96] WA 19:74 = LW 53:63.

[97] Teresa Berger, "Die Sprache der Liturgie," in *Handbuch der Liturgik. Liturgiewissenschaft in Theologie und Praxis der Kirche*, ed. Hans-Christoph Schmidt-Lauber, Michael Meyer-Blank, and Karl-Heinz Bieritz, 3rd ed. (Göttingen: Vandenhoeck & Ruprecht, 2003), 798–806, at 800.

In the Roman Catholic Church as well, after the Council of Trent, voices were repeatedly raised, calling for vernacular singing during the Latin Mass, or prayers read in the vernacular after the priest had spoken them in Latin; among these, in the sixteenth century, were those of Johann Leisentrit[98] and Georg Witzel.[99]

The Catholic Enlightenment

Around 1800 the Catholic Enlightenment discussed vernacular liturgical language in connection with the question of its interpretation of worship; theologians at the time published individual liturgical texts and especially rituals in the vernacular (see chap. 3.8 above). It was their opinion that an edifying and educative worship service must be able to be understood.

Liturgical language and the different basic understandings of liturgy

Thus we find very different reasons for the various languages (Latin or vernacular) in liturgy. At the same time we can perceive a variety of basic perceptions of liturgy: is it a time for the whole community, the people of God, all initiates, or is it something for religious specialists, the ordained? Is liturgy to be understood as a celebration by the church that is open to the public, or is it a sacred precinct to be hidden and protected by an arcane language? Should the liturgy open itself to a culture through its language and thereby influence it, or is it an event that is elevated above all inculturation?

The Liturgical Movement made it possible for the vernacular to be welcomed. This was not in the first instance about a liturgy celebrated in the vernacular but rather that the faithful might be able to join in the priest's prayer by reading along in a translation of the text of the Mass. This is shown, for example, by the publication of missals for

---

[98] Josef Gülden, *Johann Leisentrits pastoralliturgische Schriften*, Studien zur katholischen Bistums- und Klostergeschichte 4 (Leipzig: St Benno-Verlag, 1963).

[99] Karlheinz Diez, "Reform der Kirche: Georg Witzels Vorschläge zur Erneuerung des Gottesdienstes, der Predigt und der Katechese," in Werner Kathrein, et al., *Im Dienst um die Einheit und die Reform der Kirche: Zum Leben und Werk Georg Witzels*, Fuldaer Hochschulschriften 43 (Frankfurt: Knecht, 2003), 41–81.

the people (in Germany the best known was that of Anselm Schott, which first appeared in 1884). Only gradually, in the early twentieth century, did Masses begin to be celebrated in which the people took up the prayer texts and music, as in the *Missa recitata* or "dialogue Mass," the "pray-and-sing Mass" or the "community Mass." The purpose was "active participation" (*participatio actuosa*) on the part of the faithful; the concept was used as early as 1903 by Pope Pius X in his *Tra le sollecitudini* (see chap. 3.10.1 above). This pope saw a connection between the dignity of worship and the strengthening of the Christian spirit. Taking an active part in the liturgy meant, for him, being able to live from the primary source of faith.

All this was about renewal of the church and spirituality, participation in the *mysterium*. Increasingly, use of the vernacular in the liturgy was regarded as a means to that end.[100]

The extent of the use of the vernacular in the liturgy and its location remained a matter of controversy. Josef A. Jungmann suggested a solution in 1944: "making it possible for the faithful to participate more intimately even in the language of the Mass, if possible not only by reading a parallel text."[101] Other voices argued against, for example, an idea of the "universal priesthood" that was regarded as dubious; these feared that vernacular usage would loosen ties to the Roman Church.[102] Nevertheless, the goal of a vernacular liturgy was pursued at different levels within the Roman Catholic Church in the first half of the last century. Many dioceses produced diocesan appendices (*Collectio Rituum*) for the *Rituale Romanum* with texts for baptism, marriage, and burial, among others; some of these, while differing from diocese to diocese, contained many prayers and other texts in the vernacular. A number of diocesan synods also expressed positive attitudes toward the use of the vernacular in worship.

---

[100] See also Pius Parsch, *We Are Christ's Body . . .* , trans. and adapted by Clifford Howell (London: Challoner, 1962), translation of *Volksliturgie: Ihr Sinn und Umfang* (Klosterneuburg: Volksliturgischer Verlag, 1940).

[101] Quoted from Theodor Maas-Ewerd, *Die Krise der Liturgischen Bewegung in Deutschland und Österreich. Zu den Auseinandersetzungen um die "liturgische Frage" in den Jahren 1939 bis 1944*, Studien zur Pastoralliturgie 3 (Regensburg: Pustet, 1981), 616.

[102] See ibid., 174, 185, 282, 350, 424–25, and elsewhere.

The 1947 encyclical *Mediator Dei*, in contrast, showed considerable reservation: "The use of the Latin language, customary in a considerable portion of the Church, is a manifest and beautiful sign of unity, as well as an effective antidote for any corruption of doctrinal truth. In spite of this, the use of the mother tongue in connection with several of the rites may be of much advantage to the people."[103]

5.3.3 Liturgical Language at Vatican II and in the Postconciliar Liturgical Reform

The ideal: liturgy in Latin; vernacular "for pastoral reasons"

Vatican II's Constitution on the Sacred Liturgy goes far beyond *Mediator Dei*. There were repeated calls in the *aula* for an expanded space for the vernacular in worship. Of the eighty-one fathers who spoke on the corresponding passage in the Schema on the Liturgy, sixty-seven favored a greater place for the vernacular.[104] Still, liturgy in Latin remained the council's ideal. *Sacrosanctum Concilium* 36.1 emphasizes: "The use of the Latin language, except when a particular law prescribes otherwise, is to be preserved in the Latin rites." The exceptions are, among others, the right to a Roman liturgy in Slavic and permission for the German Mass. However, *SC* 36.2 concedes the right to give a larger scope to the vernacular in the liturgy for pastoral reasons. Even so, the statements favoring a vernacular liturgy are amazingly reticent. Concrete directions for the Mass are found in *SC* 54, for the sacraments and sacramentals in *SC* 63, and for the Liturgy of the Hours in *SC* 101.

---

[103] *Mediator Dei* 60.

[104] For the course of the discussion see Emil Joseph Lengeling, *Die Konstitution des Zweiten Vatikanischen Konzils über die heilige Liturgie. Lateinisch-deutscher Text*, Lebendiger Gottesdienst 5/6 (Münster: Regensberg, 1964), 81–82; Monika Selle, "Latein und Volkssprache im Gottesdienst. Die Aussagen des Zweiten Vatikanischen Konzils über die Liturgiesprache," dissertation in typescript (Munich, 2001), available at http://edoc.ub.uni-muenchen.de/3758/1/Selle_Monika.pdf (accessed 12 April 2017).

Shift to a vernacular liturgy

At least equally surprising is the speed with which the shift from Latin to vernacular liturgy took place after the council. By 1967 successive permissions had been granted for use of the vernacular for the entire Roman liturgy. Since then the Latin liturgical books have been used as *editio typica*, to be followed by vernacular liturgical books. In 1970, speaking to the Consilium (commission for carrying out the Constitution on the Liturgy), the pope indicated that efforts had been made so that "the people of God should better understand the texts of the liturgy, above all through permission for the use of the vernacular, and be able to participate more actively in the sacred celebrations" (DEL 2074). By 1979 the liturgy was being celebrated in 342 languages and dialects.[105] Since then the number can only have increased. There was internal conflict over the responsibility for church approbation of vernacular texts. While SC 36.3 accorded the corresponding right to the local churches, it was quickly reclaimed after the council by the Holy See. The *CIC* 1983 no longer mentions the right of episcopal conferences to approve vernacular liturgical texts.[106]

Basic rules for translation: the Instruction of 1969

Likewise, the question about the criteria for translations had to be clarified after the council. As early as 25 January 1969 the Consilium had issued the instruction *De interpretatione textum liturgicorum*, a legally binding document "On the translation of liturgical texts."[107] This so-called "instruction for translation" set forth some basic principles. It contains central statements about liturgical language, according

[105] Winfried Haunerland, "Liturgiesprache," *Lexikon für Theologie und Kirche* 6 (1997), 988–89, at 988.

[106] Reiner Kaczynski, "Theologischer Kommentar zur Konstitution über die heilige Liturgie *Sacrosanctum Concilium*," in *Herders Theologischer Kommentar zum Zweiten Vatikanischen Konzil*, ed. Peter Hünermann and Bernd Jochen Hilberath (Freiburg: Herder, 2004), 2:1–227, at 105–11.

[107] Consilium for Implementing the Constitution on the Sacred Liturgy, "*Comme le Prévoit:* On the Translation of Liturgical Texts for Celebrations with a Congregation," 25 January 1969, available at https://www.ewtn.com/library/curia/conslepr.htm.

to which the basis for liturgy is the text; language is the means for personal encounter through which the liturgy, as a dialogical event, develops both katabatically and anabatically.[108] The Good News is proclaimed in words, and it is in words that the church directs its prayer to God.[109] Therefore a simple, literal translation of the basic ideas of the original text from Latin into another language is insufficient. Rather, the purpose is "faithfully [to] communicate to a given people, and in their own language, that which the Church by means of this given text originally intended to communicate to another people in another time. A faithful translation, therefore, cannot be judged on the basis of individual words: the total context of this specific act of communication must be kept in mind, as well as the literary form proper to the respective language."[110] This sets the frame for such translations with great sensitivity to language: the goal is to convey the content of prayer. In this the specific communicative situation of liturgy must be taken into account. The purpose is not to achieve a translation as close as possible to the language of the original text; rather, what is crucial is that the statement of the text can be understood as a whole. The situation in which the communication takes place is more fully described: besides the communication of the prayer, the speaker, audience, and style must be considered. Translations "must be faithful to the art of communication in all its various aspects, but especially in regard to the message itself, in regard to the audience for which it is intended, and in regard to the manner of expression."[111]

Paragraphs 8–12 describe the philological principles for such translation, and this sketch is followed by examples. Notable among the communicative aspects is the classification of language: it should "be that in 'common' usage, that is, suited to the greater number of the faithful who speak it in everyday use, even 'children and persons of small education.' . . . However, the language should not be 'common' in the bad sense, but 'worthy of expressing the highest realities' . . . [and] intelligible to all."[112] No literary education should be

[108] Ibid., 4.
[109] Ibid., 5.
[110] Ibid., 6.
[111] Ibid., 7.
[112] Ibid., 15a, citing an allocution of Pope Paul VI (10 Nov. 1965).

expected of the participants; the use of poetic texts does not exclude an elevated form of ordinary language. This gives a clear outline of the possibilities for liturgical language as well as the difficulties. It is obvious that a vernacular liturgy demands at least a readiness to review the language regularly with a view to appropriateness, acceptance, and quality, because developments in language do not bypass the vernacular liturgy. The equivalence of vernacular expressions to the religious sense must be considered in making translations,[113] the possibility of inculturating liturgical language should be taken into account,[114] and the shaping of the language should correspond to the specific liturgical communication.[115] Attention to the literary genre of each text and the significant elements proper to each genre is emphasized. A distinction should be made between what is essential and what is not. The prayers should be intelligible to those who hear them.[116] Certain "euchological and sacramental formularies like the consecratory prayers, the anaphoras, prefaces, exorcisms, and those prayers which accompany an action, such as the imposition of hands, the anointing, the signs of the cross, etc., should be translated integrally and faithfully [*integre et fideliter*], without variations, omissions, or insertions."[117] In all other cases the particular form of speech should be more freely translated.[118] For sung texts, a greater freedom is desirable.[119]

Example: translation of the same oration in different missals

The following example illustrates the breadth of discretion opened by this document. It is the collect for the Nineteenth Sunday in Ordinary Time. In the 1970 *Missale Romanum* it reads:

> *Omnipotens sempiterne Deus, quem, docente Spiritu Sancto, paterno nomine invocare praesumimus, perfice in cordibus nostris spiritum adop-*

[113] Ibid., 15–16.
[114] Ibid., 19.
[115] Ibid., 24–28.
[116] Ibid., 29.
[117] Ibid., 33.
[118] Ibid., 34.
[119] Ibid., 37.

*tionis filiorum, ut promissam hereditatem ingredi mereamur. Per Domi-
num. . .*[120]

The English translation as then approved reads:

> Almighty and ever-living God, your Spirit made us your children,
> confident to call you Father. Increase your Spirit within us and
> bring us to our promised inheritance. Grant this through our Lord
> Jesus Christ. . .[121]

The Latin oration reveals typical features of this kind of text (see chap.
5.2.5), beginning with an *anaclesis* (*Omnipotens* . . .) followed by a relative clause (*quem* . . .) culminating in a petition (*perfice* . . .). The prayer
ends with a doxology (*Per* . . .). The vernacular translations retain the
literary form of the oration but deal differently with the *anaclesis*; in
this regard the English is closer to the original than is the German text.
The relative clause is eliminated, but its content (praise of God and
recollection of God's saving deeds) is retained. Part of the petition in
the Latin oration is contained in the predicate "whom, taught by the
Holy Spirit, we dare to call our Father." The German text has a clear
chiasm, the English a parallelism (Spirit—Father; Spirit—inheritance).
Both the German and the English translations dissolve *paterno nomine
invocare* and leave *in cordibus nostris* untranslated. The brevity of the English is in contrast to the greater length of the German translation.[122]

Conclusion: postconciliar practice of translation

Thus in general we can say of the translation of liturgical texts on the
basis of the Roman document in the immediate postconciliar period:

[120] *Missale Romanum* (see n. 60 above), 469.

[121] *The Sacramentary*, English translation prepared by the International Com-
mittee on English in the Liturgy (Collegeville, MN: Liturgical Press, 1985), 360.

[122] The German text reads: "Allmächtiger Gott, wir dürfen dich Vater nennen,
den du hast uns an Kindes Statt angenommen und uns den Geist deines Sohnes
gesandt. Gib, dass wir in diesem Geist wachsen und einst das verheissene Erbe
empfangen. Darum bitten wir durch Jesus Christus." (Almighty God, we dare
to call you Father because you have accepted us as your children and sent us
the Spirit of your Son. Grant us to grow in that Spirit and one day to obtain the
promised inheritance. This we ask through Jesus Christ.)

- The basis for the vernacular liturgical texts was the Latin *editiones typicae*, that is, the Latin Roman liturgical books.

- The translation should express the sense of the oration; its purpose is a faithful communication of the content, not the greatest possible similarity to the original text.

- In terms of language, the liturgical texts should be appropriate both to the congregation in its variety and to the special significance of the liturgical event involving God and humans.

- Worship is to be seen altogether as a communicative event.

- In some particular, defined instances the responsible local authorities have the right to reformulate even central liturgical texts.

It is clear that the use of the vernacular is not for purely pragmatic reasons but must consider both liturgical-theological materials and pastoral demands.

A working group commissioned by church authorities to prepare new German translations of the collects for the Mass arrived, after years of work, at a version of this one that reads:

> Gracious God, you have given us the Spirit of your Son. We may now call you Father. Help us to live in this world as your sons and daughters, and grant that one day we may receive the promised inheritance. Through Jesus Christ . . .[123]

The German Missal with this and other newly translated prayers was never published.

The explanation for the translation includes elimination of long sentences and closer adherence to the Latin text. Inclusive language is now used, so that "sons and daughters" replaces "children." The

[123] The German text reads: "Gütiger Gott, du hast uns den Geist deines Sohnes geschenkt. Wir dürfen dich Vater nennen. Hilf, dass wir in dieser Welt als deine Töchter und Söhne leben und einst das verheissene Erbe empfangen durch Jesus Christus" (from "Tagesgebete. Die Zeit im Jahreskreis. Revisionsentwurf," in *Studien und Entwürfe zur Messfeier. Texte der Studienkommission für die Messliturgie und das Messbuch der Internationalen Arbeitsgemeinschaft der Liturgischen Kommissionen im deutschen Sprachgebiet* 1, ed. Eduard Nagel with Roland Bachleitner, et al. [Freiburg: Herder, 1995], 63–98, at 83).

difficult phrase formerly translated "to grow in your Spirit" has been replaced with the more accessible formula "to live in this world as your sons and daughters."

The guidelines for this translation[124] may be sketched as follows: vernacular collects must be appropriate for the liturgical celebrations of the average congregation. They must be linked to the church's liturgical tradition, which may make the language somewhat bulky; they must be susceptible to repetition, maintain closeness to the Bible, ensure inclusivity in the sense of a holistic image of humanity and God,[125] and reflect the experience of today's people in the world. Accordingly, vernacular liturgical texts stand within the tension of the demands of Bible and liturgy, contemporaneity and liturgical pragmatics. They also follow the structures and principles of liturgical prayer as derived from liturgical theology (see chap. 5.2). Address to God must be appropriate to the God-human relationship. Liturgical language is not meant to inform, instruct, indoctrinate, or discipline. Rhetorical aspects include comprehensibility, incisiveness—including, among other things, brevity and the avoidance of an overload of content—the inclusion of fundamental Christian concepts (without falling into theological jargon), openness to associations, and a simple sentence structure, all the while maintaining an elevated style.

Liturgiam authenticam

The most recent Roman document on questions of language in the liturgy, *Liturgiam authenticam* ("On the Use of Vernacular Languages in the Publication of the Books of the Roman Liturgy," 2001), points in another direction. This instruction is binding on ecclesiastical administrative authorities. The translation of the liturgy into the vernaculars remains unquestioned; this is not about a return to the Latin liturgy. Emphasis is also placed on the necessity and rightness of active participation by the faithful. But there is a clear critique of previous translation of the Latin liturgical books, and corrections or new editions are prescribed; omissions or errors must be eliminated.

---

[124] "Leitlinien für die Revision der Gebetstexte des Messbuchs," in ibid., 55–62.

[125] Albert Gerhards, "'Einschliessende Sprache' im Gottesdienst: eine übertriebene Forderung oder Gebot der Stunde?," *Liturgisches Jahrbuch* 42 (1992): 239–48.

The Roman Rite is described as an instrument of true inculturation be-cause it is said to possess a singular capacity for cultural integration. Such an instrument must not be endangered by false translations, which is why new principles for translation are necessary. There is a sense that the unity of the Roman Rite is in danger. The new prin-ciple is to be as follows:

> It is to be kept in mind from the beginning that the translation of the liturgical texts of the Roman Liturgy is not so much a work of creative innovation as it is of rendering the original texts faithfully and accurately into the vernacular language. While it is permissible to arrange the wording, the syntax and the style in such a way as to prepare a flowing vernacular text suitable to the rhythm of popular prayer, the original text, insofar as possible, must be translated inte-grally and in the most exact manner, without omissions or additions in terms of their content, and without paraphrases or glosses.[126]

Apparently what is demanded is, above all, a translation of liturgical texts characterized by the closest possible accommodation to the Latin text. There is a call for the development of a "sacred style" that "will come to be recognized as proper to liturgical language."[127] "Inclusive" liturgical language is rejected. According to §30 its only place is in catechesis. The document is remarkable not only because it in large part represents a break with the postconciliar practice of translation; it also documents a new idea of the church that weakens the position of the local churches in favor of the Holy See. The latter, for example, retains the right, "for the good of the faithful," to "prepare transla-tions in any language, and to approve them for liturgical use."[128]

Among other criticisms of this document are that it proposes a false concept of unity that seeks uniformity even in the wording of

[126] *LA* 20.

[127] Ibid., 27. As an example of application of *Liturgiam authenticam*, compare the new translation of the collect discussed above, as it now appears in *The Roman Missal* (see n. 123 above), 479: "Almighty ever-living God, whom, taught by the Holy Spirit, we dare to call our Father, bring, we pray, to perfection in our hearts the spirit of adoption as your sons and daughters, that we may merit to enter into the inheritance which you have promised. Through our Lord Jesus Christ . . ."

[128] Ibid., 104.

liturgical texts and so contradicts statements in the Constitution on the Liturgy such as *SC* 37. There is also a lack of understanding of previous liturgical reforms and, above all, a wrong set of criteria for translations, because the Latin style of the orations cannot be reproduced in living languages without putting at risk the spiritual and intellectual gains achieved by a vernacular liturgy.[129] The new German translation of the burial liturgy on the basis of *Liturgiam authenticam* has encountered explicit criticism from those who have to celebrate it; they find its language inappropriate for liturgical use.[130] After protests, especially from priests, the German-speaking bishops' conferences published a manual of alternative texts as a supplement to the liturgical book.

5.4 Music and Hymnody in the Liturgy

5.4.1 Singing as an Integral Part of Liturgy

While we refer to the language of *the* liturgy, here we want to speak of music and singing *in* worship. This points to a difficult definition of their relationship. Still, talking of music in worship is already a step forward, given the older view that church music happened *alongside* the liturgy. The reasons for this development were given in chapter 3. In what follows our concern is to describe the importance of the audible/musical dimension of worship. On the metaphorical level that was never in doubt, but in church practice song and music were always an occasion for quarrels: from the exclusion of instrumental music in the ancient church because of its associations with pagan cults to the struggle over early polyphony to today's discussions about "praise music." This has to do in large part with the strong

---

[129] Reiner Kaczynski, "Angriff auf die Liturgiekonstitution? Anmerkungen zu einer neuen Übersetzer-Instruktion," *Stimmen der Zeit* 219 (2001): 651–68; see the response by Joseph Cardinal Ratzinger, "Um die Erneuerung der Liturgie. Antwort auf Reiner Kaczynski," *Stimmen der Zeit* 219 (2001): 837–43.

[130] See ". . . *Ohren der Barmherzigkeit.*" *Über angemessene Liturgiesprache*, ed. Benedikt Kranemann and Stephan Wahle. Theologie kontrovers (Freiburg: Herder, 2011); Peter Jeffery, *Translating Tradition: A Chant Historian Reads* Liturgiam Authenticam (Collegeville, MN: Liturgical Press, 2005).

emotional effects of music, which is the reason the Bible accords it great significance (see, e.g., Ps 150). The omnipresence of the musical dimension is evident at the very beginning of the Liturgy of the Hours every single day. The daily prayer of Jews and Christians begins with Psalm 95, whose first verse reads: "Come, let us rejoice in the Lord, let us acclaim God our salvation. Let us come before him proclaiming our thanks, let us acclaim him with songs!"

It is possible not only to speak of the God of Israel and of Jesus Christ; one must, in fact, sing! Church music—or better, singing and playing in worship—is therefore not a luxury but the appropriate way to enter into relationship with God.

No worship service without music

In the traditions of Judaism and Christianity there is practically no worship service without singing. The silent Mass or a Liturgy of the Hours that is only spoken are, basically, nothing but institutionalized exceptions. Significantly, it was the "silent Mass," performed inaudibly, that opened a space in the time of the Liturgical Movement for the introduction of community singing (see chap. 3.9 and 10). Likewise, it is unthinkable in the Eastern churches to conduct a worship service without song. Certainly, in those churches instrumental music remained almost entirely forbidden because it had been rejected by the ancient church. The Orthodox churches using Slavic languages added polyphonic singing to the originally monophonic chorales or substituted it for them entirely. In contrast, in many of the churches of the Reformation artistic vocal and instrumental music dominates because of its proclamatory character.

What is church music?

The determination of exactly what should be understood by "church music" presents some difficulties. At any rate, until Vatican II hymns were not part of it. It was only as a result of the council that such forms of popular piety were elevated to liturgical status. Despite all respect for the expansion of the concept, still the question remains whether everything that is currently sung and played in the churches is really church music. What makes music in church become church music, in particular Roman Catholic church music? Here it remains a task for liturgics (together with Gregorian chant research, hymnology, and musicology) to establish criteria.

5.4.2 Liturgical-Theological Context of the Question

Liturgy does not consist simply of texts; it is a matter of applying them (that is, the spoken and sung word) as well as sign-actions and symbols. As a result, liturgy brings those dimensions of aesthetics that previously led a more-or-less marginal existence into the purview of theology and church practice: sound (and thus music), mimicry, gestures, and dance (and so the performing arts as well). In this way the liturgy becomes a place where the church presents itself, to the extent that in it one can obtain a sense experience of everything the church believes about itself: its presence before God, its origins in God, and its future in God.

Music as the word's "sounding body"

The aesthetics of liturgy is thus an aesthetic of anamnesis, of making present.[131] It remains oriented in every dimension to the Word that God has spoken to humanity from of old and that has become flesh in Jesus Christ. The modality of the word in liturgy is threefold, observable in the performances of the (narrative) anamnesis, the (petitionary) epiclesis, and the (laudatory) doxology. Music has a key place in all three of these insofar as it gives the word a "sounding body," newly incarnating it in both space and time, that is, embodying it. This is true of all forms of liturgical singing and liturgical music, from simple spoken song (recitative tone) to artistic compositions for choir and orchestra. The theological elevation of church music beyond the decorative to becoming a necessary and integrative part of solemn liturgy (see SC 112) has rendered a good many older views of its value out of date. On the one hand church music is tied to function,

---

[131] Albert Gerhards, "Mimesis, Anamnesis, Poiesis. Überlegungen zur Ästhetik christlicher Liturgie als Vergegenwärtigung," in *Pastoralästhetik. Die Kunst der Wahrnehmung und Gestaltung in Glaube und Kirche*, ed. Walter Fürst, Quaestiones disputatae 199 (Freiburg: Herder, 2002), 169–86.

that is, arbitrary substitutions are impermissible; on the other hand the other partners, including the priest, must take into account the independent value of music as a part of the liturgy (e.g., through an attitude of attentive listening). Thus the demands made of a church music suited to the liturgy have steeply increased. Among other things, care must be taken that the congregation are not reduced to a group of silent witnesses but remain active players in this holy game.

Expressing what cannot be said

The depth dimensions of music—presupposing its correct performance and correct reception—are suited to giving a voice to the voiceless and a sound to what cannot be said. Theology is always only an attempt to get beyond the limits of the unsayable. Its reliable support in this is God's self-revelation in the "Word." That, too, is the measure of the human response. Hence every form of human response—including reflective theology and its application in preaching, creed, and prayer—is ultimately grounded in the doxology, the acknowledgment in praise of God's sovereignty, which is communicated in human freedom.

The holy game

Church music in worship, as the place for doxology, constitutes the sound-space in which the response of freedom can be made, as a "holy game." This is the reason for the superior rank—indeed, the indispensability—of music in worship: its character of constituting the acoustic side of the symbolic space of divine-human communication. In the West, since the Enlightenment, there has always been a tension between functionality and autonomy in this regard. Music in worship is the advocate of the subjective, not in order to relativize the "objective" of the divine "given," but in order to make it present and thus display its personal dimension. Church music is thus an essential factor in worship as an event of divine-human encounter.

5.4.3 Music as Art of Time and Space

Music and space are related to one another on different levels. This is not merely a matter of the "place" for church music: the Schola

Cantorum, the choir stalls, the choir screen, the organ loft. It is also and primarily about the spatial nature of music as such. It is not for nothing that we speak of "sonic space." High and low are spatial categories; the grapheme for the note is two-dimensional, but it is spatially conceived. Physically, sound waves are spatial phenomena in which space and time are interwoven. Echoes plumb the space; spatialization measures time through measures and meter.

Relationship of architecture and church music

The history of church music illustrates the profound degree to which church architecture and the practice of music influence one another. When gigantic Roman cathedrals like that at Speyer were constructed, the intervals in Gregorian chant grew larger; dwarf galleries became places for "angelic music"; vaulted Gothic architecture influenced early polyphony; the existence of multiple choirs led, in the Renaissance, to the construction of galleries and lofts; the great baroque organs, with platforms for singers, influenced the architecture of baroque churches; modern churches designed solely with the acoustics of speech in mind stifle singing and have no place for pipe organs.

In general we may say that, to a certain degree, church music represents the acoustic dimensions of the church, the church architecture its optical dimension. Characteristic—and corresponding to the architectural principle of the liturgy—is a combination of styles from different periods. It is a sign of the church's diachronic identity.

Still, music as an acoustic phenomenon should be seen primarily as a temporal art and so, as church music, enters into a particular relationship with liturgy. Before we can go into this in more detail we must first ask what, precisely, constitutes singing and music in the liturgy.

5.4.4 Determining the Use of Music in Worship

The special place of Gregorian chant

The first association that comes to mind when one speaks of Roman Catholic church music is Gregorian chant. The Constitution on the Liturgy says: "The church recognizes Gregorian chant as especially native to the Roman liturgy. Therefore, other things being equal, it should be given pride of place in liturgical services" (*SC* 116). The second part of article 116 speaks of the admissibility of other types of church music, especially polyphony, "so long as they accord with the spirit of the liturgical action as laid down in article 30"—which speaks of the active participation (*participatio actuosa*) of the people, to be expressed in acclamations, responses, the singing of psalms, antiphons (framing verses for psalms), songs, gestures, and postures, as well as through holy silence. These two statements taken together say that Gregorian chant, because of its antiquity, has a traditional place of primacy, but in principle all other forms of musical expression are permitted because the understanding of liturgy that is fundamental to all this is concerned with enabling the active participation of those present.

Principle of relationship to the texts

Certainly, the argument from tradition was unable to stem the decline of Gregorian chant in the intensive phase of liturgical reform. The theological problem in that development is more profound and is connected with the factual location of chant within the various styles of church music. Gregorian chant, while the oldest, is only one of many possible styles for *musica sacra*, comparable to the shifting design of liturgical vessels and vestments, in which stylistic variety has been admitted for long ages past (see *SC* 123). Gregorian chant is often seen primarily as a repertory of melodies worth preserving, one that is more or less closely attuned to the assigned texts of the liturgy. What is really decisive, however, is the principle of relationship to the texts that is associated with Gregorian chant. The center of every Christian and every Jewish worship service is the word of God, not merely as written or printed, but as spoken, staged, communicated word, calling for meditation and response (see chap. 5.1 and 3). All act in service to that communion in the word, whether they proclaim, preach, pray, or make music. Consequently, from a variety of perspectives Gregorian chant should be regarded as a "principle" of Roman Catholic church music.[132] While it is true that the text is, if not exclusive, certainly in the foreground, liturgy is by its nature (though

---

[132] Albert Gerhards, "Liturgiewissenschaftliche Perspektiven auf den gregorianischen Choral," *Kirchenmusikalisches Jahrbuch* 85 (2001): 17–30.

not necessarily in its actual execution) never a mere presentation of a text; it is also an expression, a speaking, a sounding.

Mutual expression

The results of recent research on the relationship between word and sound solidify the central significance of Gregorian chant and its general relevance for understanding Western liturgy: the credibility of the musical part is not independent of the textual basis, while on the other hand it is only through expression that the depth dimension of the text is revealed.

The theological development of this thesis remains a *desideratum*. Still, recent research in Gregorian chant has found its place in some important liturgics publications.

It is undeniable that in the course of time a church music largely independent of the liturgy established itself, something that has led to frictions throughout the history of music and even today. But it can be shown that it is precisely this potential for conflict, a consequence of the process of artistic emancipation, that gives birth to opportunities.[133]

5.4.5 The "Repertoire" of Liturgical Song and Church Music

Melody and its relation to the text

If we regard singing in the broadest sense as the projection of the text at correct pitch, classic liturgy contains no unsung text. Readings and prayers, if said aloud, are presented according to a fixed melodic pattern (cantillation). There are psalm tones (melodic schemata for individual verses) for the psalms in various ecclesial tonal styles. Alongside these, the antiphons in the Liturgy of the Hours and the Mass are notated according to the text: those in the Liturgy of the Hours simpler, syllabic or oligitonic (that is, only one or a few notes per syllable), those of the Mass with more ornamental, polytonic

---

[133] Albert Gerhards, "'Heiliges Spiel': Kirchenmusik und Liturgie als Rivalinnen oder Verbündete?," in *Kirchenmusik im 20. Jahrhundert. Erbe und Auftrag*, ed. idem, Ästhetik, Theologie, Liturgik 31 (Münster: LIT, 2005), 29–38.

melismatics.[134] A strict orientation to the text is even present in the Gradual hymns, whose melodic schemata are accommodated to the individual texts.[135]

Beyond this there are poetic pieces, such as hymns and sequences (strophic singing between the readings), which sometimes offer richer possibilities for musical development; in addition, there are litany-like pieces such as the *Improperia* (laments) of Good Friday.

Mass "Ordinaries"

Roman Catholic church music is associated especially with Mass "Ordinaries," musical compositions for five unchanging parts of the Order of the Mass.[136] These make up a significant portion of our Western musical tradition; they have been very popular with composers and choirs. The formal makeup of this "Ordinary" is, from the point of view of liturgics, more accidental or artistic than deliberate. Historically, the individual parts were inserted into the *Ordo Missae* at different times and for different reasons: The *Kyrie* is probably the remnant of a litany of petition from the East. The *Gloria* was originally a Greek morning hymn in the Liturgy of the Hours of the early church and was only hesitantly adopted for general use in Rome. The *Credo* was originally part of the baptismal liturgy and is a medieval addition to the *Ordo Missae* (as a result, the tradition of the Gregorian melodies is also independent of the other parts). The *Agnus Dei* is also a borrowing from the East, from around 700. Only the *Sanctus/Benedictus/Hosanna* seems to have been demonstrably part of the Eucharistic Prayer at the time when the Roman Rite arose. Nevertheless, the individual compositions for the (then four) parts of the Ordinary were collected in *troparia* (collections of textual insertions; the term is derived from *tropus*) in the Middle Ages. The names of different parts of the Ordinary (e.g., the Eastern *Kyrie* "*Lux et origo*") still recall the no longer permissible *tropus* insertions.

The later "full form" of the Ordinary of the Mass could exist only because of a general lack of interest in the question of a meaningful

[134] Gerhards, "Die Psalmen in der römischen Liturgie."

[135] Emmanuela Kohlhaas, *Musik und Sprache im Gregorianischen Gesang*, Archiv für Musikwissenschaft. Beiheft 49 (Stuttgart: Steiner, 2001).

[136] Jakob Johannes Koch, *Traditionelle mehrstimmige Messen in erneuerter Liturgie: ein Widerspruch?* (Regensburg: Pustet, 2002).

text sequence. Since in any event every text had to be spoken by the priest in order to be valid, the fixed chants could be left to the choir while the congregation played its long-practiced and mainly passive role. The choir became a substitute for the congregation rather than being given a function in service to the assembly and its singing.

In spite of this problematic development, we should not lightly dismiss this core part of Catholic church music. Classical choir and orchestral music can still be integrated in today's liturgy if an overall musical conception can be developed that does justice both to the contemporary worship event and to the composition.[137] It can be shown that many composers, through their unique approach to the text, have exposed depth dimensions of texts and internal relationships among the individual parts in their compositions; active listening and participation in such musical events can yield great spiritual gains.

Liturgy of the Hours, "paraliturgical" worship, Oratories

Besides the Ordinary of the Mass and the Requiem, the Liturgy of the Hours has offered special opportunities for the development of church music: solemn vespers, the responsories of Tenebrae, parts of Compline, the *Salve Regina*. "Paraliturgical" worship services outside the official Roman liturgy have offered space for development: these include especially the Marian Office but also processions and devotions. They incorporated sung litanies and freely composed motets that also found their way into the Mass (e.g., at the elevation of the eucharistic elements). Finally, we should mention the no-longer liturgical but similar genre of the Oratory, which constitutes a bridge to the secular musical genre of opera.

Purely instrumental music

Music that is entirely instrumental is a special case. The organ is primary,[138] but there are also traditions of use of wind instruments or

[137] Jakob Johannes Koch (ibid.) calls this a "twofold contextualization of the work."

[138] Albert Gerhards, "Jenseits der Grenze des Sagbaren . . . Zur liturgietheologischen Bestimmung der Orgelmusik im Spannungsfeld von Wort und Zeichen," in *Orgel und Liturgie. Festschrift zur Orgelweihe in St. Lamberti*, ed. Michael Zywietz with Christian Bettels, Musikwissenschaft 9 (Münster: LIT, 2004), 39–51.

strings in the context of liturgy. Their tones make church music most impressively "the sound of the unsayable."[139]

5.4.6 "Pop Music" and Liturgy

Long before the Reformation, the "paraliturgical" forms of celebration offered an opportunity for popular religious singing, something that gained only a sporadic foothold in the Mass.[140] Church hymns developed out of medieval *cantiones* and airs (that is, *Kyrie* tropes), at first stimulated by the Reformation but soon afterward in Counter-Reformation reaction. While the liturgies of the churches of the Reformation accorded congregational hymns a high liturgical status, Catholic liturgy, despite some partial successes in the baroque period and the Enlightenment, systematically kept them apart. That is one reason why one finds scarcely any tradition of hymn singing in completely Roman Catholic countries.

In fact, at the time of the Liturgical Movement hymns had already established themselves as genuine popular liturgical expression in the prayer-and-song Masses in mixed-confessional areas of Germany and elsewhere. A glance at the diocesan hymn books of the postwar period confirms it.

With the liturgical reform, in accord with the guiding principle of "active participation," congregational singing made its way into the liturgy. The instruction *Musicam Sacram* (1967) was intended to set the parameters at the very beginning of the reform period.[141] The post–Vatican II common hymnal *Gotteslob* (1975) could link to traditions of the prewar and postwar periods, as one can see by looking at the dates of composition of many hymns and the names of the

---

[139] Wolfgang Bretschneider, "Stimme der Sehnsucht und der Klage. Klang des Unsagbaren: Musik im Gottesdienst," in *Gott feiern in nachchristlicher Gesellschaft. Die missionarische Dimension der Liturgie*, part 1, ed. Benedikt Kranemann, Klemens Richter, and Franz-Peter Tebart-van Elst (Stuttgart: Katholisches Bibelwerk, 2000), 93–101.

[140] Christian Möller, *Kirchenlied und Gesangbuch. Quellen zu ihrer Geschichte. Ein hymnologisches Arbeitsbuch*, Mainzer Hymnologische Studien 1 (Tübingen: Francke, 2000).

[141] Eckhard Jaschinski, *Kleine Geschichte der Kirchenmusik* (Freiburg: Herder, 2004); Gerhards, "Heiliges Spiel."

authors. An ongoing problem lies in the fact that the older tradition of church hymnody was shaped by paraliturgies. Essentially, the celebration of the Eucharist offers little room for hymns with multiple verses, and the older versions of the Ordinary of the Mass are at best paraphrases of the liturgical texts. So there remains a tension between what the church's liturgy prescribes and what people like to sing. This is especially evident in the decades-long controversies over "praise music." Here the tension between an "objective" rendition and "subjective" sensibility is especially evident. Resolving the tension by authoritative pronouncements, as recent documents seek to do[142] only serves to stifle singing in worship.[143]

5.4.7 Theological Basis for Singing in Worship

Singing as making-present in space-time

The thesis of these reflections is that singing produces a making-present in space-time, an overcoming of the flow of time through celebration and festival. The way in which singing makes present can be described from a formal and a content perspective:[144]

Formal aspects:

> Formally: singing produces communication in a holistic sense. This can be shown in terms of the categories of movement, perception, and play:[145]
>
> a) *Movement: as actio,* singing belongs to the dimension of movement. The singers express themselves, stepping out of a purely passive, receptive attitude. They document their presence

---

[142] See Albert Gerhards, "Liturgietheologische und -ästhetische Überlegungen zur Instruktion 'Sakrament der Erlösung,'" *Zeitschrift für katholische Theologie* 127 (2005): 253–70.

[143] Wolfgang Bretschneider, "'Dem Sprachlosen eine Stimme geben': Verstummt das Singen im Gottesdienst?" in *Kirchenmusik im 20. Jahrhundert*, 39–50.

[144] Albert Gerhards, "Mehr als Worte sagt ein Lied. Theologische Dimensionen des liturgischen Singens," *Musica Sacra* 113 (1993): 509–13.

[145] Felbecker, *Die Prozession* (see n. 74 above).

through their action. Movement is essentially a rhythm of breathing and speaking (speaking in word and speaking in tone), with meter. We can also consider dance in this context, in its stylized liturgical shape (processions, movement from place to place). These are intimately connected with music and singing and expand the gesture of movement.

b) *Perception:* because singing represents an acoustic articulation, what is at stake is first of all hearing—hearing one's own voice and those of others. Only in that way can there be harmony, that is, an experience of community in song. Second to it is perception through vision. Those who see others as fellow singers experience themselves as part of a community, and that effects a making-present. This is experienced with special intensity in circumstances influenced by mass psychology: for example, in a stadium at a big game. The associated dangers—especially depersonalizing and ideologizing—can certainly not be dismissed out of hand.

c) *Play:* in singing, *homo ludens*, the playful person, is brought into being. While singing is part of all Christian liturgies in East and West, it was left to the West to regard it as inessential. The development of the silent Mass and the corresponding usage *missa recitata* ("saying Mass") make it clear that the liturgy—and especially the Mass—had been functionalized and so stripped of its real meaning: pure purposelessness as an expression of grace-filled event. But that is precisely the essence of song. Singing at worship is "playing before God."

Content aspects:

In terms of content: Singing expresses the basic actions of liturgical speech, with their multiple differentiations. It is essentially about the three actions of *anaclesis*, *anamnesis*, and *epiclesis*. (See also chap. 5.2.)

a) *Address (anaclesis):* In approaching God, those praying become self-aware. This happens at the beginning of worship when the people call upon God; this action establishes the thou-I or thou-we relationship. In the Liturgy of the Hours it is the appeal: *Deus in adiutorium meum intende!* ("O God, come to my assistance!"); in the Gregorian "Introit" at Mass the same is expressed by the approach to the altar accompanied by the singing of a psalm. Here music and movement are inseparable and constitute a single expressive action. However, the opening chant or hymn in the Liturgy of the Hours or the Mass (*Gloria*) also function as address insofar as in them God is named and praised.

b) *Anamnesis (recollection):* Songs tell of God's saving deeds in the history of Israel and the church. In all ages songs have also been the vessels of memory; they were and are therefore a component of historical memory and thus a guarantee of a community's identity. The content expressed in song is at the same time made present and appropriated as one's own.

c) *Epiclesis (appeal):* A longing for the presence of God can find intense expression in song, as in the "O-antiphons" of Advent that musically develop *Veni!* ("come"). It is about appealing to God to continue bestowing the salvation assured throughout history. Ultimately this concerns the eschatological dimension, and it can find profound expression in song—in forms not only of petition but also of lament. Here we find the expression of the preliminary character of every earthly liturgy in relation to the promised "heavenly liturgy."

Choral song as image of redemption

The Jewish philosopher of religion Franz Rosenzweig, in his major work *The Star of Redemption*, written during World War I, inquired about the form of expression within which the promise of salvation is preserved as a certain future. "So it is not prophecy that is the particular form where Redemption can become the content of Revelation; rather, this must be a form belonging entirely to Redemption, which consequently expresses the event not-yet-having-taken-place and yet still-to-come-one-day. But this is the form of the communal song of the community."[146] Thomas Eicker comments on this statement: "Thus singing brings the individual human person together with her or his fellow humans, with the (nearby) world, in witness and sung confession of faith. For Rosenzweig, choral song is an image of redemption. It is a first fruit of redemption because prayer has already

---

[146] Franz Rosenzweig, *The Star of Redemption*, trans. Barbara E. Galli (Madison: University of Wisconsin Press, 2005), 268.

been heard, because all pray and have come together and found one another in common praise."[147]

Ultimately, however, even singing is something preliminary. It is necessary, first, in order to afford a new acoustic space for the Word drowned out by the many words. Before we can hear the word of revelation, many other voices that draw us away from the essential one must be silenced. It is only through reduction and concentration that human beings can come to themselves and their center. Whether through the fading of worship music to a collective silence or through its voicing in confession, praise, thanks, petition, or lament, what always happens is what Rosenzweig calls, in regard to the way of redemption, "the sowing of eternity into the living."[148]

In this comprehensive sense, then, church music is the sound of the unsayable. It is ultimately the servant, the echo of the sighing of the Holy Spirit within us (Rom 8:26), but not the medium of what is humanly made. To bring that to expression is a high calling that requires both spirituality and professional musical ability.

5.5 Sign and Sign-Character of the Liturgy

5.5.1 Sign-Character of Worship

Sign and function

The liturgy is made up of an abundance of sign systems that are difficult to systematize because of their complexity. Recent years have seen the publication of a significant number of relevant studies in liturgics related to American initiatives in linguistics and semiotics.[149] The terminology is uneven, for example, with regard to the

---

[147] Thomas Eicker, "Einsäen der Ewigkeit ins Lebendige. Impulse einer Theologie der Kirchenmusik im Dialog mit Franz Rosenzweig," in *Kirchenmusik im 20. Jahrhundert*, 153–68, at 155.

[148] Ibid., 168; Rosenzweig, *Star of Redemption*, 391.

[149] Gerard Lukken and Mark Searle, *Semiotics and Church Architecture: Applying the Semiotics of A. J. Greimas and the Paris School to the Analysis of Church Buildings* (Kampen: Kok Pharos, 1993); Karl-Heinrich Bieritz, *Liturgik* (Berlin and New York: de Gruyter, 2004); Michael B. Merz, *Liturgisches Gebet als Geschehen*.

meanings of "sign" and "symbol." What is relevant for liturgics is Umberto Eco's statement that, essentially, there are no signs but only sign-functions,[150] that is, a sign becomes a sign when it enters into a relationship, a process of presentation, apprehension, and interpretation. Its function is traditionally described in a two-part model that distinguishes the signifier from the signified.

Semiotic triangle

This model is often expanded into a "semiotic triangle" by the addition of a third element, the "referent": what common "reality" underlies the signifier and the signified? Umberto Eco modifies the traditional model by introducing, in place of the referent, the concept of the "interpretant," which he adopts from Charles Sanders Peirce:

> Appeal to a referent never clarifies what is signified by the sign. . . . What is signified by a sign can only be understood by reference to an interpretant, which in turn points to another interpretant, and so on *ad infinitum*, beginning a process of unlimited semiosis, in the course of which the recipient of the original sign decodifies the process to the extent necessary for the purpose of the pertinent communication and the contexts in which he or she wants to use it.[151]

In other words: human culture is a system of interpretation from which we cannot escape. In the realm of human communication

---

Liturgiewissenschaftlich-linguistische Studie anhand der Gebetsgattung Eucharistisches Hochgebet, Liturgiewissenschaftliche Quellen und Forschungen 70 (Münster: Aschendorff, 1988); Bernhard Meffert, *Liturgie teilen. Akzeptanz und Partizipation in der erneuerten Messliturgie. Mit einer Einführung von Albert Gerhards*, Praktische Theologie heute 52 (Stuttgart: Kohlhammer, 2000); Michael Meyer-Blanck, *Vom Symbol zum Zeichen. Symboldidaktik und Semiotik* (Rheinbach: CMZ-Verlag, 2002); Stephan Winter, *Eucharistische Gegenwart. Liturgische Redehandlung im Spiegel mittelalterlicher und analytischer Sprachtheorie*, Ratio fidei 13 (Regensburg: Pustet, 2002), etc.

[150] Bieritz, *Liturgik*, 38.

[151] Translated from the German of Umberto Eco, *Zeichen. Einführung in einem Begriff und seine Geschichte* (Frankfurt: Suhrkamp, 1977), 172–73; translation of his *Il Segno* (Milan: ISEDI, 1973). [This work went through 119 editions and printings in Italian, French, Spanish, Portuguese, and German, but none in English, though we now have an extensive body of Eco's later work in English as well.—Trans.]

there are no referents independent of culture and communication but only ongoing processes of signification through which the "world" repeatedly acquires a new and perceptible form.

Liturgy as a process of signification

Liturgy as a whole, with all its differing (optical, acoustic, tactile, etc.) sign-systems (codes), is such a process of signification. This statement, not derived in the first instance from theology, nevertheless has theological relevance. Clearly, sacramental theology has operated throughout the ages with the idea of signs; thus the transformation of the eucharistic elements can be described as "transsignification." But the core sacramental event is embedded in a surrounding communicative or significative context whose individual systems can be called "languages." Karl-Heinrich Bieritz distinguishes the following "languages" in worship:[152]

1. *Word languages:* linguistic and written codes (liturgical languages) as well as speech codes (including loudness, tone, intonation, etc.)

2. *Body languages:* mimicry, gestures, postures, movements in space, placement within the space, touching, taste, smell

3. *Sound languages:* acoustic codes such as sounds, noises, and especially musical codes

4. *Object languages:* clothing, decoration of the space, liturgical vessels and instruments, images, symbols of varying degrees of perceptibility to the senses, especially the space and its decoration

5. *Social languages:* persons and community as representatives of Christ, staging, division of time, festal codes

Sequences of signs can be established within the elements of a code (e.g., dress code), and these can be called "text." It is within this context that we seek the "coherence" (that is, the grammatical correctness, so to speak) and the meaning (semantics) of a sign. The question of the effects of the sign brings us to the pragmatic aspect.

---

[152] Bieritz, *Liturgik*, 42–46.

Structuring

Finally, we should make reference to the structure, or structuring, a process essential to all levels of communication. To speak of structuring is to view communicative systems "from without." Structures are also subject to conventions; in the liturgy, for example, this means sustaining the liturgical "role-play" and fixed elements. Structures are also significant for interpretation. Beneath the superstructure lie depth-structures that, for example, in the case of ecumenical worship services, may work themselves out in different ways.

For worship as a ritual event and part of the authentic church tradition we may ask: how should we deal with the tension between existing and prescribed structures and restructuring? Simply referring to fundamental structures that have evolved through history and (in the case of Roman Catholicism) are prescribed by magisterial decree does not excuse us from the task of steadily developing new structurings (see chaps. 3 and 4). The rule here is this: "Traditional liturgy encounters us with the dignity and power of a text that—even at the level of its 'structure'—suggests certain readings of God and the world, life and faith. Those who want to write this text forward must first not only have read and grasped it, but must also have been grasped by it."[153]

Sign-systems in liturgy

In what follows we will give a more extended treatment of some of the sign-systems in the liturgy in the realm of "objective language." What was previously known as "the study of material objects" and enjoyed a rather marginal existence has acquired a new value as a result of being regarded through the lens of sign-theory. Consequently there is nothing in worship that is insignificant. The Constitution on the Liturgy devoted a separate chapter to this subject: "Sacred Art and Furnishings."[154] The documents of the liturgical reform gave concrete

---

[153] Ibid., 54.

[154] *SC* 122–30; see Albert Gerhards, "'. . . zu immer vollerer Einheit mit Gott und untereinander gelangen' (*SC* 48): Die Neuordnung der Kirchenräume durch die Liturgiereform," in *Liturgiereform. Eine bleibende Aufgabe. 40 Jahre Konzilskonstitution über die heilige Liturgie*, ed. Klemens Richter and Thomas Sternberg (Münster: Aschendorff, 2004), 126–43.

instructions, though some determinations were and are the province of the territorial authorities.[155]

5.5.2 The Liturgical Space

The church building presents a highly complex sign-system.[156] Historic structures are subject, in the course of their history, to repeatedly renewed processes of signification; they maintain their "identity" only through changes in interpretation and form. The meaning of a space can be learned only from its context, that is, by including the liturgical and extra-liturgical actions that take place there.[157] Liturgy and space are thus relational entities that unfold their meaning not only from the perspective of a given agenda or the architectural plan but also through perception or experience. Our view must include not only the classic sources of liturgics and the history of art and architecture but also previously unexploited resources. Autobiographical sources are of special interest with regard to experiences of liturgy and space as well as forms of popular piety.[158]

[155] See "Leitlinien für den Bau und die Ausgestaltung von gottesdienstlichen Räumen. Handreichung der Liturgiekommission der Deutschen Bischofskonferenz. 25 Oktober 1988," 6th rev. ed., Sekretariat der Deutschen Bischofskonferenz. Arbeitshilfen 132 (Bonn, 1996); see also "Built of Living Stones: Art, Architecture, and Worship," issued by NCCB/USCC (now USCCB), November 16, 2000 (guidelines of National Conference of Catholic Bishops, USA), the guidelines of Canada, Ireland, England and Wales, and the United States. Tiziano Ghirelli, Ierotopi cristiani alla luce della riforma liturgica del Concilio Vaticano II. Dettami di Conferenze Episcopali nazionali per la progettazione di luoghi liturgici. Prime indagini (Città dei Vaticano: Libreria Editrice Vaticana, 2012).

[156] Gerard Lukken, "Liturgie und Sinnlichkeit. Über die Bedeutung der Leiblichkeit in der Liturgie," in idem, Per visibilia ad invisibilia. Anthropological, Theological, and Semiotic Studies on the Liturgy and the Sacraments, coll. and ed. Louis van Tongeren and Charles Caspers (Kampen: Kok Pharos, 1994), 118–39; Rainer Volp, Liturgik. Die Kunst, Gott zu feiern, vol. 1: Einführung und Geschichte (Gütersloh: Mohn, 1992).

[157] Albert Gerhards, Wo Gott und Welt sich begegnen. Kirchenräume verstehen (Kevelaer: Butzon & Bercker, 2011).

[158] Friedrich Lurz, Erlebte Liturgie. Autobiografische Schriften als liturgiewissenschaftliche Quellen, Ästhetik, Theologie, Liturgik 28 (Münster: Lit, 2003); for the whole subject see Albert Gerhards, "St. Gereon: Identität eines Kirchenraums

Church space as a place for movement

The spatial dimension is traditionally regarded as something static. That was associated by no means least with the introduction of pews during the Reformation period. Catholic churches became places where people gathered for instruction in the faith, but above all for private prayer together. But in late antiquity and the Middle Ages the churches were primarily places for movement that enabled a varied experience of the space—which likewise means experience of the self. It makes a difference whether a congregation only watches an entrance procession or takes an active part in it themselves. The rediscovery of the dimension of movement as part of the liturgy is a necessary consequence of a renewed understanding of liturgy. We ought to remember that it was only in the phase of liturgical reform that many elements of the movement dimension were abolished (processions, interactions); these were not regarded as real liturgy. But the traditional concept of liturgy as *actio* points, in fact, to active events, the "sacred drama," whereby liturgy approaches the modern artistic concept. From this point of view we can also describe worship as "performance," though from the point of view of the faithful that refers to only a small part of the reality of worship. Christian worship is a descriptive-representative action in which God's history of salvation acquires a present form and in this way is not only believed in as something effective and open toward the future but is also experienced as such.

Spatial antinomy: centering and orientation

The consequences of the post–Vatican II liturgical reform for Roman Catholic worship space were considerable (see chap. 3.10). However, the changes made, for example, in the wake of the Tridentine reform were no less substantial (dissolution of the medieval sequence of spaces into a single room through removal of the choir stalls, shift of the tabernacle for reservation of the Eucharist to the high altar, intro-

---

im Wandel der Geschichte," in *Märtyrergrab, Kirchenraum, Gottesdienst. Interdisziplinäre Studien zur ehemaligen Stiftskirche St. Gereon in Köln*, ed. Andreas Odenthal and Albert Gerhards, Studien zur Kölner Kirchengeschichte 35 (Siegburg: Franz Schmitt, 2006), 9–23.

duction of church pews and confessionals). From the point of view of sign-theory, today's church spaces exist in an unsolved and possibly insoluble state of spatial antinomy between orientation and centralization, illustrated by the newly revived question of the direction of celebration *versus populum*. Both dimensions—centralized assembly and extrinsic orientation—belong to Christian worship (like that of the synagogue) and must be kept in balance, though the emphases may be different. The plurality of biblical images for church and the statement in *SC* 7 about the different ways in which Christ is present in the liturgy suggest a plurality of spatial concepts.[159] Different from previous directives, the "guidelines" for building begin with the idea of the fundamental unity of the church space. The community of the baptized priesthood is not eliminated by the hierarchical internal structure. Hence the space is divided into places for different kinds of participants (e.g., the presider's chair) and different functions (e.g., the altar). This is not about a leveling of differences.[160]

Communio *spaces*

Greater value has recently been accorded to the idea of differentiation in regard to the multiple forms of celebration. In this, architectonic quality and liturgical dignity are of equal worth. This has led to considerations and arrangements tending toward "*communio* spaces" that are supposed to make the *specificum* of God-human community in worship available to experience.[161] These spatial concepts once again raise the question of the "center" of the church space. In the documents it appears to be identified with the altar. But can the altar, which is a thing, symbolize a person or a personal event? The "center" of Christian worship is also not to be equated simply with Christ. Christocentrism was questioned even during the Liturgical

[159] See "Leitlinien für den Bau," chaps. 1, 3; see also "Built of Living Stones" (see n. 155 above), chap. 1 (635–42): "The Living Church," chap. 2 (642–63): "The Church Building and the Sacred Rites Celebrated There."

[160] "Liturgie und Bild. Eine Orientierungshilfe," Handreichung der Liturgiekommission der Deutschen Bischofskonferenz, 23 April 1996, Sekretariat der Deutschen Bischofskonferenz. Arbeitshilfen 132 (Bonn: 1996), chap. 3.1.

[161] See Gerhards, Sternberg, and Zahner, eds., *Communio-Räume*.

Movement and was corrected by a trinitarian view.[162] The center of the celebratory space is more accurately perceived as relationship in a twofold sense: relationship within God and between God and humans. The Holy Spirit is the principle of unity in God and also of the church celebrating liturgy, as is expressed in the concluding doxology of the Eucharistic Prayer (see chap. 5.2).

Form of the place of assembly

What accordingly crystallizes is a spatial form that equally encourages expression through body language (postures, orientations, movements) in the various elements of worship and the "hierarchical codes." The central question is whether the concentric assembly of the congregation (which has come together around a center) is, of itself, something closed or whether it is also open. According to Reinhard Messner the assembly for Eucharist does not have a twofold shape (word and meal) but is threefold (proclamation, prayer, and eucharistic table fellowship/communion). The "center" of the assembly is in each case extrinsically located.[163] It must therefore retain the shape of an assembly that, in praying, somehow keeps its orientation. It is about an encounter with God the Father through Jesus Christ in the Holy Spirit. This partner, according to Messner, cannot be portrayed by a human representative. In that sense Rudolf Schwarz's suggestion of an assembly shaped as an open circle is still important.[164] Of course, this concept lacks the second focus, the place for proclamation of the Word. In a further development of the concept of *communio* space the place for proclamation of the Word is in the open segment of the circle, now extended to form an oval or ellipsis, or taking the form

[162] Rudolf Schwarz; see Albert Gerhards, "Räume für eine tätige Teilnahme. Katholischer Kirchenbau aus theologisch-liturgischer Sicht // Spaces for Active Participation. Theological and Liturgical Perspectives on Catholic Church Architecture," in *Europäischer Kirchenbau 1950–2000 // European Church Architecture*, ed. Wolfgang Jean Stock (Munich: Prestel, 2002), 16–51.

[163] Reinhard Messner, "Gebetsrichtung, Altar und die exzentrische Mitte der Gemeinde," in *Communio-Räume*, 27–36, at 29.

[164] Rudolf Schwarz, *Vom Bau der Kirche*, 3rd ed. with altered title and form, and with the addition of original hand-drawn sketches (Salzburg: Pustet, 1998; original pub. 1938).

of a U. In this way, according to Messner, the figure of the subject who speaks to us in the word of Scripture is, in fact, embodied in the human representative. Hence at the moment when the Word is proclaimed, the open segment can be closed. The priest goes behind the altar to prepare the gifts and looks, together with the community, toward the open segment. In this way the shape of prayer demanded by Messner is achieved. For the third figure, that of participation, communion in semicircles corresponding to the seating order of the faithful seems appropriate; it expresses, on the one hand, the aspect of community and on the other the orientation to the altar from which the eucharistic gifts are received.

5.5.3 Liturgical Places

5.5.3.1 The Altar

Sacrificial and meal dimensions

The charged relationship between sacrifice and meal we have mentioned is attested in the very tradition of Christian altars, beginning when separate church buildings were erected in the period after the Constantinian shift. There were probably both fixed and portable altars from the beginning; they could symbolize a sacrificial stone or a grave but were adorned and decorated like festal boards. We can see from liturgical texts as well as the discoveries of archaeologists and art historians that the dimensions of sacrifice and meal always coexisted, though with different emphases depending on the time and the cultural context. In Christian understanding, in contrast to Jewish and pagan sacrificial rituals, the altar is always something figurative: not exactly a place of sacrifice and yet a base on which the gifts can be laid; not exactly a dining table and yet a table from which the gifts of the meal are received. Of signal importance is the question of whether the integration is successful—a highly demanding artistic-aesthetic task.[165]

---

[165] Albert Gerhards, "Teologia dell'altare," in *L'altare. Mistero di presenza, opera dell'arte. Atti de II Convegno liturgico internazionale Bose, 31 ottobre–2 novembre 2003*, ed. Goffredo Boselli (Magnano: Edizione Qiqajon, 2005), 213–32.

Communication between divine and human

The altar in a Christian church takes its significance not from any material sacrificial action in the sense of a cult owed to God. This links Christianity to the other two monotheistic world religions, Judaism and Islam, neither of which has a sacrificial altar. There have been movements, for example, in the Reformed churches, against any kind of materialist idea, which was countered by a purely spiritual view. The altar instead draws its significance from the unique character of the church's central liturgical action, the Eucharist, which is a fabric of verbal and sign actions on and with material gifts of food and drink. This accomplishes an actualizing memorial of the history of God with humanity. The altar is the place on which these verbal and physical-gestural acts are performed. In that sense the altar is the place of divine-human communication.

On closer view we should here distinguish between the material and formal character of the Eucharist.

Four directions of movement

The material character is observable from the series of actions within the celebration. With respect to the altar, four directions of movement are significant: a *centripetal* orientation of the procession with the gifts, whose goal is the altar; a *descending* motion of placing the gifts on the altar, where they are prepared, and the epicletic gesture during the Eucharistic Prayer; an *ascending* movement in the concluding doxology with elevation of the species at the end of the Eucharistic Prayer; and a *centrifugal* movement in the distribution of the eucharistic gifts from the altar at communion.[166] It is made clear that the material character is not put forth as in an ordinary meal but in view of the cultic meal, with a speech-act at its center: the Eucharistic Prayer with its three basic aspects of praise, memorial, and appeal (see chap. 5.2).

---

[166] Albert Gerhards, "Vorbedingungen, Dimensionen und Ausdrucksgestalten der Bewegung in der Liturgie," in *Volk Gottes auf dem Weg. Bewegungselemente im Gottesdienst*, ed. Wolfgang Meurer (Mainz: Matthias Grünewald, 1989), 11–24.

The altar is the focal point in space of the eucharistic actions. Its position and shape reflect the eucharistic concept of a particular time and cultural space.

Eschatological dimension

The altar is part of the present creation renewed in Christ and at the same time points to the ultimate new creation in divine glory. It is the place that joins the praises of earth and heaven (*Sanctus*). The eschatological orientation is expressed very early, through the direction toward which one prays. In churches with an Eastern apse this view led to a withdrawal of the altar from the common assembly and its elevation, with steps leading up to it. But the altar, as a threshold, belongs to the present creation also. For a long time its form and materials expressed that fact, and formal and material correctness are still important criteria at present.

Place of remembrance

Memorial occupies a considerable space in the Eucharistic Prayer, especially in the anaphorae of Syrian provenience. This remembering has to do not only with God's history with Israel and humanity but also with the church in its present, its past, and its future completion. The altar becomes the place for remembering, with the *mysterium paschale* at the center, as expressed in the so-called special anamnesis. Hence the altar is always also a symbol of God's history with humanity. In attempts at interpretation throughout its history it also became a Christ-symbol representing manger, Golgotha, tomb, as well as the table of the Last Supper. Here we must deal with the question of an appropriate iconography for the altar, and in any case for its image.

Symbol of the heavenly wedding banquet

The Eucharistic Prayer is not only an actualizing memorial of the past; it also has a "forward-leaning" dynamic. In reference to the celebration it aims toward the communion (communion epiclesis); as regards the time-structure it ends in a double eschatological perspective with a view to fulfillment now and in the *eschatōn*, on the last day. Epiclesis and intercessions are the logical continuation of the anamnetic prayer and take up the universal perspectives of the first part. Thus the earthly altar, as the place of the eucharistic meal, becomes a symbol of the heavenly wedding banquet in the end time. But there is a "foretaste" of it in the sacramental eucharistic meal. The table fellowship of Christian Eucharist is not virtual but real-symbolic. Therefore the altar is also the center of the community, the family table of God-human communication. This is the justification for the aim of the Liturgical Movement and the post–Vatican II renewal to make the altar the perceived center of the assembly.

The task for the future consists of finding a balance between the desire for experience of real community (*communio*) through a concentric form of assembly around the altar and the other desire to express the openness of the community to the not-yet perfected community with God.

Tabernacle

The question of the place of reservation for the consecrated hosts (tabernacle) has, indeed, been detached from a direct connection to the altar (the tabernacle can also be placed in a separate chapel), but in the search for an appropriate form of eucharistic topography of the church space it must still be taken into consideration.

5.5.3.2 *The Ambo*

Ambo and pulpit

Probably second in importance among the innovations in Catholic church spaces, after the free-standing altar for celebration *versus populum*, is the (re-)introduction of the ambo as a fixed liturgical place, corresponding to the revaluation of the Word in the Roman liturgy (see chap. 5.1). It also led to an emptying of the traditional pulpits of their meaning and function. As regards the ambo, both the terminology and functional definition present a significant problem. Still more difficult is the issue of the placement of the ambo in the altar or church space. Is it a monument comparable to the altar, a second table alongside or opposite that of the altar? Or is the expression "table of the Word" only a metaphor (*SC* 51, *DV* 21)?

In terms of its origins the ambo is nothing but an elevated place from which one can be heard and seen. The bookstand was, accordingly, only an artificial addition that could easily be replaced by a person holding the book. Between monumentalism and minimalism lie a near-infinite number of possible variations reflecting an array of different ideas about the act of proclamation and other liturgical actions.

Place of the act of proclamation

The ambo's importance derives from its character as the place of the *event* of proclamation. Thus what is essential is the action that takes place there, through which the word of God is made present in the celebrating assembly. To the extent that anamnesis and making present take place at the ambo, its full significance is altogether comparable to that of the altar as the place of the eucharistic anamnesis. Since faith comes from hearing, the proclamation of the word is prior to the sacramental celebration. In the proclamation of the word it is made really present, analogously to the real presence in the Eucharist. God's self-donation takes place in God's word. However, in worship services today there is often an inappropriate treatment of the Word; it seems that no one any longer believes in its power to effect change. Thus the Liturgy of the Word is often reduced to the conveyance of information and the ambo to a lectern. However, a look at the history of the ambo can reveal the astonishing riches and variety of possibilities for its use, and so of the effective dimensions of liturgy.

From a current point of view a number of problem fields can be listed: what is the relationship of functionalism and symbolism? What is the relationship of the ambo to the altar, in terms both of material and formal shape and position? How should it be situated in relation to the presider's chair and the people's places?

The gospel and other readings

A theology of the ambo derives from the anamnetic character of the Liturgy of the Word, in accord with the medium whereby the worship service is made audible in making present the story that is told in it. The anamnetic character of the Liturgy of the Word is especially evident in the ritual staging of the reading of the gospel. The gradient from the rather simple presentation of the other readings from the Old and New

Testaments is striking. In the Byzantine liturgy the position of the "little entrance" at the beginning of the Liturgy of the Word more clearly marks the unity of the whole action than is the case in the Roman Rite, in which the gospel procession takes place immediately before the reading of the gospel. In fact, the topography of the Roman basilicas, with their two ambos, corresponds to the clear division between the proclamation of the gospel and that of the other Scripture readings. In contrast, the documents of Vatican II, and especially its teaching about the fundamental unity of the Scriptures, suggest concentration on a single place for proclamation of the Word as well as a ritual staging worthy of the action. In light of the forms of the Liturgy of the Word (see chap. 5.1.4) we may say that the Liturgy of the Word in the Mass is *primarily* anamnetic, although didactic and paracletic moments are not altogether absent. The optimal communicative situation called for in the church documents (comprehensibility, visibility) is therefore essentially a necessary but not in-itself-determinative aspect as regards the concrete position and form of the ambo. Rather, it is analogous to the altar as a place for anamnesis of Christ in the Eucharist. Here we may also consider, in analogy to the place of reservation of the Eucharist, the possibility of a place of reservation for the gospel book or Bible when liturgy is not being celebrated.

5.5.3.3 The Font

The font, the place of baptism, is the third anamnetic locus within the room for liturgical celebration; like the ambo, it had largely surrendered its function and has experienced a revaluation through the reordering prescribed in the liturgical reform.

As early as New Testament times, baptism was regarded as a many-layered event. The multiple text passages and sign-actions around the baptismal font in the strands of ancient church tradition correspond to the biblical record, as do the different forms of the place for baptism. We will give a summary account of these in what follows, though one must consider that in reality a number of motifs always coexisted.

Place of repentance and purification

First we should speak of the baptism of John, which should be seen in connection with Jewish proselyte baptism. Here repentance was a central motif and the metaphor of judgment was significant. We find the baptism of repentance in New Testament times (Acts 13:24). Liturgically, the idea of repentance resides in the rite of *apotaxis* (renunciation of Satan, toward the West) and *syntaxis* (acceptance of Christ, toward the East); for this, a passage with a West-East orientation was an important feature of some baptisteries. The associated motif of forgiveness of sins is imaged with different connotations. Thus 1 Corinthians 6:11 and Revelation 22:16 speak of washing clean, while Hebrews 10:22b refers to sprinkling (with the blood of Christ). These correspond to baptism through perfusion (pouring) and immersion. Here the font is primarily a fount of purification in both function and form.

Place of burial and rebirth

The motif of baptism and death, as in Mark 10:38-39, points to a different symbolism. This corresponds to baptism through descent and immersion as symbolic drowning. Cruciform fonts and baptisteries indicate a staurocentric level of interpretation. In the course of the fourth century (Ambrose) being immersed corresponded to the image of burial (see Rom 6:4), and large, flat baptisteries were created. The idea of baptism as rebirth (John 3:5) was obviously connected to all of these themes. It seems natural to interpret coming up out of the font as rising from the grave or the underworld. In the Roman liturgy that motif occurs especially in the symbolism of the blessing of the baptismal water, which interprets the font as a mother's womb. The symbolism of the white garment can also be interpreted in that context.

Place of rescue (Exodus; Passover)

Finally, we should point to the theme of baptism and rescue in the sense of the paschal *transitus* (see Mark 16:16). The underlying typology is that of the exodus event. The font is interpreted and designed as the place of passage through the Reed Sea (toward the East).[167]

---

[167] Albert Gerhards, "Die fortdauernde Wirksamkeit der Taufe im christlichen Leben: *simul iustus et peccator*. Liturgiewissenschaftliche Erkenntnisse," in *Gerecht und Sünder zugleich? Ökumenische Klärungen*, ed. Christine Axt-Piscalar,

Basin for storing water

The fonts of the developed baptismal liturgy in the ancient church evolved into basins for keeping the water consecrated for baptism during the Easter Vigil. The originally quite voluminous Roman fonts (made of stone or bronze) shrank over time. For the individual act of baptism, conducted as a rule without much ceremony, nothing more was needed but a basin and shell. With the reorganization of the baptismal liturgy (possibly including baptism through immersion) and the reintroduction of the catechumenate, the font has now acquired a new significance in action and also as an anamnetic sign, a monumental memorial of baptism. The question is: to which of the New Testament typologies do we want to refer? The design of the font is also associated with the question of the appropriate place for storing the three holy oils (chrism, oil of catechumens, and oil of the sick).

5.5.4 Vessels and Utensils

Costliness of vessels

Precious vessels—chalice and paten, ciborium and monstrance— were the heart of the cathedrals of the High Middle Ages. They contained the relics of the saints over whose tombs the buildings were erected, and above all they received the eucharistic species. Silver and gold symbolized proximity to the holy. Traditionally, only those precious metals could be used for the vessels that received the bread and wine during the celebration of Mass, because only the most precious were regarded as worthy to touch the Most Holy. On the human side this corresponded to the fear of receiving the Body and Blood of the Lord unworthily. The image-character of the costly vessels supported that attitude on the part of priests and people.

After a phase of general disregard for liturgical vessels and utensils, this sphere has quite recently received a good deal of attention once again.[168] The classic literature distinguished between *vasa sacra*

Theodor Schneider, and Gunther Wenz, Dialog der Kirchen 11 (Freiburg: Herder; Göttingen: Vandenhoeck & Ruprecht, 2001), 376–95.

[168] See *LiturgieGefässe, Kirche und Design. Eine Ausstellung anlässlich des 50jährigen Bestehens des Deutschen Liturgischen Instituts* (Trier: Deutsches Liturgisches Institut, 1997).

and *vasa non sacra*, depending on how close they were to the eucharistic event. The *vasa sacra* were primarily the ciboria and chalice. But the cup for wine, a constant in Christian worship, was already part of Jewish liturgy. The book of Psalms speaks repeatedly of the cup of blessing or salvation (e.g., Ps 116:12-14). Paul adjures his audience in Corinth: "The cup of blessing that we bless, is it not a sharing in the blood of Christ?" (1 Cor 10:16). The elevation of the chalice and the spoken expressions of praise that accompany it are a particular expression of the festal character of Christian liturgy. Thus a twofold action is central: praise and thanksgiving over the bread and wine as well as eating and drinking the consecrated gifts, for which appropriate vessels are necessary.

Changes over time

The vessels for the eucharistic gifts, as they developed over time, speak eloquently about how the eucharistic transformation is perceived. A great two-handled cup such as we see, for example, in a sixth-century mosaic in St. Vitale in Ravenna has nothing in common with a baroque chalice beyond its function as a drinking vessel. While the ancient cup was intended to be handed around and drunk from by a large number of people, the baroque chalice, with its broad foot and small cup, is designed to be blessed and consumed by only one person. It demonstrates that, at the time it was created, the people's communion in the cup was only visual. Still more serious were the changes in the vessels for the eucharistic bread. The bread plate (still the *diskos* in the East even today) was replaced by a ciborium for preserving hosts for communion outside Mass and the small paten was for the priest's host, received during Mass by the priest alone.

Vessels and utensils were also used for other worship actions: for baptism with water and anointing with oil; for light (lamp, candlestand); later for incense and, since the High Middle Ages, for ritual signings; for relics (small boxes, shrines, "speaking" reliquaries); and for the eucharistic bread (pyxes, ciboria, eucharistic doves, monstrances). The form of the vessel was usually associated with the unique character of the action connected with it; form and function maintained a kind of mutual relationship.

Influence of the changing forms of liturgy on the vessels

The formal changes in liturgical celebrations could not remain inconsequential for the form of the vessels and utensils used. The shape of the "periphery" derives from the liturgical action. The medieval sign-ritual, the elevation, determined the form of the chalice and created a new form: the monstrance, a show-vessel that enabled signing with the bread. The rule that, after the consecration, the priest must keep thumbs and index fingers together until the post-communion ablutions led to another rule, that a thickening (node) must be added to the chalice so the vessel could be held in the hand. Although that practical necessity no longer exists, chalices continue to be made with nodes since for many people it is an identifying sign of a chalice.

This brings us to the question of the illustrative character of liturgical vessels. We should distinguish primary and secondary illustrative functions; their hierarchy has changed with time.[169] This is true especially when dogmatic considerations influence the form. So the ciborium, the "bread chalice" for the people's communion, took on the form of a drinking vessel in order to make it clear that communion under the form of bread alone contained the whole Christ. With the reintroduction of the "cup for the laity" after Vatican II that relic of the Reformation period was eliminated, but in the process the "bread chalice" lost its plausibility. So we ought to ask what form corresponds to today's liturgy. Here the council, with its statement that the rites (and everything associated with them) should "radiate a noble simplicity" (*SC* 34), chose an important, if misconstruable, basic option. Appropriateness for the liturgical action-event is to be primary. Material and form must correspond to the dignity of the event. The use of particular materials (e.g., precious metals for chalice and vessels for the host) is rightly no longer a matter of universal church regulation; it is left to the territorial authorities. In addition, the reality of the form is not to be obscured by a questionable secondary "shaping."

---

[169] *Liturgie und Licht. Eine Orientierungshilfe*, ed. Albert Gerhards, Liturgie & Gemeinde, Impulse & Perspektiven 7 (Trier: Deutsches Liturgisches Institut, 2006).

Hence efforts to reverse the process of reduction of liturgical actions and the vessels and utensils necessary for them should be increased. This is true, for example, of the reduction of the font, already mentioned, and the vessels and utensils of the baptismal liturgy: we have spoken of the font itself. A traditional small jug is no longer adequate for the solemn epiclesis of blessing the baptismal water that is now repeated at each baptism (outside the Easter season). Miniaturized oil stocks scarcely suffice to illustrate the symbolism of blessing, healing, and strengthening. With the rediscovery of processions, certain vessels and utensils that had often vanished, even quite recently, have come to light again: monstrances and reliquaries, processional crosses and lamps, pictures and banners.

5.5.5 Vestments and Textiles

The words "text" and "textile" are etymologically related: *textum* (Lat.) is the fabric, texture the structure of the weave. Complex weaving techniques developed out of primitive basketwork, just as complex linguistic structures gave rise to literary texts. Textile work is among the most elementary craft achievements of humanity, while working with texts is one of the late forms of the human power of abstraction. The production of cloth and textiles is, along with other culture-related creations such as ceramics, jewelry, and weapons, part of the incunabula of human culture and an indicator of cultural differentiations (e.g., robes of state). Thus the remains of garments (for example, in tombs) are among the most eloquent archaeological witnesses.

Symbolic value of clothing

Textiles—especially pieces of clothing—have a high symbolic value that cannot be reduced to function (e.g., protection against cold, concealment of pudenda). "The origins of human clothing lie . . . in the human need for adornment."[170] Textiles are transitional objects to a special degree;[171] they are an important component of

---

[170] Rupert Berger, "Liturgische Gewänder und Insignien," in idem, et al., *Gestalt des Gottesdienstes*, 309–46, at 313.

[171] Barbara Schimmel, *Tuchbestimmungen, Schweigeschrift, Ritualkleider. Album zu den textilen Universalien*, Studien zur Phänomenologie der gestalterischen Erfahrung 1 (Münster: Lit, 1999), 22–23, following Donald W. Winnicott.

anthropogenesis as well as of religious rituals: covering and uncovering are central moments in the back-and-forth of sacred and profane. Clothing always plays a dominant role in both the profane-social and the religious spheres. It signals identities and differences even in an apparently permissive society that has moved away from thinking in terms of class. So in the youth scene today, clothing represents an important point of identification.

In contrast, the subject of textiles has long been marginalized or even taboo in church circles. The widespread neglectful treatment of paraments, antependia, or altar linens in the second half of the twentieth century speaks for itself. In reaction, we can observe a creative recovery of sensibility to materials that quite often reaches back for lost objects such as paraments and other textile indicators.

Garments in the book of Revelation

We should not be surprised at the rediscovery of textiles when we consider the wealth of biblical symbolism and metaphor associated with robes and cloths. The question is whether and how a real liturgical symbol can and should be derived from the word-symbols. The Johannine Apocalypse offers one possible starting point; there, according to many authors, concrete liturgical usages have entered into the text. In the depiction of the "heavenly liturgy" it is said of the martyrs: "they have washed their robes and made them white in the blood of the Lamb" (Rev 7:14). The white garment unifies the heavenly liturgy: all who are allowed to appear before the heavenly throne wear it or have it given to them (Rev 3:4, 5, 18; 4:4; 6:11; 7:9, 13); likewise, the Bride of the Lamb wears a white robe (Rev 19:8). At the end we read: "Blessed are those who wash their robes, so that they will have the right to the tree of life and may enter the city by the gates" (Rev 22:14).

It is clear that washing of garments and the white color are allusions to the Christian baptismal liturgy. The step to a prescribed baptismal garment is not a long one, and from that other initiation robes derived (above all the monastic habit, but wedding gowns also).

Robes and hierarchy

Textiles played an increasing role in later church tradition. Everyday clothing developed over time into liturgical garments to which—

with reference to Old Testament models—ever greater significance was assigned. This was true especially of episcopal robes and insignia. Garments serve to represent the hierarchically organized church and therefore have a primarily representative function. Concentration of artistic effort on the priest's chasuble (and the robes of the other clergy) since the Middle Ages corresponds to the narrowing of eucharistic theology to the priestly power of consecration.

Developments in the churches of the Reformation

Reformation critique was directed against such a concept. But reduction of the symbols alone was not a lasting solution. The pastor's gown was no equivalent for Catholic paraments. The Protestant liturgical movement in the twentieth century accordingly rediscovered liturgical colors, not so much for the pastor's robe as for the antependia. Recently there has also been increasing use of the stole. On the Catholic side, after the reductive phase in the 1960s and 1970s, later decades have seen a rediscovery of the textile dimension. Here again we should warn against one-sidedness: if the priest's garment is seen only in its function of hierarchical representation it shrinks to mere insignia.

Functions of the robe

Besides the robe's pragmatic function of designating an office-holder we should consider a number of theological levels of meaning. With the Pauline motif of putting on Christ or being clothed with immortality the robe takes on a soteriological connotation and symbolism that is present primarily in the baptismal garment, but secondarily also in the priest's chasuble (*casula*: little house; see 2 Cor 5:1).[172]

Liturgical garments participate in a special way in the basic anamnetic dimension of the liturgy, as Dietmar Thönnes has said: "Clothing supports memory. The church's textile memory, as a figurative appropriation of revelation, can become a part of the liturgy

---

[172] Michael Kunzler, "*Indumentum Salutis*. Überlegungen zum liturgischen Gewand," *Theologie und Glaube* 81 (1991): 52–78.

that can be experienced by the senses through appropriate action, a mnemotechnique of faith."[173]

Dimensions of the robe

Under the title "Dimensions of the Form of the Sign," Klara Antons, OSB, describes these purposes of the robe:

1. the *functional* dimension, separated in the church's official documents into festal and service character; to be distinguished from this is the functionality of the robe itself, that is, its appropriateness for the particular liturgical action

2. the *sacral* dimension: covering (as a dimension of the religious), the principle of representation, the principle of the beautiful, fullness, superfluity, as well as the eschatological principle

3. the *personal* dimension: the incarnational principle, *communio*-theology, the dimension of attunement, the sense-side (including therapeutic and integrative aspects) as well as the special form of the monastic as a dimension of the *humanum*.[174]

Textiles are closer to the human person than any other product of human activity other than food; the feel of the cloth is of the essence. Liturgics has a task before it in regard to "textile memory." This applies first of all to the garments of the liturgy. The Working Group for Sacred Art and Architecture of the German Bishops' Liturgical Commission held a discussion a few years ago about a new way of dealing with this question and proposed some new garments and insignia (stole, baptismal scarf).[175] In the meantime many pastors have been experimenting with robes and textile insignia, though a number of fundamental questions remain: should the liturgical

---

[173] Dietmar Thönnes, "Das textile Gedächtnis der Kirche. Mnemotechniken und anamnetische Aspekte liturgischer Kleidung," *Liturgisches Jahrbuch* 47 (1997): 78–88, at 88.

[174] Klara Antons, *Paramente: Dimensionen der Zeichengestalt*, Bild, Raum, Feier, Kirche und Kunst im Gespräch 3 (Regensburg: Schnell & Steiner, 1999).

[175] *Gottes Volk: neu gekleidet: ein Versuch, entwickelt von der Arbeitsgruppe "Kirchliche Architektur und Sakrale Kunst" der Liturgiekommission der Deutschen Bischofskonferenz* (Trier: Deutsches Liturgisches Institut, 1994).

ministers (lector, communion minister) wear liturgical garments? Should those be clearly distinct from the clergy's robes? There is also dispute over the question of a unified set of garments for children at First Communion. In particular, the baptismal scarf has encountered critique from church leaders because it could be confused with the priest's stole.

Alongside the question of a basic liturgical garment there is a great deal of new interest in classic paraments. The chasuble display in the art gallery of St. Peter in Cologne (1992) and the subsequent projects[176] brought the artistic dimension of the question newly into play and inaugurated a discussion whose effects have on the whole been positive. Even if fixation on the cultic aspect does not seem altogether unproblematic, still, perception of the necessary quality of older and newer paraments and textiles in the context of the liturgy has been rendered more acute.

In the realm of signs and symbols there are no "trivia," because every sign that is falsely placed can become a dominant and disturbing factor. This is true, for example, of flowers on and around the altar or the decoration of the entrance area. The "Guidelines for the Building and Furnishing of Churches" as well as the aids "Liturgie und Bild" and "Liturgie und Licht" from the Liturgical Commission of the German Bishops' Conference thus focus also on such often-neglected details. It is the task of liturgics to study these *realia* historically, in terms of sign-theory, and also in the context of systematic theology, and so to establish criteria for the proper way of dealing with them.

---

[176] *Casula: Gregory Amenoff, James Brown, Paolo d'Orazio . . . . Kunst-Station Sankt Peter Köln, 3 Juni–16 August 1992, Galerie in der Finkenstrasse München, 3 September–9 Oktober 1992, Sankt Petri Lübeck, 18 Oktober–18 November 1992* (Cologne: Kunst-Station Sankt Peter, 1992).

Appendix 1

Initiation

1.1 Rites of Initiation

1.1.1 Rite of Christian Initiation of Adults

Steps of Initiation	1. First Step: Acceptance into the Order of Catechumens	2. Second Step: Election or Enrollment Of Names	3. Third Step: Celebration of the Sacraments of Initiation
Periods of Time	"usually celebrated on some annual date or dates" (14)	"usually celebrated on the First Sunday of Lent" (14)	"usually integrated into the Easter Vigil" (14)

ACCEPTANCE INTO THE ORDER OF CATECHUMENS

✦ Receiving the Candidates
   • Greeting
   • Opening Dialogue
   • Candidates' First Acceptance of the Gospel
   • Affirmation by the Sponsors and the Assembly
   • Signing of the Candidates with the Cross
      – Signing of the Forehead
      – [Signing of the Other Senses]
      – Concluding Prayer
   • Invitation to the Celebration of the Word of God

✦ Liturgy of the Word
  • Instruction
  • Readings
  • Homily
  • [Presentation of a Bible]
  • Intercessions for the Catechumens
  • Prayer over the Catechumens
  • Dismissal of the Catechumens

✦ Liturgy of the Eucharist

RITE OF ELECTION OR ENROLLMENT OF NAMES

✦ Liturgy of the Word
  • Homily
  • Presentation of the Catechumens
  • Affirmation by the Godparents [and the Assembly]
  • Invitation and Enrollment of Names
  • Act of Admission or Election
  • Intercessions for the Elect
  • Prayer over the Elect
  • Dismissal of the Elect

✦ Liturgy of the Eucharist

PERIOD OF PURIFICATION AND ENLIGHTENMENT

First Scrutiny
Presentation of the Creed
Second Scrutiny
Third Scrutiny
Presentation of the Lord's Prayer
Preparation Rites on Holy Saturday
  • Recitation of the Creed
  • Ephphatha Rite
  • [Choosing a Baptismal Name]
  • Concluding Rites

SCRUTINIES ON THE THIRD, FOURTH, AND FIFTH SUNDAY OF LENT

✦ Liturgy of the Word

- Readings
- Homily
- Invitation to Silent Prayer
- Intercessions for the Elect
- Exorcism
- Dismissal of the Elect

✦ Liturgy of the Eucharist

CELEBRATION OF THE SACRAMENTS OF INITIATION

✦ Celebration of Baptism
  - Presentation of the Candidates
  - Invitation to Prayer
  - Litany of the Saints
  - Prayer over the Water
  - Profession of Faith
    - Renunciation of Sin
    - Profession of Faith
  - Baptism
  - Explanatory Rites
    - [Anointing after Baptism]
    - [Clothing with a Baptismal Garment]
    - Presentation of a Lighted Candle

✦ Celebration of Confirmation
  - Invitation
  - Laying on of Hands
  - Anointing with Chrism

✦ [Renewal of Baptismal Promises (at the Easter Vigil)]
  - Invitation
  - Renewal of Baptismal Promises
    - Renunciation of Sin
    - Profession of Faith
  - Sprinkling with Baptismal Water

✦ Liturgy of the Eucharist

(Source: "Rite of Christian Initiation of Adults," in *The Rites*, vol. 1 [College-ville, MN: Liturgical Press, 1990]).

1.1.2 Rite of Baptism for Children

A: All
P: Parents
GP: Godparents
C: Celebrant

Reception of the child	ENTRANCE OF THE CHURCH or part of the church where the parents and godparents are waiting with the child
C	Greeting
	Questions for the parents
	Address for the parents and the godparents
C / P/ GP	Sign of the cross of the child's forehead
A	[Procession to the place of the Liturgy of the Word]

Liturgy of the Word	The baptism takes place in the CHURCH.
	One or two gospel passages
	[between responsorial psalms and verses]
C	Short homily
	[Silence]
	[Song]
C/L/A	General intercession
C/A	Invocation of saints
C	Prayer of exorcism
C	[Anointing before baptism]

Celebration of the sacrament	BAPTISTERY or sanctuary
	Introduction
C	Blessing and invocation of God over baptismal water
C/P/GP	Renunciation of sin
A	Profession of faith or a suitable song
C	Baptism

Explanatory rites
C	Anointing after baptism
C	Clothing with the white garment
C/P/GP	Lighted candle
	[Ephphatha or prayer over ears and mouth]

Conclusion of the rite	Procession to the ALTAR

A	Baptismal song at the procession
A	Lord's prayer
C	Blessing over the mother, the father, and the assembly; dismissal
A	[Hymn of thanksgiving and Easter joy or the *Magnificat*]

1.2 Blessing and Invocation of God over Baptismal Water (A)

C: Father,
you give us grace through sacramental signs,
which tell us of the wonders of your unseen power.
In baptism we use your gift of water,
which you have made a rich symbol of the grace
you give us in this sacrament.

[Anamnesis with Paradigms from the Old and New Testaments]

At the very dawn of creation
your Spirit breathed on the waters,
making them the wellspring of all holiness.
The waters of the great flood
you made a sign of the waters of baptism
that make an end of sin
and a new beginning of goodness.
Through the waters of the Red Sea
you led Israel out of slavery
to be an image of God's holy people,
set free from sin by baptism.
In the waters of the Jordan
your Son was baptized by John
and anointed with the Spirit.
Your Son willed that water and blood should flow from his side
as he hung upon the cross.
After his resurrection he told his disciples:
"Go out and teach all nations,
baptizing them in the name of the Father, and of the Son, and of the
  Holy Spirit."
Father,
look now with love upon your Church
and unseal for it the fountain of baptism.

By the power of the Holy Spirit
give to this water the grace of your Son,
so that in the sacrament of baptism
all those whom you have created in your likeness
may be cleansed from sin
and rise to a new birth of innocence
by water and the Holy Spirit.
   The celebrant touches the water with his right hand and continues:
   [Epiclesis]
We ask you, Father, with your Son
to send the Holy Spirit upon the waters of this font.
May all who are buried with Christ in the death of baptism
rise also with him to newness of life.
We ask this through Christ our Lord.

All: Amen.

(Source: "Rite of Christian Initiation of Adults," in *The Rites*, vol. 1 [College-ville, MN: Liturgical Press, 1990]).

Appendix 2

The Canon of the Mass
Eucharistic Prayer II as an Example

Dialogue
Pr(iest): The Lord be with you.
P(eople): And with your spirit.
Pr.: Lift up your hearts.
P.: We lift them up to the Lord.
Pr.: Let us give thanks to the Lord our God.
P.: It is right and just.

Preface
Priest:
It is truly right and just, our duty and our salvation, always and everywhere to give you thanks, Father most holy, through your beloved Son, Jesus Christ, your Word through whom you made all things, whom you sent as our Savior and Redeemer, incarnate by the Holy Spirit and born of the Virgin. Fulfilling your will and gaining for you a holy people, he stretched out his hands as he endured his Passion, so as to break the bonds of death and manifest the resurrection. And so, with the Angels and all the Saints we declare your glory, as with one voice we acclaim:

Sanctus
All:
Holy, Holy, Holy Lord God of hosts.
Heaven and earth are full of your glory.
Hosanna in the highest.
Blessed is he who comes in the name of the Lord.
Hosanna in the highest.

Transition

Priest:

You are indeed Holy, O Lord, the fount of all holiness.

Consecration Epiclesis

Make holy, therefore, these gifts, we pray, by sending down your Spirit upon them like the dewfall, so that they may become for us the Body and Blood of our Lord Jesus Christ.

Account of Institution

At the time he was betrayed and entered willingly into his Passion, he took bread and, giving thanks, broke it, and gave it to his disciples, saying:

Take this, all of you, and eat of it, for this is my Body, which will be given up for you.

In a similar way, when supper was ended, he took the chalice and, once more giving thanks, he gave it to his disciples, saying:

Take this, all of you, and drink from it, for this is the chalice of my Blood, the Blood of the new and eternal covenant, which will be poured out for you and for many for the forgiveness of sins. Do this in memory of me.

Acclamation

The mystery of faith.

People:

We proclaim your Death, O Lord, and profess your Resurrection until you come again.

Or:

When we eat this Bread and drink this Cup, we proclaim your Death, O Lord, until you come again.

Or:

Save us, Savior of the world, for by your Cross and Resurrection you have set us free.

Special Anamnesis

Therefore, as we celebrate the memorial of his Death and Resurrection, we offer you, Lord, the Bread of life and the Chalice of salvation, giving thanks that you have held us worthy to be in your presence and minister to you.

Communion Epiclesis

Humbly we pray that, partaking of the Body and Blood of Christ, we may be gathered into one by the Holy Spirit.

Intercessions

C1. Remember, Lord, your Church, spread throughout the world, and bring her to the fullness of charity, together with N. our Pope and N. our Bishop and all the clergy.

(In Masses for the Dead, the following may be added.
2C. Remember your servant N., whom you have called [today] from this world to yourself. Grant that he [she] who was united with your Son in a death like his, may also be one with him in his Resurrection.)

C2. Remember also our brothers and sisters who have fallen asleep in the hope of the resurrection, and all who have died in your mercy: welcome them into the light of your face. Have mercy on us all, we pray, that with the Blessed Virgin Mary, Mother of God, with the blessed Apostles, and all the Saints who have pleased you throughout the ages, we may merit to be coheirs to eternal life, and may praise and glorify you through your Son, Jesus Christ.

Doxology

Through him, and with him, and in him, O God, almighty Father, in the unity of the Holy Spirit, all glory and honor is yours, for ever and ever.

Closing Acclamation

People:
Amen.

(Source: *The Roman Missal, Third Edition* [Collegeville, MN: Liturgical Press, 2011], 645–49).

Appendix 3

Structures of the Liturgies of the Hours

Morning and Evening Prayer as Major Hours

Lauds	Vespers
Opening verse	Opening verse
Hymn	Hymn
Psalmody	Psalmody
Morning psalm	Psalm
OT canticle	Psalm
Psalm of praise	NT canticle
Short Scripture lesson	Short Scripture lesson
Short Response	Short Response
Gospel canticle: *Benedictus* (Canticle of Zechariah)	Gospel canticle: *Magnificat* (Canticle of Mary)
Invocations	Intercessions
Lord's Prayer	Lord's Prayer
Concluding collect	Concluding collect
Blessing	Blessing
	Marian antiphon

Compline
Opening verse
Examination of conscience or penitential rite
Hymn
Psalmody: one or two psalms with antiphons
Short Scripture lesson
Short Response
Gospel canticle: *Nunc dimittis* (Canticle of Simeon)
Concluding collect
Blessing
Marian antiphon

Office of Readings
(Invitatory) Opening verse Hymn Psalmody: three psalms with antiphons Verse Scripture lesson with response Readings from the writings of the Fathers or church writers or a reading connected with the saints (On Sundays outside Lent, on days within the octaves of Easter and Christmas, on solemnities and feasts: *Te Deum*) Concluding collect Acclamation

Appendix 4

Structure and Content of the Constitution on the Liturgy, Sacrosanctum Concilium

Introduction (1–4)

Chapter I: General Principles for the Restoration and Promotion of the Sacred Liturgy (5–46)

Edition quoted in this book

Vatican Council II: The Conciliar and Postconciliar Documents, edited by Austin Flannery, OP, © 1996. Used with permission of Liturgical Press, Collegeville, Minnesota.

Overviews

Bugnini, Annibale. *The Reform of the Liturgy, 1948–1975*. Translated by Matthew J. O'Connell. Collegeville, MN: Liturgical Press, 1990.

Ferrone, Rita. *Liturgy:* Sacrosanctum Concilium. Rediscovering Vatican II. New York: Paulist Press, 2007.

Marini, Piero. *A Challenging Reform: Realizing the Vision of the Liturgical Renewal, 1963–1975*. Edited by Mark R. Francis, John R. Page, and Keith F. Pecklers. Collegeville, MN: Liturgical Press, 2007.

Commentaries

Crichton, James D. *The Church's Worship: Considerations on the Liturgical Constitution of the Second Vatican Council*. New York: Sheed & Ward, 1964.

Jungmann, Josef Andreas. "Commentary on Constitution on the Sacred Liturgy." In *Commentary on the Documents of Vatican II*, edited by Herbert Vorgrimler, translated by Lalit Adolphus, Kevin Smyth, and Richard Strachan, 1:1–87. New York: Herder and Herder, 1967–.

Kaczynski, Reiner. "Sacrosanctum Concilium." In *Sacrosanctum Concilium, Inter mirifica, Lumen gentium*, edited by Peter Hünermann, et al., 1–227. Herders Theologischer Kommentar zum Zweiten Vatikanischen Konzil 2. Freiburg: Herder, 2004.

Lengeling, Emil Joseph. *Die Konstitution des Zweiten Vatikanischen Konzils über die Heilige Liturgie*. Lateinisch-deutscher Text mit einem Kommentar. Lebendiger Gottesdienst 5/6. Münster: Regensberg, 1965.

Bibliographies

Ancient Authors

Ambrose of Milan. "The Mysteries." In *Ambrose: Theological and Dogmatic Works*. Translated by Roy J. Deferrari. Fathers of the Church 44. Washington, DC: Catholic University of America Press, 1963.

———. "The Sacraments." In *Ambrose: Theological and Dogmatic Works*.

Aurelius Augustinus. *Letters*. Volume 1. Translated by Sister Wilfrid Parsons. Fathers of the Church 12. Washington, DC: Catholic University of America Press, 2008.

Cyril of Jerusalem. *Catecheses*. In *Select Library of Nicene and Post-Nicene Fathers of the Church 2, vol. 7: Cyril of Jerusalem, S. Gregory Nazianzen*. Edited by Philip Schaff. Grand Rapids: Eerdmans, 1989.

Dionysius the Areopagite. *Works* (1897). Translated by John Parker. London: James Parker, 1897–1899. Available at http://www.ccel.org/ccel/dionysius/works.pdf.

Egeria: Diary of a Pilgrimage. Translated by George E. Gingras. Ancient Christian Writers 38. New York and Mahwah, NJ: Newman Press, 1968.

Gregory the Great. *Homilies on the Book of the Prophet Ezekiel*. Translated by Theodosia Tomkinson. Etna, CA: Center for Traditionalist Orthodox Studies, 2008.

Innocent I, Pope. "Epistle 25." Patrologia Latina 20:554B–55A; 559B–61A.

John Chrysostom. *Baptismal Instructions*. Translated by Paul W. Harkins. Ancient Christian Writers 31. New York: Paulist Press, 1963.

———. "Homily on the Birth of Christ." Patrologia Graeca 49:351–62.

Justin Martyr, *The First and Second Apologies*. Translated with introduction and notes by Leslie William Barnard. Ancient Christian Writers 56. New York and Mahwah, NJ: Paulist Press, 1997.

Milavec, Aaron. *The Didache: Text, Translation, Analysis, and Commentary*. Collegeville, MN: Liturgical Press, 2003.

Origen. *Homilies on Numbers*. Translated by Thomas P. Scheck. Edited by Christopher A. Hall. Ancient Christian Texts. Downers Grove, IL: IVP Academic Press, 2009.

The Rule of Benedict. See esp. Terrence G. Kardong. *Benedict's Rule: A Transla-tion and Commentary.* Collegeville, MN: Liturgical Press, 1996.

Rupert of Deutz. *Ruperti Tuitiensis Liber de divinis officiis.* Edited by Rhabanus Maurus Haacke. Corpus Christianorum, Continuatio Mediae-valis 7. Turnhout: Brepols, 1967.

Sicard of Cremona. *Sicardi cremonensis episcopi Mitrale, sive De officiis ecclesi-asticis summa.* Patrologia Latina 213:9–436.

Theodore of Mopsuestia. *Katechetische Homilien.* Translated by Peter Bruns. Fontes christiani 17. Freiburg and New York: Herder, 1994–1995. Selections in Frederick G. McLeod, *Theodore of Mopsuestia.* Early Church Fathers. London and New York: Routledge, 2009, 158–70.

William Durandus of Mende. *Rationale divinorum officiorum.* Edited by Anselme Davril and Timothy M. Thibodeau. Corpus Christianorum, Continuatio Mediaevalis 140, 140A, 140B. Turnhout: Brepols, 1995–2000.

Modern Authors

Altermatt, Urs. "Von der Volksreligion zur Massenreligiosität," 33–51 in *Liturgie in Bewegung/Liturgie en mouvement. Beiträge zum Kolloquium Gottesdienstliche Erneuerung in den Schweizer Kirchen im 20. Jahrhundert 1.–3. März 1999 an der Universität Freiburg/Schweiz // Actes du Colloque Renouveau liturgique des Églises en Suisse au XXe siècle. 1–3 mars 1999, Université de Fribourg/Suisse.* Edited by Bruno Bürki and Martin Klöckener, with Arnaud Join-Lambert. Fribourg: Universitätsverlag; Geneva: Labor et Fides, 2000.

Andrieu, Michel. *Les "Ordines Romani" du haut moyen âge.* Vol. 2, *Les textes (Ordines I–XIII).* Spicilegium Sacrum Lovaniense 23. Louvain: SSL, 1948.

Angenendt, Arnold. *Das Frühmittelalter. Die abendländische Christenheit von 400 bis 900.* 3rd ed. Stuttgart: Kohlhammer, 2001.

———. *Liturgik und Historik. Gab es eine organische Liturgie-Entwicklung?* 2nd ed. Quaestiones Disputatae 189. Freiburg: Herder, 2001.

———. *Liturgie im Mittelalter. Ausgewählte Aufsätze zum 70. Geburtstag.* Edited by Thomas Flammer and Daniel Meyer. Ästhetik, Theologie, Liturgik 35. Münster: LIT, 2004.

———. "Religiösität und Theologie. Ein spannungsreiches Verhältnis im Mittelalter." In idem, *Liturgie im Mittelalter,* 3–33.

———. "Missa specialis. Zugleich ein Beitrag zur Entstehung der Privatmessen." In idem, *Liturgie im Mittelalter,* 111–90.

———. *Geschichte der Religiosität im Mittelalter.* 3rd ed. Darmstadt: Wissenschaftliche Buchgesellschaft, 2005.

Antons, Klara. *Paramente: Dimensionen der Zeichengestalt.* Bild, Raum, Feier. Kirche und Kunst im Gespräch 3. Regensburg: Schnell & Steiner, 1999.

Assmann, Jan. *Cultural Memory and Early Civilization: Writing, Remembrance, and Political Imagination.* Cambridge: Cambridge University Press, 2011.

Auf der Maur, Hansjörg. *Feiern im Rhythmus der Zeit I. Herrenfeste in Woche und Jahr.* Volume 5 of *Gottesdienst der Kirche. Handbuch der Liturgiewissenschaft.* Edited by Hans Bernhard Meyer, et al. Regensburg: Pustet, 1983.

———. *Die Osterfeier in der alten Kirche. Aus dem Nachlass.* Edited by Reinhard Messner and Wolfgang G. Schöpf, mit einem Beitrag von Clemens Leonhard. Liturgica Oenipotana 2. Münster: LIT, 2003.

Baumstark, Anton. *Missale Romanum. Seine Entwicklung, ihre wichtigsten Urkunden und Probleme.* Eindhoven-Nijmegen: Wilhelm van Eupen, 1929.

———. *Nocturna laus: Typen frühchristlicher Vigilienfeier und ihr Fortleben vor allem im römischen und monastischen Ritus.* Münster: Aschendorff, 1957.

———. *Comparative Liturgy.* Revised by Bernard Botte. Edited by F. L. Cross. London: Mowbray, 1958.

———. *On the Historical Development of the Liturgy.* Collegeville, MN: Liturgical Press, 2011.

Becker, Hansjakob. "Wortgottesdienst als Dialog der beiden Testamente. Der Stellenwert des Alten Testaments bei einer Weiterführung der Reform des Ordo Lectionum Missae." In *Streit am Tisch des Wortes? Zur Deutung und Bedeutung des Alten Testaments und seiner Verwendung in der Liturgie.* Edited by Ansgar Franz. Pietas liturgica 8. St. Ottilien: EOS Verlag, 1997, 659–89.

———. "'Es ist ein Ros entsprungen." In *Geistliches Wunderhorn. Grosse deutsche Kirchenlieder.* Edited by Hansjakob Becker, et al. Munich: Beck, 2001, 135–45.

———, Bernd Jochen Hilberath, and Ulrich Willers, eds. *Gottesdienst, Kirche, Gesellschaft. Interdisziplinäre und ökumenische Standortbestimmungen nach 25 Jahren Liturgiereform.* Pietas Liturgica 5. St. Ottilien: EOS Verlag, 1991.

Bell, Catherine. *Ritual: Perspectives and Dimensions.* New York and Oxford: Oxford University Press, 1997.

Belliger, Andrea, and David J. Krieger, eds. *Ritualtheorien. Ein einführendes Handbuch.* 5th ed. Wiesbaden: Verlag für Sozialwissenschaften, 2013.

Berger, Klaus. "Volksversammlung und Gemeinde Gottes. Zu den Anfängen der christlichen Verwendung von 'ekklesia.'" *Zeitschrift für Theologie und Kirche* 73 (1976): 167–207.

Berger, Rupert A. "Ostern und Weihnachten. Zum Grundgefüge des Kirchenjahres." *Archiv für Liturgiewissenschaft* 8 (1963): 1–20.

———. "Liturgische Gewänder und Insignien." In idem, et al., *Gestalt des Gottesdienstes*, 309–46.

———, et al. *Gestalt des Gottesdienstes. Sprachliche und nichtsprachliche Ausdrucksformen.* 2nd rev. ed. Gottesdienst der Kirche 3. Regensburg: Pustet, 1990.

Berger, Teresa. *Liturgie. Spiegel der Kirche. Eine systematisch-theologische Analyse des liturgischen Gedankenguts im Traktarianismus.* Forschungen zur systematischen und ökumenischen Theologie 52. Göttingen: Vandenhoeck & Ruprecht, 1986.

———. "'Erneuerung und Pflege der Liturgie'—'Einheit aller, die an Christus glauben.' Ökumenische Aspekte der Liturgiekonstitution." In *Gottesdienst—Kirche—Gesellschaft. Interdisziplinäre und ökumenische Standortbestimmungen nach 25 Jahren Liturgiereform.* Edited by Hansjakob Becker, Bernd Jochen

Hilberath, and Ulrich Willers. Pietas liturgica 5. St. Ottilien: EOS Verlag, 1991, 339–56.

———. "Die Sprache der Liturgie." In *Handbuch der Liturgik. Liturgiewissenschaft in Theologie und Praxis der Kirche*. Edited by Hans-Christoph Schmidt-Lauber, Michael Meyer-Blank, and Karl-Heinz Bieritz. 3rd ed. Göttingen: Vandenhoeck & Ruprecht, 2003, 798–806.

———. *Gender Differences and the Making of Liturgical History: Lifting a Veil on Liturgy's Past*. Farnham, England, and Burlington, VT: Ashgate, 2011.

Bertsch, Ludwig. *Der neue Messritus im Zaire. Ein Beispiel kontextueller Liturgie*. Theologie der Dritten Welt 18. Freiburg: Herder, 1993.

Bieritz, Karl-Heinrich. "Liturgik II. Forschungsstand." *Religion in Geschichte und Gegenwart* 5 (2001): 452–57.

———. "Anthropologische Grundlegung." In *Handbuch der Liturgik. Liturgiewissenschaft in Theologie und Praxis der Kirche*. Edited by Hans-Christoph Schmidt-Lauber, Michael Meyer-Blanck, and Karl-Heinrich Bieritz. 3rd ed. Göttingen: Vandenhoeck & Ruprecht, 2003, 95–128.

———. *Liturgik*. Berlin and New York: de Gruyter, 2004.

———. "Einladung zum Mitspielen? Riten-Diakonie und Ritualtheorie: Anregungen und Einwürfe." In *Die diakonale Dimension der Liturgie*. Edited by Benedikt Kranemann, Thomas Sternberg, and Walter Zahner. Quaestiones disputatae 218. Freiburg: Herder 2006, 284–304.

Bishop, Edmund. *Liturgica Historica: Papers on the Liturgy and Religious Life of the Western Church*. Oxford: Clarendon Press, 1918.

The Book of Blessings. Collegeville MN: Liturgical Press, 1992.

The Book of Common Prayer and Administration of the Sacraments and Other Rites and Ceremonies of the Church, together with The Psalter or Psalms of David, According to the use of The Episcopal Church. New York: Church Publishing, 1979.

Bradshaw, Paul F. "The Use of the Bible in Liturgy: Some Historical Perspectives." *Studia liturgica* 22 (1992): 35–52.

Brakmann, Heinzgerd. "Der christlichen Bibel erster Teil in den gottesdienstlichen Traditionen des Ostens und Westens. Liturgiehistorische Anmerkungen zum sog. Stellenwert des Alten/Ersten Testaments im Christentum." In *Streit am Tisch des Wortes? Zur Deutung und Bedeutung des Alten Testaments und seiner Verwendung in der Liturgie*. Edited by Ansgar Franz. Pietas liturgica 8. St. Ottilien: EOS Verlag, 1997, 565–99.

———. "*Foedera pluries hominibus*. Anmerkungen zur Revision des Eucharistischen Hochgebets IV." *Liturgisches Jahrbuch* 50 (2000): 211–34.

Braulik, Georg. "Die Tora als Bahnlesung. Zur Hermeneutik einer zukünftigen Auswahl der Sonntagsperikopen." In *Bewahren und Erneuern. Studien zur Messliturgie. Festschrift für Hans Bernhard Meyer SJ zum 70. Geburtstag*.

Edited by Reinhard Messner, Eduard Nagel, and Rudolf Pacik. Innsbrucker theologische Studien 42. Innsbruck and Vienna: Tyrolia, 1995, 50–76.

Bretschneider, Wolfgang. "Stimme der Sehnsucht und der Klage. Klang des Unsagbaren: Musik im Gottesdienst." In *Gott feiern in nachchristlicher Gesellschaft. Die missionarische Dimension der Liturgie*, Part 1. Edited by Benedikt Kranemann, Klemens Richter, and Franz-Peter Tebart-van Elst. Stuttgart: Katholisches Bibelwerk, 2000, 93–101.

———. "'Dem Sprachlosen eine Stimme geben': Verstummt das Singen im Gottesdienst?" In *Kirchenmusik im 20. Jahrhundert. Erbe und Auftrag.* Edited by Albert Gerhards. Ästhetik, Theologie, Liturgik 31. Münster: LIT, 2005, 39–50.

Brunner, Peter. "Zur Lehre vom Gottesdienst der im Namen Jesu versammelten Gemeinde." In *Geschichte und Lehre des evangelischen Gottesdienstes*. Edited by Karl Ferdinand Müller and Walter Blankenburg. Leiturgia n.s. 1. Kassel: Stauda, 1954, 83–364.

Brüske, Gunda. "Plädoyer für liturgische Sprachkompetenz. Thesen zur Sprachlichkeit der Liturgie." *Archiv für Liturgiewissenschaft* 42 (2000): 317–43.

———. "Die Liturgie als Ort des kulturellen Gedächtnisses. Anregungen für ein Gespräch zwischen Kulturwissenschaften und Liturgiewissenschaft." *Liturgisches Jahrbuch* 51 (2001): 151–71.

———. "Lesen und Wiederkäuen: *Lectio divina*, Liturgie und Intertextualität. Zugleich ein Beitrag zur Hermeneutik liturgischer Texte." *Erbe und Auftrag* 78 (2002): 94–103.

Buchinger, Harald. "Zur Hermeneutik liturgischer Psalmenverwendung. Methodologische Überlegungen im Schnittpunkt von Bibelwissenschaft, Patristik und Liturgiewissenschaft." *Heiliger Dienst* 54 (2000): 193–222.

Budde, Achim. "Improvisation im Hochgebet. Zur Technik freien Betens in der Alten Kirche." *Jahrbuch für Antike und Christentum* 44 (2001): 127–41.

———. *Die ägyptische Basilios-Anaphora. Text, Kommentar, Geschichte.* Jerusalemer Theologisches Forum 7. Münster: Aschendorff, 2004.

Built of Living Stones: Art, Architecture, and Worship. Issued by the NCCB/USCC (now USCCB). November 16, 2000.

Casanova, José. *Public Religions in the Modern World*. Chicago: University of Chicago Press, 1994.

———. "Religion und Öffentlichkeit. Ein Ost-/Westvergleich." In *Religion und Gesellschaft. Texte zur Religionssoziologie.* Edited by Karl Gabriel and Hans-Richard Reuter. UTB 2510. Paderborn: Schöningh, 2004, 271–93.

Casel, Odo. *Die Liturgie als Mysterienfeier*. Ecclesia Orans 9. Freiburg: Herder, 1922.

———. "Glaube, Gnosis und Mysterium." *Jahrbuch für Liturgiewissenschaft* 15 (1935): 155–305.

Casula: Gregory Amenoff, James Brown, Paolo d'Orazio . . . . Kunst-Station Sankt Peter Köln, 3 Juni–16 August 1992, Galerie in der Finkenstrasse München, 3 September–9 Oktober 1992, Sankt Petri Lübeck, 18 Oktober–18 November 1992. Cologne: Kunst-Station Sankt Peter, 1992.

Chupungco, Ansgar J. *Liturgical Inculturation: Sacramentals, Religiosity, and Catechesis.* Collegeville, MN: Liturgical Press, 1992.

———. "Liturgy and Inculturation." In *Handbook for Liturgical Studies.* Vol. 2: *Fundamental Liturgy.* Edited by Ansgar J. Chupungco. Collegeville, MN: Liturgical Press, 1998, 337–75.

Collet, Giancarlo. "Inkulturation." *Neues Handbuch theologischer Grundbegriffe* 2 (1991): 394–407.

Consilium for Implementing the Constitution on the Sacred Liturgy. "*Comme le Prévoit:* On the Translation of Liturgical Texts for Celebrations with a Congregation," 25 January 1969. Available at https://www.ewtn.com /library/curia/conslepr.htm.

Crichton, John D. *Lights in Darkness: Forerunners of the Liturgical Movement.* Collegeville, MN: Liturgical Press, 1996.

Deeg, Alexander. "Gottesdienst in Israels Gegenwart: Liturgie als intertextuelles Phänomen." *Liturgisches Jahrbuch* 54 (2004): 34–52.

De Zan, Renato. "Bible and Liturgy," 33–51, and "Criticism and Interpretation of Liturgical Texts," 331–65. In *Handbook for Liturgical Studies.* Vol. 1: *Introduction to the Liturgy.* Edited by Ansgar J. Chupungco. Collegeville, MN: Liturgical Press, 1997.

Diez, Karlheinz. "Reform der Kirche: Georg Witzels Vorschläge zur Erneuerung des Gottesdienstes, der Predigt und der Katechese." In Werner Kathrein, et al., *Im Dienst um die Einheit und die Reform der Kirche: Zum Leben und Werk Georg Witzels.* Fuldaer Hochschulschriften 43. Frankfurt: Knecht, 2003, 41–81.

Ebenbauer, Peter. "Eingekehrt in Gottes Zeit. Gebetstheologische Beobachtungen zu Lobpreis und Danksagung in biblischen und nachbiblischen Kontexten." In *Kontinuität und Unterbrechung. Gottesdienst und Gebet in Judentum und Christentum.* Edited by Albert Gerhards and Stephan Wahle. Studien zu Judentum und Christentum. Paderborn: Schöningh, 2005, 63–106.

———. *Mehr als ein Gespräch. Zur Dialogik von Gebet und Offenbarung in jüdischer und christlicher Liturgie.* Studien zu Judentum und Christentum. Paderborn: Schöningh, 2010.

Eco, Umberto. *Il Segno.* Milan: ISEDI, 1973.

———. *The Open Work.* Cambridge, MA: Harvard University Press, 1989.

Eicker, Thomas. "Einsäen der Ewigkeit ins Lebendige. Impulse einer Theologie der Kirchenmusik im Dialog mit Franz Rosenzweig." In *Kirchenmusik im 20. Jahrhundert. Erbe und Auftrag.* Edited by Albert Gerhards. Ästhetik, Theologie, Liturgik 31. Münster: LIT, 2005, 153–68.

Eisenbach, Franziskus. *Die Gegenwart Jesu Christi im Gottesdienst. Systematische Studien zur Liturgiekonstitution des II. Vatikanischen Konzils.* Mainz: Matthias-Grünewald, 1982.

Eisenhofer, Ludwig. *Handbuch der katholischen Liturgik.* 2 vols. 2nd ed. Freiburg: Herder, 1941.

Emminghaus, Johannes H. *The Eucharist: Essence, Form, Celebration.* Translated by Linda M. Maloney. Collegeville, MN: Liturgical Press, 2005.

Faber, Eva-Maria. *Einführung in die katholische Sakramentenlehre.* 3rd ed. Darmstadt: Wissenschaftliche Buchgesellschaft, 2011.

———. *Die Feier der Trauung in den katholischen Bistümern des deutschen Sprachgebietes.* 2nd ed. By order of the Bishops' Conferences of Germany, Austria, and Switzerland, as well as the (arch)bishops of Bozen-Brixen, Lüttich [Liège, Belgium], Luxemburg, and Strassburg. Zürich: Benziger; Freiburg: Herder; Regensburg: Pustet; Salzburg: St. Peter; Linz: Veritas, 1992.

Felbecker, Sabine. *Die Prozession. Historische und systematische Untersuchungen zu einer liturgischen Ausdruckshandlung.* Münsteraner theologische Abhandlungen 39. Altenberge: Oros, 1995.

Felmy, Karl Christian. *Einführung in die orthodoxe Theologie der Gegenwart.* Lehr- und Studienbücher zur Theologie 5. Münster: LIT, 2011.

Finger, Heinz, ed. *Das Lob Gottes im Rheinland. Mittelalterliche Handschriften und alte Drucke zur Geschichte von Liturgie und Volksfrömmigkeit im Erzbistum Köln. Eine Ausstellung der Diözesan- und Dombibliothek Köln (7. März bis 25. April 2002).* Libelli Rhenani 1. Cologne: Erzbischöfliche Diözesan- und Dombibliothek, 2002.

Fischer, Balthasar. "Das 'Mechelner Ereignis' vom 23. September 1909." *Liturgisches Jahrbuch* 9 (1959): 203–19.

———. "Zehn Jahre danach. Zur gottesdienstlichen Situation in Deutschland zehn Jahre nach Erscheinen der Liturgie-Konstitution" (1963). In idem, et al., *Kult in der säkularisierten Welt.* Regensburg: Pustet, 1974, 117–27.

———. "Östliches Erbe in der jüngsten Liturgiereform des Westens." *Liturgisches Jahrbuch* 27 (1977): 92–106.

———. *Die Psalmen als Stimme der Kirche. Gesammelte Studien zur christlichen Psalmenfrömmigkeit.* Edited by Andreas Heinz. Trier: Paulinus-Verlag, 1982.

Foley, Edward, et al. *A Commentary on the General Instruction of the Roman Missal.* Collegeville, MN: Liturgical Press, 2007.

Fortescue, Adrian. *The Mass: A Study of the Roman Liturgy*. London and New York: Longmans, Green, 1912.

———. *The Orthodox Eastern Church*. New York: B. Franklin, 1969.

———. *The Lesser Eastern Churches*. Piscataway, NJ: Gorgias Press, 2001.

Franz, Ansgar. *Wortgottesdienst der Messe und Altes Testament. Katholische und ökumenische Lektionarreform nach dem II. Vatikanum im Spiegel von* Ordo Lectionum Missae, Revised Common Lectionary *und* Four Year Lectionary: *Positionen, Probleme, Perspektiven*. Pietas liturgica 14. Tübingen and Basel: Francke, 2002.

Fuchs, Gotthard, ed. *Angesichts des Leids an Gott glauben? Zur Theologie der Klage*. Frankfurt: J. Knecht, 1996.

Gabriel, Karl. "Säkularisierung und öffentliche Religion. Religionssoziologische Anmerkungen mit Blick auf den europäischen Kontext." *Jahrbuch für Christliche Sozialwissenschaften* 44 (2003): 13–36.

Gahn, Philipp. "Joseph Thomas von Haiden und das Reformbrevier von St. Stephan zu Augsburg. Einige Anmerkungen zum Aufsatz von Liobgid Koch, 'Ein deutsches Brevier der Aufklärungszeit.'" *Archiv für Liturgiewissenschaft* 42 (2000): 84–96.

Gärtner, Heribert W., and Michael B. Merz. "Prolegomena für eine integrative Methode in der Liturgiewissenschaft. Zugleich ein Versuch zur Gewinnung der empirischen Dimension." *Archiv für Liturgiewissenschaft* 24 (1982): 165–89.

Genette, Gérard. *Palimpsests: Literature in the Second Degree*. Translated by Channa Newman and Claude Doubinsky. Lincoln: University of Nebraska Press, 1997.

Gerhards, Albert. "Zu wem beten? Die These Josef Andreas Jungmanns († 1975) über den Adressaten des Eucharistischen Hochgebets im Licht der neueren Forschung." *Liturgisches Jahrbuch* 32 (1982): 219–30.

———. "La doxologie, un chapitre définitif de l'histoire du dogme?" In *Trinité et liturgie. Conférences Saint-Serge, XXXᵉ semaine d'études liturgiques, Paris, 28 juin–1er juillet 1983*. Edited by Achille M. Triacca and Alessandro Pistoia. Bibliotheca Ephemerides liturgicae. Subsidia 32. Rome: C.L.V.-Edizioni liturgiche, 1984, 103–18.

———. "Der liturgische Hintergrund der Palestrina-Renaissance im 19. Jahrhundert." In *Palestrina und die Idee der klassischen Vokalpolyphonie im 19. Jahrhundert. Zur Geschichte eines kirchenmusikalischen Stilideals*. Edited by Winfried Kirsch. Palestrina und die Kirchenmusik im 19. Jahrhundert 1. Regensburg: Bosse, 1989, 181–94.

———. "Vorbedingungen, Dimensionen und Ausdrucksgestalten der Bewegung in der Liturgie." In *Volk Gottes auf dem Weg. Bewegungselemente im*

Gottesdienst. Edited by Wolfgang Meurer. Mainz: Matthias Grünewald, 1989, 11–24.

———. "'Einschliessende Sprache' im Gottesdienst: eine übertriebene Forderung oder Gebot der Stunde?" *Liturgisches Jahrbuch* 42 (1992): 239–48.

———. "Mehr als Worte sagt ein Lied. Theologische Dimensionen des liturgischen Singens." *Musica Sacra (D)* 113 (1993): 509–13.

———. "Romano Guardini als Prophet des Liturgischen. Eine Rückbesinnung in postmoderner Zeit." In *Guardini weiterdenken.* Edited by Hermann Josef Schuster. Schriftenreihe des Forum Guardini 1. Berlin: Dreieck, 1993, 140–53.

———. "Zur Frage der Gebetsanrede im Zeitalter des jüdisch-christlichen Dialogs." *Trierer theologische Zeitschrift* 102 (1993): 245–57.

———. "Gottesdienst und Menschwerdung. Vom Subjekt liturgischer Feier." In *Markierungen. Theologie in den Zeichen der Zeit.* Edited by Mariano Delgado and Andreas Lob-Hüdepohl. Schriften der Diözesanakademie Berlin 11. Berlin: Morus, 1995, 275–92.

———. "Improperia." *Reallexikon für Antike und Christentum* 17 (1996): 1198–1212.

———. "Prozession II. In der Kirchengeschichte." *Theologische Realenzyklopädie* 27 (1997): 593–97.

———. "Schriftgebrauch im Gottesdienst. Zur Bewertung der Rolle des Gottesdienstes in den Überlegungen des Ökumenischen Arbeitskreises evangelischer und katholischer Theologen unter besonderer Berücksichtigung des Alten Testaments." In *Streit am Tisch des Wortes? Zur Deutung und Bedeutung des Alten Testaments und seiner Verwendung in der Liturgie.* Edited by Ansgar Franz. Pietas liturgica 8. St. Ottilien: EOS Verlag, 1997, 491–503.

———. "Die Psalmen in der römischen Liturgie. Eine Bestandsaufnahme des Psalmengebrauchs in Stundengebet und Messfeier." In *Der Psalter in Judentum und Christentum.* Edited by Erich Zenger. Herders biblische Studien 18. Freiburg: Herder, 1998, 355–79.

———. "Die liturgische Entwicklung zwischen 1600 und 1800." In *Hirt und Herde. Religiosität und Frömmigkeit im Rheinland des 18. Jahrhunderts.* Edited by Frank Günter Zehnder. Der Riss im Himmel 5. Köln: DuMont, 2000, 19–36.

———. "'Blickt nach Osten!' Die Ausrichtung von Priester und Gemeinde bei der Eucharistie—eine kritische Reflexion nachkonziliarer Liturgiereform vor dem Hintergrund der Geschichte des Kirchenbaus." In *Liturgia et Unitas. Liturgiewissenschaftliche und ökumenische Studien zur Eucharistie und zum gottesdienstlichen Leben in der Schweiz. Études liturgiques et oecuméniques sur l'Eucharistie et la vie liturgique en Suisse. In honorem Bruno Bürki.* Edited by Martin Klöckener and Arnaud Join-Lambert. Fribourg: Universitätsverlag; Geneva: Labor et Fides, 2001, 197–217.

———. "Die fortdauernde Wirksamkeit der Taufe im christlichen Leben: *simul iustus et peccator*. Liturgiewissenschaftliche Erkenntnisse." In *Gerecht und Sünder zugleich? Ökumenische Klärungen*. Edited by Christine Axt-Piscalar, Theodor Schneider, and Gunther Wenz. Dialog der Kirchen 11. Freiburg: Herder; Göttingen: Vandenhoeck & Ruprecht, 2001, 376–95.

———. "Kraft aus der Wurzel. Zum Verhältnis christlicher Liturgie gegenüber dem Jüdischen: Fortschreibung oder struktureller Neubeginn?" *Kirche und Israel* 16 (2001): 25–44.

———. "Liturgiewissenschaftliche Perspektiven auf den gregorianischen Choral." *Kirchenmusikalisches Jahrbuch* 85 (2001): 17–30.

———. "Mimesis, Anamnesis, Poiesis. Überlegungen zur Ästhetik christlicher Liturgie als Vergegenwärtigung." In *Pastoralästhetik. Die Kunst der Wahrnehmung und Gestaltung in Glaube und Kirche*. Edited by Walter Fürst. Quaestiones Disputatae 199. Freiburg: Herder, 2002, 169–86.

———. "Die Synode von Pistoia 1786 und ihre Reform des Gottesdienstes." In *Liturgiereformen. Historische Studien zu einem bleibenden Grundzug des christlichen Gottesdienstes*. Vol. 1: *Biblische Modelle und Liturgiereformen von der Frühzeit bis zur Aufklärung*. Edited by Martin Klöckener and Benedikt Kranemann. Liturgiewissenschaftliche Quellen und Forschungen 88. Münster: Aschendorff, 2002, 16–51.

———. "*Versus orientem, versus populum*. Zum gegenwärtigen Stand einer alten Streitfrage." *Theologische Revue* 98 (2002): 15–22.

———. "Impulse des christlich-jüdischen Dialogs für die Liturgiewissenschaft." In *Methodische Erneuerung der Theologie. Konsequenzen der wiederentdeckten jüdisch-christlichen Gemeinsamkeiten*. Edited by Peter Hünermann and Thomas Söding. Quaestiones Disputatae 200. Freiburg: Herder, 2003, 183–211.

———. "Ein Reformprojekt am Vorabend der Reformation: der *Libellus ad Leonem X* (1513)." In *Frömmigkeitsformen in Mittelalter und Renaissance*. Edited by Johannes Laudage. Studia humaniora 37. Düsseldorf: Droste, 2004, 391–408.

———. "Jenseits der Grenze des Sagbaren . . . Zur liturgietheologischen Bestimmung der Orgelmusik im Spannungsfeld von Wort und Zeichen." In *Orgel und Liturgie. Festschrift zur Orgelweihe in St. Lamberti*. Edited by Michael Zywietz with Christian Bettels. Musikwissenschaft 9. Münster: LIT, 2004, 39–51.

———. "Räume für eine tätige Teilnahme. Katholischer Kirchenbau aus theologisch-liturgischer Sicht // Spaces for Active Participation. Theological and Liturgical Perspectives on Catholic Church Architecture." In *Europäischer Kirchenbau 1950–2000 // European Church Architecture*. Edited by Wolfgang Jean Stock. Munich: Prestel, 2002, 16–51.

————. "'. . . zu immer vollerer Einheit mit Gott und untereinander gelangen' (SC 48): Die Neuordnung der Kirchenräume durch die Liturgiereform." In *Liturgiereform. Eine bleibende Aufgabe. 40 Jahre Konzilskonstitution über die heilige Liturgie.* Edited by Klemens Richter and Thomas
Sternberg. Münster: Aschendorff, 2004, 126–43.

————. "Geschichtskonstruktionen in liturgischen Texten des Judentums
und Christentums." In *Kontinuität und Unterbrechung. Gottesdienst und
Gebet in Judentum und Christentum.* Edited by Albert Gerhards and Stephan
Wahle. Studien zu Judentum und Christentum. Paderborn: Schöningh,
2005, 269–85.

————. "'Heiliges Spiel': Kirchenmusik und Liturgie als Rivalinnen oder
Verbündete?" In *Kirchenmusik im 20. Jahrhundert. Erbe und Auftrag.* Edited
by Albert Gerhards. Ästhetik, Theologie, Liturgik 31. Münster: LIT, 2005,
29–38.

————. "*In persona Christi in nomine Ecclesiae.* Zum Rollenbild des priesterlichen Dienstes nach dem Zeugnis orientalischer Anaphoren." In *Priester
und Liturgie. Manfred Probst zum 65. Geburtstag.* Edited by George Augustin, et al. Paderborn: Bonifatius, 2005, 59–73.

————. "Liturgietheologische und -ästhetische Überlegungen zur Instruktion 'Sakrament der Erlösung.'" *Zeitschrift für Katholische Theologie* 127
(2005): 253–70.

————. "Teologia dell'altare." In *L'altare. Mistero di presenza, opera dell'arte.
Atti de II Convegno liturgico internazionale Bose, 31 ottobre–2 novembre 2003.*
Edited by Goffredo Boselli. Magnano: Edizione Qiqajon, 2005, 213–32.

————. "Theologische und sozio-kulturelle Bedingungen religiöser Konflikte
mit dem Judentum. Beispiele aus der katholischen Liturgie und ihrer
Wirkungsgeschichte." In *Kontinuität und Unterbrechung. Gottesdienst und
Gebet in Judentum und Christentum.* Edited by Albert Gerhards and Stephan
Wahle. Studien zu Judentum und Christentum. Paderborn: Schöningh,
2005, 269–85.

————. "Liturgie." *Neues Handbuch theologischer Grundbegriffe* 3 (2005): 7–22.

————. "St. Gereon: Identität eines Kirchenraums im Wandel der Ge-
schichte." In *Märtyrergrab, Kirchenraum, Gottesdienst. Interdisziplinäre
Studien zur ehemaligen Stiftskirche St. Gereon in Köln.* Edited by Andreas
Odenthal and Albert Gerhards. Studien zur Kölner Kirchengeschichte 35.
Siegburg: Franz Schmitt, 2006, 9–23.

————. *Ein Ritus, zwei Formen. Die Richtlinie Papst Benedikts XVI. Zur Liturgie.*
Theologie kontrovers. Freiburg: Herder, 2008.

————. *Wo Gott und Welt sich begegnen. Kirchenräume verstehen.* Kevelaer:
Butzon & Bercker, 2011.

————. *Erneuerung kirchlichen Lebens aus dem Gottesdienst. Beiträge zur Reform der Liturgie*. Praktische Theologie heute 120. Stuttgart: Kohlhammer, 2012.

————. "Gipfelpunkt und Quelle. Intention und Rezeption der Liturgiekonstitution *Sacrosanctum Concilium*." In *Erinnerung an die Zukunft. Das Zweite Vatikanische Konzil*. Edited by Jan Heiner Tück. Freiburg: Herder, 2012, 107–26.

————, ed. *Liturgie und Licht. Eine Orientierungshilfe*. Liturgie & Gemeinde, Impulse & Perspektiven 7. Trier: Deutsches Liturgisches Institut, 2006.

————, and Birgit Osterholt-Kootz. "Kommentar zur 'Standortbestimmung der Liturgiewissenschaft.'" *Liturgisches Jahrbuch* 42 (1992): 122–38.

————, and Andreas Odenthal. "Auf dem Weg zu einer Liturgiewissenschaft im Dialog. Thesen zur wissenschaftstheoretischen Standortbestimmung." *Liturgisches Jahrbuch* 50 (2000): 41–53.

————, and Andreas Odenthal. *Kölnische Liturgie und ihre Geschichte. Studien zur interdisziplinären Erforschung des Gottesdienstes im Erzbistum Köln*. Liturgiewissenschaftliche Quellen und Forschungen 87. Münster: Aschendorff, 2000.

————, Andrea Doeker, and Peter Ebenbauer, eds. *Identität durch Gebet. Zur gemeinschaftsbildenden Funktion institutionalisierten Betens in Judentum und Christentum*. Studien zu Judentum und Christentum. Paderborn: Schöningh, 2003.

————, Thomas Sternberg, and Walter Zahner, eds. *Communio-Räume. Auf der Suche nach der angemessenen Raumgestalt katholischer Liturgie*. Bild, Raum, Feier. Studien zu Kirche und Kunst 2. Regensburg: Pustet, 2003.

————, and Hans Hermann Henrix, eds. *Dialog oder Monolog? Zur liturgischen Beziehung zwischen Judentum und Christentum*. Quaestiones Disputatae 208. Freiburg: Herder, 2004.

————, Heinzgerd Brakmann, and Martin Klöckener, eds. *Prex Eucharistica*, III. *Studia, pars prima, "Ecclesia antiqua et occidentalis."* Fribourg: Academic Press, 2005.

Ghirelli, Tiziano. *Ierotopi cristiani alla luce della riforma liturgica del Concilio Vaticano II. Dettami di Conferenze Episcopali Nazionali per la progettazione di luoghi liturgici*. Prime indagini. Città del Vaticano: Libreria Editrice Vaticana, 2012.

Golitzin, Alexander. *Et introibo ad altare Dei: The Mystagogy of Dionysius Areopagita: with special reference to its predecessors in the Eastern Christian tradition*. Thessalonikē: Patriarchikon Idruma Paterikōn Meletōn, 1994.

Gott feiern in nachchristlicher Gesellschaft. Die missionarische Dimension der Liturgie. Edited by Benedikt Kranemann, Klemens Richter, and Franz-Peter Tebartz-van Elst. Stuttgart: Katholisches Bibelwerk, 2000.

Gottesdienst als Feld theologischer Wissenschaft im 20. Jahrhundert. Deutschsprachige Liturgiewissenschaft in Einzelporträts. Edited by Benedikt Kranemann and Klaus Raschzok. Liturgiewissenschaftliche Quellen und Forschungen 98. Münster: Aschendorff, 2011.

"Gottesdienst. Beschluss." In *Gemeinsame Synode der Bistümer in der Bundesrepublik Deutschland. Beschlüsse der Vollversammlung. Offizielle Gesamtausgabe 1.* Edited by order of the Presidium of the General Synod by Ludwig Bertsch, et al. Freiburg: Herder, 1976, 196–225.

Gottes Volk, neu gekleidet: ein Versuch, entwickelt von der Arbeitsgruppe "Kirchliche Architektur und Sakrale Kunst" der Liturgiekommission der Deutschen Bischofskonferenz. Trier: Deutsches Liturgisches Institut, 1994.

Gnilka, Joachim. *Das Matthäusevangelium 1, Kommentar zu Kap. 1,1–13,58.* Herders Theologischer Kommentar 1.1. Freiburg: Herder, 1989.

Gotteslob. Katholisches Gebet und Gesangbuch. Edited by the Bishops of Germany, Austria, and the Dioceses of Bozen Brixen and Liège. Stammausgabe. Stuttgart: Katholische Bibelanstalt, 1975; new and rev. ed. Stuttgart, et. al.: Katholisches Bibelwerk, 2013.

Greule, Albrecht. "Die liturgischen Text- und Redesorten." *Heiliger Dienst* 56 (2002): 231–39.

Guardini, Romano. "Über die systematische Methode in der Liturgiewissenschaft." *Jahrbuch für Liturgiewissenschaft* 1 (1921): 97–108.

———. "Der Kultakt und die gegenwärtige Aufgabe der Liturgie." In idem, *Liturgie und liturgische Bildung.* Würzburg: Werkbund-Verlag, 1966, 9–18.

———. *The Spirit of the Liturgy.* Chicago: Biretta Books, 2015.

Guéranger, Prosper, and Lucien Fromage. *The Liturgical Year.* 15 volumes. Translated by Laurence Shepherd and the Benedictines of Stanbrook. Westminster, MD: Newman Press, 1951–1955.

Gülden, Josef. *Johann Leisentrits pastoralliturgische Schriften.* Studien zur katholischen Bistums- und Klostergeschichte 4. Leipzig: St Benno-Verlag, 1963.

Güntner, Diana. *Das Gedenken des Erhöhten im Neuen Testament. Zur ekklesialen Bedeutung des Gedenkens am Modell des Psalms 110.* Benediktbeurer Studien 6. Munich: Don Bosco, 1998.

Gy, Pierre-Marie. "Les réformes liturgiques et la sociologie historique de la liturgie." In *Liturgiereformen. Historische Studien zu einem bleibenden Grundzug des christlichen Gottesdienstes.* Vol. 1: *Biblische Modelle und Liturgiereformen von der Frühzeit bis zur Aufklärung.* Edited by Martin Klöckener and Benedikt Kranemann. Liturgiewissenschaftliche Quellen und Forschungen 88. Münster: Aschendorff, 2002, 262–72.

Hahne, Werner. *De arte celebrandi oder Von der Kunst, Gottesdienst zu feiern. Entwurf einer Fundamentalliturgik.* 2nd ed. Freiburg: Herder, 1991.

————. *Gottes Volksversammlung. Die Liturgie als Ort lebendiger Erfahrung.* Freiburg: Herder, 1999.

Halbwachs, Maurice. *On Collective Memory.* Translated by Lewis A. Coser. Chicago: University of Chicago Press, 1992.

Harnoncourt, Philipp. "Vom Beten im Heiligen Geist." In *Gott feiern. Theologische Anregung und geistliche Vertiefung zur Feier von Messe und Stundengebet.* Edited by Josef G. Plöger. Freiburg: Herder, 1980, 100–115.

————. "Die Gegenwart des Mysteriums Christi in den Sakramenten. Entwurf eines Modells zur Sakramententheologie." In *Die Feier der Sakramente in der Gemeinde. Festschrift für Heinrich Rennings.* Edited by Martin Klöckener and Winfried Glade. Kevelaer: Butzon & Bercker, 1986, 31–46.

Haspelmath-Finatti, Dorothea. *Theologia Prima. Liturgische Theologie für den evangelischen Gottesdienst.* Arbeiten zur Pastoraltheologie, Liturgik und Hymnologie 80. Göttingen: Vandenhoeck & Ruprecht, 2014.

Hauke, Reinhard. "Die Feier der Lebenswende. Eine christliche Hilfe zur Sinnfindung für Ungetaufte." In *Gott feiern in nachchristlicher Gesellschaft. Die missionarische Dimension der Liturgie.* Edited by Benedikt Kranemann, Klemens Richter, and Franz-Peter Tebartz-van Elst. Stuttgart: Katholisches Bibelwerk, 2000, 2:32–48.

Haunerland, Winfried. *Die Eucharistie und ihre Wirkungen im Spiegel der Euchologie des Missale Romanum.* Liturgiewissenschaftliche Quellen und Forschungen 71. Münster: Aschendorff, 1989.

————. "*Lingua Vernacula.* Zur Sprache der Liturgie nach dem II. Vatikanum." *Liturgisches Jahrbuch* 42 (1992): 219–38.

————. "Liturgiesprache." *Lexikon für Theologie und Kirche* 6 (1997): 988–89.

————. "Authentische Liturgie. Der Gottesdienst der Kirche zwischen Universalität und Individualität." *Liturgisches Jahrbuch* 52 (2002): 135–57.

————. "Einheitlichkeit als Weg der Erneuerung. Das Konzil von Trient und die nachtridentinische Reform der Liturgie." In *Liturgiereformen. Historische Studien zu einem bleibenden Grundzug des christlichen Gottesdienstes.* Vol. 1: *Biblische Modelle und Liturgiereformen von der Frühzeit bis zur Aufklärung.* Edited by Martin Klöckener and Benedikt Kranemann. Liturgiewissenschaftliche Quellen und Forschungen 88. Münster: Aschendorff, 2002, 436–65.

————. "*Mysterium paschale.* Schlüsselbegriff liturgietheologischer Erneuerung." In *Liturgie als Mitte des christlichen Lebens.* Edited by George Augustin and Kurt Kardinal Koch. Theologie im Dialog 7. Freiburg, et al.: Herder, 2012, 189–209.

Häussling, Angelus A. *Mönchskonvent und Eucharistiefeier. Eine Studie über die Messe in der abendländischen Klosterliturgie des frühen Mittelalters und zur Geschichte der Messhäufigkeit.* Liturgiewissenschaftliche Quellen und Forschungen 58. Münster: Aschendorff, 1973.

————. "Odo Casel—noch von Aktualität? Eine Rückschau in eigener Sache aus Anlass des hundertsten Geburtstages des ersten Herausgebers." *Archiv für Liturgiewissenschaft* 28 (1986): 357–87.

————. "Liturgy: Memorial of the Past and Liberation in the Present." In idem, ed., *The Meaning of the Liturgy.* Collegeville, MN: Liturgical Press, 1994, 107–18.

————. "Gottesdienst III. Liturgiegeschichtlich." "IV. Liturgisch-theologisch." *Lexikon für Theologie und Kirche* 4 (1995): 891–903.

————. "Die Psalmen des Alten Testaments in der Liturgie des Neuen Bundes." In *Christologie der Liturgie. Der Gottesdienst der Kirche: Christusbekenntnis und Sinaibund.* Edited by Klemens Richter and Benedikt Kranemann. Quaestiones Disputatae 159. Freiburg: Herder, 1995, 87–102.

————. "Liturgiereform und Liturgiefähigkeit." *Archiv für Liturgiewissenschaft* 38/39 (1996/97): 1–24.

————. "'Pascha-Mysterium.' Kritisches zu einem Beitrag in der dritten Auflage des 'Lexikon für Theologie und Kirche.'" *Archiv für Liturgiewissenschaft* 41 (1999): 157–65.

————. *Christliche Identität aus der Liturgie. Theologische und historische Studien zum Gottesdienst der Kirche.* Edited by Martin Klöckener, Benedikt Kranemann, and Michael B. Merz. Liturgiewissenschaftliche Quellen und Forschungen 79. Münster: Aschendorff, 1997. Includes:

————. "Die kritische Funktion der Liturgiewissenschaft" [1970], 284–301.

————. "Liturgiewissenschaftliche Aufgabenfelder vor uns" [1970], 321–33.

————. "Liturgiewissenschaft zwei Jahrzehnte nach Konzilsbeginn. Eine Umschau im deutschen Sprachgebiet" [1982], 302–20.

————. "Liturgiereform. Materialien zu einem neuen Thema der Liturgiewissenschaft" [1989], 41–43.

————. "Liturgie: Gedächtnis eines Vergangenen und doch Befreiung in der Gegenwart" [1991], 2–10.

————. "Wie beginnt Gottesdienst? Beobachtungen an den Horen der Tagzeitenliturgie" [1991], 257–70.

————. "Die Übung der Tagzeiten in der Geschichte der Kirche. Gebet und Bekenntnis." *Heiliger Dienst* 57 (2003): 23–37.

Heckel, Ulrich. "Segnung und Salbung. Theologische und praktische Überlegungen zur Einführung einer neuen Gottesdienstform." *Kerygma und Dogma* 47 (2001): 126–55.

Heimbach-Steins, Marianne, and Georg Steins. "Sehnsucht nach dem umfassenden Heil. Liturgie und Diakonie im österlichen Triduum." *Gottesdienst* 34 (2000): 33–35.

Heinz, Andreas. "Papst Gregor der Grosse und die römische Liturgie. Zum Gregorius-Gedenkjahr 1400 Jahre nach seinem Tod († 604)." *Liturgisches Jahrbuch* 54 (2004): 69–84.

Henrix, Hans Hermann, ed. *Jüdische Liturgie. Geschichte, Struktur, Wesen.* Quaestiones Disputatae 86. Freiburg: Herder, 1979.

Hock, Klaus. *Einführung in die Religionswissenschaft.* 4th ed. Darmstadt: Wissenschaftliche Buchgesellschaft, 2011.

Hoffman, Lawrence A. "How Ritual Means: Ritual Circumcision in Rabbinic Culture and Today." *Studia liturgica* 23 (1993): 78–97.

Hollerweger, Hans. *Die Reform des Gottesdienstes zur Zeit des Josephinismus in Österreich.* Studien zur Pastoralliturgie 1. Regensburg: Pustet, 1976.

Hoping, Helmut, and Birgit Jeggle-Merz, eds. *Liturgische Theologie. Aufgaben systematischer Liturgiewissenschaft.* Paderborn: Schöningh, 2004.

Hossfeld, Frank-Lothar, and Erich Zenger. *Die Psalmen, 1. Psalm 1–50.* Neue Echter Bibel. Altes Testament 29. Würzburg: Echter Verlag, 1993.

Hucke, Helmut, and Heinrich Rennings. *Die gottesdienstlichen Versammlungen der Gemeinde.* Pastorale 2. Mainz: Matthias-Grünewald, 1973.

Hug, Elisabeth. *Reden zu Gott. Überlegungen zur deutschen liturgischen Gebetssprache.* Zürich: Benziger, 1985.

Huonder, Vitus. *Die Psalmen in der Liturgia Horarum.* Studia Friburgensia n.s. 74. Fribourg: Universitätsverlag, 1991.

The Hymnal 1982, according to the use of The Episcopal Church. New York: Church Hymnal Corporation, 1982.

Iser, Wolfgang. "The Reading Process: A Phenomenological Approach." *New Literary History* 3, no. 2: On Interpretation: I (Winter 1972): 279–99.

Jaschinski, Eckhard. *Kleine Geschichte der Kirchenmusik.* Freiburg: Herder, 2004.

Jeffery, Peter. *Translating Tradition: A Chant Historian Reads* Liturgiam Authenticam. Collegeville, MN: Liturgical Press, 2005.

Jeggle-Merz, Birgit. *Erneuerung der Kirche aus dem Geist der Liturgie. Der Pastoralliturgiker Athanasius Wintersig/Ludwig A. Winterswyl.* Liturgiewissenschaftliche Quellen und Forschungen 84. Münster: Aschendorff, 1998.

Joas, Hans. "Glaube und Moral im Zeitalter der Kontingenz." In idem, *Braucht der Mensch Religion? Über Erfahrungen der Selbsttranszendenz.* Freiburg: Herder, 2004, 32–49. English: *Do We Need Religion? On the Experience of Self-Transcendence.* Translated by Alex Skinner. Yale Cultural Sociology Series. Boulder, CO: Paradigm Publishers, 2008.

Jungmann, Josef A. *Liturgical Worship.* Translated by a monk of Saint John's Abbey. New York: Pustet, 1941.

―――. *The Mass of the Roman Rite: Its Origins and Development (Missarum Sollemnia)*. 2 vols. Translated by Francis A. Brunner. New York: Benziger, 1951–1955.

―――. *The Place of Christ in Liturgical Prayer*. Staten Island: Alba House, 1965.

―――. *The Liturgy of the Word*. Translated from the 4th revised edition by H. E. Winstone. London: Burns & Oates, 1966.

―――. "Vordringliche Aufgaben liturgiewissenschaftlicher Forschung. Referat auf der Studientagung der Liturgikdozenten des deutschen Sprachgebietes in München (28 März 1967)." Introduced, transcribed, and explained by Rudolf Pacik. *Archiv für Liturgiewissenschaft* 42 (2000): 3–28.

―――. *Pastoral Liturgy*. Translated by Francis Brunner with an Introduction by John F. Baldovin. Notre Dame, IN: Ave Maria Press, 2014.

Kaczynski, Reiner. "Die Benediktionen." In Bruno Kleinheyer, et al., *Sakramentliche Feiern* II. Gottesdienst der Kirche 8. Regensburg: Pustet, 1984, 233–74.

―――. "Angriff auf die Liturgiekonstitution? Anmerkungen zu einer neuen Übersetzer-Instruktion." *Stimmen der Zeit* 219 (2001): 651–68.

―――. "Theologischer Kommentar zur Konstitution über die heilige Liturgie *Sacrosanctum Concilium*." In *Herders Theologischer Kommentar zum Zweiten Vatikanischen Konzil*. Edited by Peter Hünermann and Bernd Jochen Hilberath. Freiburg: Herder, 2004, 2:1–227.

Kavanagh, Aidan. *On Liturgical Theology*. The Hale Memorial Lectures of Seabury-Western Theological Seminary 1981. New York: Pueblo, 1984.

Keller, Klaus. *Die Liturgie der Eheschliessung in der katholischen Aufklärung. Eine Untersuchung der Reformentwürfe im deutschen Sprachraum*. Münchener theologische Studien, II. Systematische Abteilung 51. St. Ottilien: EOS Verlag, 1996.

Kieffer, Georg. *Rubrizistik oder Ritus des katholischen Gottesdienstes nach den Regeln der heiligen römischen Kirche*. 9th ed. Wissenschaftliche Handbibliothek. Paderborn: Schöningh, 1947.

Kilmartin, Edward J. *Christian Liturgy: Theology and Practice*. Vol. 1: *Systematic Theology of Liturgy*. Kansas City: Sheed & Ward, 1988.

Kirchberg, Julie. *Theo-logie in der Anrede als Weg zur Verständigung zwischen Juden und Christen*. Innsbrucker theologische Studien 31. Innsbruck: Tyrolia, 1991.

Kirchschläger, Walter. "Begründung und Formen des liturgischen Leitungsdienstes in den Schriften des Neuen Testaments." In *Wie weit trägt das gemeinsame Priestertum? Liturgischer Leitungsdienst zwischen Ordination und Beauftragung*. Edited by Martin Klöckener and Klemens Richter. Quaestiones Disputatae 171. Freiburg: Herder, 1998, 20–45.

―――. "Die liturgische Versammlung. Eine neutestamentliche Bestandsaufnahme." *Heiliger Dienst* 52 (1998): 11–24.

Klauser, Theodor. *A Short History of the Western Liturgy: An Account and Some Reflections.* Translated by John Halliburton. Oxford and New York: Oxford University Press, 1979.

Klöckener, Martin. "Die 'Feier vom Leiden und Sterben Jesu Christi' am Karfreitag. Gewordene Liturgie vor dem Anspruch der Gegenwart." *Liturgisches Jahrbuch* 41 (1991): 210–51.

———. *Die liturgischen Bücher im deutschen Sprachgebiet. Verzeichnis für die pastoralliturgische Arbeit, die liturgische Bildung und das liturgiewissenschaftliche Studium* [as of 1 October 1995]. Pastoralliturgische Hilfen 9. Trier: Deutsches Liturgisches Institut, 1995.

———. "Zeitgemässes Beten. Messorationen als Zeugnisse einer sich wandelnden Kultur und Spiritualität." In *Bewahren und Erneuern. Studien zur Messliturgie. Festschrift für Hans Bernhard Meyer SJ zum 70. Geburtstag.* Edited by Reinhard Messner, Eduard Nagel, and Rudolf Pacik. Innsbrucker theologische Studien 42. Innsbruck and Vienna: Tyrolia, 1995, 114–42.

———. "Freiheit und Ordnung im Gottesdienst: ein altes Problem mit neuer Brisanz." *Freiburger Zeitschrift für Philosophie und Theologie* 43 (1996): 368–419.

———. "Das Eucharistische Hochgebet in der nordafrikanischen Liturgie der christlichen Spätantike." In *Prex Eucharistica, III. Studia, pars prima, "Ecclesia antiqua et occidentalis."* Edited by Albert Gerhards, Heinzgerd Brakmann, and Martin Klöckener. Spicilegium Friburgense 42. Fribourg: Academic Press, 2005, 43–128.

———. "Wie Liturgie verstehen? Anfragen an das Motu proprio 'Summorum Pontificum' Papst Benedikts XVI." *Archiv für Liturgiewissenschaft* 50 (2008): 268–305.

———, and Benedikt Kranemann, eds. *Liturgiereformen. Historische Studien zu einem bleibenden Grundzug des christlichen Gottesdienstes.* Vol. 1: *Biblische Modelle und Liturgiereformen von der Frühzeit bis zur Aufklärung.* Vol. 2: *Liturgiereformen seit der Mitte des 19. Jahrhunderts bis zur Gegenwart.* Liturgiewissenschaftliche Quellen und Forschungen 88. Münster: Aschendorff, 2002.

———, and Klemens Richter, eds. *Wie weit trägt das gemeinsame Priestertum? Liturgischer Leitungsdienst zwischen Ordination und Beauftragung.* Quaestiones Disputatae 171. Freiburg: Herder, 1998.

———, and Benedikt Kranemann, eds. *Gottesdienst in Zeitgenossenschaft. Positionsbestimmungen 40 Jahre nach der Liturgiekonstitution des Zweiten Vatikanischen Konzils.* Fribourg: Academic Press, 2006.

Kluger, Florian. *Benediktionen. Studium zur kirchlichen Segensfeiern.* Studien zur Pastoralliturgie 31. Regensburg: Pustet, 2011.

Knop, Julia. *Ecclesia orans. Liturgie als Herausforderung für die Dogmatik.* Freiburg: Herder, 2012.

Koch, Jakob Johannes. *Traditionelle mehrstimmige Messen in erneuerter Liturgie—ein Widerspruch?* Regensburg: Pustet, 2002.

Koch, Liobgid. "Ein deutsches Brevier der Aufklärungszeit. Thaddäus Dereser und sein Deutsches Brevier für Stiftsdamen, Klosterfrauen und jeden guten Christen." *Archiv für Liturgiewissenschaft* 17/18 (1975–76): 80–144.

Kohlhaas, Emmanuela. *Musik und Sprache im Gregorianischen Gesang.* Beihefte zum Archiv für Musikwissenschaft 49. Stuttgart: Steiner, 2001.

Kohlschein, Franz. "Die Tagzeitenliturgie als 'Gebet der Gemeinde' in der Geschichte." *Heiliger Dienst* 41 (1987): 12–40.

———, ed. *Aufklärungskatholizismus und Liturgie. Reformentwürfe für die Feier von Taufe, Firmung, Busse, Trauung und Krankensalbung.* Pietas liturgica, Studia 6. St. Ottilien: EOS Verlag, 1989.

———. "Liturgiereform und deutscher Aufklärungskatholizismus." In *Liturgiereformen. Historische Studien zu einem bleibenden Grundzug des christlichen Gottesdienstes.* Vol. 1: *Biblische Modelle und Liturgiereformen von der Frühzeit bis zur Aufklärung.* Edited by Martin Klöckener and Benedikt Kranemann. Liturgiewissenschaftliche Quellen und Forschungen 88. Münster: Aschendorff, 2002, 511–33.

———, and Kurt Küpper, eds. *"Der grosse Sänger David: euer Muster." Studien zu den ersten diözesanen Gesang- und Gebetbüchern der katholischen Aufklärung.* Liturgiewissenschaftliche Quellen und Forschungen 73. Münster: Aschendorff, 1993.

Konzil und Diaspora. Die Beschlüsse der Pastoralsynode der katholischen Kirche in der DDR. Berlin: Morus Verlag, 1977.

Kranemann, Benedikt. "Feier des Glaubens und soziales Handeln. Überlegungen zu einer vernachlässigten Dimension christlicher Liturgie." *Liturgisches Jahrbuch* 48 (1998): 203–21.

———. "Liturgiewissenschaft angesichts der 'Zeitenwende.' Die Entwicklung der theologischen Disziplin zwischen den beiden Vatikanischen Konzilien." In *Die katholisch-theologischen Disziplinen in Deutschland 1870–1962. Ihre Geschichte, ihr Zeitbezug.* Edited by Hubert Wolf. Programm und Wirkungsgeschichte des II. Vatikanums 3. Paderborn: Schöningh, 1999, 351–75.

———. "Die Liturgiereform im Bistum Münster nach dem II Vatikanum. Eine Skizze." In *Kirche, Staat und Gesellschaft nach 1945. Konfessionelle Prägungen und sozialer Wandel.* Edited by Bernd Hey. Beiträge zur Westfälischen Kirchengeschichte 21. Bielefeld: Luther Verlag, 2001, 67–85.

———. "Wort–Buch–Verkündigungsort. Zur Ästhetik der Wortverkündigung im Gottesdienst." In *Liturgia et Unitas. Liturgiewissenschaftliche und ökumenische Studien zur Eucharistie und zum gottesdienstlichen Leben in der Schweiz. Études liturgiques et oecuméniques sur l'Eucharistie et la vie liturgique en Suisse. In honorem Bruno Bürki.* Edited by Martin Klöckener and Arnaud Join-Lambert. Fribourg: Universitätsverlag; Geneva: Labor et Fides, 2001, 57–72.

———. "Gottesdienst als ökumenisches Projekt." In *Liturgisches Kompendium.* Edited by Christian Grethlein and Günter Ruddat. Göttingen: Vandenhoeck & Ruprecht, 2003, 77–100.

———. "'Lesejahr D?' Das Johannesevangelium in der Liturgie." *Bibel und Kirche* 59 (2004): 167–70.

———. "Zwischen Tradition und Zeitgeist. Programm und Durchführung der Liturgiereform in der deutschen katholischen Aufklärung." *Jaarboek voor liturgie-onderzoek* 20 (2004): 25–47.

———. "Die Wiederentdeckung des Rituals. Ein kulturelles Phänomen in liturgiewissenschaftlicher Perspektive." *Religionsunterricht an höheren Schulen* 48 (2005): 24–35.

———. "Gottesdienstformen und die Rezeption der Liturgiereform des Zweiten Vatikanischen Konzils in Deutschland." In *Katholiken in den USA und Deutschland. Kirche, Gesellschaft und Politik.* Edited by Wilhelm Damberg and Antonius Liedhegener. Münster: Aschendorff, 2006, 62–72.

———. "Funktionswandel der Rhetorik in der katholischen Liturgie. Deutschsprachige Gebetstexte von der Aufklärung des 19. Jahrhunderts bis zur Liturgiereform des späten 20. Jahrhunderts." In *Religion und Rhetorik.* Edited by Holt Meyer and Dirk Uffelmann. Religionswissenschaft heute 4. Stuttgart: Kohlhammer, 2007, 102–21.

———, Thomas Sternberg, and Walter Zahner, eds. *Die diakonale Dimension der Liturgie.* Quaestiones Disputatae 218. Freiburg: Herder, 2006.

———, and Paul Post, eds. *Modern Ritual Studies as a Challenge for Liturgical Studies.* Liturgia condenda 20. Leuven: Peeters, 2009.

———, and Stephan Wahle, eds. ". . . Ohren der Barmherzigkeit." Über angemessene Liturgiesprache.* Theologie kontrovers. Freiburg, et al.: Herder, 2011.

Kranemann, Daniela. *Israelitica dignitas? Studien zur Israeltheologie Eucharistischer Hochgebete.* Münsteraner theologische Abhandlungen 66. Altenberge: Oros, 2001.

———. "Mehr als eine Statistenrolle! Israel in der Dramaturgie der christlichen Liturgie." *Bibel und Liturgie* 76 (2003): 16–27.

Kretschmar, Georg. "Kirchensprache." *Theologische Realenzyklopädie* 19 (1990): 74–92.

Kunzler, Michael. "*Indumentum Salutis.* Überlegungen zum liturgischen Gewand." *Theologie und Glaube* 81 (1991): 52–78.

———. *Die Liturgie der Kirche.* Associazione di Manuali di Teologia Cattolica 10. Paderborn: Bonifatius, 1995.

Ladrière, Jean. "The Performativity of Liturgical Language." Translated by John Griffiths. *Concilium* 9/1 (1973): 50–62 (= Herman A. P. Schmidt and David N. Power, eds., *Liturgical Experience of Faith* [New York: Herder and Herder, 1973], 50–62).

Lang, Bernhard. "Ritual/Ritus." *Handbuch religionswissenschaftlicher Grundbegriffe* 4 (1998): 442–58.

Lang, Uwe Michael. *Conversi ad Dominum. Zu Geschichte und Theologie der christlichen Gebetsrichtung*. Neue Kriterien 5. Einsiedeln: Johannesverlag, 2003.

Langer, Susanne K. *Philosophy in a New Key: A Study in the Symbolism of Reason, Rite, and Art*. Cambridge, MA: Harvard University Press, 1957.

Lathrop, Gordon. *Holy Things: A Liturgical Theology*. Minneapolis: Fortress Press, 1993.

Lechner, Joseph. *Liturgy of the Roman Rite*. Translated by Edward Francis Peeler and Harold Edgar Winstone. Freiburg, Edinburgh, and London: Nelson, 1961.

Lectionary for Mass. Collegeville, MN: Liturgical Press, 1998.

Le Gall, Robert. "Die Namen Gottes in der Liturgie." *Internationale katholische Zeitschrift "Communio"* 22 (1993): 63–77.

Legner, Anton. *Kölner Heilige und Heiligtümer. Ein Jahrtausend europäischer Reliquienkultur*. Cologne: Greven, 2003.

Lehner, Ulrich L. *The Catholic Enlightenment: The Forgotten History of a Global Movement*. New York: Oxford University Press, 2016.

"Leitlinien für den Bau und die Ausgestaltung von gottesdienstlichen Räumen. Handreichung der Liturgiekommission der Deutschen Bischofskonferenz. 25. Oktober 1988." 5th rev. ed. Sekretariat der Deutschen Bischofskonferenz. Die deutschen Bischöfe – Liturgiekommission 9. Bonn, 2000.

"Leitlinien für die Revision der Gebetstexte des Messbuchs." In *Studien und Entwürfe zur Messfeier. Texte der Studienkommission für die Messliturgie und das Messbuch der Internationalen Arbeitsgemeinschaft der Liturgischen Kommissionen in deutschen Sprachgebiet* 1. Edited by Eduard Nagel with Roland Bachleitner, et al. Freiburg: Herder, 1995, 55–62.

Lengeling, Emil Joseph. "Liturgie." *Handbuch theologischer Grundbegriffe* 3 (1970): 77–100 [first pub. 1962].

———. "Von der Erwartung des Kommenden." In *Gott feiern. Theologische Anregung und geistliche Vertiefung zur Feier von Messe und Stundengebet*. Edited by Josef G. Plöger. Freiburg: Herder, 1980, 193–238.

———. *Liturgie: Dialog zwischen Gott und Mensch*. Edited by Klemens Richter. Altenberge: Telos, 1988. Includes:

———. "Wort, Bild und Symbol als Elemente der Liturgie." [1980]: 91–108.

————. "Liturgie/Liturgiewissenschaft." *Neues Handbuch theologischer Grundbegriffe* 3 (1991): 279–305.

Lentes, Thomas. "*A maioribus tradita*. Zur Kommunikation von Mythos und Ritus im mittelalterlichen Messkommentar." In *Literarische und religiöse Kommunikation in Mittelalter und Früher Neuzeit*. Edited by Peter Strohschneider. DFG-Symposion 2006. Berlin and New York: de Gruyter, 2009, 324–70.

Lentner, Leopold. *Volkssprache und Sakralsprache. Geschichte einer Lebensfrage bis zum Ende des Konzils von Trient*. Wiener Beiträge zur Theologie 5. Vienna: Herder, 1964.

Leonhard, Clemens. "Die Erzählung Ex 12 als Festlegende für das Pesachfest am Jerusalemer Tempel." In *Das Fest: Jenseits des Alltags*. Edited by Martin Ebner. Jahrbuch für Biblische Theologie 18. Neukirchen-Vluyn: Neukirchener Verlag, 2003, 233–60.

"Liturgie und Bild. Eine Orientierungshilfe. Handreichung der Liturgiekommission der Deutschen Bischofskonferenz. 23. April 1996." Sekretariat der Deutschen Bischofskonferenz. Arbeitshilfen 132. Bonn, 1996.

LiturgieGefässe, Kirche und Design. Eine Ausstellung anlässlich des 50jährigen Bestehens des Deutschen Liturgischen Instituts. Trier: Deutsches Liturgisches Institut, 1997.

Liturgiewissenschaft. Studien zur Wissenschaftsgeschichte. Edited by Franz Kohlschein and Peter Wünsche. Liturgiewissenschaftliche Quellen und Forschungen 78. Münster: Aschendorff, 1996.

The Liturgy of the Hours. 4 vols. New York: Catholic Book Publishing, 1975–1976.

Liturgy's Imagined Past/s: Methodologies and Materials in the Writing of Liturgical History Today. Edited by Teresa Berger and Bryan D. Spinks. Collegeville, MN: Liturgical Press, 2016.

Lohfink, Norbert. "Moses Tod, die Tora und die alttestamentliche Sonntagslesung." In *Leseordnung. Altes und Neues Testament in der Liturgie*. Edited by Georg Steins. Gottes Volk S/97. Stuttgart: Katholisches Bibelwerk, 1997, 122–37.

————. "The Old Testament and the Course of the Christian's Day: The Songs in Luke's Infancy Narrative." In idem, *In the Shadow of Your Wings: New Readings of Great Texts from the Bible*. Translated by Linda M. Maloney. Collegeville, MN: Liturgical Press, 2003, 136–50.

Luckmann, Thomas. *The Invisible Religion: The Problem of Religion in Modern Society*. New York: Macmillan, 1974.

————. *Die unsichtbare Religion*. 3rd ed. Frankfurt: Suhrkamp, 1996.

Lüddeckens, Dorothea. "Neue Rituale für alle Lebenslagen. Beobachtungen zur Popularisierung des Ritualdiskurses." *Zeitschrift für Religions- und Geistesgeschichte* 56 (2004): 37–53.

Lukken, Gerard. "Liturgie und Sinnlichkeit. Über die Bedeutung der Leib-lichkeit in der Liturgie." In idem, *Per visibilia ad invisibilia. Anthropological, Theological, and Semiotic Studies on the Liturgy and the Sacraments*. Collected and edited by Louis Van Tongeren and Charles Caspers. Kampen: Kok Pharos, 1994, 118–39.

————, and Mark Searle. *Semiotics and Church Architecture: Applying the Semiotics of A. J. Greimas and the Paris School to the Analysis of Church Buildings*. Kampen: Kok Pharos, 1993.

Lurz, Friedrich. *Die Feier des Abendmahls nach der Kurpfälzischen Kirchenordnung von 1563. Ein Beitrag zu einer ökumenischen Liturgiewissenschaft*. Praktische Theologie heute 38. Stuttgart: Kohlhammer, 1998.

————. "Für eine ökumenische Liturgiewissenschaft." *Trierer theologische Zeitschrift* 108 (1999): 273–90.

————. *Erlebte Liturgie. Autobiografische Schriften als liturgiewissenschaftliche Quellen*. Ästhetik, Theologie, Liturgik 28. Münster: LIT, 2003.

Luz, Ulrich. *Matthew 8–20: A Commentary*. Hermeneia. Minneapolis: Fortress Press, 2001.

Maas-Ewerd, Theodor. *Die Krise der Liturgischen Bewegung in Deutschland und Österreich. Zu den Auseinandersetzungen um die "liturgische Frage" in den Jahren 1939 bis 1944*. Studien zur Pastoralliturgie 3. Regensburg: Pustet, 1981.

März, Claus-Peter. "Das 'Wort vom Kult' und der 'Kult des Wortes.' Der Hebräerbrief und die rechte Feier des Gottesdienstes." In *Wie das Wort Gottes feiern? Der Wortgottesdienst als theologische Herausforderung*. Edited by Benedikt Kranemann and Thomas Sternberg. Quaestiones Disputatae 194. Freiburg: Herder, 2002, 82–98.

Mayer, Anton Ludwig. "Die geistesgeschichtliche Situation der Liturgischen Erneuerung in der Gegenwart." *Archiv für Liturgiewissenschaft* 4 (1955): 1–51. Also in: *Die Liturgie in der europäischen Geistesgeschichte. Gesammelte Aufsätze*. Edited by Emmanuel von Severus. Darmstadt: Wissenschaftliche Buchgesellschaft, 1971, 388–438.

Meffert, Bernhard. *Liturgie teilen. Akzeptanz und Partizipation in der erneuerten Messliturgie*, with an introduction by Albert Gerhards. Praktische Theologie heute 52. Stuttgart: Kohlhammer, 2000.

Merz, Michael B. *Liturgisches Gebet als Geschehen. Liturgiewissenschaftlich-linguistische Studie anhand der Gebetsgattung Eucharistisches Hochgebet*. Liturgiewissenschaftliche Quellen und Forschungen 70. Münster: Aschendorff, 1988.

Messner, Reinhard. "Was ist systematische Liturgiewissenschaft? Ein Entwurf in sieben Thesen." *Archiv für Liturgiewissenschaft* 40 (1998): 257–74.

————. "Unterschiedliche Konzeptionen des Messopfers im Spiegel von Bedeutung und Deutung der Interzession des römischen Canon missae." In *Das Opfer. Biblischer Anspruch und liturgische Gestalt*. Edited by Albert Gerhards and Klemens Richter. Quaestiones Disputatae 186. Freiburg: Herder, 2000, 128–84.

————. "Der Gottesdienst in der vornizänischen Kirche." In *Die Zeit des Anfangs (bis 250)*. Edited by Luce Pietri. Die Geschichte des Christentums 1. Freiburg: Herder, 2003, 340–441.

————. "Gebetsrichtung, Altar und die exzentrische Mitte der Gemeinde." In *Communio-Räume. Auf der Suche nach der angemessenen Raumgestalt katholischer Liturgie*. Bild, Raum, Feier. Studien zu Kirche und Kunst 2. Regensburg: Pustet, 2003, 27–36.

————. "Grundlinien der Entwicklung des eucharistischen Gebets in der Frühen Kirche." In *Prex Eucharistica, III. Studia, pars prima, "Ecclesia antiqua et occidentalis."* Edited by Albert Gerhards, Heinzgerd Brakmann, and Martin Klöckener. Spicilegium Friburgense 42. Fribourg: Academic Press, 2005, 3–41.

————. *Einführung in die Liturgiewissenschaft*. 2nd ed. Paderborn: Schöningh, 2009.

————, and Martin Lang. "Die Freiheit zum Lobpreis des Namens. Identitätsstiftung im eucharistischen Hochgebet und in verwandten jüdischen Gebeten." In *Identität durch Gebet. Zur gemeinschaftsbildenden Funktion institutionalisierten Betens in Judentum und Christentum*. Studien zu Judentum und Christentum. Paderborn: Schöningh, 2003, 371–411.

Metzger, Marcel. *Histoire de la liturgie: les grands étapes*. Petite encyclopédie moderne du christianisme. Paris: Desclée de Brouwer, 1994.

Meyer, Hans Bernhard. "Zur Frage der Inkulturation der Liturgie." *Zeitschrift für katholische Theologie* 105 (1983): 1–31.

————. "Liturgie in lebenden Sprachen. Das 2. Vatikanum und die Folgen." In *Die Feier der Sakramente in der Gemeinde. Festschrift für Heinrich Rennings*. Edited by Martin Klöckener and Winfried Glade. Kevelaer: Butzon & Bercker, 1986, 331–45.

————. *Eucharistie. Geschichte, Theologie, Pastoral*, mit einem Beitrag von Irmgard Pahl. Volume 4 of *Gottesdienst der Kirche. Handbuch der Liturgiewissenschaft*. Edited by Hans Bernhard Meyer, et al. Regensburg: Pustet, 1989.

Meyer-Blanck, Michael. *Vom Symbol zum Zeichen. Symboldidaktik und Semiotik*. Rheinbach: CMZ-Verlag, 2002.

————, ed. *Liturgiewissenschaft und Kirche. Ökumenische Perspektiven*. Rheinbach: CMZ, 2003.

Missale Romanum ex decreto sacrosancti oecumenici Concilii Vaticani II instaura-tum auctoritate Pauli PP. VI promulgatum Ioannis Pauli PP. II cura recognitum. Editio typica tertia. Rome: Typ. Vaticanis 2002.

Mitchell, Nathan. *Liturgy and the Social Sciences.* American Essays in Liturgy. Collegeville, MN: Liturgical Press, 1999.

Möller, Christian. *Kirchenlied und Gesangbuch. Quellen zu ihrer Geschichte. Ein hymnologisches Arbeitsbuch.* Mainzer Hymnologische Studien 1. Tübingen: Francke, 2000.

Moltmann, Jürgen. "The First Liberated Men in Creation." Translated by Reinhard Ulrich. In Jürgen Moltmann, et al., *Theology of Play.* London: SCM, 1973, 26–90.

Müller, Cornelia. "Der Gottesgeist weht wie ein Wind." In *Kirchenlied im Kirchenjahr. Fünfzig neue und alte Lieder zu den christlichen Festen.* Edited by Ansgar Franz. Mainzer hymnologische Studien 8. Tübingen and Basel: Francke, 2002, 517–23.

Müller, Karlheinz. "Das Vater-Unser als jüdisches Gebet." In *Identität durch Gebet. Zur gemeinschaftsbildenden Funktion institutionalisierten Betens in Judentum und Christentum.* Edited by Albert Gerhards, Andrea Doeker, and Peter Ebenbauer. Studien zu Judentum und Christentum. Paderborn: Schöningh, 2003, 159–204.

Neijenhuis, Jörg, ed. *Liturgie lernen und lehren. Aufsätze zur Liturgiedidaktik.* Beiträge zu Liturgie und Spiritualität 6. Leipzig: Evangelische Verlags-Anstalt, 2001.

Neunheuser, Burkhard. "Die klassische Liturgische Bewegung (1909–1963) und die nachkonziliare Liturgiereform. Vergleich und Versuch einer Würdigung." In *Mélanges liturgiques. Offerts au R. P. Dom Bernard Botte O.S.B.* Louvain: Abbaye du Mont César, 1972, 401–16.

Nübold, Elmar. *Entstehung und Bewertung der neuen Perikopenordnung des Römischen Ritus für die Messfeier an Sonn- und Festtagen.* Paderborn: Bonifatius, 1986.

Nussbaum, Otto. "Von der Gegenwart Gottes im Wort." In *Gott feiern. Theologische Anregung und geistliche Vertiefung zur Feier von Messe und Stundengebet.* Edited by Josef G. Plöger. Freiburg: Herder, 1980, 116–32.

Odenthal, Andreas. *Der älteste Liber Ordinarius der Stiftskirche St. Aposteln in Köln. Untersuchungen zur Liturgie eines mittelalterlichen kölnischen Stifts.* Studien zur Kölner Kirchengeschichte 28. Siegburg: F. Schmitt, 1994.

———. "Die Palmsonntagsfeier in Köln im Mittelalter. Zu ihrer Genese anhand liturgischer Quellen des Domstiftes und des Gereonstiftes." *Kölner Domblatt* 62 (1997): 275–92.

——. *Liturgie als Ritual. Theologische und psychoanalytische Überlegungen zu einer praktisch-theologischen Theorie des Gottesdienstes als Symbolgeschehen.* Praktische Theologie heute 60. Stuttgart: Kohlhammer, 2002.

——. "'Häresie der Formlosigkeit' durch ein 'Konzil der Buchhalter'? Überlegungen zur Kritik an der Liturgiereform nach 40 Jahren 'Sacrosanctum Concilium.'" *Liturgisches Jahrbuch* 53 (2003): 242–57.

——. "'. . . et communicatio sancti spiritus sit cum omnibus vobis.' Thesen zu einer praktisch-theologischen Liturgiewissenschaft im Kontext der 'Kommunikativen Theologie.'" In *Communicative Theology: Approaches, Discussions, Differentiation.* Edited by Matthias Scharer, Bradford E. Hinze, and Bernd Jochen Hilberath. Communicative Theology: Interdisciplinary Studies 14. Vienna: LIT, 2010, 108–29.

——. *Liturgie vom Frühen Mittelalter zum Zeitalter der Konfessionalisierung.* Studien zur Geschichte des Gottesdienstes. Spätmittelalter, Humanismus, Reformation 62. Tübingen: Mohr Siebeck, 2011.

The Order of Celebrating Matrimony. Collegeville, MN: Liturgical Press, 2016.

Pahl, Irmgard. *Coena Domini I. Die Abendmahlsliturgie der Reformationskirchen im 16./17. Jahrhundert.* Spicilegium Friburgense 29. Fribourg: Universitätsverlag, 1983.

——. "Die Stellung Christi in den Präsidialgebeten der Eucharistiefeier. Textbefund des heutigen Messbuchs und Anforderungen an eine Revision." In *Christologie der Liturgie. Der Gottesdienst der Kirche: Christusbekenntnis und Sinaibund.* Edited by Klemens Richter and Benedikt Kranemann. Quaestiones Disputatae 159. Freiburg: Herder, 1995, 243–57.

——. "Das Paschamysterium in seiner zentralen Bedeutung für die Gestalt christlicher Liturgie." *Liturgisches Jahrbuch* 46 (1996): 71–93.

——. *Coena Domini II. Die Abendmahlsliturgie der Reformationskirchen vom 18. bis zum frühen 20. Jahrhundert.* Spicilegium Friburgense 43. Fribourg: Universitätsverlag, 2005.

——. "Die Feier des Abendmahls in den Kirchen der Reformation." In *Eucharistie. Geschichte, Theologie, Pastoral,* mit einem Beitrag von Irmgard Pahl. Volume 4 of *Gottesdienst der Kirche. Handbuch der Liturgiewissenschaft.* Edited by Hans Bernhard Meyer, et al. Regensburg: Pustet, 1989, 393–440.

Parsch, Pius. *We Are Christ's Body . . . .* Translated and and adapted by Clifford Howell. London: Challoner, 1962.

Pecklers, Keith F. *The Unread Vision: The Liturgical Movement in the United States of America: 1926–1955.* Collegeville, MN: Liturgical Press, 1998.

——. *Dynamic Equivalence: The Living Language of Christian Worship.* Collegeville, MN: Liturgical Press, 2003.

——, ed. *Liturgy in a Postmodern World.* London and New York: Continuum, 2003.

————. *The Genius of the Roman Rite: On the Reception and Implementation of the New Missal.* Collegeville, MN: Liturgical Press, 2009.

————. *Liturgy: The Illustrated History.* Mahwah, NJ: Paulist Press, 2012.

Peterson, Erik. *Das Buch von den Engeln. Stellung und Bedeutung der heiligen Engel im Kultus.* Leipzig: J. Hegner, 1935. English: "The Angels and the Liturgy: Their Place and Meaning in the Liturgy." In *Theological Tractates,* edited and translated by Michael J. Hollerich, 106–42. Stanford: Stanford University Press, 2011.

Pius X, Pope St. *Tra le Sollecitudini* (Instruction on Sacred Music), 22 Nov. 1903. See http://www.adoremus.org/MotuProprio.html.

Plank, Peter. *Phos hilaron. Christushymnus und Lichtdanksagung der frühen Christenheit.* Hereditas 20. Bonn: Borengässer, 2001.

Pontifical Biblical Commission. *The Interpretation of the Bible in the Church.* London: SCM Press, 1995.

Popp, Friedrich. "Die deutsche Vesper im Zeitalter der Aufklärung unter besonderer Berücksichtigung des Bistums Konstanz." *Freiburger Diözesan-Archiv* 87. Freiburg: Herder, 1967, 87–495.

Post, Paul. "Liturgical Movements and Feast Culture: A Dutch Research Program." In *Christian Feast and Festival: The Dynamics of Western Liturgy and Culture.* Edited by Paul Post, Gerard Rouwhorst, Louis van Tongeren, and Anton Scheer. *Liturgia condenda* 12. Leuven: Peeters, 2001, 3–43.

————. "Ritual Studies: Einführung und Ortsbestimmung im Hinblick auf die Liturgiewissenschaft." *Archiv für Liturgiewissenschaft* 45 (2003): 21–45.

————. "Überfluss und Unvermögen. Ritualkompetenz oder Kompetenzverlust: rituell-liturgische Erkundungen im Lichte der Ritual Studies." In *Wiederkehr der Rituale. Zum Beispiel die Taufe.* Edited by Benedikt Kranemann, Gotthard Fuchs, and Joachim Hake. Stuttgart: Kohlhammer, 2004, 47–71.

Probst, Manfred. "Das Schöpfungsmotiv im Eucharistischen Hochgebet." *Liturgisches Jahrbuch* 31 (1981): 129–44.

Ratzinger, Joseph (Pope Benedict XVI). "Um die Erneuerung der Liturgie. Antwort auf Reiner Kaczynski." *Stimmen der Zeit* 219 (2001): 837–43.

————. *Summorum Pontificum. On the Use of the Roman Liturgy Prior to the Reform of 1970.* Available at http://w2.vatican.va/content/benedict-xvi/en/motu_proprio/documents/hf_ben-xvi_motu-proprio_20070707_summorum-pontificum.html.

————. *Theology of the Liturgy: The Sacramental Foundation of Christian Existence.* Translated by Michael J. Miller. San Francisco: Ignatius Press, 2014.

Rau, Stefan. *Die Feiern der Gemeinden und das Recht der Kirche. Zu Aufgabe, Form und Ebenen liturgischer Gesetzgebung in der katholischen Kirche.* Münsteraner theologische Abhandlungen 12. Altenberge: Telos, 1990.

Redtenbacher, Andreas, ed. *Die Zukunft der Liturgie. Gottesdienst 40 Jahre nach dem Konzil*. Innsbruck: Tyrolia, 2004.

Reichert, Franz Rudolf. *Die älteste deutsche Gesamtauslegung der Messe. Erstausgabe ca. 1480*. Corpus Catholicum 29. Münster: Aschendorff, 1967.

Reifenberg, Hermann. "Bemühungen um die Zeichen in der Liturgie. Ansatz der Liturgiekonstitution, Ergebnisse, Möglichkeiten." In *Lebt unser Gottesdienst? Die bleibende Aufgabe der Liturgiereform*. Edited by Theodor Maas-Ewerd. Freiburg: Herder, 1988, 63–74.

Richter, Klemens. "Liturgie und Seelsorge in der katholischen Kirche seit Beginn des 20. Jahrhunderts." In *Seelsorge und Diakonie in Berlin. Beiträge zum Verhältnis von Kirche und Grosstadt im 19. und beginnenden 20. Jahrhundert*. Edited by Kaspar Elm and Hans-Dietrich Loock. Berlin and New York: de Gruyter, 1990, 585–608.

———. "Soziales Handeln und liturgisches Tun als der eine Gottesdienst des Lebens." *Gemeinsame Arbeitsstelle für gottesdienstliche Fragen* 27 (1996): 15–30.

———. *Kirchenräume und Kirchenträume. Die Bedeutung des Kirchenraums für eine lebendige Gemeinde*. 2nd ed. Freiburg: Herder, 1999.

———, et al., eds. *Liturgie: ein vergessenes Thema der Theologie?* 2nd ed. Quaestiones Disputatae 107. Freiburg: Herder, 1987.

———, and Thomas Sternberg, eds. *Liturgiereform. Eine bleibende Aufgabe. 40 Jahre Konzilskonstitution über die heilige Liturgie*. Münster: Aschendorff, 2004.

Ringseisen, Paul, ed. *Morgenlob / Abendlob. Mit der Gemeinde feiern*. [Service Book]. 3 volumes. Planegg: promultis, 2000, 2004.

———. *Morgen- und Abendlob mit der Gemeinde. Geistliche Erschliessung, Erfahrungen und Modelle. Mit einem Beitrag von Martin Klöckener*. New edition Freiburg: Herder, 2002.

"Rite of Baptism for Children." In *The Rites*. Vol. 1. Collegeville, MN: Liturgical Press, 1990.

"Rite of Christian Initiation of Adults." In *The Rites*. Vol. 1. Collegeville, MN: Liturgical Press, 1990.

Rosenzweig, Franz. *The Star of Redemption*. Translated by Barbara E. Galli. Madison: University of Wisconsin Press, 2005.

Rouwhorst, Gerhard. "Identität durch Gebet. Gebetstexte als Zeugen eines jahrhundertelangen Ringens um Kontinuität und Differenz zwischen Judentum und Christentum." In *Identität durch Gebet. Zur gemeinschaftsbildenden Funktion institutionalisierten Betens in Judentum und Christentum*. Studien zu Judentum und Christentum. Paderborn: Schöningh, 2003, 37–55.

———. "Christlicher Gottesdienst und der Gottesdienst Israels. Forschungs-geschichte, historische Interaktionen, Theologie." In Karl-Heinrich Bie-ritz, et al., *Theologie des Gottesdienstes: Gottesdienst im Leben der Christen. Christliche und jüdische Liturgie.* Gottesdienst der Kirche 2.2. Regensburg: Pustet, 2008, 491–572.

The Sacramentary. Collegeville, MN: Liturgical Press, 1985.

Salmann, Elmar. *Zwischenzeit. Postmoderne Gedanken zum Christsein heute.* Warendorf: Schnell, 2004.

Sattler, Dorothea. "Gegenwart Gottes im Wort. Systematisch-theologische Aspekte." In *Wie das Wort Gottes feiern? Der Wortgottesdienst als theologische Herausforderung.* Edited by Benedikt Kranemann and Thomas Sternberg. Quaestiones Disputatae 194. Freiburg: Herder, 2002, 123–43.

Schaeffler, Richard. "Kultisches Handeln. Die Frage nach Proben seiner Be-währung und nach Kriterien seiner Legitimation." In Richard Schaeffler and Peter Hünermann, *Ankunft Gottes und Handeln des Menschen. Thesen über Kult und Sakrament.* Quaestiones Disputatae 77. Freiburg: Herder, 1977, 9–50.

———. "Das Gebet: Schule des Glaubens und Schule des Lebens im Ju-dentum." In *Lebenserfahrung und Glaube.* Edited by Gisbert Kaufmann. Düsseldorf: Patmos, 1983, 73–90.

———. *Kleine Sprachlehre des Gebets.* Sammlung Horizonte, n.s. 26. Einsiedeln and Trier: Johannes Verlag, 1988.

———. "'Darum sind wir eingedenk.' Die Verknüpfung von Erinnerung und Erwartung in der Gegenwart der gottesdienstlichen Feier. Religi-onsphilosophische Überlegungen zur religiös verstandenen Zeit." In *Vom Sinn der Liturgie. Gedächtnis unserer Erlösung und Lobpreis Gottes.* Edited by Angelus A. Häussling. Schriften der Katholischen Akademie in Bayern 140. Düsseldorf: Patmos, 1991, 16–44.

Schermann, Josef. *Die Sprache im Gottesdienst.* Innsbrucker theologische Stu-dien 18. Innsbruck and Vienna: Tyrolia, 1987.

Schierse, Franz Joseph. *Verheissung und Heilsvollendung. Zur theologi-schen Grundfrage des Hebräerbriefes.* Münchener theologische Studien I. Historische Abteilung 9. Munich: Karl Zink, 1955.

Schillebeeckx, Edward. *Christ: The Christian Experience in the Modern World.* Translated by John Bowden. The Collected Works of Edward Schille-beeckx 7. London: Bloomsbury, 2014.

Schilson, Arno. *Theologie als Sakramententheologie. Die Mysterientheologie Odo Casels.* Tübinger theologische Studien 18. Mainz: Matthias Grünewald, 1982.

———. "Romano Guardini: Wegbereiter und Wegbegleiter der liturgischen Erneuerung." *Liturgisches Jahrbuch* 36 (1986): 3–27.

———. "Erneuerung aus dem Geist der Restauration. Ein Blick auf den Ursprung der Liturgischen Bewegung bei Prosper Guéranger." *Rottenburger
Jahrbuch für Kirchengeschichte* 12 (1993): 213–34.

———. "'Gedachte Liturgie' als Mystagogie. Überlegungen zum Verhältnis
von Dogmatik und Liturgie." In *Dogma und Glaube. Bausteine für eine
theologische Erkenntnislehre. Festschrift für Bischof Walter Kasper.* Edited by
Eberhard Schockenhoff and Peter Walter. Mainz: Matthias Grünewald,
1993, 213–34.

Schimmel, Barbara. *Tuchbestimmungen, Schweigeschrift, Ritualkleider. Album zu
den textilen Universalien.* Studien zur Phänomenologie der gestalterischen
Erfahrung 1. Münster: LIT, 1999.

Schlierf, Wilhelm-Josef. "Die Stadtkölnische Gottestracht und die Fronleichnamsprozession in Köln im Lichte ihrer Geschichte." *Kölner Domblatt* 62
(1997): 293–334.

Schmemann, Alexander. *Introduction to Liturgical Theology.* Crestwood, NY:
St Vladimir's Seminary Press, 1986.

Schmid, Franz Xaver. *Grundriss der Liturgik der christkatholischen Religion.*
Passau: Friedrich Winkler, 1836.

Schmidt-Lauber, Christoph, Michael Meyer-Blanck, and Karl-Heinrich Bieritz, eds. *Handbuch der Liturgik. Liturgiewissenschaft in Theologie und Praxis
der Kirche.* 3rd rev. ed. Göttingen: Vandenhoeck & Ruprecht, 2003.

Schmitz, Josef. "Canon Romanus." In *Prex Eucharistica*, III. *Studia, pars prima,
"Ecclesia antiqua et occidentalis."* Edited by Albert Gerhards, Heinzgerd
Brakmann, and Martin Klöckener. Spicilegium Friburgense 42. Fribourg:
Academic Press, 2005, 281–310.

Schöttler, Heinz-Günther. "'Per Christum . . .' Christus als Weg. In memoriam Friedrich-Wilhelm Marquardt († 25 Mai 2002)." *Bibel und Liturgie*
76 (2003): 4–15.

Schulz, Frieder. "Gottesdienstreform im ökumenischen Kontext. Katholische
Einflüsse auf den evangelischen Gottesdienst." *Liturgisches Jahrbuch* 47
(1997): 202–20.

Schütz, Christian. *Einführung in die Pneumatologie.* Darmstadt: Wissenschaftliche Buchgesellschaft, 1985.

Schwarz, Rudolf. *Vom Bau der Kirche* (1938), 3d ed. with altered title and
form, and with the addition of original hand-drawn sketches. Salzburg:
Pustet, 1998.

Selle, Monika. "Latein und Volkssprache im Gottesdienst. Die Aussagen des
Zweiten Vatikanischen Konzils über die Liturgiesprache." Dissertation
in typescript (Munich, 2001) (http://edoc.ub.uni-muenchen.de/3758/1
/Selle_Monika.pdf).

Senn, Frank C. *The People's Work: A Social History of the Liturgy.* Minneapolis: Augsburg Fortress, 2006.

Sequeira, A. Ronald. "Gottesdienst als menschliche Ausdruckshandlung." In Rupert Berger, et al., *Gestalt des Gottesdienstes. Sprachliche und nichtsprachliche Ausdrucksformen.* 2nd ed. Gottesdienst der Kirche 3. Regensburg: Pustet, 1990, 7–39.

Sidur Sefa Emet = Hebrew Prayer Book. Halberstadt: League of Orthodox Jewish Congregations, 1923.

Söding, Thomas. "Wort des lebendigen Gottes? Die neutestamentlichen Briefe im Wortgottesdienst der Eucharistiefeier." In *Wie das Wort Gottes feiern? Der Wortgottesdienst als theologische Herausforderung.* Edited by Benedikt Kranemann and Thomas Sternberg. Quaestiones Disputatae 194. Freiburg: Herder, 2002, 41–81.

Steins, Georg, ed. *Schweigen wäre gotteslästerlich. Die heilende Kraft der Klage.* Würzburg: Echter Verlag, 2000.

Stolz, Fritz. *Grundzüge der Religionswissenschaft.* Kleine Vandenhoeck-Reihe 1527. Göttingen: Vandenhoeck & Ruprecht, 1988.

Stringer, Martin D. "Liturgy and Anthropology: The History of a Relationship." *Worship* 63 (1989): 503–21.

Stuflesser, Martin. *Memoria Passionis. Das Verhältnis von lex orandi und lex credendi am Beispiel des Opferbegriffs in den Eucharistischen Hochgebeten nach dem II. Vatikanischen Konzil.* Münsteraner theologische Abhandlungen 51. Altenberge: Oros, 1998.

———, and Stefan Winter. "Liturgiewissenschaft—Liturgie und Wissenschaft? Versuch einer Standortbestimmung im Kontext des Gesprächs zwischen Liturgiewissenschaft und Systematischer Theologie." *Liturgisches Jahrbuch* 51 (2001): 90–118.

———, and Stefan Winter, eds. *"Ahme nach, was du vollziehst . . ." Positionsbestimmungen zum Verhältnis von Liturgie und Ethik.* Studien zur Pastoralliturgie 22. Regensburg: Pustet, 2009.

Taft, Robert F. "Über die Liturgiewissenschaft heute." *Theologische Quartalschrift* 177 (1997): 243–55.

———, and Gabriele Winkler, eds. *Comparative Liturgy: Fifty Years after Anton Baumstark (1872–1948).* Acts of the International Congress, Rome, 25–29 September 1998. Orientalia Christiana analecta 265. Rome: Pontificio Istituto Orientale, 2001.

"Tagesgebete. Die Zeit im Jahreskreis. Revisionsentwurf." In *Studien und Entwürfe zur Messfeier.* Texte der Studienkommission für die Messliturgie und das Messbuch der Internationalen Arbeitsgemeinschaft der Liturgischen Kommissionen im deutschen Sprachgebiet 1. Edited by Eduard Nagel with Roland Bachleitner, et al. Freiburg: Herder, 1995, 63–98.

Tambiah, Stanley J. "A Performative Approach to Ritual." *Proceedings of the British Academy* 65 (1979): 113–69.

Taylor, Charles. *A Secular Age*. Cambridge, MA: Harvard University Press, 2007.

Thaler, Anton. *Gemeinde und Eucharistie. Grundlegung einer eucharistischen Ekklesiologie*. Praktische Theologie im Dialog 2. Fribourg: Universitätsverlag, 1988.

Thönnes, Dietmar. "Das textile Gedächtnis der Kirche. Mnemotechniken und anamnetische Aspekte liturgischer Kleidung." *Liturgisches Jahrbuch* 47 (1997): 78–88.

Trepp, Leo. *Der jüdische Gottesdienst. Gestalt und Entwicklung*. 2nd ed. Stuttgart: Kohlhammer, 2004.

Triacca, Achille Maria. "Le preghiere eucaristiche ambrosiane." In *Prex Eucharistica*, III. *Studia*, pars prima, "Ecclesia antiqua et occidentalis." Edited by Albert Gerhards, Heinzgerd Brakmann, and Martin Klöckener. Spicilegium Friburgense 42. Fribourg: Academic Press, 2005, 145–202.

Trippen, Norbert. "Gottesdienst und Volksfrömmigkeit im Kölner Dom während des 19. Jahrhunderts." In *Der Kölner Dom im Jahrhundert seiner Vollendung 2. Essays zur Ausstellung der Historischen Museen in der Josef-Haubrich-Kunsthalle Köln*. Edited by Hugo Borger. Cologne: Historische Museen der Stadt Köln, 1980, 182–98.

Turner, Victor W. *The Ritual: Structure and Anti-Structure*. Chicago: Aldine, 1969.

Valenziano, Crispino. "Liturgy and Anthropology: The Meaning of the Question and the Method for Answering It." In *Handbook for Liturgical Studies*. Vol. 2: *Fundamental Liturgy*. Edited by Ansgar J. Chupungco. Collegeville, MN: Liturgical Press, 1998, 189–225.

Van Gennep, Arnold. *The Rites of Passage* (1909). Translated by Monika B. Vizedom and Gabrielle L. Caffee. Chicago: University of Chicago Press, 1960.

Volp, Rainer. *Liturgik. Die Kunst, Gott zu feiern*. Vol. 1: *Einführung und Geschichte*. Gütersloh: Gerd Mohn, 1992.

Wagner, Johannes. *Mein Weg zur Liturgiereform 1936–1986. Erinnerungen*. Freiburg: Herder, 1993.

Wainwright, Geoffrey. *Doxology: The Praise of God in Worship, Doctrine and Life; A Systematic Theology*. New York: Oxford University Press, 1980.

———, and Karen B. Westerfield Tucker, eds. *The Oxford History of Christian Worship*. Oxford and New York: Oxford University Press, 2006.

Wannenwetsch, Bernd. *Political Worship: Ethics for Christian Citizens*. Oxford and New York: Oxford University Press, 2004.

Wegman, Hermann A. J. *Liturgie in der Geschichte des Christentums*. Regensburg: Pustet, 1994.

Welker, Michael. *Was geht vor beim Abendmahl?* 2nd ed. Stuttgart: Quell, 2004.

Werbick, Jürgen. "Bibel Jesu und Evangelium Jesu Christi. Systematisch-theologische Perspektiven." *Bibel und Liturgie* 70 (1997): 213–18.

West, Fritz. *The Comparative Liturgy of Anton Baumstark.* Alcuin/Grove Joint Liturgical Studies 31. Nottingham: Grove, 1995.

Wick, Peter. *Die urchristlichen Gottesdienste. Entstehung und Entwicklung im Rahmen der frühjüdischen Tempel-, Synagogen- und Hausfrömmigkeit.* 2nd ed. Beiträge zur Wissenschaft vom Alten und Neuen Testament 150. Stuttgart: Kohlhammer, 2003.

Wiese, Hans-Ulrich. *Karsamstagsexistenz. Auseinandersetzung mit dem Karsamstag in Liturgie und moderner Kunst.* Bild, Raum, Feier. Studien zu Kirche und Kunst 1. Regensburg: Schnell & Steiner, 2002.

Winkler, Gabriele. "Überlegungen zum Gottesgeist als mütterlichem Prinzip und zur Bedeutung der Androgynie in einigen frühchristlichen Quellen." In *Liturgie und Frauenfrage. Ein Beitrag zur Frauenforschung aus liturgiewissenschaftlicher Sicht.* Edited by Teresa Berger and Albert Gerhards. Pietas liturgica 7. St. Ottilien: EOS Verlag, 1990, 7–29.

———, and Reinhard Messner. "Überlegungen zu den methodischen und wissenschaftstheoretischen Grundlagen der Liturgiewissenschaft." *Theologische Quartalschrift* 178 (1998): 229–43.

Winter, Stephan. *Eucharistische Gegenwart. Liturgische Redehandlung im Spiegel mittelalterlicher und analytischer Sprachtheorie.* Ratio fidei 13. Regensburg: Pustet, 2002.

———. "'Wir übergeben den Leib der Erde . . .' Überlegungen zu mystagogischer Bestattungsliturgie." *Arbeitsstelle Gottesdienst* 16 (2002): 12–25.

———. "Am Grund des rituellen Sprachspiels. Notwendige Klärungen zu 'Performance' und 'Performativität' in liturgiewissenschaftlichem Interesse." *Bibel und Liturgie* 84 (2011): 12–27.

Wintersig, Athanasius. "Methodisches zur Erklärung von Messformularen." *Jahrbuch für Liturgiewissenschaft* 4 (1924): 135–52.

———. "Pastoralliturgik. Ein Versuch über Wesen, Weg, Einteilung und Abgrenzung einer seelsorgswissenschaftlichen Behandlung der Liturgie." *Jahrbuch für Liturgiewissenschaft* 4 (1924): 153–67.

Wirth, Uwe, ed. *Performanz. Zwischen Sprachphilosophie und Kulturwissenschaft.* Frankfurt: Suhrkamp, 2002.

Wohlmuth, Josef. *Jesu Weg, unser Weg. Kleine mystagogische Christologie.* Würzburg: Echter, 1992.

———. "Eucharistie: Feier des neuen Bundes." In *Christologie der Liturgie. Der Gottesdienst der Kirche: Christusbekenntnis und Sinaibund.* Edited by Klemens Richter and Benedikt Kranemann. Quaestiones Disputatae 159. Freiburg: Herder, 1995, 187–206.

————. "Trinitarische Aspekte des Gebetes." In *Beten: Sprache des Glaubens, Seele des Gottesdienstes. Fundamentaltheologische und liturgiewissenschaftliche Aspekte.* Edited by Ulrich Willers. Pietas liturgica 15. Tübingen and Basel: Francke, 2000, 83–101.

"'Zeit zur Aussaat.' Missionarisch Kirche sein," 26 November 2000. Die deutschen Bischöfe 68. Bonn: Sekretariat der Deutschen Bischofskonferenz, 2000.

Zenger, Erich. *A God of Vengeance? Understanding the Psalms of Divine Wrath.* Translated by Linda M. Maloney. Louisville: Westminster John Knox, 1996.

Index of Subjects

Easter, 2, 14, 72, 73, 95, 110, 116, 117, 120–21, 158, 186, 190, 222, 244, 249–50, 283, 335
editio typica, 300, 304
Eighteen Benedictions, 272–74
elevation, 315, 329, 336–37
embolism, 277
epiclesis, 101, 184, 206–10, 211, 224–25, 226, 274–75, 277, 278–79, 309, 330, 338
Epiphany, 110, 117, 125, 218, 252
Epistolary, 104
eschatological tension, 180, 230–31, 246
Eucharist, 2, 24–25, 89, 94, 97–100, 171, 172, 178–79, 198, 199–202, 234, 242, 277, 329, 332–33
ecclesiology, 161, 178–79
place of reservation, 162–63, 325, 331, 333
Sunday, 91, 121, 175
vessels, 335–38
Eucharistic Prayer, 20, 25, 93, 108, 129, 135, 161–63, 190, 207–9, 273–75, 285, 327, 329–30
Anaphora of Addai and Mari, 111
Anaphora of Basil, 278
Anaphora of Gregory, 193
concluding doxology, 283, 327, 329
congregational acclamation, 190–91, 282–83, 290
Eucharistic Prayer II, 279
Eucharistic Prayer IV, 184–87, 279
Masses for Various Needs, 241–42
Roman Canon, 80, 99–101, 134, 279, 274, 283
Evangeliar (Gospel Book), 102, 104, 107, 199, 251, 333

exorcism, 75, 77, 100, 302
explanation of the liturgy, 21, 23–30, 35, 122

fermentum, 107
formula of greeting, 173, 289

General Intercessions, 64, 226, 284
German Mass, 136, 139, 296, 299
Gloria, 107, 175, 180, 228, 260, 264, 281, 314
God images in liturgy, 185–89
Good Friday, 95, 120, 191, 244
liturgy, 286
petitions, 195, 284
Gospel, 235, 237, 242, 248, 296
Gregorian chant, 36, 101–2, 151–52, 311–13

heavenly liturgy, 92, 169, 180, 226–31, 339
Hear, O Israel, 272
Holy Spirit, 66, 99, 161, 179, 201, 204–17, 240, 327
homily, 134, 251, 255
"Hymn to the Sun" (Francis), 129
hymnals, prayer books, 34, 138, 142
hymnody, 92, 93, 138, 214, 228, 307–20

imposition of hands, 95, 100, 211, 302
Improperia, 120, 314
incense, 190, 238, 251, 336
inculturation, 2, 20, 70, 81, 84–86, 118, 137, 151, 160, 297, 306
initiation, 4, 25, 75, 100, 111, 175, 177–78, 211, 232, 236, 241
insignia, 105, 340, 341
intertextuality, 262–66
introit, 107, 318
invitatory, 174, 269–70, 273

ordination, 134, 175, 208, 211, 286
Ordines Romani, 105
organ, 149, 311, 315
orientation to the east, 26, 107, 124, 334
Our Father, 89, 135, 136, 203, 260, 268–69, 273

Palm Sunday, 110, 126, 127
paraliturgies, 315–17
parish liturgy, 103
Pasch, 194
paschal mystery, 9, 13, 48, 64, 117–18, 158, 160, 167, 172, 186, 194–99, 202, 205, 232, 236, 240, 244, 255, 261, 272, 278
pastoral liturgics, 49, 69
pastoral theology, 33, 34, 38, 51, 266
paten, 28, 335–38
patriarchates, 111–12
patrocinium, 126
penance, penitential order, 62, 136, 163
Pentecost, 95, 117, 118, 205, 210, 214–15
Phos hilarion, 96, 222
physicality, 238–40
pilgrimage, 15, 110–11, 127, 139, 142, 146, 286
to Jerusalem, 88, 109, 110
plenary missal, 103, 104
pontifical, 104, 168
popular hymnody, 138
popular piety, 109–10, 128–29, 156, 283, 308, 234
prayer, 266–87
address/addressee, 78, 115–17, 191–93, 198
gestures, 284–87
Jewish, 87–88, 92, 93–94, 272–74, 308
posture, 26, 183, 284–87

preaching service, 130, 134
preface, 135–36
presence of Christ in the liturgy, 9–10, 172–73, 199–204
presider's chair, 326, 332
presider's prayer, 101, 191, 289
private Masses, 102–3, 121, 151
processions, 14–15, 60, 105–10, 120, 122, 125–27, 130, 138–39, 142, 144, 146, 286, 315, 325
proclamation of the Word, 53, 54, 162, 163, 198, 200, 249, 251, 262, 327, 332–33
prostration, 286
Psalter, 255–57, 267–68

reform, 34, 41, 53, 81–82, 93, 157–60, 164–68, 299, 312, 316, 323, 325, 333
Requiem, 315
rites of passage, 4, 13
ritual, 11–16, 21–22, 57–58, 76, 103–4
ritual studies, 21, 63–64
roles
identification of, 102, 165, 172, 175, 203, 270–71, 289–90
liturgical, 53, 70, 149, 151, 170, 231
Roman ceremonial, 105, 109, 124
Romanum Rituale, 298
rubricism, 23, 31–33, 38

Sabbath, 87, 88, 94, 95, 260
sacramental, 57, 159, 175, 198, 299
Sacramentary, 102–4
sacred oils, 75, 163, 335, 338
Sacred Scripture, 35, 92–93, 131–32, 144, 160, 247–66
sacrifice of the Mass, 128, 203
Sanctus, 107, 135–36, 180, 184, 227, 314

Index of Names